Ethical Practices

Modern Techniques

Roland Berry

ISBN: 978-1-77961-326-4
Imprint: Bedlam Buster

Contents

Introduction to Ethical Practices

The Importance of Ethics in Modern Society

The Role of Ethics in Business

Ethics plays a crucial role in modern society, particularly in the field of business. Business operations and practices have a significant impact on various stakeholders, including employees, customers, shareholders, and the broader community. Ethical behavior in business is not only morally right but also contributes to the success and sustainability of organizations. In this section, we will explore the role of ethics in business and its importance in creating a positive and responsible business environment.

Business Ethics and Stakeholders

Business ethics refers to the moral principles and values that guide business decision-making and conduct. It encompasses how businesses should behave in their interactions with various stakeholders, considering their rights, interests, and well-being. Stakeholders in a business context include employees, customers, shareholders, suppliers, the community, and the environment.

Ethical business practices promote trust and confidence among stakeholders, leading to beneficial relationships and sustainable business growth. By considering the interests of stakeholders, businesses can avoid short-term gains that may harm others or the environment. For example, a company that prioritizes customer satisfaction by providing high-quality products and services builds a loyal customer base, leading to long-term success.

Creating a Positive Organizational Culture

Ethics in business is not only about adhering to legal requirements but also about fostering a positive organizational culture. A strong ethical culture improves employee morale, attracts top talent, and enhances the company's reputation. It sets the foundation for ethical decision-making at all levels of the organization.

Ethical leadership is key in shaping an ethical culture within a business. Leaders who demonstrate integrity, transparency, and fairness, and who hold themselves accountable for ethical behavior, inspire employees to follow suit. They promote a culture where ethical considerations are integrated into all aspects of the business, from daily operations to strategic planning.

Customer Trust and Reputation

Ethical practices are essential in establishing and maintaining customer trust. Customers are more likely to engage with businesses that demonstrate ethical behavior. When a company acts in a transparent and honest manner, customers feel confident in their transactions. Ethical practices such as truthful advertising, fair pricing, and effective complaint handling build a positive reputation and customer loyalty.

On the other hand, unethical practices can lead to a loss of customer trust and damage a company's reputation. For example, when a business engages in deceptive advertising or fails to deliver on promises, customers may feel deceived and choose to take their business elsewhere. Negative publicity related to unethical behavior can have long-lasting consequences, impacting the financial performance and sustainability of the organization.

Long-Term Sustainability

Ethics in business contribute to long-term sustainability by considering the social, environmental, and economic impacts of business operations. By embracing ethical practices, businesses can contribute positively to the well-being of the community and minimize harm to the environment. This approach not only fulfills corporate social responsibility but also aligns with the expectations of customers and society as a whole.

Sustainable business practices, such as reducing carbon footprint, promoting diversity and inclusion, and supporting local communities, are increasingly valued in the marketplace. Ethical considerations also extend to supply chain management, ensuring fair treatment of suppliers and labor conditions.

Emphasizing sustainability builds credibility and positions businesses as responsible industry leaders.

Navigating Ethical Challenges in Business

While ethical practices are beneficial, businesses often face ethical challenges that require careful navigation. For instance, conflicts of interest may arise when personal interests of employees or managers interfere with their obligation to act in the best interests of the organization. Bribery and corruption can undermine fair competition and damage the integrity of the business environment.

Ethical decision-making models provide frameworks to address these challenges. The Utilitarian Model, for example, suggests making decisions that maximize the overall well-being of all stakeholders. The Rights-based Model focuses on respecting and protecting individual rights, while the Virtue-based Model emphasizes personal character and moral virtues. These models provide guidance in evaluating ethical dilemmas and making decisions aligned with ethical principles.

Conclusion

Ethics plays a vital role in business by guiding decision-making, fostering a positive organizational culture, building customer trust, ensuring long-term sustainability, and addressing ethical challenges. Implementing ethical practices in business operations and interactions with stakeholders creates a foundation for success, reputation, and responsible business conduct. By prioritizing ethics, businesses can contribute to the betterment of society while achieving their organizational goals.

Ethics in Politics and Governance

Politics and governance play a crucial role in shaping the society we live in. Ethical considerations are fundamental to ensuring that political systems and governance structures operate in a fair, just, and accountable manner. In this section, we will explore the ethical dimensions of politics and governance, including the principles that guide ethical decision-making, the challenges faced in ethical governance, and the importance of transparency and integrity in political processes.

Principles of Ethical Politics

Ethics in politics and governance are anchored in a set of principles that guide decision-making and behavior. These principles provide a moral compass for politicians, policymakers, and public officials, helping them navigate complex issues and make choices that uphold the public interest. Some of the principles that underpin ethical politics include:

- **Accountability**: Politicians and public officials are accountable to the people they represent and serve. They have a responsibility to act honestly, transparently, and with integrity. This principle ensures that those in power can be held responsible for their actions and decisions.

- **Justice**: Politics should be guided by the principle of justice, which means treating every individual fairly and impartially. Inequities and discrimination should be challenged, and measures should be taken to ensure equal access to resources and opportunities.

- **Democratic Values**: Politics and governance should adhere to democratic values such as openness, participation, and inclusion. Decision-making processes should be participatory and transparent, allowing citizens to have a voice in shaping policies and holding their representatives accountable.

- **Rule of Law**: Political systems and governance structures should operate within the framework of the rule of law. This means that laws should be applied equally to all individuals, regardless of their political power or influence. It ensures that no one is above the law and that everyone is subject to legal processes.

- **Integrity**: Ethical politics requires individuals in power to act with honesty, transparency, and consistency. Public officials should avoid conflicts of interest and act in the best interests of the public rather than their personal gain. Integrity builds trust and credibility in the political process.

These principles form the foundation for ethical decision-making in politics and governance. By adhering to these principles, politicians and public officials can ensure that their actions contribute to the common good and create a just and inclusive society.

Challenges in Ethical Governance

Ethical governance faces various challenges that can undermine the trust and effectiveness of political systems. Some of the key challenges include:

1. **Corruption:** Corruption is a major threat to ethical governance. It involves the abuse of power for personal gain, eroding public trust in political institutions. Measures such as transparent financial disclosure, anti-corruption legislation, and strong enforcement mechanisms are vital to combat corruption.

2. **Lobbying and Special Interests:** The influence of lobbying groups and special interests can create conflicts of interest and compromise ethical decision-making. It is essential to regulate lobbying activities and ensure transparency in the interactions between policymakers and interest groups.

3. **Misuse of Public Resources:** Ethical governance requires the responsible and fair use of public resources. Misuse of public funds or assets for personal gain undermines public trust and diverts resources away from public welfare.

4. **Nepotism and Cronyism:** Favoritism in political appointments and the allocation of resources based on personal relationships rather than merit can erode the principles of fairness and equal opportunity.

5. **Transparency and Accountability:** Lack of transparency and accountability in political processes can lead to corruption, favoritism, and the erosion of public trust. Robust mechanisms for transparency, such as freedom of information laws and public reporting, are crucial to ensuring ethical governance.

Transparency and Integrity in Political Processes

Transparency and integrity are key pillars of ethical politics and governance. They promote public trust, accountability, and informed decision-making. Here are some important aspects of transparency and integrity in political processes:

1. **Disclosure of Interests:** Politicians and public officials should disclose their financial interests, assets, and potential conflicts of interest. This ensures transparency and helps identify potential conflicts that could compromise ethical decision-making.

2. **Openness in Decision-Making:** Political decisions should be made openly, allowing for public scrutiny and participation. Openness promotes accountability and reduces the risk of corruption and favoritism.

3. **Access to Information:** Citizens have the right to access information held by public institutions. Freedom of information laws and mechanisms for proactive disclosure enable citizens to hold politicians and public officials accountable.

4. **Whistleblower Protection:** Whistleblowers play a critical role in exposing corruption and unethical behavior. Robust legal protections for whistleblowers encourage the reporting of misconduct and help create a culture of integrity.

5. **Ethical Codes and Standards:** The development and enforcement of ethical codes and standards for politicians and public officials promote integrity and guide ethical behavior. These codes provide guidance on issues such as conflicts of interest, gifts and hospitality, and campaign financing.

Case Study: Ethical Leadership

Ethical leadership is crucial in politics and governance, setting the tone and standards for ethical behavior. One notable example of ethical political leadership is the late Nelson Mandela, who demonstrated integrity, moral courage, and a commitment to justice throughout his life.

Mandela's leadership was characterized by a strong sense of accountability and a commitment to democratic values. He prioritized the welfare of the people over personal gain and was dedicated to the principles of justice and equality. Mandela's ability to forgive and reconcile with his oppressors showcased his ethical approach to leadership.

Ethical leaders in politics and governance inspire trust, foster transparency, and promote the common good. They lead by example, uphold ethical principles, and make decisions that consider the long-term well-being of society.

Conclusion

Ethics in politics and governance are essential for creating a just and inclusive society. Adherence to ethical principles, transparency, and integrity in political processes are vital to building public trust, promoting accountability, and ensuring the common good. By addressing the challenges and fostering ethical leadership, we can create political systems that serve the interests of all citizens and uphold democratic values.

Summary
- Politics and governance require ethical considerations to ensure fair and accountable systems. - Principles of ethical politics include accountability, justice, democratic values, rule of law, and integrity. - Challenges in ethical governance include corruption, lobbying, misuse of public resources, nepotism, and lack of transparency/accountability. - Transparency and integrity are crucial for ethical political processes, including disclosure of interests, openness, access to information, whistleblower protection, and ethical codes. - Ethical leadership sets the standard for ethical behavior in politics and governance. - Nelson Mandela is an example of ethical political leadership. - Adherence to ethical principles promotes public trust, accountability, and the common good.

Ethics in Healthcare

Ethics in healthcare is a fundamental aspect of providing quality and compassionate medical care to individuals and communities. It involves the application of moral principles and values to guide the actions and decisions of healthcare professionals, organizations, and policymakers. This section explores the ethical considerations and challenges that arise in various areas of healthcare, such as patient care, medical research, end-of-life care, global health, and reproductive medicine.

Ethical Principles in Healthcare

Ethical decision making in healthcare is guided by several fundamental principles that prioritize the well-being of patients and respect for their autonomy. These principles provide a framework for healthcare professionals to navigate complex ethical dilemmas.

1. **Informed Consent and Patient Autonomy:** In healthcare, it is crucial to respect patients' autonomy and their right to make informed decisions about their medical care. Healthcare providers must ensure that patients have access to all relevant information about their condition, treatment options, and potential risks and benefits. Informed consent is obtained when patients voluntarily agree to undergo a specific medical intervention after fully understanding its nature and implications.

   For example, when a patient is diagnosed with a critical illness, such as cancer, the healthcare provider should explain the available treatment options, potential side effects, and prognosis. The patient can then make an informed decision based on their values and preferences.

2. **Beneficence and Non-maleficence in Medical Practice:** Beneficence emphasizes the healthcare professionals' obligation to act in the best interest of their patients and promote their well-being. Non-maleficence, on the other hand, requires avoiding harm and minimizing risks to patients. These principles guide healthcare professionals in providing competent and compassionate care while ensuring the highest standards of safety and avoiding unnecessary harm.

   For instance, a surgeon conducting a complex procedure should have the necessary skills and experience to ensure the best possible outcome for the patient. Additionally, healthcare professionals should regularly update their knowledge and skills to provide evidence-based care and avoid medical errors.

3. **Justice and Fair Allocation of Healthcare Resources:** The principle of justice focuses on the fair distribution of healthcare resources, including access to quality care and health insurance coverage. It highlights the importance of ensuring equal opportunities and avoiding discrimination in healthcare delivery. Healthcare professionals and policymakers should strive to allocate resources equitably, prioritize the needs of underserved populations, and address health disparities.

   An example of justice in healthcare is the implementation of policies and healthcare systems that provide affordable and accessible healthcare to all individuals, regardless of their socio-economic background.

4. **Honesty and Truth-Telling with Patients:** Healthcare professionals have an ethical obligation to be honest and truthful with their patients. Open and transparent communication enhances the trust between healthcare providers and patients, enabling shared decision making and fostering a therapeutic relationship. Patients have the right to accurate and understandable information about their condition, treatment options, and prognosis.

   For instance, when a patient receives a diagnosis of a terminal illness, the healthcare provider should convey the information compassionately and truthfully, while respecting the patient's emotional and psychological well-being.

5. **Confidentiality and Privacy in Healthcare:** Healthcare providers must protect patients' personal and medical information and maintain confidentiality, thereby respecting their right to privacy. Strict guidelines and legal frameworks govern the collection, storage, access, and sharing of

patient information to maintain confidentiality and prevent unauthorized use or disclosure.

For example, medical professionals should ensure that patient records and electronic health information systems are secure, and only authorized personnel have access to sensitive patient data.

These ethical principles provide a foundation for healthcare professionals to make ethically sound decisions and ensure the provision of patient-centered care. However, applying these principles in real-world scenarios often presents complex ethical challenges, requiring the use of ethical frameworks and decision-making models.

Ethical Issues in Medical Research

Medical research plays a crucial role in advancing knowledge, improving healthcare practices, and developing new treatments. However, it also raises important ethical considerations due to potential risks to participants, the need for informed consent, and the protection of vulnerable populations.

1. **Informed Consent and Voluntary Participation:** Ethical research requires obtaining informed consent from participants, ensuring they have a clear understanding of the study's purpose, procedures, risks, and potential benefits. Participants must voluntarily agree to participate without any form of coercion or undue influence.

   Researchers should also respect participants' right to withdraw from the study at any time without penalty. Informed consent ensures that individuals can make autonomous decisions about their involvement in research, balancing potential benefits with potential risks.

2. **Ethical Guidelines and Institutional Review Boards (IRBs):** Ethical guidelines and review boards play a pivotal role in protecting participants' rights and welfare in research. Institutional Review Boards (IRBs) review research proposals to ensure they meet ethical standards and regulatory requirements. They assess the study's scientific merit, risk-benefit ratio, participant recruitment strategies, and consent procedures to ensure the protection of participants' rights and well-being.

   Researchers must comply with ethical guidelines and obtain ethical approval from relevant authorities before initiating any research involving human subjects.

3. **Animal Research and Ethical Considerations:** Animal research is vital to advance biomedical knowledge and develop medical treatments. However, it raises ethical questions regarding the welfare and rights of animals used in research. Researchers must justify the necessity of animal research, minimize harm to animals, and adhere to ethical guidelines for animal experimentation.

   Ethical considerations in animal research include using the minimum number of animals required, ensuring proper housing and care, minimizing pain and distress, and considering alternatives, such as cell cultures or computer simulations, when feasible.

4. **Gene Editing and Human Genetic Engineering:** The advent of gene-editing technologies, such as CRISPR-Cas9, has opened new possibilities for modifying the human genome. However, ethical dilemmas arise concerning the potential for designer babies, the alteration of inheritable traits, and unintended consequences.

   Discussions about the ethical boundaries of human genetic engineering involve considering the principles of autonomy, beneficence, justice, and long-term implications for individuals and society.

5. **Data Sharing and Open Science in Research:** Data sharing promotes scientific collaboration, transparency, and reproducibility. However, it also raises ethical challenges, including the protection of participants' privacy, ensuring proper data de-identification, and addressing intellectual property concerns. Researchers must balance the benefits of data sharing with the potential risks and develop ethical practices that respect participants' rights and preserve the integrity of research findings.

   Ethical guidelines and institutional policies on data sharing play a critical role in guiding researchers on responsible and ethical data handling practices.

Addressing these ethical issues in medical research is essential to protect the rights and well-being of research participants, maintain public trust in scientific research, and ensure the integrity and validity of research findings.

Ethics in End-of-Life Care

End-of-life care involves providing compassionate and supportive care to individuals approaching the end of their lives. Ethical considerations in end-of-life care revolve around supporting patients' autonomy, relieving suffering, maintaining dignity, and respecting cultural and religious beliefs.

1. **Euthanasia and Assisted Suicide:** Euthanasia and assisted suicide are controversial topics that raise ethical and legal debates. Euthanasia involves a deliberate act to end a patient's life, typically at their request, to relieve suffering. Assisted suicide involves providing the means for a patient to end their own life.

   Different countries and states have varying legal and ethical perspectives on euthanasia and assisted suicide, and healthcare professionals must navigate these complex and sensitive issues with compassion, respect, and adherence to legal and ethical guidelines.

2. **Palliative Care and Pain Management:** Palliative care focuses on providing comprehensive, holistic care to patients with life-limiting illnesses. It aims to alleviate suffering, relieve pain, and improve the quality of life for patients and their families. Ethical considerations in palliative care involve ensuring access to palliative care services, addressing patients' physical, emotional, and spiritual needs, and respecting their wishes regarding pain management and end-of-life decisions.

   Healthcare providers in palliative care must approach pain management with empathy and a commitment to balancing pain relief with the potential risks and side effects of medications.

3. **Withholding and Withdrawing Life-Sustaining Treatment:** End-of-life care often involves decisions regarding the initiation, continuation, withholding, or withdrawal of life-sustaining treatments. Ethical considerations in these decisions include respecting patient autonomy, assessing the benefits and burdens of treatment, considering medical futility, and involving patients, families, and healthcare professionals in shared decision-making processes.

   Healthcare professionals must ensure clear and empathetic communication with patients and their families, informing them about treatment options, potential outcomes, and the ethical considerations surrounding end-of-life decisions.

4. **Advance Directives and Decision Making:** Advance directives are legal documents that allow individuals to express their preferences for medical care in the event that they cannot make their own decisions. Ethical considerations involve respecting patients' advance directives, ensuring their wishes are followed, and involving surrogate decision-makers when necessary.

Healthcare professionals should regularly discuss advance care planning with patients and encourage the creation and review of advance directives to guide medical decision making when patients are unable to communicate their preferences.

5. **Cultural and Religious Perspectives on Death and Dying:** End-of-life care should respect diverse cultural and religious beliefs and practices concerning death and dying. Healthcare professionals should be aware of and sensitive to cultural and religious preferences regarding family involvement, spiritual rituals, and the handling of the deceased body.

   Respecting cultural and religious perspectives promotes patient-centered care and supports patients and their families in maintaining their cultural and religious practices during the end-of-life journey.

Addressing ethical considerations in end-of-life care requires healthcare professionals to provide compassionate and comprehensive care that respects patients' autonomy, relieves suffering, and upholds their dignity and cultural values.

Ethical Challenges in Global Health

Global health encompasses efforts to address health issues and disparities that transcend national boundaries. It raises several ethical challenges related to access to healthcare, resource allocation, infectious disease control, and social determinants of health.

1. **Access to Healthcare in Developing Countries:** Global health ethics places a strong emphasis on addressing health inequities, particularly in developing countries that face resource constraints and limited access to healthcare. Healthcare professionals and policymakers should work towards promoting universal access to quality healthcare, ensuring fair allocation of resources, and strengthening health systems in resource-limited settings.

   International collaborations, aid programs, and technological innovations play a crucial role in improving access to healthcare in these contexts.

2. **Medical Tourism and Ethical Considerations:** Medical tourism involves traveling to another country to seek medical treatment, often to take advantage of cost savings or specialized procedures. This phenomenon raises ethical concerns regarding the exploitation of healthcare workers, potential harm to patients, and the impact on the local healthcare infrastructure.

Healthcare professionals should critically evaluate medical tourism practices and ensure that patients are well-informed about potential risks, benefits, and ethical considerations before engaging in medical tourism.

3. **Infectious Disease Outbreaks and Public Health Ethics:** Public health ethics is an essential aspect of managing infectious disease outbreaks and health emergencies. It involves balancing individual rights and public health interests, ensuring accurate and transparent communication, and implementing effective preventive measures.

For example, during a pandemic, healthcare professionals must prioritize resource allocation based on the principles of equity, need, and maximizing overall population health.

4. **Allocation of Scarce Medical Resources:** In resource-limited settings or during health emergencies, healthcare professionals may face challenging decisions regarding the allocation of scarce medical resources, such as ventilators, vaccines, or medications. Ethical considerations in resource allocation include maximizing benefits, promoting fairness, and minimizing harm.

Healthcare professionals must adhere to ethical frameworks and guidelines to ensure fair and transparent allocation of scarce resources, taking into account factors such as medical need, prognosis, and the potential to save lives.

5. **Health Disparities and Social Determinants of Health:** Addressing health disparities requires recognizing and addressing social determinants of health, such as poverty, education, housing, and access to clean water and healthcare. Global health ethics aims to reduce health inequities by advocating for policies that promote social justice, equitable resource distribution, and comprehensive healthcare systems.

Healthcare professionals should work collaboratively to address the root causes of health disparities and promote health equity, acknowledging the structural and systemic factors that contribute to health inequalities.

Ethical practices in global health involve balancing the needs of individuals and populations, promoting equitable access to healthcare, engaging in culturally sensitive approaches, and addressing the social determinants that shape health outcomes.

The ethical considerations discussed in this section serve as a foundation for healthcare professionals, policymakers, and researchers to navigate the complex ethical landscape in healthcare. By prioritizing patient autonomy, beneficence, justice, honesty, confidentiality, and respect for cultural and religious beliefs, ethical healthcare practices can ensure the provision of compassionate care that respects the rights and dignity of individuals and communities.

Ethics in Technology and Artificial Intelligence

As technology continues to advance at an unprecedented rate, ethical considerations surrounding its use have become increasingly important. In this section, we will explore the ethical implications of technology and artificial intelligence (AI), and delve into the key principles that should guide our decision-making in these areas.

Understanding Technology Ethics

Technology ethics refers to the moral principles and values that govern the development, deployment, and use of technology. It encompasses ethical considerations related to privacy, security, transparency, accountability, fairness, and the impact of technology on individuals and society as a whole.

Ethical Concerns in Artificial Intelligence

Artificial Intelligence, with its growing presence in various aspects of our lives, brings about unique ethical challenges. It raises questions about accountability, bias, privacy, and the potential impact on job markets and socioeconomic disparities. Here are some specific areas of ethical concern in AI:

1. Accountability   As AI systems become more autonomous and make decisions that impact human lives, questions arise about who should be held accountable when things go wrong. Ensuring clear lines of responsibility and establishing mechanisms for recourse and redress in case of AI failures is essential.

2. Bias and Fairness   AI systems learn from vast amounts of data, which may contain biases inherent in human society. If these biases are not properly addressed, AI algorithms can perpetuate or even amplify discrimination and inequality. It is crucial to develop AI systems that are fair, unbiased, and transparent in their decision-making processes.

3. Privacy and Data Protection   AI often relies on vast amounts of personal and sensitive data to function effectively. Balancing the benefits of AI with the rights of individuals to privacy and data protection is a significant ethical challenge. Adequate safeguards and regulations must be in place to ensure the responsible and ethical use of personal data.

4. Transparency and Explainability The inherent complexity of AI algorithms can make it challenging to understand how they arrive at their decisions. Ensuring transparency in AI systems is crucial to build trust and allow individuals to understand the underlying reasoning behind AI-generated outcomes. Explainable AI is an area of research that aims to address this ethical concern.

5. Socioeconomic Impact AI has the potential to disrupt job markets and contribute to socioeconomic disparities. As AI technology advances, ethical considerations must address the impact on employment, income inequality, and access to resources. It is essential to ensure that the benefits of AI are distributed equitably and that measures are in place to mitigate negative consequences.

Ethical Guidelines and Frameworks

To navigate the ethical complexities of technology and AI, several ethical guidelines and frameworks have been proposed. These frameworks provide a set of principles and best practices to guide ethical decision-making. Here are some commonly referenced frameworks:

1. The IEEE Global Initiative on Ethics of Autonomous and Intelligent Systems The IEEE (Institute of Electrical and Electronics Engineers) developed a framework that emphasizes the need for transparency, accountability, and the consideration of societal impact. The framework encourages involving multiple stakeholders, ensuring diversity and inclusion, and prioritizing human well-being in the design and deployment of AI systems.

2. The European Commission's Ethics Guidelines for Trustworthy AI The European Commission's guidelines emphasize the development of AI systems that are lawful, ethical, and robust. The guidelines focus on the principles of human agency and oversight, technical robustness, privacy, and data governance, as well as societal well-being. They stress the importance of respecting fundamental rights and avoiding harm.

3. The Partnership on AI's Ethical Guidelines for AI   The Partnership on AI, a collaboration between major technology companies and nonprofits, has developed ethical guidelines for AI that emphasize fairness, transparency, and accountability. The guidelines promote the responsible use of AI, safeguarding individual privacy, and ensuring that AI technologies prioritize social benefit and avoid harmful uses.

Case Study: Facial Recognition Technology

Facial recognition technology is an example that highlights the ethical complexities surrounding technology and AI. While this technology has various beneficial applications, such as improving security and identifying missing persons, it also raises significant concerns. Here are some ethical considerations related to facial recognition technology:

Privacy and Surveillance   The widespread use of facial recognition technology raises concerns about individual privacy and the potential for surveillance. There is a need to establish regulations and safeguards to protect individuals' privacy rights and prevent the misuse of this technology.

Accuracy and Bias   Facial recognition algorithms may produce inaccurate results, especially when it comes to recognizing individuals from marginalized communities. This can lead to biased outcomes and reinforce existing societal disparities. Ensuring the accuracy and fairness of facial recognition technology is crucial to mitigate these biases.

Consent and Informed Decision-making   When deploying facial recognition technology in public spaces or private establishments, obtaining informed consent and providing individuals with the necessary information about data collection and use is essential. Ethical considerations should prioritize consent and empower individuals to make informed choices about their personal data.

Resources for Further Reading

Ethics in technology and AI is a complex and evolving field. For those interested in exploring these topics further, the following resources provide valuable insights and perspectives:

- *The Ethics of Artificial Intelligence* by Nick Bostrom and Eliezer Yudkowsky

- *Artificial Intelligence: A Guide to Ethical and Legal Issues* edited by Wendell Wallach and Colin Allen

- *Ethics of Artificial Intelligence and Robotics* edited by Vincent C. Müller

- *Ethical AI: The Ten Commandments of AI Ethics* by Daniel Shapiro

- *The Ethical Algorithm: The Science of Socially Aware Algorithm Design* by Michael Kearns and Aaron Roth

Conclusion

As technology and AI continue to shape our world, it is vital to approach their development and use with a strong ethical foundation. By considering principles of fairness, transparency, accountability, and social impact, we can navigate the complexities of technology ethics and ensure that our technological advancements align with our values and contribute to a better future. Remember, the decisions we make today will shape the world of tomorrow.

Ethics in Education

In today's rapidly changing world, ethics plays a crucial role in every aspect of society. Education, as a fundamental pillar of society, is no exception. Ethics in education encompasses a wide range of principles and values that guide the actions and decisions of educators, administrators, and students. It involves not only ethical conduct but also the development of ethical awareness and decision-making skills among all stakeholders in the educational system.

The Importance of Ethics in Education

Ethics in education is essential for several reasons. Firstly, it provides a moral framework for educators to uphold the highest standards of professional conduct. Teachers and administrators must act with integrity and treat all students fairly and equitably, regardless of their background or circumstances. This ensures that educational institutions serve as safe and inclusive spaces for learning and growth.

Secondly, ethics in education helps instill moral values and promote character development in students. Education is not just about imparting knowledge; it also involves shaping individuals' values, attitudes, and behaviors. By incorporating ethical principles into the curriculum and fostering a moral climate within schools, educators can help students cultivate virtues such as empathy, respect, honesty, and responsibility.

Furthermore, ethics in education prepares students for the complexities of the modern world. It equips them with the skills to critically analyze ethical dilemmas, make informed decisions, and navigate ethical challenges they may encounter in their personal and professional lives. Education should not only focus on academic achievements but also on fostering ethical intelligence, social awareness, and ethical reasoning abilities.

Ethical Principles in Education

The ethical framework in education is based on a set of fundamental principles that guide the behavior and decision-making of educational professionals. These principles serve as a compass to ensure that educators act responsibly and ethically in all aspects of their work. Some of the key ethical principles in education include:

1. **Respect for autonomy:** This principle emphasizes the importance of recognizing and honoring the autonomy and dignity of each student. It requires educators to treat students as individuals with their own unique perspectives, abilities, and needs. Respecting autonomy involves providing students with choices, involving them in the decision-making process, and empowering them to voice their opinions and concerns.

2. **Beneficence:** Educators have a duty to promote the well-being and development of their students. This principle entails taking actions that benefit students' learning, growth, and overall welfare. It involves providing a supportive and nurturing learning environment, offering personalized instruction, and adapting teaching methods to meet students' diverse needs.

3. **Non-maleficence:** This principle states that educators must do no harm to their students. It requires them to actively avoid actions that could cause physical, emotional, or psychological harm. Educators should prioritize the safety and well-being of their students and take measures to prevent and address any form of abuse, bullying, discrimination, or harassment.

4. **Justice:** The principle of justice emphasizes fairness and equitable treatment in education. It requires educators to promote equal access to educational opportunities for all students, regardless of their socioeconomic status, cultural background, or abilities. Educators should strive to create an inclusive and diverse learning environment that celebrates and respects individual differences.

5. **Integrity**: Integrity is a fundamental ethical principle in education. It involves honesty, transparency, and adherence to ethical standards. Educators should act in a manner consistent with their professional and ethical responsibilities, maintaining the trust of students, parents, and the community. Integrity also encompasses fostering academic honesty and preventing cheating and plagiarism among students.

Ethical Challenges in Education

While ethics provides a guiding framework, educators often face challenging ethical dilemmas in their day-to-day work. These challenges require a thoughtful and principled approach to navigate effectively. Some common ethical challenges in education include:

1. **Conflicts of interest**: Educators may encounter situations where their personal interests conflict with their professional responsibilities. For example, accepting gifts from students or their families may compromise fairness and impartiality. Addressing conflicts of interest requires educators to prioritize the best interests of students and make decisions based on ethical principles rather than personal gain.

2. **Inclusivity and diversity**: Creating an inclusive and equitable learning environment can be challenging due to the diverse needs, backgrounds, and abilities of students. Educators must find ways to respect and value individual differences while ensuring fairness and equal opportunities for all. This may involve adapting teaching methods, providing accommodations, and promoting cultural sensitivity and awareness.

3. **Testing and assessment**: Balancing the need for assessments to measure student progress with the ethical considerations of fairness and accountability can be complex. Educators must ensure that assessments accurately reflect students' abilities and provide opportunities for growth and improvement. They should avoid excessive pressure and competition and consider alternative assessment methods that accommodate different learning styles.

4. **Digital citizenship and online behavior**: With the increasing use of technology in education, educators must address ethical challenges related to digital citizenship and online behavior. This includes teaching students about responsible and ethical use of technology, promoting digital privacy and safety, and preventing cyberbullying and inappropriate online behaviors.

5. **Teacher-student boundaries:** Maintaining appropriate boundaries between educators and students is crucial to ensure the well-being and safety of students. Educators must be vigilant to avoid any behavior that could be misinterpreted or contribute to an unhealthy power dynamic. Establishing clear expectations and guidelines for professional conduct helps maintain a safe and respectful learning environment.

Ethical Decision Making in Education

To navigate ethical challenges effectively, educators can utilize ethical decision-making models. These models provide a systematic approach to analyze ethical dilemmas, consider alternative courses of action, and make informed decisions based on ethical principles. Some commonly used ethical decision-making models in education include:

1. **The Utilitarian Model:** This model focuses on maximizing overall happiness or well-being for the majority of individuals involved. Educators using this model would consider the potential benefits and harms of each decision and choose the option that leads to the greatest happiness or well-being for the most students.

2. **The Rights-based Model:** Based on the concept of individual rights, this model prioritizes ensuring that each student's rights and dignity are respected. Educators employing this model would analyze how each decision impacts the fundamental rights of students and choose the alternative that upholds and protects those rights.

3. **The Virtue-based Model:** This model emphasizes the cultivation of virtues and character development. It involves reflecting on the educator's moral virtues and values and considering how each decision aligns with those virtues. Educators using this model would choose the course of action that promotes traits such as honesty, empathy, and fairness.

4. **The Duty-based Model:** Rooted in principles of duty and obligation, this model focuses on performing actions that fulfill one's moral responsibilities. Educators employing this model would consider their professional obligations to students, parents, and society and choose the decision that best fulfills those duties.

5. **The Consequence-based Model:** This model examines the potential consequences of each decision and weighs them in determining the ethical

course of action. Educators using this model would analyze the short-term and long-term consequences of each option and select the alternative that minimizes harm and maximizes benefits.

It is important to note that ethical decision-making is a complex process, and different models may be more applicable depending on the specific circumstances and context of the ethical dilemma. Educators should engage in reflective practice, seek advice from colleagues, and consult relevant policies and guidelines when facing challenging ethical decisions.

Conclusion

Ethics in education is a vital component of creating a nurturing and inclusive learning environment. By integrating ethical principles into the education system, educators can help shape responsible and compassionate individuals who contribute positively to society. By navigating ethical challenges with thoughtful decision-making, educators can uphold the highest standards of integrity and promote the well-being and development of their students. Ultimately, ethics in education is not only about imparting knowledge but also about fostering ethical awareness, compassion, and character in the next generation of leaders.

Historical Evolution of Ethics

Ancient Philosophical Perspectives on Ethics

In order to understand the development of ethical thought, it is important to explore the ancient philosophical perspectives on ethics. Ancient civilizations made significant contributions to ethical philosophy, laying the foundation for the ethical theories and principles that we use today. This section will examine some of the key ancient philosophical perspectives on ethics, including those from Ancient Greece, India, and China.

Ancient Greek Philosophical Perspectives

Ancient Greece was a hotbed of intellectual activity, giving rise to several philosophical schools of thought that continue to influence ethical thinking. Three prominent philosophers of ancient Greece who contributed significantly to the understanding of ethics are Socrates, Plato, and Aristotle.

Socrates: The Pursuit of Wisdom Socrates, one of the most influential philosophers of all time, believed in the intrinsic value of knowledge and the pursuit of wisdom. He emphasized the importance of self-examination and questioning one's own beliefs and values. Socrates used a method of inquiry called the Socratic Method to engage in dialogue and challenge conventional wisdom. His ethical philosophy centered around the notion that knowledge and virtue are inseparable, and that true happiness is derived from living a virtuous life.

Plato: The Realm of Ideas Plato, a student of Socrates, emphasized the metaphysical realm of ideas and believed that the ultimate reality exists beyond the physical world. In his famous work "The Republic," Plato set forth his theory of Forms, arguing that the material world is a mere reflection of perfect and unchanging ideal Forms. Plato believed that the highest good is the pursuit of knowledge and the realization of the eternal truths found in the realm of ideas. He also introduced the concept of the tripartite soul, composed of the rational, spirited, and appetitive parts, which he believed should be harmoniously balanced to achieve a virtuous life.

Aristotle: Virtue Ethics Aristotle, a student of Plato, developed a comprehensive ethical theory known as virtue ethics. He believed that the ultimate goal of human life is eudaimonia, often translated as "flourishing" or "the good life." According to Aristotle, eudaimonia is achieved through the cultivation of virtues, such as courage, temperance, and wisdom. Unlike Plato, Aristotle focused on the ethical virtues that could be developed through habituation and practical reasoning. He emphasized the importance of finding the "golden mean" between extremes, arguing that ethical behavior lies in striking a balance between deficiency and excess.

Ancient Indian Philosophical Perspectives

Ancient Indian philosophy also made significant contributions to ethics, particularly through the teachings of Hinduism and Buddhism.

Hinduism: Karma and Dharma Hinduism, one of the oldest religions in the world, places great emphasis on the concepts of karma and dharma. Karma refers to the law of cause and effect, where one's present actions determine their future destiny. Good actions result in positive karma, while bad actions lead to negative karma. Dharma, on the other hand, refers to one's duty or moral obligations based on their caste, occupation, and stage of life. Hindu ethical philosophy revolves around the idea of fulfilling one's dharma and accumulating good karma to achieve liberation from the cycle of birth and death.

Buddhism: The Middle Way   Buddhism, founded by Siddhartha Gautama (the Buddha) in the 6th century BCE, offers a unique perspective on ethics. The Buddha taught the concept of the Middle Way, which advocates for moderation and balance in all aspects of life. Buddhism emphasizes the importance of moral conduct, known as the Five Precepts, which include refraining from killing, stealing, sexual misconduct, lying, and intoxication. The ultimate goal in Buddhism is to attain enlightenment and liberation from suffering through the practice of mindfulness and the cultivation of ethical virtues, such as compassion, generosity, and wisdom.

Ancient Chinese Philosophical Perspectives

Ancient Chinese philosophy, particularly Confucianism and Daoism, provides valuable insights into ethical thinking.

Confucianism: The Way of Moral Cultivation   Confucianism, founded by Confucius in the 5th century BCE, emphasizes the importance of moral cultivation and social harmony. Confucius believed that the key to a harmonious society lies in the cultivation of ethical virtues, such as benevolence, righteousness, and filial piety. He emphasized the importance of maintaining proper relationships and fulfilling one's roles and responsibilities within society. Confucian ethics focus on creating an ethical society through the practice of rituals, respect for authority, and the cultivation of moral character.

Daoism: The Way of Nature   Daoism, attributed to the ancient Chinese philosopher Laozi, emphasizes living in harmony with the Dao, which can be translated as the "way" or the "path." Daoism encourages individuals to embrace the natural flow of life and to avoid excessive striving and attachment. Ethical values in Daoism revolve around simplicity, spontaneity, and humility. Daoist ethics emphasize the importance of non-action, or wu-wei, which involves not interfering with the natural course of events and allowing things to unfold naturally.

Key Takeaways

The ancient philosophical perspectives on ethics provide a rich and diverse foundation for ethical thinking. From the Greeks to the Indians and the Chinese, these ancient civilizations explored the nature of virtue, the pursuit of wisdom, the importance of moral conduct, and the quest for harmony and balance. Understanding these ancient perspectives allows us to appreciate the historical evolution of ethical thought and to engage in contemporary ethical discourse with a broader perspective.

Aristotle's Virtue Ethics

Aristotle's Virtue Ethics is a philosophical approach to ethics that focuses on the development of moral character and the cultivation of virtues in individuals. It is based on the belief that moral qualities or virtues are essential for human flourishing and the attainment of eudaimonia, which can be translated as "flourishing" or "fulfillment."

1. Historical Context: Aristotle (384-322 BCE) was a Greek philosopher and one of the most influential thinkers in Western philosophy. He was a student of Plato and the teacher of Alexander the Great. Aristotle's moral philosophy differs from the earlier theories of Socrates and Plato, who focused on the abstract nature of morality. Instead, Aristotle emphasized the role of virtue in human life and how it contributes to a good and meaningful existence.

2. Key Concepts: 2.1. Telos: Aristotle believed that everything in nature has a specific purpose or end goal, referred to as its telos. For human beings, the ultimate telos is eudaimonia, which encompasses the highest form of human flourishing. Virtuous actions and living in accordance with one's moral virtues are essential for achieving eudaimonia.

2.2. Moral Virtues: According to Aristotle, moral virtues are acquired through habituation and practice. They are qualities of character that enable individuals to act in the right way and develop a virtuous disposition. Examples of moral virtues include courage, honesty, generosity, and justice. Aristotle identified twelve moral virtues, which he considered to be the golden mean between extremes.

2.3. Golden Mean: Aristotle believed that virtue lies between two extremes. For example, courage is the virtue that lies between the vices of recklessness (excessive courage) and cowardice (deficiency of courage). The golden mean is not an exact midpoint between extremes but rather a relative balance that depends on the situation and individual.

2.4. Ethical Eudaimonism: Aristotle's ethics is a form of eudaimonism, which means that the ultimate goal of human life is the achievement of eudaimonia. Eudaimonia is not simply happiness but a state of well-being that encompasses flourishing, fulfillment, and the realization of one's potential. Virtuous actions and the cultivation of moral virtues are essential for attaining eudaimonia.

3. Application of Virtue Ethics: 3.1. Ethical Decision Making: Virtue ethics provides a framework for making ethical decisions based on the development of moral character. Instead of focusing on rules or consequences, virtue ethics emphasizes the importance of developing virtuous habits and virtues that guide ethical behavior.

3.2. Moral Education: Aristotle believed that moral virtues can be cultivated through education and practice. Education plays a crucial role in shaping individuals' characters and inculcating moral virtues. Virtue ethics, therefore, has implications for moral education, both in formal educational settings and in society at large.

3.3. Virtuous Leadership: Aristotle argued that virtuous character traits are essential for effective leadership. Leaders who possess virtues such as integrity, courage, and justice are more likely to make ethical decisions and inspire trust and respect in their followers. Virtue ethics can, therefore, inform and guide ethical leadership practices.

4. Criticisms and Limitations: 4.1. Cultural Relativism: Critics argue that virtue ethics can lead to cultural relativism, as it allows for a wide range of moral virtues and values based on cultural norms. This flexibility can make it challenging to determine universal moral standards and can lead to variation in ethical judgments across different cultures.

4.2. Lack of Guidance in Difficult Moral Dilemmas: Virtue ethics may not provide clear-cut guidance in complex moral dilemmas where there are conflicting virtues or where the right course of action is not evident. Other ethical frameworks, such as consequentialism or deontology, may offer more specific guidance in such situations.

4.3. Incomplete Account of Moral Obligations: Critics argue that virtue ethics focuses primarily on the development of moral character and does not provide a comprehensive account of moral obligations towards others, such as duties, responsibilities, and rights.

5. Resources and Further Reading: 5.1. "Nicomachean Ethics" by Aristotle: This is Aristotle's major work on ethics, where he presents his ideas on virtue, character, and eudaimonia. It provides a detailed account of his ethical framework and is a fundamental text in virtue ethics.

5.2. "Virtue Ethics" by Rosalind Hursthouse: This book provides a contemporary exploration of virtue ethics, including its historical development, key concepts, and application to various ethical issues. It offers a comprehensive introduction to the topic for students and scholars alike.

5.3. Stanford Encyclopedia of Philosophy: The Stanford Encyclopedia of Philosophy offers an in-depth article on virtue ethics, providing a scholarly overview of the historical development, key concepts, criticisms, and contemporary debates within the field.

5.4. Virtue Ethics Research Centre: This research center, based at the University of Oxford, focuses on the study of virtue ethics from an interdisciplinary perspective. It offers resources, publications, and events related to virtue ethics research.

Example:

Consider the example of a business executive faced with a difficult decision. They discover that a competitor is engaging in unethical practices that could harm consumers. The executive believes it is their duty to report this information to the relevant authorities. However, doing so would result in negative consequences for their own company and potentially lead to the loss of their job.

Using Aristotle's Virtue Ethics, the executive would consider the virtues relevant to the situation. They would balance the virtue of honesty, which urges them to report the unethical practices, with the virtues of loyalty and integrity, which urge them to protect their company and its employees. In this case, the executive would need to find the golden mean that balances these competing virtues and leads to the best overall outcome.

By weighing the virtues and seeking the appropriate balance, the executive can make a decision that aligns with their moral character and contributes to their eudaimonia, as well as the well-being of consumers and the wider society. This example illustrates how virtue ethics can guide ethical decision making in complex situations where multiple virtues are at play.

Remember, virtue ethics is just one ethical framework among many, and its application may vary depending on the context and individual beliefs. In practice, individuals often draw on different ethical approaches to make informed and morally considered decisions.

Kant's Deontological Ethics

In this section, we will explore the ethical theory known as deontological ethics, as developed by the philosopher Immanuel Kant. Deontological ethics focuses on the moral duties and obligations that individuals have, rather than the consequences of their actions. Kant believed that moral principles should be based on reason and universal principles, rather than subjective desires or inclinations.

Background

Immanuel Kant (1724-1804) was a German philosopher who made significant contributions to the field of ethics. His work in this area is often referred to as deontological ethics, which comes from the Greek word "deon" meaning duty or obligation. Kant's ethical theory is grounded in the idea that individuals have moral duties that they must fulfill, regardless of the consequences.

Principles of Kantian Ethics

Kantian ethics is based on a few key principles that guide ethical decision making:

1. **Categorical Imperative:** The categorical imperative is a fundamental concept in Kantian ethics. It states that individuals must act according to rules that they could rationally will to be universal laws. In other words, an action is morally right if it can be universally applied without contradiction. For example, if lying is considered immoral, then according to Kant, lying is always wrong, regardless of the situation or the consequences.

2. **Autonomy and Rationality:** Kant emphasized the importance of human autonomy and rationality. He believed that individuals have the capacity to make moral decisions based on reason alone, independent of desires or emotions. This rational autonomy allows individuals to freely choose to act in accordance with moral principles.

3. **Respect for Persons:** Kantian ethics places a strong emphasis on the inherent value and dignity of every human being. Individuals should be treated as ends in themselves, never merely as means to an end. This principle requires respecting the autonomy and rationality of others, and not using them as a mere tool for personal gain.

Universalizability and Duty

One of the key aspects of Kant's deontological ethics is the idea of universalizability. The principle of universalizability states that moral principles must be applicable to all rational agents in similar situations. If an action cannot be consistently applied to everyone without contradiction, then it is considered morally impermissible.

Kant argued that moral duties are derived from reason and apply universally to all rational beings. He believed that moral duties are obligations that individuals have, regardless of their personal desires or interests. These duties are not based on the consequences of actions but on the principles that govern them.

Examples and Applications

To illustrate Kant's deontological ethics, let's consider a few examples:

1. **Promise-keeping:** According to Kantian ethics, making and keeping promises is a moral duty. Suppose you have promised to meet a friend for lunch, but on the day of the meeting, you receive a more tempting offer to attend a concert. In this situation, a Kantian would argue that you have a moral duty to keep your promise to your friend, even if it means missing out on the concert.

2. **Truth-telling:** According to Kant, telling the truth is a moral duty. Consider a scenario where a friend asks you for your opinion on their new haircut. Even if you dislike the haircut, a Kantian would argue that you have a moral duty to be honest and provide your sincere opinion, rather than lying to spare their feelings.

3. **Helping others:** Kantian ethics also emphasizes the importance of helping others. According to Kant, we have a moral duty to assist others in need, regardless of our personal desires or interests. For example, if you come across someone who is injured on the street, a Kantian would argue that you have a moral duty to offer assistance, even if it inconveniences you.

Challenges and Criticisms

Like any ethical theory, Kant's deontological ethics has faced its fair share of challenges and criticisms. Some of the common criticisms include:

1. **Conflicting Duties:** Kantian ethics does not provide clear guidance when faced with conflicting duties. For example, if telling the truth leads to harm or injustice, while lying would prevent harm, it is not clear how Kant's theory would resolve this dilemma.

2. **Inflexibility:** Kant's theory is often criticized for its rigidity and lack of flexibility. Since it places a heavy emphasis on moral duties, it may not adequately account for the complexities and nuances of real-life situations.

3. **Emphasis on Reason:** Some critics argue that Kant's theory places too much emphasis on reason and neglects the role of emotions and personal inclinations in moral decision making.

Despite these criticisms, Kant's deontological ethics remains a significant and influential ethical theory. Its emphasis on moral duties and principles continues to shape our understanding of ethics and guide our moral decision making.

Conclusion

Kant's deontological ethics provides a unique perspective on ethics, focusing on the moral duties and obligations individuals have, rather than the consequences of their actions. The principles of universalizability and duty guide ethical decision making in this framework, emphasizing autonomy, rationality, and respect for persons. While it has faced criticisms, Kant's ethical theory continues to be relevant and influential in modern ethical practices.

Mill's Utilitarianism

Background

Utilitarianism is a consequentialist ethical theory that was developed by Jeremy Bentham and later refined by John Stuart Mill in the 19th century. It is based on the premise that the rightness or wrongness of an action is determined by its consequences. According to utilitarianism, the morally right action is the one that maximizes overall happiness or well-being and minimizes overall suffering or harm.

John Stuart Mill, in his work "Utilitarianism" published in 1863, expanded upon Bentham's utilitarianism and introduced important modifications to the theory. Mill believed that happiness should be understood in terms of higher pleasures and that the quality of pleasure should be given more importance than the quantity.

Principles of Mill's Utilitarianism

Mill's utilitarianism is guided by several key principles:

Greatest Happiness Principle: The ultimate principle of morality is to seek the greatest amount of happiness for the greatest number of people. Mill argued that actions are right in proportion as they tend to promote happiness and wrong as they tend to produce the reverse of happiness.

Higher and Lower Pleasures: Mill distinguished between higher and lower pleasures. Higher pleasures are those that appeal to our intellectual and moral faculties, while lower pleasures are more sensual and immediate in nature. Mill argued that higher pleasures are of greater value and should be pursued over lower pleasures.

Quality over Quantity: Mill emphasized the importance of the quality of pleasure over the quantity of pleasure. He believed that a life of intellectual pursuits, virtues, and meaningful relationships can bring a deeper and more lasting sense of happiness compared to a life focused solely on sensory pleasures.

Rule Utilitarianism: Mill introduced the concept of rule utilitarianism, which suggests that actions should be judged based on their conformity to general rules that, if followed consistently, would lead to the greatest happiness. This approach contrasts with act utilitarianism, which evaluates each individual action on a case-by-case basis. Mill argued that rule utilitarianism provides more stability and consistency in moral decision-making.

Application of Mill's Utilitarianism

Mill's utilitarianism can be applied to various ethical dilemmas and situations. Let's consider a few examples:

Example 1: The Trolley Problem

In the famous ethical dilemma known as the Trolley Problem, a runaway train is heading towards five people tied to the tracks. You have the option to divert the train onto another track where only one person is tied. According to Mill's utilitarianism, the morally right action would be to divert the train, sacrificing one life to save five lives. This decision is based on the principle of maximizing overall happiness by minimizing overall suffering.

Example 2: Environmental Ethics

In the context of environmental ethics, Mill's utilitarianism can be used to determine the right course of action for the protection of the environment. For instance, in the case of building a new factory, utilitarianism would consider the overall consequences of the factory's construction on the environment, wildlife, and human well-being. If the negative impacts outweigh the benefits, such as job creation, utilitarianism would argue against building the factory.

Critiques and Limitations

While Mill's utilitarianism offers a comprehensive ethical framework, it is not without its critiques and limitations. Some common criticisms include:

Utilitarian Calculus: Critics argue that the calculation of overall happiness or well-being is subjective and difficult to quantify. Different individuals have different definitions of happiness, and it may be challenging to weigh the value of various pleasures and pains.

Rights and Justice: Utilitarianism is also criticized for potentially sacrificing individual rights and justice for the sake of maximizing happiness. Critics argue that utilitarianism could endorse actions that violate basic human rights or principles of justice if they maximize overall happiness.

Mind vs. Body: Mill's distinction between higher and lower pleasures has been criticized for its inherent bias towards intellectual and moral pursuits. Critics argue that pleasure and happiness derived from physical and sensory experiences should also be given equal consideration.

Conclusion

Mill's utilitarianism provides a practical and flexible ethical theory that takes into account the overall consequences of actions and seeks to maximize happiness. It incorporates the notion of higher pleasures, the importance of quality over quantity, and the concept of rule utilitarianism. However, it is not without its critiques and limitations, such as the challenges in calculating happiness and potential conflicts with individual rights and justice. Nonetheless, Mill's utilitarianism continues to be influential in contemporary ethical debates and decision-making.

Ethical Theories in the Renaissance and Enlightenment

During the Renaissance and Enlightenment period, there was a significant shift in the way ethics was understood and studied. This era saw the emergence of new philosophical perspectives and ethical theories that challenged traditional beliefs and paved the way for modern ethical thought. In this section, we will explore some of the key ethical theories that emerged during the Renaissance and Enlightenment.

Humanism and the Ethics of the Renaissance

The Renaissance was a period of humanistic revival, where scholars and thinkers placed a strong emphasis on the potential and dignity of human beings. Humanism rejected the dominant religious worldview of the Middle Ages and sought to ground morality in reason and human experience.

One prominent ethical theory that emerged during this period was the concept of virtue ethics. Inspired by the ancient Greek philosophers, particularly Aristotle, virtue ethics emphasized the cultivation of virtuous character traits as the foundation of ethical behavior. Renaissance humanists like Pico della Mirandola and Leonardo da Vinci believed that humans have the capacity to develop their moral character through reason and personal growth.

Virtue ethics in the Renaissance emphasized the importance of qualities such as wisdom, courage, temperance, and justice. For example, Leonardo da Vinci, known not only for his artistic genius but also his scientific advancements, believed that cultivating virtues like curiosity and open-mindedness would lead to a more ethical and fulfilling life.

Enlightenment and the Ethics of Reason

The Enlightenment was a period characterized by the pursuit of reason, science, and individual freedom. Enlightenment thinkers sought to challenge traditional authority and dogma, advocating for the use of reason and evidence in all areas of life, including ethics.

Immanuel Kant was one of the most influential philosophers of the Enlightenment, and his ethical theory, known as deontological ethics, had a profound impact on moral philosophy. Kant argued that morality should be based on rational principles and universal moral laws.

According to Kant, actions are morally right if they are done out of a sense of duty and in accordance with the categorical imperative, which is a principle that commands respect for the inherent dignity and autonomy of all rational beings. This universal principle requires treating others as ends in themselves, rather than as mere means to our own ends.

Kant's deontological ethics emphasized moral rules and duties, rather than outcomes or consequences. For example, lying is always morally wrong, regardless of the potential benefits it may bring. Kant believed that ethical decisions should be guided by reason and moral principles, rather than subjective desires or preferences.

Contrasting Hedonism and Utilitarianism

While virtue ethics and deontological ethics were gaining prominence during the Renaissance and Enlightenment, other ethical theories were also being explored and developed. One such theory was hedonism, which advocated for the pursuit of pleasure and the avoidance of pain as the ultimate aim of human life.

The philosopher Jeremy Bentham, a key figure in the development of utilitarianism, built upon the hedonistic tradition by proposing a consequentialist ethical theory. Utilitarianism holds that actions are morally right if they produce the greatest amount of happiness for the greatest number of people.

Bentham believed in the quantification of pleasure and proposed a method of measurement called the "hedonic calculus." This calculus sought to assign numerical values to different pleasures and pains, taking into account their intensity, duration, certainty, and other relevant factors.

Utilitarianism gained further traction during the Enlightenment period through the work of philosophers like John Stuart Mill. Mill developed a more nuanced version of utilitarianism, known as rule utilitarianism, which focused on the establishment of general moral rules that maximize overall happiness.

However, utilitarianism faced critiques from other ethical theories, including the deontological perspective. Critics argued that utilitarianism could lead to the violation of individual rights and the sacrifice of certain individuals for the greater good.

Implications and Relevance

The ethical theories that emerged during the Renaissance and Enlightenment continue to shape our understanding of morality and guide ethical decision-making in various fields today. Virtue ethics reminds us of the importance of character development and the cultivation of virtues in our personal and professional lives.

Deontological ethics, with its emphasis on duty and universal moral laws, provides a framework for ethical decision-making that is not solely based on outcomes but also on ethical principles. Utilitarianism, while criticized by some, highlights the importance of considering the overall consequences of our actions and aiming for the greatest happiness for the largest number of people.

These ethical theories are not mutually exclusive, and different perspectives can be integrated to provide a comprehensive ethical framework. It is essential to consider the complexities and nuances of ethical issues, taking into account both individual and societal values.

In the modern era, these theories continue to be relevant in addressing contemporary ethical challenges. For example, in healthcare, the principles of beneficence and non-maleficence draw upon virtue ethics, while issues of patient autonomy and justice align with deontological principles.

In business, considerations of corporate social responsibility and ethical decision-making often involve weighing the outcomes and consequences of actions, as well as adherence to moral principles. And in the realm of technology and artificial intelligence, questions of privacy, fairness, and accountability necessitate the application of various ethical theories.

Ethical theories provide a valuable framework for analyzing and evaluating moral issues, but it is crucial to remember that ethics is a complex and evolving field. As we navigate the challenges of the modern world, it is important to engage in ongoing dialogue and critical reflection on ethical matters, recognizing the multifaceted nature of ethical decision-making.

Contractualism and Social Contract Theory

Contractualism and social contract theory are ethical frameworks that aim to provide principles for moral decision-making based on agreements and contracts between individuals or groups. These theories emphasize the role of rationality, fairness, and mutual consent in determining the moral rules that govern society. In this section, we will explore the key concepts, principles, and implications of contractualism and social contract theory.

Background

Contractualism and social contract theory have their roots in the works of philosophers such as Thomas Hobbes, John Locke, and Jean-Jacques Rousseau. These thinkers explored the idea of a social contract, which is an implicit or explicit agreement among individuals to establish a society and live together under a set of rules.

Hobbes, in his book "Leviathan," proposed that individuals enter into a social contract out of a fundamental self-interest, seeking protection and security in a society governed by a sovereign authority. Locke expanded upon this idea, arguing that the purpose of a social contract is to protect natural rights, including life, liberty, and property. Rousseau, on the other hand, emphasized the collective will of the people and the need for a general will to guide societal decision-making.

Principles of Contractualism and Social Contract Theory

1. **Mutual Agreement:** Contractualism and social contract theory posit that moral principles are derived from a process of mutual agreement and consent among individuals. The focus is on the fair and voluntary consent of all parties involved.

2. **Rationality:** Rationality plays a crucial role in contractualist and social contract theories. Individuals are expected to act rationally and consider the long-term consequences of their actions, taking into account the interests of others as well as their own.

3. **Universalizability:** Contractualist principles are intended to be universalizable, meaning they apply equally to all individuals in similar situations. Moral rules should be applicable to everyone, without any arbitrary distinctions or biases.

4. **Impartiality and Fairness**: Contractualism emphasizes the importance of impartiality and fairness in decision-making. Individuals should choose principles that they would agree to under conditions of fairness, without favoring their own interests over others.

Application

To illustrate the application of contractualism and social contract theory, let's consider the example of taxation. In a society, individuals agree to contribute a portion of their income through taxes to fund public services such as healthcare, education, and infrastructure.

From a contractualist perspective, taxation is justified because it is based on a mutual agreement among citizens. It is in the collective interest to contribute to the common good, ensuring the provision of essential services. However, the principles of fairness and proportionality should also be considered, so that the burden of taxation is distributed equitably among individuals based on their ability to pay.

Social contract theory provides a broader framework for understanding the legitimacy of political authority. According to this theory, individuals consent to be governed by a state in exchange for the protection of their rights and the fulfillment of their needs. This agreement forms the basis for the establishment of laws and institutions that govern society.

Critiques and Limitations

Contractualism and social contract theory have faced various critiques and limitations. Some of the key criticisms include:

1. **Non-existent consent**: Critics argue that individuals may not have explicitly consented to the social contract or agreed upon the specific terms of the agreement. The notion of implicit consent is also questioned, as it assumes that individuals have a choice to opt out of the social contract.

2. **Inequality and power dynamics**: The social contract may not always reflect the interests and perspectives of all individuals equally. Power imbalances, systemic injustices, and social inequalities can influence the terms of the social contract, compromising its fairness.

3. **Cultural and moral diversity**: Contractualism and social contract theory may not adequately account for cultural diversity and moral pluralism. Different cultures and communities may have distinct moral principles and values that may not align with the universalizable principles of contractualism.

Despite these critiques, contractualism and social contract theory continue to provide valuable insights into the foundations of morality and the functioning of societies. These theories remind us of the importance of consent, fairness, and rationality in establishing moral principles and promoting the well-being of individuals and communities.

Further Readings and Resources

1. Rawls, J. (1971). "A Theory of Justice". Harvard University Press. 2. Gaus, G. F. (2011). "The Order of Public Reason: A Theory of Freedom and Morality in a Diverse and Bounded World". Cambridge University Press. 3. Simmons, A. J. (2009). "On the Edge of Anarchy: Locke, Consent, and the Limits of Society". Princeton University Press. 4. Hampton, J. (1986). "Hobbes and the Social Contract Tradition". Cambridge University Press. 5. Rousseau, J. J. (1762). "The Social Contract". Penguin Classics. 6. Stanford Encyclopedia of Philosophy - Contractualism: plato.stanford.edu/entries/contractualism 7. Stanford Encyclopedia of Philosophy - Social Contract Theory: plato.stanford.edu/entries/contractarianism-contemporary

Hedonism and Utilitarian Calculus

Hedonism is a philosophical concept that suggests that the ultimate goal of human life is to maximize pleasure and minimize pain. It is based on the belief that pleasure and happiness are the highest forms of good, and individuals should strive to maximize their own well-being.

Utilitarianism, on the other hand, is a moral theory that focuses on the consequences of actions. It states that the right action is the one that maximizes overall happiness or utility for the greatest number of people. Utilitarians believe that actions that lead to the greatest amount of happiness and the least amount of suffering are morally right.

Hedonism and utilitarianism are closely related, as they both prioritize the pursuit of happiness and pleasure. However, while hedonism focuses on individual well-being, utilitarianism takes a more collective approach, considering the happiness and suffering of all individuals affected by an action.

Principles of Hedonism

Hedonism is rooted in the belief that pleasure and happiness are intrinsically valuable. It recognizes two main principles:

1. **Pleasure Principle:** The ultimate aim of human life is to experience pleasure and avoid pain. Pleasure is the only intrinsic good, and pain is the only intrinsic evil. According to hedonism, pleasure encompasses both physical and mental enjoyment, while pain includes physical and mental suffering.

2. **Felicity Calculus:** Hedonism suggests that individuals should make decisions based on a felicity calculus, in which they assess the balance of pleasure and pain that is likely to result from their actions. This calculus involves considering the intensity, duration, certainty, and propinquity of the pleasure or pain.

Principles of Utilitarianism

Utilitarianism is guided by the principle of maximizing overall happiness or utility. It is based on several key principles:

1. **Utility Principle:** The morality of an action is determined by its overall contribution to happiness or overall utility. Actions that maximize happiness are morally right, while those that decrease overall happiness are morally wrong. Utility is defined as the net balance of pleasure and pain.

2. **Consequentialism:** Utilitarianism focuses on the consequences of actions rather than the intentions or motives behind them. The morality of an action is evaluated based on its outcomes and the resulting happiness or suffering it produces.

3. **Impartiality:** Utilitarianism requires individuals to consider the happiness and suffering of all individuals equally. It promotes a sense of fairness and impartiality, emphasizing the need to maximize the overall happiness of the greatest number of people.

Applying Utilitarian Calculus

Utilitarian calculus involves a systematic approach to decision-making, considering the balance of happiness and suffering that is likely to result from different actions. It takes into account several factors:

1. **Quantitative Assessment:** Utilitarian calculus quantifies happiness and suffering, allowing for a comparative analysis of different outcomes. It involves assigning values to pleasure and pain and calculating their overall impact.

2. **Consideration of All Affected Parties:** Utilitarian calculus requires considering the happiness and suffering of all individuals affected by an action. This includes not only the direct participants but also indirect stakeholders, such as future generations or those in distant geographical locations.

3. **Long-term Perspective:** Utilitarian calculus looks beyond immediate consequences and considers the long-term impact of actions. It takes into account future happiness or suffering that may result from present decisions.

4. **Moral Dilemmas:** Utilitarianism acknowledges that ethical decision-making can involve conflicting values and interests. In cases of moral dilemmas, where different actions lead to different amounts of overall happiness, utilitarian calculus provides a framework for evaluating and choosing the morally right course of action.

Example: Ethical Considerations in Resource Allocation

Utilitarian calculus can be applied to ethical dilemmas, such as the fair allocation of scarce resources in healthcare. In situations where there is a limited supply of life-saving treatments or organs, utilitarianism can help determine the most ethical distribution.

For example, suppose there are two patients in critical condition, both in need of a heart transplant. Patient A is a young adult with a higher chance of survival, while patient B is an older adult with a lower chance of survival. Utilitarian calculus would involve considering the overall happiness that would result from each decision.

By quantifying the potential happiness and suffering of each patient, including factors such as the expected quality of life and the potential years of happiness gained, utilitarian calculus can help determine the most ethical allocation of the scarce resource. In this case, if the expected happiness from saving patient A is significantly higher than that of patient B, a utilitarian approach would prioritize patient A for the heart transplant.

Caveats and Criticisms

While hedonism and utilitarianism offer valuable frameworks for ethical decision-making, they are not without criticism. Some common criticisms include:

1. **Challenges in Measuring Happiness:** Quantifying pleasure and pain, and measuring overall happiness, can be subjective and difficult. It raises questions about whose values and preferences should be considered when assessing utility.

2. **Treatment of Minority Interests:** Utilitarianism's focus on maximizing overall happiness may overlook the needs and interests of minority groups or individuals. Critics argue that it can lead to the oppression or disregard of minority rights.

3. **Moral Integrity**: Some argue that utilitarianism may require individuals to compromise their moral integrity or act against their deeply held values in order to maximize overall happiness.

Despite these criticisms, hedonism and utilitarianism offer valuable perspectives on ethical practices. By considering the pursuit of pleasure, happiness, and overall utility, individuals and societies can engage in meaningful reflections on the consequences of their actions and strive for ethical decision-making.

Kantian Ethics

Kantian ethics is a philosophical theory developed by Immanuel Kant in the 18th century. It is a deontological ethical framework that focuses on the principles and duties that guide moral behavior. According to Kant, ethical judgments are based on reason and rationality rather than subjective emotions or consequences. In this section, we will explore the key concepts of Kantian ethics and how they shape our understanding of ethical practices.

Principle of Moral Law

At the core of Kantian ethics lies the principle of moral law, which Kant refers to as the categorical imperative. The categorical imperative is a universal and unconditional moral principle that applies to all rational beings. It is a command that we must follow regardless of our desires or personal circumstances. Kant presents several formulations of the categorical imperative, each highlighting a different aspect of moral duty.

First Formulation: Universalizability

The first formulation of the categorical imperative states that we should act only according to the maxim that we can will to become a universal law. In other words, our actions should be guided by principles that can be universally applied without contradiction. This formulation emphasizes the importance of consistency and coherence in moral decision-making.

For example, consider the act of lying. According to Kant, lying is morally wrong because if lying were to become a universal law, trust and communication would break down, rendering lying ineffective. Therefore, lying is not permissible under the first formulation of the categorical imperative.

Second Formulation: Humanity as an End in Itself

The second formulation of the categorical imperative states that we should always treat humanity, whether in ourselves or others, as an end and never merely as a means to an end. This formulation highlights the inherent worth and dignity of rational beings.

Kant argues that using someone merely as a means to achieve our own goals is a violation of their autonomy and diminishes their humanity. Treating others with respect, dignity, and fairness is essential in Kantian ethics.

For example, suppose a person needs help with a project, and you offer your assistance genuinely out of a sense of care and concern. In this case, you treat the person as an end in themselves, acknowledging their worth and autonomy.

Duty and Moral Obligation

According to Kant, ethical actions are not based on consequences or personal desires, but on a sense of duty. Moral obligations arise from our rational nature and the recognition of the moral law. Kant argues that we have a moral obligation to follow the categorical imperative because it is in line with reason and the principles of moral duty.

Kant distinguishes between two types of duties: perfect and imperfect duties. Perfect duties are those that must be universally upheld without exception, such as the duty to honesty and respecting the autonomy of others. Imperfect duties, on the other hand, are more flexible and allow for personal discretion, such as the duty to help others in need.

Universal Intent and Moral Luck

In Kantian ethics, the morality of an action is determined by the intention behind it, rather than the outcome or consequences. According to Kant, we should not be held responsible for factors beyond our control, such as external circumstances or luck. This concept is referred to as moral luck.

For example, suppose you make a donation to a charitable organization with the intention of helping others. Even if the organization mismanages the funds, your action is still morally praiseworthy because your intention was noble.

Freedom and Autonomy

Central to Kantian ethics is the notion of human freedom and autonomy. Kant argues that morality is inherently tied to our ability to reason and make rational choices. Rational beings possess the capacity for autonomy, the ability to act according to one's own free will, guided by reason and moral principles.

Kant emphasizes the importance of individuals taking responsibility for their actions and making choices based on their own rational judgment. Autonomy requires self-governance and the ability to resist external pressures or influences.

Critiques and Limitations

While Kant's ethical framework provides valuable insights into moral duty and rational decision-making, it is not without its critiques and limitations. Some of the common criticisms include:

1. Overemphasis on duty: Critics argue that Kantian ethics may undermine the importance of compassion, empathy, and the consideration of consequences in ethical decision-making.

2. Lack of practical guidance: Kantian ethics does not offer concrete guidance on how to navigate complex moral dilemmas or conflicting duties.

3. Ignoring the role of emotions: Kantian ethics downplays the significance of emotions in ethical decision-making, focusing solely on rationality.

Despite these critiques, Kantian ethics continues to be a significant and influential school of thought in ethical philosophy. Its emphasis on universality, autonomy, and moral duty provides a foundation for understanding ethical practices in various domains of human activity.

Further Reading

- Kant, Immanuel. *Groundwork of the Metaphysics of Morals.* Cambridge University Press, 1997.

- Hill, Thomas E. *Human Welfare and Moral Worth: Kantian Perspectives.* Oxford University Press, 2002.

- O'Neill, Onora. *Constructions of Reason: Explorations of Kant's Practical Philosophy.* Cambridge University Press, 1990.

Exercises

1. Choose an ethical dilemma from everyday life and analyze it from a Kantian perspective. How would Kantian ethics guide you in making a moral decision?

2. Critically evaluate the first formulation of the categorical imperative. Are there any situations in which it may lead to conflicting moral obligations?

Remember, Kantian ethics emphasizes the importance of reason, duty, and treating individuals as ends in themselves. Consider these principles when tackling the exercise questions.

Modern Ethical Theories

In this section, we will explore some of the main modern ethical theories that have emerged in the field of ethics. These theories provide frameworks for understanding and making moral decisions in various contexts. While there are numerous ethical theories, we will focus on four influential ones: consequentialism, deontology, virtue ethics, and feminist ethics.

Consequentialism

Consequentialism, also known as teleological ethics, is a moral theory that emphasizes the consequences or outcomes of actions. According to consequentialism, the moral rightness or wrongness of an action is determined by its consequences. The primary goal of consequentialism is to maximize overall happiness, well-being, or some other desirable outcome.

One prominent form of consequentialism is utilitarianism, which was developed by Jeremy Bentham and John Stuart Mill. Utilitarianism holds that the right action is the one that produces the greatest amount of happiness or utility for the greatest number of people. It focuses on the general welfare and aims to minimize suffering and maximize pleasure.

For example, in the context of healthcare, a consequentialist approach might prioritize allocating medical resources to those who will benefit the most, in terms of saving the most lives or improving quality of life the most. This approach values efficiency and cost-effectiveness.

Deontology

Deontological ethics, in contrast to consequentialism, emphasizes the inherent nature of actions themselves rather than their outcomes. Deontologists believe that there are certain inherent moral duties or principles that govern human actions and should be followed, regardless of the consequences.

Immanuel Kant's deontological theory, known as Kantian ethics, is one of the most well-known deontological frameworks. According to Kant, moral actions are those that are carried out in accordance with categorical imperatives - universal principles that apply to all rational beings. He emphasizes the importance of acting out of a sense of duty rather than personal inclination or desired outcomes.

For instance, in business, a deontologist might argue that lying is inherently wrong, regardless of the potential positive consequences. Thus, in a situation where lying might lead to more sales, a deontologist would argue that honesty and integrity should prevail.

Virtue Ethics

Virtue ethics focuses on the moral character of an individual and the virtues or qualities that make someone a good person. This ethical theory places importance on developing virtuous character traits, such as honesty, compassion, and fairness. Virtue ethics emphasizes the cultivation of these virtues through practice and habituation.

One of the most influential figures in virtue ethics is Aristotle. He believed that practicing virtues leads to eudaimonia, which can be translated as human flourishing or living a fulfilled life. According to Aristotle, virtues lie between extremes, known as vices, and the moral agent should aim to strike a balance.

In the context of education, virtue ethics can inform decisions about what virtues and character traits should be cultivated in students. For example, a virtue ethicist might argue that the development of empathy and kindness is essential for creating a positive and caring educational environment.

Feminist Ethics

Feminist ethics is a branch of ethical theory that focuses on the experiences and perspectives of women and highlights the ways in which gender influences moral reasoning. It critiques traditional ethical theories for their male-centric biases and seeks to include women's experiences in ethical discourse.

Feminist ethics emphasizes the values of care, empathy, and interconnectedness. It rejects the notion of impartiality and argues for the importance of relational ethics.

Relational ethics acknowledges the significance of relationships and social contexts in moral decision-making.

For instance, in healthcare, feminist ethics might highlight the importance of considering the unique needs and experiences of women in medical research, treatment, and reproductive rights. It also draws attention to issues such as gender inequality, domestic violence, and sexual harassment.

Conclusion

In this section, we have explored four major modern ethical theories: consequentialism, deontology, virtue ethics, and feminist ethics. Each of these theories offers a distinct framework for understanding and evaluating moral actions. It is important to note that these theories are not mutually exclusive and often complement one another in practice.

By studying and understanding these ethical theories, individuals can enhance their ability to analyze complex moral questions, make informed decisions, and engage in ethical discussions in various fields and contexts. The application of these theories can contribute to creating a more just and compassionate society. As you delve deeper into the field of ethics, remember that ethical theories are tools for guiding moral reasoning and should be used thoughtfully and critically.

Rawls' Theory of Justice

John Rawls, a prominent American philosopher, developed a comprehensive theory of justice that has had a significant impact on both political philosophy and ethics. Rawls' theory, often referred to as "justice as fairness," provides a framework for understanding how to create a just society and make fair decisions.

Background

To appreciate Rawls' theory, it is important to understand the historical context in which it emerged. Rawls was writing in response to the dominant utilitarian and libertarian theories of justice. Utilitarianism, championed by philosophers like Jeremy Bentham and John Stuart Mill, holds that the morally right action is the one that maximizes overall happiness or pleasure. Libertarianism, on the other hand, emphasizes the importance of individual liberty and minimal government intervention.

Rawls sought to move beyond these theories by addressing the inherent flaws and inequalities they failed to adequately address. He proposed a theory of justice that prioritizes principles of fairness and equal opportunity.

The Original Position

At the core of Rawls' theory is the concept of the "original position." The original position represents a hypothetical situation in which individuals are tasked with designing a just society from behind a "veil of ignorance." In this hypothetical scenario, individuals have no knowledge of their own social position, wealth, talents, or personal characteristics. They are effectively ignorant of everything that could potentially bias their decision-making.

Rawls argues that behind the veil of ignorance, rational individuals would choose principles that maximize fairness and equal opportunity. They would seek to create a society where the least advantaged members are still provided with a decent quality of life.

Principles of Justice

Rawls proposes two principles of justice that individuals in the original position would agree upon:

1. **The Principle of Equal Liberty:** This principle states that each person has an equal right to basic liberties, such as freedom of speech, association, and religion. This principle ensures that individuals have the necessary freedoms to pursue their own conception of the good life.

2. **The Difference Principle:** This principle focuses on the distribution of social and economic goods within society. It states that inequalities are acceptable as long as they benefit the least advantaged members and are attached to positions open to all under fair conditions. In other words, inequalities should be arranged so as to provide the most benefit to those with the least advantages.

Veil of Ignorance and Fairness

The veil of ignorance plays a crucial role in ensuring fairness in Rawls' theory. By imagining a scenario where no one knows their own position in society, individuals are more likely to choose principles that are fair and unbiased. They cannot prioritize their own self-interest or ignore the plight of the least advantaged.

The original position and the veil of ignorance compel individuals to consider the needs of the most vulnerable members of society. This leads to the development of principles that ensure equal access to resources, opportunities, and social benefits.

Critiques and Controversies

Rawls' theory of justice has not been without criticism. One notable critique is the challenge of defining what counts as fair, as individuals may have differing interpretations of the principles of justice. Additionally, some argue that Rawls' theory places too much emphasis on the distribution of resources and may not sufficiently consider other aspects of justice, such as recognition and capabilities.

Another criticism of Rawls' theory is its potential incompatibility with certain cultural and religious values. Critics argue that the theory's focus on individualism and the veil of ignorance may clash with communitarian or collectivist perspectives.

Despite these criticisms, Rawls' theory of justice continues to be influential and widely studied. It offers a valuable framework for understanding the principles and considerations necessary for a just society.

Applying Rawls' Theory in a Contemporary Context

To apply Rawls' theory of justice in a contemporary context, consider the following scenario:

In a society with significant income inequality, the debate arises over whether to implement a progressive tax system. A progressive tax system imposes higher tax rates on individuals with higher incomes and lower rates on those with lower incomes.

Using Rawls' theory, we can analyze this issue. Behind the veil of ignorance, individuals would prioritize the well-being of the least advantaged members of society. They would recognize that a progressive tax system helps redistribute wealth and resources, ensuring a more equal distribution of benefits.

By applying Rawls' theory and considering the principles of justice from the original position, we can argue that implementing a progressive tax system aligns with the goal of creating a just society.

Additional Resources

To further explore Rawls' theory of justice, the following resources are recommended:

+ *A Theory of Justice* by John Rawls: Rawls' original book where he presents his theory in detail.

+ *Justice: What's the Right Thing to Do?* by Michael J. Sandel: Explores various theories of justice, including Rawls' theory, in a engaging and accessible manner.

+ *Rawls's "A Theory of Justice": A Reader's Guide* by Paul Graham: Provides a comprehensive analysis and commentary on Rawls' theory, helping readers navigate its complexities.

Exercises

1. Discuss and debate the merits of Rawls' theory of justice. What are its strengths and weaknesses? Can it adequately address contemporary societal challenges?

2. Imagine you are tasked with designing a healthcare system from behind the veil of ignorance. How would Rawls' theory influence your decision-making? How would you ensure equitable access to healthcare for all members of society?

3. Explore a real-life policy or social issue (e.g., income inequality, climate change) through the lens of Rawls' theory. Analyze how the principles of justice from the original position might inform potential solutions.

Remember to think critically and engage in respectful dialogue when discussing these exercises.

Gilligan's Care Ethics

Gilligan's Care Ethics is a framework for ethical decision making that emphasizes the importance of relationships, care, and empathy. Developed by psychologist Carol Gilligan, this theory emerged as a response to the predominantly male-centered perspectives in traditional ethical theories. Care Ethics provides a valuable alternative that highlights the ethical significance of caring for others and maintaining connections within our moral decision-making processes.

Background

In contrast to traditional ethical theories that prioritize principles and rules, Gilligan argues that women often approach ethical dilemmas from a perspective centered around caring relationships. She suggests that women tend to prioritize the well-being of others, nurture connections, and consider the impact of their actions on the people involved. Gilligan's research revealed that women tend to base their ethical decisions on empathy, compassion, and the desire to prevent harm.

Principles of Care Ethics

Care Ethics is based on several principles that guide ethical decision making:

1. **Interconnectedness:** Care Ethics emphasizes the interconnectedness of individuals and the recognition of our mutual dependence on each other. It emphasizes the importance of maintaining relationships and acknowledging the impact of our actions on others.

2. **Responsiveness to Need:** Care Ethics emphasizes the importance of recognizing and responding to the needs of others. It involves actively engaging with the experiences and perspectives of others and providing support and care when necessary.

3. **Emphasis on Relationships:** Care Ethics recognizes the significance of relationships in ethical decision making. It encourages the consideration of how our actions affect the well-being and relationships of others, and strives to maintain and nurture those relationships.

4. **Empathy and Compassion:** Care Ethics emphasizes the importance of empathy and compassion in understanding the experiences and needs of others. It encourages individuals to consider the emotions and perspectives of others when making ethical decisions.

5. **Nonviolence and Care:** Care Ethics promotes nonviolence and care as fundamental values. It requires actively working towards preventing harm to others, both physically and emotionally, and fostering a nurturing and supportive environment.

Application of Care Ethics

Care Ethics can be applied to various domains, including healthcare, education, politics, and personal relationships. By highlighting the importance of care and empathy, this framework can help individuals make more compassionate and inclusive decisions.

In healthcare, Care Ethics can guide medical professionals in providing patient-centered care. It encourages healthcare providers to consider the patients' emotional well-being, preferences, and needs when making decisions about their treatment plans.

In education, Care Ethics can inform the development of nurturing and inclusive learning environments. It emphasizes the importance of educators building trusting relationships with their students, understanding their unique needs, and providing individualized support.

In politics and governance, Care Ethics challenges traditional power structures and encourages leaders to prioritize the well-being and needs of their constituents. It promotes policies that prioritize care, inclusivity, and social justice.

Example: Applying Care Ethics in a Business Context

Imagine a business executive faced with a decision that could potentially harm a group of employees in the interest of maximizing profits. A Care Ethics perspective would encourage the executive to consider the impact of their decision on the well-being and relationships of the employees.

Instead of solely focusing on financial gains, the executive would evaluate the potential harm caused to the employees and explore alternative solutions that prioritize their well-being. This may involve considering options such as providing additional support, training, or seeking alternative ways to achieve business goals without compromising the employees' welfare.

By applying Care Ethics in this scenario, the executive acknowledges the importance of maintaining relationships, empathy, and compassion in the decision-making process. This approach promotes a more caring and conscientious business environment, emphasizing the well-being of employees and fostering a positive organizational culture.

Resources and Critiques

To further explore Care Ethics, additional resources are available, such as Carol Gilligan's book "In a Different Voice: Psychological Theory and Women's Development." This seminal work delves deeper into the theory and presents compelling arguments for the inclusion of care-based ethics in ethical discourse.

Critics of Care Ethics argue that it may prioritize emotions over rationality and undervalue principles and rules. They contend that a sole focus on care might lead to biased decision making or inconsistent moral judgments. However, advocates assert that Care Ethics should not be seen as a replacement for other ethical theories but rather as a complementary perspective that brings attention to the importance of care and relationships in ethical decision making.

Exercise: Applying Care Ethics in Your Life

Reflect on a recent ethical dilemma you have encountered in your personal or professional life. Using the principles of Care Ethics, analyze the situation from a caring perspective. Consider the impact on relationships, responsiveness to needs, empathy, and the avoidance of harm. How might your decision have differed if you had prioritized care in that situation? Reflect on the potential benefits and challenges of applying Care Ethics in your own life.

Ethical Frameworks and Decision Making

Ethical Principles and Values

In ethical decision making, individuals and organizations rely on a set of principles and values to guide their actions. These principles and values serve as the foundation for ethical behavior and help individuals navigate complex ethical dilemmas. In this section, we will explore some of the key ethical principles and values that are commonly used in ethical frameworks.

Autonomy

Autonomy is the principle that emphasizes an individual's right to self-determination and freedom of choice. It recognizes that individuals have the capacity to make decisions about their own lives and should be respected as autonomous agents. Autonomy is particularly important in the context of healthcare, where it is closely tied to the concept of informed consent. Healthcare professionals must respect the autonomy of their patients and ensure that they have the information and understanding necessary to make informed decisions about their medical care.

Beneficence

Beneficence is the principle that requires individuals to act in a way that promotes the well-being and best interests of others. It is the ethical obligation to do good and to prevent harm. In healthcare, beneficence guides healthcare professionals to provide the best possible care for their patients and to prioritize their health and welfare. It also extends to other areas such as business, where organizations are expected to act in the best interests of their stakeholders, employees, and the wider society.

Non-maleficence

Non-maleficence is the principle that emphasizes the duty to do no harm. It requires individuals to avoid causing harm or injury to others. In healthcare, non-maleficence is a fundamental principle that guides medical professionals to prioritize the safety and well-being of their patients. In other contexts, non-maleficence also applies to avoiding harm to employees, consumers, and the environment.

Justice

Justice is the principle that focuses on fairness and equity. It involves treating all individuals fairly and equally, and ensuring that resources and opportunities are distributed in a just manner. In healthcare, justice is closely tied to the allocation of healthcare resources, as healthcare professionals and policymakers must make decisions about how to allocate limited resources in a fair and equitable way. In business, justice is important in areas such as hiring practices, pay equity, and corporate social responsibility.

Integrity

Integrity is the principle that emphasizes honesty, truthfulness, and adherence to ethical principles. It involves acting in a manner that is consistent with one's values and principles, and being transparent and accountable for one's actions. In healthcare, integrity is essential for maintaining trust between healthcare professionals and patients, as well as ensuring the integrity of research and data. In business, integrity is important for building trust with customers, stakeholders, and the wider community.

Ethical Decision Making Models

Ethical decision making models provide a systematic approach for evaluating ethical dilemmas and making ethical choices. These models help individuals and organizations navigate complex ethical situations by providing a framework for analyzing the relevant ethical principles and values. Some commonly used ethical decision making models include:

- The Utilitarian Model: This model focuses on maximizing overall happiness or utility for the greatest number of people. It involves weighing the potential benefits and harms of different courses of action and choosing the option that maximizes overall utility.

- The Rights-based Model: This model emphasizes the protection of individual rights and respect for autonomy. It involves identifying the rights that are at stake in a particular situation and choosing the course of action that best respects and protects those rights.

- The Virtue-based Model: This model focuses on developing and embodying virtuous character traits such as honesty, compassion, and fairness. It involves considering what a virtuous person would do in a given situation and choosing the course of action that aligns with virtuous principles.

- The Duty-based Model: This model emphasizes the importance of fulfilling one's moral duties and obligations. It involves identifying the moral duties and obligations that apply to a particular situation and choosing the course of action that best fulfills those duties.

- The Consequence-based Model: This model focuses on the potential consequences of different courses of action. It involves considering the potential positive and negative consequences of each option and choosing the course of action that minimizes harm and maximizes benefits.

Ethical decision making is a complex process that often requires balancing competing ethical principles and values. It is important to consider the specific context and circumstances of each situation, as well as the potential impact of different choices on various stakeholders. By applying ethical principles and using ethical decision making models, individuals and organizations can make informed and ethical choices that align with their values and uphold ethical standards.

Additional Resources and Exercises

To further explore ethical principles and values, consider the following resources and exercises:

- Readings:

    - "Principles of Biomedical Ethics" by Tom L. Beauchamp and James F. Childress

    - "Ethics: Theory and Contemporary Issues" by Barbara MacKinnon

    - "Business Ethics: Concepts and Cases" by Manuel G. Velasquez

    - "Ethics and Technology: Controversies, Questions, and Strategies for Ethical Computing" by Herman T. Tavani

    - "Ethics and Education" by Kate Bullock

- Discussion: Engage in a group discussion or debate about the importance and application of different ethical principles in a specific field of interest, such as healthcare, business, or education.

+ Case Studies: Analyze and discuss case studies that present ethical dilemmas, and apply the principles and values discussed in this section to propose ethical solutions or courses of action.

+ Reflection: Reflect on your own values and how they align with the ethical principles discussed in this section. Consider examples from your own life or professional experiences where these principles played a role in decision making.

+ Research: Conduct research on current ethical issues or controversies in a particular field, and explore how different ethical principles and values are being applied or challenged in these contexts.

Remember, ethical principles and values provide a framework for ethical decision making, but ethical dilemmas are often complex and require thoughtful analysis and consideration. It is important to continually engage in ethical reflection and seek out additional resources and perspectives to enhance ethical understanding and practice.

Autonomy

In the realm of ethics, autonomy refers to the principle that individuals have the right to make decisions for themselves and have control over their own lives. It is a foundational principle in many ethical frameworks and plays a crucial role in various areas of society, including healthcare, business, and education.

Autonomy is derived from the Greek words "autos," meaning self, and "nomos," meaning rule or law. In essence, it embodies the idea of self-rule. Autonomy recognizes that individuals possess the capacity for rational thought, free will, and self-determination. It embraces the belief that individuals should have the freedom to act according to their own values, beliefs, and interests, within the boundaries of respecting the rights and well-being of others.

The principle of autonomy is closely associated with the concept of informed consent. In healthcare, for example, informed consent requires that healthcare professionals provide patients with all relevant information about their condition, treatment options, and potential risks and benefits. This empowers patients to make informed decisions about their own healthcare.

Autonomy also extends to the business realm. A company's employees should have the autonomy to make decisions within their area of expertise, as long as those decisions align with the ethical standards of the organization. Autonomy fosters employee empowerment, creativity, and a sense of ownership towards their work.

In education, autonomy recognizes the importance of students' active participation and engagement in the learning process. Students who are given the freedom to explore their own interests and make choices regarding their education are more likely to become independent and motivated learners.

However, autonomy is not an absolute principle. It is subject to various limitations and considerations. For instance, the principle of autonomy must be balanced with other ethical principles, such as beneficence and non-maleficence. In healthcare, for example, a patient's autonomy may be limited in cases where their decision would result in harm to themselves or others. Similarly, in business, the autonomy of employees must be balanced with the organization's goals and ethical obligations.

Additionally, autonomy may be limited by legal frameworks and societal norms. For example, in certain situations, the law may require individuals to act in a certain way, restricting their autonomy. Society also sets certain limits on individuals' autonomy to ensure the well-being and safety of its members.

In conclusion, autonomy is a fundamental ethical principle that recognizes an individual's right to self-rule and decision-making. It is essential in various domains, including healthcare, business, and education. However, it is important to acknowledge the limitations and considerations that are necessary to balance autonomy with other ethical principles and societal norms. By respecting and promoting autonomy, we can empower individuals to lead self-directed and meaningful lives.

Beneficence

In the field of ethics, the principle of beneficence plays a crucial role in guiding ethical decision making. Beneficence refers to the ethical obligation to promote the well-being and welfare of others, to act in their best interests, and to do good.

The Importance of Beneficence

Beneficence is rooted in the belief that individuals and institutions have a moral responsibility to actively contribute to the betterment of society and the welfare of others. It recognizes that human beings have the capacity to act in ways that promote positive outcomes for others and enhance their overall well-being. By prioritizing the principle of beneficence, ethical practices aim to create a more just and compassionate society.

Principles of Beneficence

The principle of beneficence encompasses several key principles that guide ethical decision making:

1. **Non-maleficence:** The principle of non-maleficence states that one should do no harm and avoid actions that could cause harm to others. It emphasizes the importance of minimizing or preventing harm while actively promoting well-being.

2. **The duty to care:** The duty to care is a fundamental principle of beneficence that highlights the moral obligation to provide assistance and support to those in need. It encourages individuals and institutions to act compassionately, showing empathy and concern for others.

3. **Promoting the greater good:** Beneficence requires considering the broader impact of actions and decisions on society as a whole. It involves making choices that maximize the overall well-being and welfare of individuals and communities, even if it requires sacrificing some individual interests.

4. **Alleviating suffering and improving quality of life:** Beneficence involves actively working to reduce suffering and enhance the quality of life for individuals. This can be achieved through interventions, support systems, and programs that address physical, emotional, and social needs.

Applying Beneficence in Ethical Decision Making

In a practical sense, beneficence guides ethical decision making by providing a framework for evaluating actions and their potential consequences. It helps individuals and institutions assess the ethical implications of their decisions and consider the impact on the well-being of others. When faced with ethical dilemmas, the following steps can help apply the principle of beneficence:

1. **Identify the stakeholders:** Identify all individuals or groups who may be affected by the decision or action in question. Consider their needs, interests, and well-being.

2. **Evaluate potential benefits and harms:** Assess the potential positive and negative outcomes of each available course of action. Consider short-term and long-term consequences, as well as any risks involved.

3. **Promote autonomy:** Respect the autonomy and self-determination of individuals involved in the decision-making process. Seek their input and involve them in the decision to the extent possible.

4. **Seek expert opinions and advice:** Consult with professionals, experts, or relevant stakeholders who can provide valuable insights and expertise regarding the potential impact of the decision.

5. **Make an informed decision:** Consider all relevant factors, ethical principles, and available options to make a well-informed and morally justifiable decision that promotes the well-being and welfare of others.

Case Study: Ethical Dilemma in Healthcare

Consider the following real-world example to illustrate the application of the principle of beneficence in an ethical dilemma:

Scenario: A physician is treating a terminally ill patient who is experiencing severe pain. The patient is considering euthanasia as an option to alleviate their suffering. The physician is conflicted between respecting the patient's autonomy and the ethical obligation to prevent harm.

Application of beneficence: In this case, the principle of beneficence requires the physician to prioritize the patient's well-being and quality of life. The physician should explore all available options to effectively manage the patient's pain and suffering. They should engage in active dialogue with the patient, addressing their concerns and exploring alternative palliative care strategies. By valuing the principle of beneficence, the physician can strike a balance between respecting the patient's autonomy and fulfilling their moral duty to alleviate suffering.

Ethical Dilemma Discussion

Here is an ethical dilemma for you to ponder and reflect upon:

Scenario: You are a manager in a manufacturing company and have recently discovered that one of your employees has been stealing valuable supplies from the company's inventory. You are conflicted between reporting the employee's actions, which could lead to their termination and potential legal consequences, and providing them with a second chance, considering they are the sole breadwinner for their family.

Discussion questions:

1. How would you apply the principle of beneficence in this situation?

2. What are the potential benefits and harms associated with each available course of action?

3. How might you balance the employee's well-being with the need to maintain a fair and ethical work environment?

4. What ethical principles, apart from beneficence, might you consider in making this decision?

Further Reading

To deepen your understanding of beneficence and its applications, you may find the following resources helpful:

- *Ethics: Theory and Practice* by Jacques P. Thiroux and Keith W. Krasemann

- *Ethics and the Conduct of Business* by John R. Boatright

- *Contemporary Issues in Bioethics* by Tom L. Beauchamp and James F. Childress

- *Ethics and Technology: Controversies, Questions, and Strategies for Ethical Computing* by Herman T. Tavani

Remember, beneficence is not only a principle to be applied in professional settings but also in our everyday lives. By embracing the principle of beneficence, we can contribute to a more compassionate and ethical society that values the well-being of all its members.

Non-maleficence

Non-maleficence is a fundamental principle in ethics that requires individuals to avoid causing harm or inflicting unnecessary suffering. In the context of healthcare, non-maleficence is often referred to as the principle of "do no harm." The ethical obligation of healthcare professionals to prioritize the well-being and safety of their patients is based on this principle.

Background

The principle of non-maleficence has its roots in the historical evolution of ethical thought. Ancient philosophers, such as Hippocrates, emphasized the importance of avoiding harm to patients. This principle was later reinforced by the rise of modern medical ethics in the 20th century, which codified non-maleficence as a core principle in healthcare.

Non-maleficence is closely related to the principle of beneficence, which requires healthcare professionals to act in the best interests of their patients. While beneficence focuses on promoting positive outcomes, non-maleficence focuses on minimizing and preventing harm.

Scope of Non-maleficence in Healthcare

Non-maleficence applies to all aspects of healthcare, including diagnosis, treatment, research, and end-of-life care. Healthcare professionals must constantly assess the potential risks and benefits of their actions to ensure that the harm inflicted is minimized or completely avoided.

In the context of clinical practice, non-maleficence requires healthcare professionals to:

- Use their knowledge and skills responsibly and with competence to prevent harm.

- Carefully weigh the potential risks and benefits of medical interventions.

- Ensure the safety and well-being of patients during procedures and treatments.

- Protect patient confidentiality to prevent harm caused by the disclosure of sensitive information.

- Provide accurate and understandable information to patients to support their decision-making process.

- Adhere to evidence-based guidelines and best practices to minimize harm.

- Continuously learn and update their knowledge to provide the best possible care.

Challenges and Solutions

The application of the non-maleficence principle in healthcare can be complex and challenging. Healthcare professionals often encounter situations where the potential benefits of an intervention are uncertain or where there is a conflict of interest between different stakeholders. In such cases, ethical decision-making frameworks can help guide healthcare professionals in balancing the principle of non-maleficence with other ethical considerations.

One such framework is the principle-based approach, which involves considering the ethical principles of autonomy, beneficence, non-maleficence, and justice in decision-making. By carefully analyzing each principle and weighing its importance in a given situation, healthcare professionals can make ethical decisions that prioritize the well-being of their patients.

In addition to ethical decision-making frameworks, clear communication and shared decision-making with patients can play a crucial role in upholding non-maleficence. By involving patients in the decision-making process, healthcare professionals can ensure that potential risks and benefits are adequately discussed and understood, allowing patients to make informed choices about their own healthcare.

Examples and Real-World Application

Non-maleficence is essential in various areas of healthcare, and its application can be seen in multiple scenarios. For example, in prescribing medications, healthcare professionals must consider potential adverse effects and drug interactions to prevent harm to their patients. Surgical procedures also require careful consideration of the risks and benefits to minimize the potential for harm during and after the operation.

In the realm of medical research, the principle of non-maleficence guides researchers and ethics committees in ensuring the safety and well-being of study participants. Strict ethical guidelines and oversight mechanisms are in place to prevent any harm caused by research procedures or interventions.

Furthermore, non-maleficence is particularly important in end-of-life care, where the principle guides decisions around withholding or withdrawing life-sustaining treatments. In these delicate situations, healthcare professionals must balance the desire to alleviate suffering with the principle of not causing harm, taking into account the wishes and values of the patient.

Resources and Further Reading

- Beauchamp, T. L., & Childress, J. F. (2019). *Principles of biomedical ethics.* Oxford University Press.

- Kuhse, H., Singer, P., & Batavia, A. I. (Eds.). (2018). *A companion to bioethics.* Wiley.

- National Academies of Sciences, Engineering, and Medicine. (2021). *Ethical considerations for research involving prisoners.* The National Academies Press.

- Royal College of Nursing. (2018). *The Code: Professional standards of practice and behavior for nurses, & midwives.* Royal College of Nursing.

Summary

Non-maleficence is a foundational principle in healthcare ethics, requiring healthcare professionals to prioritize the avoidance of harm and unnecessary suffering. It guides decision-making in clinical practice, research, and end-of-life care. The application of non-maleficence can be challenging, but ethical decision-making frameworks and open communication with patients can help healthcare professionals navigate complex situations while upholding this important ethical principle.

Justice

Justice is a fundamental ethical principle that plays a crucial role in guiding ethical decision-making across various fields, including business, politics, healthcare, technology, and education. It involves the fair and equitable treatment of individuals and the distribution of benefits and burdens in society. In this section, we will explore the concept of justice in depth, examine different theories of justice, and discuss its applications in different domains.

The Concept of Justice

At its core, justice refers to the principle of fairness and equality. It is concerned with ensuring that individuals receive their due rights and entitlements and that resources and opportunities are distributed in a just manner. Justice requires impartiality, transparency, and adherence to established rules and principles.

In a broader societal context, justice also encompasses notions of social justice, which involves addressing systemic inequalities and promoting equal access to resources, opportunities, and basic human rights. It seeks to correct historical injustices and create a more equitable and inclusive society.

Theories of Justice

There are various theories of justice that provide different frameworks for defining and achieving justice. Let's explore some of the prominent ones:

1. **Distributive Justice:** This theory focuses on the fair distribution of resources, wealth, and opportunities in society. It seeks to address the

question of how goods and benefits should be distributed among individuals and groups. One influential theory of distributive justice is John Rawls' theory of justice as fairness, which emphasizes the equal distribution of resources and the prioritization of the least advantaged members of society.

2. **Retributive Justice:** Retributive justice is concerned with the punishment of wrongdoers and the restoration of balance in society. It seeks to ensure that those who commit crimes or harm others face proportionate consequences for their actions. Retributive justice includes principles such as proportionality, reformation, and deterrence.

3. **Restorative Justice:** This theory focuses on repairing the harm caused by wrongdoing and promoting healing and reconciliation. It emphasizes the active involvement of all affected parties and seeks to address the root causes of conflict and crime. Restorative justice aims to provide a more humane and transformative approach to justice.

4. **Procedural Justice:** Procedural justice emphasizes the fairness and transparency of decision-making processes. It is concerned with ensuring that fair procedures, such as impartial hearings, unbiased judgments, and the right to appeal, are in place. Procedural justice is particularly relevant in legal and organizational contexts where due process and equitable treatment are vital.

5. **Interactional Justice:** Interactional justice focuses on the fairness of interpersonal interactions and relationships. It involves treating individuals with respect, dignity, and honesty. Interactional justice is often pertinent in areas such as healthcare, education, and workplace environments where the quality of interactions can significantly impact individuals' well-being and satisfaction.

Applications of Justice

Justice has wide-ranging applications in various domains, influencing ethical practices and decision-making. Let's explore some examples:

1. **Justice in Business:** In the business world, justice guides decisions related to fair wages, equal opportunities, and ethical treatment of employees. It encompasses issues such as pay equity, diversity and inclusion, labor rights, and responsible corporate governance.

2. **Justice in Healthcare:** In healthcare, justice plays a crucial role in ensuring equal access to quality care and the fair allocation of limited resources. It involves ethical considerations surrounding the distribution of healthcare services, healthcare disparities, and the prioritization of patient needs.

3. **Justice in Technology and AI:** In the evolving field of technology and artificial intelligence, justice is essential for addressing issues such as algorithmic bias, privacy concerns, and ethical decision-making by autonomous systems. It involves ethical guidelines for the development and deployment of technology to prevent discrimination and promote fairness.

4. **Justice in Education:** In education, justice entails providing equal opportunities for all students, regardless of their background, and promoting inclusive and equitable learning environments. It involves addressing issues such as educational disparities, access to resources, and treating students and teachers with fairness and respect.

Case Study: Ensuring Justice in Resource Allocation

Consider the following scenario: A small rural community is facing a shortage of clean drinking water due to a prolonged drought. The community relies on a single water source, and there is not enough water to meet the needs of all residents.

To ensure justice in resource allocation, several ethical considerations come into play. Distributive justice requires a fair and equal distribution of available water among community members. However, given the limited supply, it may be necessary to prioritize certain groups, such as those with medical needs or vulnerable populations like children and the elderly.

Procedural justice comes into play in deciding how to determine who gets priority access to water. A transparent and inclusive decision-making process involving community members, local authorities, and stakeholders can help ensure fairness and avoid potential favoritism or discrimination.

Furthermore, social justice considerations should be taken into account to address underlying factors contributing to the water shortage, such as climate change, inadequate infrastructure, or unequal access to resources. Efforts should be made to advocate for sustainable water management practices, equitable distribution of resources, and long-term solutions to prevent future water crises.

This case study illustrates the complex interplay of different theories of justice in addressing real-world challenges and highlights the importance of considering multiple ethical perspectives in decision-making processes.

Key Takeaways

+ Justice is a fundamental ethical principle that promotes fairness, equality, and the equitable distribution of resources and opportunities.

+ Different theories of justice, such as distributive justice, retributive justice, restorative justice, procedural justice, and interactional justice, provide frameworks for understanding and achieving justice in various contexts.

+ Justice has applications in business, healthcare, technology and AI, and education, helping guide ethical decision-making and practices.

+ Ensuring justice often involves considering various ethical considerations, such as fairness, transparency, inclusivity, and addressing systemic inequalities.

Summary

Justice, as a fundamental ethical principle, plays a crucial role in guiding ethical practices and decision-making across different fields. It encompasses notions of fairness, equality, and the equitable distribution of resources and opportunities. Different theories of justice provide frameworks for defining and achieving justice, and it finds applications in diverse domains such as business, healthcare, technology and AI, and education. By considering justice in decision-making processes, individuals and organizations can contribute to creating a more just and ethical society.

Integrity

Integrity is a fundamental ethical principle that guides decision making and behavior. It refers to the adherence to moral and ethical principles and the consistency between one's actions and values. In the context of ethical practices, integrity plays a crucial role in creating trust, maintaining ethical standards, and promoting a culture of ethical behavior.

Definition of Integrity

Integrity can be defined as the quality of being honest, truthful, and morally upright. It encompasses a range of virtues such as honesty, transparency, dependability, and credibility. A person with integrity acts in accordance with their values and principles, even when faced with challenges or temptations.

Importance of Integrity

Integrity is essential in various aspects of life, including personal relationships, professional settings, and society as a whole. Here are some reasons why integrity is important:

- **Trustworthiness:** Integrity is the foundation of trust. When individuals consistently demonstrate integrity, they gain the trust and respect of others. This is crucial in personal relationships, as well as in professional settings such as business and leadership roles.

- **Ethical Behavior:** Acting with integrity means following ethical principles and values. It helps individuals make ethical decisions and ensures that their actions are in line with their moral compass. Integrity serves as a guide for ethical behavior, even in challenging situations.

- **Accountability:** Integrity promotes accountability. Individuals with integrity take responsibility for their actions, admit their mistakes, and make amends when necessary. This fosters a culture of accountability and encourages others to do the same.

- **Credibility and Reputation:** Having integrity enhances an individual's credibility and reputation. When people consistently act with integrity, they are seen as trustworthy, reliable, and honest, which positively impacts their personal and professional relationships.

- **Organizational Culture:** Integrity is a key component of a positive organizational culture. When integrity is valued and practiced by leaders and employees, it creates a culture of openness, fairness, and ethical conduct. This contributes to a harmonious and productive work environment.

Challenges to Integrity

While integrity is highly valued, there can be challenges that individuals and organizations face in upholding it. Some common challenges include:

- **Pressure to Compromise:** In certain situations, individuals may face pressure to compromise their integrity, such as when faced with unethical requests or temptations. This can be particularly challenging in business settings where financial gain or perceived career advancement may be at stake.

* **Conflicting Interests:** Conflicting interests can pose a challenge to integrity. When individuals have personal or professional interests that are in conflict with their ethical principles, they may struggle to make decisions that align with their values.

* **Lack of Role Models:** The absence of ethical role models can make it difficult for individuals to uphold integrity. Without positive examples to emulate, individuals may be more susceptible to engaging in unethical behavior.

* **Organizational Culture:** A toxic or unethical organizational culture can erode integrity. When an organization prioritizes short-term gains over ethical conduct, it can create an environment that discourages integrity and rewards unethical behavior.

* **Lack of Accountability:** A lack of accountability can undermine integrity. When individuals are not held accountable for unethical actions, it can create a culture where integrity is disregarded, leading to a decline in ethical standards.

Promoting Integrity

Promoting and upholding integrity requires conscious effort and proactive measures. Here are some strategies to foster integrity:

* **Lead by Example:** Leaders play a crucial role in promoting integrity. By consistently demonstrating integrity in their actions and decisions, leaders set a positive example for others to follow.

* **Establish Policies and Codes of Conduct:** Organizations should develop clear policies and codes of conduct that explicitly outline expectations for ethical behavior. These guidelines provide a reference point for individuals to make ethical decisions and maintain integrity.

* **Encourage Ethical Decision Making:** Organizations should encourage employees to engage in ethical decision-making processes. This involves considering the potential impact of their actions on stakeholders, evaluating ethical dilemmas, and seeking guidance when needed.

* **Promote Open Communication:** Creating a culture of open communication encourages individuals to speak up when they witness unethical behavior or face ethical dilemmas. It is important to establish

channels for reporting unethical conduct and protect whistleblowers from retaliation.

- **Provide Training and Education:**   Offering training programs and educational resources on ethics and integrity can enhance individuals' understanding and awareness. This empowers individuals to make informed decisions and gives them the tools to navigate ethical challenges.

- **Recognize and Reward Integrity:** Recognizing and rewarding individuals who demonstrate integrity reinforces its importance. This can be done through performance evaluations, awards, or other forms of acknowledgment that highlight ethical behavior.

Case Study: Enron Corporation

The Enron Corporation scandal serves as a cautionary tale highlighting the consequences of a lack of integrity in an organization. Enron, a former energy company, collapsed in 2001 due to widespread accounting fraud and unethical practices.

Enron's corporate culture prioritized short-term financial gains and rewarded unethical behavior.   Executives engaged in fraudulent accounting practices to manipulate the company's financial statements, resulting in the deception of shareholders and investors.

The lack of integrity within Enron reverberated throughout the organization and had a devastating impact on employees, stakeholders, and the broader business community. The scandal led to the dissolution of Arthur Andersen, Enron's auditing firm, and prompted significant regulatory changes to prevent similar occurrences in the future.

This case study illustrates the importance of integrity in organizational practices and the severe consequences that can arise when it is compromised.

Summary

Integrity is a fundamental ethical principle that guides decision making and behavior. It involves the adherence to moral and ethical principles, consistency between actions and values, and the creation of a culture of trust and accountability.   Upholding integrity is essential in personal relationships, professional settings, and society as a whole. However, it can face challenges such as pressure to compromise, conflicting interests, lack of role models, toxic organizational culture, and lack of accountability. To promote integrity, leaders should lead by example, establish policies and codes of conduct, encourage ethical decision making, promote open communication, provide training and education, and recognize and reward integrity. By prioritizing integrity, individuals and organizations can foster a culture of ethical behavior and contribute to a better society.

Ethical Decision Making Models

Ethical decision making is a critical process that individuals and organizations go through to evaluate different options and choose the most ethically sound course of action. To guide this process, various ethical decision-making models have been developed. These models provide a framework for assessing ethical dilemmas and making decisions that align with ethical principles and values.

The Utilitarian Model

The utilitarian model, also known as consequentialism, focuses on the consequences of different actions to determine their ethical value. According to utilitarianism, the morally right action is the one that produces the greatest overall happiness or the greatest amount of utility for the greatest number of people. In other words, the decision that maximizes the overall well-being of all stakeholders is considered ethically right.

To apply this model, one must assess the potential outcomes of each available option and determine the one that will result in the greatest net benefit. This requires considering the short-term and long-term consequences, both positive and negative, for all affected parties. The utilitarian model often involves weighing different quantities and qualities of happiness or utility.

For example, imagine a company is deciding whether to introduce a new product that may provide substantial financial gains but could harm the environment. By using the utilitarian model, the company would evaluate the potential benefits to consumers and shareholders against the negative impact on the environment. If the overall net benefit to society outweighs the harm caused, the decision to introduce the product might be considered ethically justified.

The Rights-based Model

The rights-based model, also known as deontological ethics, focuses on respecting and protecting individual rights when making ethical decisions. According to this model, certain rights and principles are considered inherent and inviolable, regardless of the consequences. Actions are evaluated based on whether they uphold or violate these rights.

In the rights-based model, individuals have a set of fundamental rights, such as the right to life, liberty, and equality. The ethical decision-making process involves considering these rights and ensuring that actions do not infringe upon them. This model emphasizes the importance of principles such as honesty, integrity, and fairness.

For example, consider an organization facing a decision to lay off a group of employees to cut costs. In using the rights-based model, the organization would consider the rights of the affected employees, such as the right to fair treatment and a just process. If the organization determines that the proposed action violates these rights, an alternative approach that respects the employees' rights should be pursued.

The Virtue-based Model

The virtue-based model focuses on the development of virtues or positive character traits in individuals when making ethical decisions. According to this model, ethical actions are those that align with virtues such as honesty, integrity, compassion, and courage. The emphasis is placed on the overall ethical character of an individual rather than specific actions or consequences.

To apply this model, individuals must cultivate virtues through education, self-reflection, and practice. Ethical decision making involves considering which virtues are relevant to a given situation and choosing the action that best embodies these virtues.

For example, suppose a teacher witnesses another teacher engaging in unfair grading practices. In using the virtue-based model, the ethical decision-making process would involve reflecting on the virtues of honesty, fairness, and professionalism. The teacher may then choose to confront the colleague privately to address the issue and uphold these virtues.

The Duty-based Model

The duty-based model, also known as deontological ethics, focuses on fulfilling one's duty or moral obligations when making ethical decisions. According to this model, individuals have a set of moral duties or principles that are independent of the consequences of their actions. Ethical decisions are determined by adhering to these duties.

This model places importance on universal rules and principles. It suggests that individuals have duties to act honestly, keep promises, be respectful, and avoid causing harm to others. Actions are evaluated based on whether they fulfill these duties or violate them.

For example, imagine a healthcare professional who discovers a colleague engaging in unethical behavior that could harm patients. In applying the duty-based model, the healthcare professional would be obliged to report this behavior to the appropriate authorities, as it aligns with the duty to prioritize patient welfare and uphold the ethical standards of the profession.

The Consequence-based Model

The consequence-based model, also known as ethical pragmatism, focuses on assessing the potential consequences of different actions to determine their ethical value. It acknowledges that ethical decisions must consider both the short-term and long-term consequences for all stakeholders involved.

In this model, individuals evaluate the outcomes of different options by considering the potential benefits and harms they may cause. The decision that maximizes overall happiness, minimizes suffering, and promotes the greatest balance of benefits over harms is considered ethically right.

For example, suppose a government is considering whether to implement a new policy that may lead to short-term economic growth but could also exacerbate income inequality. By using the consequence-based model, the government would evaluate the potential outcomes of the policy, weighing the economic benefits against the social costs. If the overall consequence is a net positive for society, the policy may be considered ethically justified.

Ethical Decision Making Models in Practice

When faced with ethical dilemmas, individuals and organizations can use a combination of these ethical decision-making models to fully assess the situation and make informed choices. It is essential to consider the specific context, values, and principles relevant to the given situation.

It is important to note that ethical decision-making is not always straightforward, and different models may yield conflicting results. In such cases, individuals must carefully consider the underlying principles and values of each model and make judgments based on the best course of action that balances competing ethical considerations.

Furthermore, ethical decision-making requires critical thinking, empathy, and consideration of diverse perspectives. It is also essential to continuously reflect on and evaluate the ethical frameworks and models being used to ensure their alignment with evolving societal values and ethical standards.

Summary

Ethical decision making models provide a structured framework for assessing ethical dilemmas and making decisions that align with ethical principles and values. The utilitarian model focuses on maximizing overall happiness or utility, while the rights-based model emphasizes respecting and protecting individual rights. The virtue-based model emphasizes developing positive character traits, and the duty-based model emphasizes fulfilling moral obligations. The consequence-based model assesses the potential outcomes of different actions to determine their ethical value.

When making ethical decisions, it is crucial to consider the specific context, values, and principles relevant to the situation. It is also essential to engage in critical thinking, empathy, and reflection, as well as to be aware of the potential conflicts and limitations of different ethical decision-making models. By adopting a comprehensive approach to ethical decision making, individuals and organizations can navigate complex ethical challenges and promote a culture of ethical behavior.

The Utilitarian Model

The Utilitarian Model is a consequentialist ethical theory that focuses on maximizing overall happiness or utility. It is based on the principle of utility, which states that actions are morally right if they produce the greatest amount of happiness or pleasure for the greatest number of people.

1. Overview of the Utilitarian Model

Utilitarianism was first introduced by Jeremy Bentham in the late 18th century and later developed by John Stuart Mill in the 19th century. The central idea behind utilitarianism is that the morality of an action depends solely on its outcomes or consequences.

According to the Utilitarian Model, the right action is the one that leads to the greatest amount of overall happiness or utility. Happiness, in this context, is understood as the presence of pleasure and the absence of pain. Utility refers to the overall well-being or welfare of individuals.

2. Principles of the Utilitarian Model

2.1 The Principle of Hedonistic Calculus

The Utilitarian Model utilizes a framework known as the Hedonistic Calculus to determine the overall utility of an action. The Hedonistic Calculus assigns values and weights to different aspects of pleasure and pain, such as intensity, duration, certainty, propinquity, fecundity, purity, and extent.

By quantifying these factors, the Hedonistic Calculus allows for a comparative analysis of different actions and their potential consequences, enabling decision-makers to choose the action that maximizes overall utility.

2.2 The Greatest Happiness Principle

The Greatest Happiness Principle is the core principle of the Utilitarian Model. It states that actions are morally right if they promote the greatest happiness for the greatest number of people.

According to this principle, the well-being of each individual is of equal importance. The Utilitarian Model does not discriminate between individuals based on their characteristics such as race, gender, or social status.

3. Application of the Utilitarian Model

The Utilitarian Model can be applied to various ethical dilemmas and decision-making situations. It provides a flexible framework for evaluating the consequences of actions and making morally informed choices.

3.1 Evaluating the Consequences

To apply the Utilitarian Model, one needs to evaluate the potential consequences of each available action. This involves predicting the positive and negative impacts of each option on the overall happiness or utility of all affected individuals.

For example, in a healthcare setting, a doctor might need to decide whether to allocate a limited supply of a life-saving drug to a group of patients with different chances of survival. The doctor would consider factors such as the potential number of lives saved, the relief of pain and suffering, and the long-term consequences for the patients and their families.

3.2 Maximizing Overall Happiness

Once the consequences are evaluated, the Utilitarian Model requires decision-makers to choose the action that maximizes overall happiness or utility. This means selecting the option that provides the most benefits and minimizes the negative impacts for the greatest number of people.

In the healthcare example, the doctor would administer the drug to the patients who have the highest chance of survival and the greatest potential for future well-being.

4. Criticisms and Limitations of the Utilitarian Model

4.1 Lack of Consideration for Individual Rights

One major criticism of the Utilitarian Model is that it can neglect individual rights and justice in favor of maximizing overall happiness. In some situations, the model may allow for actions that violate the rights of a few individuals if it leads to a greater overall benefit.

4.2 Difficulty in Predicting Consequences

Another limitation is the difficulty of accurately predicting the consequences of actions. The Hedonistic Calculus relies on subjective evaluations of pleasure and pain, making it challenging to accurately quantify and compare the impacts of different choices.

4.3 Ignoring Distribution of Utility

The Utilitarian Model also faces criticism for its lack of attention to the distribution of utility. It may lead to situations where a minority suffers greatly while the majority experiences only a slight increase in happiness.

5. Case Study: Utilitarian Model in Environmental Decision Making

An example of applying the Utilitarian Model is in environmental decision making. Suppose a company plans to build a factory that would create jobs and stimulate economic growth but would also pollute the nearby river and harm local wildlife.

Using the Utilitarian Model, decision-makers would evaluate the potential consequences of building the factory and weigh them against the benefits. They would consider factors such as economic growth, job creation, pollution reduction measures, and impacts on the local community and ecosystem.

The decision would be made by choosing the option that maximizes the overall happiness or utility for all affected parties. This might include implementing pollution control measures, investing in alternative energy sources, or even deciding against building the factory altogether.

6. Conclusion

The Utilitarian Model offers a consequentialist approach to ethical decision making, focusing on maximizing overall happiness or utility. By evaluating the consequences of actions and considering the well-being of all affected individuals, decision-makers can make informed choices that aim to promote the greatest amount of happiness for the greatest number of people.

While the Utilitarian Model has its criticisms and limitations, it provides a valuable framework for analyzing ethical dilemmas and balancing competing interests in various domains, including business, healthcare, technology, and education. By understanding the principles and application of the Utilitarian Model, individuals can approach ethical decision making in a thoughtful and rational manner.

The Rights-based Model

In the realm of ethical decision making, the rights-based model is a prominent framework that focuses on the protection and promotion of individual rights. It is derived from the ethical principle of respect for autonomy, which asserts that individuals have the right to make decisions and pursue their own interests without interference from others.

Principles of the Rights-based Model

The rights-based model is based on several key principles that guide ethical decision making. These principles include:

1. **Human Rights:** The rights-based model emphasizes the importance of upholding fundamental human rights. Human rights are inherent to all individuals by virtue of their humanity and include rights such as the right to life, liberty, and security of person, freedom of thought, conscience, and religion, and the right to a fair trial.

2. **Universalism:** The rights-based model embraces the concept of universal human rights, meaning that these rights apply to all individuals, regardless of their nationality, race, gender, or any other characteristic. This principle rejects any form of discrimination or inequality in the enjoyment of rights.

3. **Inviolability:** The rights-based model acknowledges that human rights are inviolable and should not be violated or restricted except in certain limited circumstances, such as when the exercise of one person's rights infringes upon the rights of others.

4. **Empowerment:** The rights-based model seeks to empower individuals by recognizing and protecting their rights. It aims to ensure that individuals have the freedom and ability to exercise their rights and make informed decisions about their own lives.

Applying the Rights-based Model

The rights-based model provides a framework for ethical decision making in various contexts, including politics, law, healthcare, and business. To apply the rights-based model, one must consider the following steps:

1. **Identification of Rights:** Identify the specific rights that are relevant to the situation at hand. This involves understanding the applicable legal and ethical frameworks and determining which rights are at stake.

2. **Balancing of Rights:** Assess the potential conflicts or tensions between different rights. In some situations, the exercise of one person's rights may limit or infringe upon the rights of others. It is important to carefully consider and balance various rights to arrive at a fair and just decision.

3. **Respect for Autonomy**: Prioritize respect for individual autonomy and the right to self-determination. Individuals should be given the opportunity to freely exercise their rights, as long as their actions do not harm or infringe upon the rights of others.

4. **Ethical Constraints**: Recognize that the exercise of certain rights may be subject to ethical constraints. While individuals have the right to freedom of expression, for example, it is generally accepted that hate speech or incitement to violence should be prohibited.

Case Study: Balancing Rights in Free Speech

To illustrate the application of the rights-based model, let's consider the case of hate speech and its potential conflict with the right to freedom of expression. In many democratic societies, freedom of expression is considered a fundamental right. However, hate speech is often seen as a form of harmful speech that can incite violence and perpetuate discrimination.

In using the rights-based model to analyze this case, we would first identify the relevant rights, namely, the right to freedom of expression and the right to be free from discrimination and harm. We would then need to balance these rights and consider any ethical constraints.

The rights-based model would prioritize freedom of expression but also recognize the ethical constraint of preventing harm and discrimination. In this case, limitations on hate speech may be justified, as it infringes upon the rights of others to live free from harm and discrimination. Balancing these rights would involve crafting legislation or policies that prohibit hate speech while still allowing for a wide range of expression.

Resources for Further Exploration

To delve deeper into the rights-based model and its applications, the following resources may be useful:

+ Books:

    - "The Rights of Others: Aliens, Residents, and Citizens" by Seyla Benhabib

    - "The Idea of Human Rights" by Charles R. Beitz

    - "Human Rights: Politics and Practice" by Michael Goodhart

+ Websites:

- United Nations Human Rights: `https://www.un.org/en/universal-declaration-human-rights/`

- Human Rights Watch: `https://www.hrw.org/`

- Amnesty International: `https://www.amnesty.org/`

+ Academic Journals:

  - *Human Rights Quarterly*

  - *Ethics & International Affairs*

  - *Journal of Human Rights*

Ethics in Action

To apply the principles of the rights-based model, consider the following scenario:

A university is facing a dilemma regarding the establishment of a controversial student club that promotes extremist ideologies. On one hand, allowing the club to form would uphold the right to freedom of association and expression. On the other hand, such a club may pose a threat to the safety and well-being of other students.

As an ethical decision-maker, how would you apply the rights-based model to determine the appropriate course of action? Consider the identification of rights, the balancing of rights, the respect for autonomy, and any ethical constraints that may be present.

The Virtue-based Model

The virtue-based model is a prominent ethical framework that focuses on cultivating moral character and virtues. This model emphasizes the importance of developing virtuous traits in individuals and making ethical decisions based on these virtues. It draws inspiration from ancient philosophical perspectives on ethics and provides a practical approach to ethical decision-making in various contexts.

Background

The virtue-based model has its roots in ancient Greek philosophy, particularly the works of Plato and Aristotle. Plato believed that virtues were universal ideals that could be attained through education and introspection. Aristotle, on the other hand, emphasized the practical aspect of virtues and believed that they could be developed through habituation and moral education.

The virtue-based model gained renewed attention in modern ethical theory through the works of philosophers like Alasdair MacIntyre and Rosalind Hursthouse. MacIntyre argued for the importance of virtues in constructing a moral framework rooted in traditions and community practices. Hursthouse further developed the virtue-based model by examining how virtues guide ethical decision-making in specific cases.

Key Concepts

The virtue-based model revolves around the concept of virtues and moral character. Virtues are positive character traits that enable individuals to act ethically and lead a good life. They are not innate qualities but can be cultivated through practice and moral education. Some examples of virtues include honesty, compassion, courage, fairness, and integrity.

Central to the virtue-based model is the idea of eudaimonia, which can be translated as "flourishing" or "living well." Eudaimonia represents the ultimate goal of human life and is achieved through the development and practice of virtues. It is not simply about the pursuit of personal happiness but entails leading a morally good and fulfilling life.

Application

In the virtue-based model, ethical decision-making involves evaluating actions based on the virtues they promote or hinder. Instead of focusing solely on the consequences or principles, this model emphasizes the character of the individual and the moral virtues they embody. It encourages individuals to cultivate virtues and act in ways that promote the development of their moral character.

To apply the virtue-based model, one must first identify the relevant virtues associated with a particular situation. For example, in a business context, virtues such as honesty, integrity, and fairness may be relevant. Then, one must consider how the various courses of action align with these virtues and choose the one that promotes the development of virtuous character.

It is important to note that the virtue-based model does not provide a set of specific rules or guidelines for ethical behavior. Instead, it encourages individuals to exercise practical wisdom and judgment in evaluating ethical dilemmas. By cultivating virtuous character, individuals are better equipped to make morally sound decisions in complex and challenging situations.

Critiques

The virtue-based model, like any ethical framework, has its critiques. One criticism is that it lacks a universal set of virtues and can be culturally biased. Different cultures may prioritize and value different virtues, leading to variations in ethical judgments. Additionally, some argue that the emphasis on virtues may neglect the significance of actions and consequences in ethical decision-making.

Another critique is that the virtue-based model may not provide clear guidance in situations where virtues conflict. It may be challenging to determine which virtue should take precedence in complex moral dilemmas. However, proponents of the virtue-based model argue that cultivating virtuous character helps individuals navigate such dilemmas by developing practical wisdom and discernment.

Real-World Example

To illustrate the virtue-based model, let's consider a real-world example. Imagine a manager who has discovered that one of their employees made a mistake that resulted in a financial loss for the company. The manager has to decide how to address the situation.

In applying the virtue-based model, the manager would consider virtues such as honesty, fairness, and integrity. They would recognize the importance of honesty in acknowledging and addressing the mistake. They would also consider fairness in determining an appropriate response that takes into account the employee's intentions, the impact of the mistake, and any mitigating factors.

The manager's decision would be guided by their commitment to promoting virtuous character within the organization. They would aim to create a culture of integrity and accountability, where mistakes are acknowledged and learned from rather than punished harshly. By considering the virtues involved, the manager can make an ethical decision that aligns with the values of the organization and promotes the development of virtuous character.

Further Resources

For further exploration of the virtue-based model and its applications, the following resources are recommended:

- Hursthouse, R. (1999). *On Virtue Ethics*. Oxford University Press.

- MacIntyre, A. (2007). *After Virtue: A Study in Moral Theory*. University of Notre Dame Press.

- Slote, M. (2001). *Virtue Ethics.* Oxford University Press.

These resources provide in-depth analysis, case studies, and philosophical discussions on the virtue-based model and its relevance in contemporary ethical discourse.

Conclusion

The virtue-based model offers a valuable approach to ethical decision-making by focusing on the cultivation of virtues and the development of moral character. By considering the virtues associated with a situation, individuals can make ethical choices that promote personal growth and flourishing. While it may have its critiques, the virtue-based model provides a nuanced and practical perspective on ethics that is applicable in various domains of life.

The Duty-based Model

The duty-based model is a foundational ethical framework that places a strong emphasis on one's moral obligations and responsibilities. Also known as deontological ethics, this model derives its principles from the concept of duty, rather than solely focusing on the consequences of actions or the character of individuals involved.

Background

The duty-based model can be traced back to the moral philosophy of Immanuel Kant, who believed that moral actions should be guided by a sense of duty rather than personal desires or consequences. According to Kant, individuals have a moral duty to act in accordance with universal moral laws, which he referred to as categorical imperatives. These principles are binding on all individuals, regardless of personal inclinations.

Principles of the Duty-based Model

The duty-based model is centered around a few key principles that guide ethical decision-making. These principles include:

- **Universalizability:** According to the duty-based model, moral actions are those that can be universally applied. In other words, individuals should act in a way that they would want everyone else to act in similar situations. This principle helps ensure fairness and consistency in moral reasoning.

+ **Respect for autonomy:** Autonomy, or the ability of individuals to make informed choices and act according to their own will, is highly valued in the duty-based model. This principle emphasizes treating others as rational beings who have the capacity to make their own moral decisions.

+ **Respect for human dignity:** The duty-based model holds that all individuals possess intrinsic worth and should be treated with dignity. This principle dictates that we should never use others merely as a means to an end but instead recognize them as ends in themselves.

+ **Acting out of duty:** According to the duty-based model, the morality of an action is not determined by the consequences it produces but rather by the intention behind the action. Acting out of a sense of moral duty, even if it leads to unfavorable outcomes, is considered morally praiseworthy.

Application of the Duty-based Model

The duty-based model has broad applications across various domains, including personal ethics, professional ethics, and societal ethics. It provides individuals with a framework for making ethical decisions based on principles rather than subjective preferences or desired outcomes.

In personal ethics, the duty-based model can guide individuals in determining their moral obligations and how they should act in difficult situations. For example, if faced with a moral dilemma, such as whether to tell the truth or lie, individuals following this model would prioritize their duty to be truthful, regardless of the potential consequences.

In professional ethics, the duty-based model provides a foundation for ethical decision-making in various fields. For instance, healthcare professionals are guided by the duty to prioritize patient well-being and respect patient autonomy. This means that even if disclosing unfavorable medical information may cause distress, healthcare professionals have an obligation to provide patients with accurate information.

In societal ethics, the duty-based model plays a crucial role in shaping laws, policies, and social norms. By establishing principles that prioritize human dignity and universalizability, the duty-based model helps promote fairness, justice, and respect for human rights within a society.

Critiques and Limitations

While the duty-based model provides a valuable ethical framework, it is not without its critiques and limitations. Critics argue that focusing solely on moral duties can lead to rigid and inflexible decision-making. The model may not adequately address complex ethical dilemmas that require consideration of multiple factors and consequences.

Additionally, determining one's moral duties in practice can be challenging, as different interpretations and conflicts between duties can arise. Balancing various moral obligations can pose difficulties for individuals and may require careful ethical reasoning and reflection.

Ethical Dilemma and Solution

To illustrate the application of the duty-based model, let's consider an ethical dilemma in the context of business ethics:

Scenario: A company executive discovers that a competitor is planning to release a product that poses significant health risks to consumers. The executive is torn between the duty to protect the public from harm and the duty to respect their competitor's intellectual property rights by not disclosing the information.

Solution: In the duty-based model, the executive would prioritize the duty to protect the public from harm. By acting in accordance with this duty, the executive would consider it their moral obligation to report the potential health risks to the appropriate regulatory authorities or consumer protection agencies. While there may be legal and professional implications, the executive would base their decision on the duty to prevent harm and uphold public safety.

Key Takeaways

The duty-based model emphasizes the importance of moral obligations and universal principles in ethical decision-making. Key takeaways from this model include:

+ Moral actions should be guided by a sense of duty, rather than personal desires or consequences.

+ Ethical decisions should be based on principles that are universally applicable.

+ Autonomy and human dignity are central values in the duty-based model.

- The morality of an action is determined by the intention behind it, rather than the outcomes it produces.

By considering these principles, individuals can navigate ethical dilemmas and make decisions that align with their moral duties and responsibilities.

The Consequence-based Model

In ethical decision-making, the consequence-based model, also known as the consequentialist or teleological model, focuses on the outcomes or consequences of an action. According to this model, the rightness or wrongness of an act is determined by the overall balance of its beneficial and harmful consequences.

1. **Principle of Utility**: The consequence-based model is often associated with the principle of utility, which states that an action is morally right if it produces the greatest amount of overall happiness or utility for the greatest number of people. This principle is commonly referred to as utilitarianism, and it is one of the most influential ethical theories in modern philosophy.

2. **Calculating Consequences**: To apply the consequence-based model, one needs to assess the consequences of an action and evaluate their impact on the well-being of individuals or society as a whole. This evaluation can involve both quantitative and qualitative considerations.

- **Quantitative Considerations**: When assessing consequences, factors such as the number of people affected, the intensity of the consequences, and the duration of those consequences should be taken into account. For instance, an action that brings a small benefit to a large number of people might be favored over an action that brings a greater benefit to a smaller number of people.

- **Qualitative Considerations**: In addition to the quantitative aspects, qualitative aspects should also be considered. These include factors such as the nature of the consequences (e.g., pleasure or pain), the distribution of those consequences, and the preferences or values of individuals affected by the action.

3. **Application to Ethical Dilemmas**: The consequence-based model can be useful in addressing ethical dilemmas where there are conflicting moral obligations. By evaluating the consequences of different courses of action, individuals can choose the option that maximizes overall well-being or utility.

For example, consider a healthcare professional faced with the dilemma of allocating a limited supply of a life-saving drug to two patients. Using the consequence-based model, the professional may weigh the potential benefits and harms for each patient and decide to administer the drug to the patient with a higher chance of survival and longer life expectancy, thus maximizing overall well-being.

4. **Critiques and Limitations:** While the consequence-based model offers a systematic approach to ethical decision-making, it is not without its critiques and limitations.

- **Difficulty in Measuring and Comparing Consequences:** Quantifying and comparing the various consequences of an action can be challenging. Assigning numerical values to factors such as happiness or suffering is subjective and may not fully capture the complexity of human experiences.

- **Rights and Justice Concerns:** Critics argue that the consequence-based model may neglect individual rights or fail to address issues of justice and fairness. For instance, the model could potentially justify sacrificing the well-being of a minority group for the greater good of the majority.

- **Unintended and Unforeseen Consequences:** Predicting all possible consequences of an action is often impossible. Unintended or unforeseen consequences may arise and have significant ethical implications, leading to moral dilemmas or contradictory outcomes.

5. **Real-World Examples:** The consequence-based model can be applied to various real-world scenarios to guide ethical decision-making. Let's consider two examples:

- **Environmental Conservation:** When making decisions regarding environmental policies, the consequence-based model can help assess the impact on ecosystems, wildlife, and future generations. By considering the long-term consequences of actions such as deforestation or pollution, policymakers can strive to promote sustainability and protect the well-being of the planet.

- **Public Health Measures:** In public health emergencies, such as the COVID-19 pandemic, the consequence-based model can inform decisions on implementing measures like lockdowns or vaccination campaigns. By weighing the potential benefits of reducing virus transmission and saving lives against any negative consequences like economic impacts, policymakers can make informed choices to maximize overall welfare.

6. **Ethical Considerations:** When applying the consequence-based model, it is essential to consider ethical considerations.

- **Unintended Harms:** While optimizing overall utility is the aim of the consequence-based model, it is crucial to be mindful of the unintended harms that might result from an action. Actively seeking to minimize harm, even at the expense of some utility, is an ethical imperative.

- **Moral Responsibility:** In assessing consequences, it is important to consider the moral responsibility of individuals or institutions. Actions that may lead to severe negative consequences, such as environmental pollution or human rights violations, should be ethically evaluated and avoided if possible.

- **Fairness and Equity:** Although the consequence-based model evaluates actions based on overall utility, fairness and equity should also be considered. Ensuring a just distribution of benefits and avoiding unjust discrimination is crucial to maintaining ethical standards.

In conclusion, the consequence-based model provides an ethical framework for decision-making that focuses on evaluating the consequences of actions. By assessing the overall well-being or utility generated by different options, this model offers a systematic approach to address ethical dilemmas. However, it is essential to consider critiques and limitations, while also incorporating ethical considerations such as unintended harms, moral responsibility, and fairness.

Ethical Practices in Business

Ethics in Corporate Governance

Corporate Social Responsibility

Corporate Social Responsibility (CSR) refers to the ethical obligations and responsibilities that businesses have towards society. It involves considering the impact of business operations on various stakeholders, including employees, customers, communities, and the environment. CSR has become increasingly important in the modern business landscape, as companies are expected to go beyond mere profit-making and contribute positively to society.

The Importance of CSR

CSR is important for several reasons. Firstly, it helps build and maintain a positive reputation for the company. Businesses that engage in socially responsible practices are often viewed favorably by customers, employees, and the general public. This can enhance brand image, attract talent, and ultimately lead to increased profits.

Secondly, CSR can help mitigate risks and prevent potential legal and reputational damage. By adopting responsible practices, companies can avoid lawsuits, fines, and negative publicity associated with unethical behavior. Additionally, it can help build strong relationships with regulators and government agencies, fostering trust and cooperation.

Moreover, CSR allows businesses to contribute to the well-being of society. Through initiatives such as philanthropy, environmental conservation, and community development, companies can address social issues and actively participate in the betterment of the communities in which they operate. This not only benefits society but also creates a positive work environment and enhances employee morale.

Principles of CSR

Several principles guide the practice of CSR:

1. **Sustainability:** Businesses should adopt sustainable practices that minimize their impact on the environment. This includes reducing waste, conserving resources, and adopting renewable energy sources. Sustainability extends beyond ecological considerations to include social and economic sustainability as well.

2. **Ethical Conduct:** Companies should uphold high ethical standards in all their activities. This includes being honest and transparent in their business dealings, treating employees fairly, and respecting human rights. Ethical conduct also involves ensuring that suppliers and partners adhere to similar standards.

3. **Stakeholder Engagement:** Businesses should actively engage with their stakeholders to understand their needs and concerns. This includes consulting with employees, customers, local communities, and other relevant groups to ensure that business decisions take into account their interests. Stakeholder engagement fosters trust and helps identify potential areas for improvement.

4. **Philanthropy and Community Investment:** Companies should contribute to the social and economic development of the communities in which they operate. This can be done through initiatives such as donations, volunteering, and partnerships with non-profit organizations. Philanthropic efforts should align with the company's core values and address pressing societal needs.

5. **Responsible Marketing and Consumer Protection:** Businesses should engage in truthful and responsible marketing practices. This includes providing accurate and reliable information about products and services, ensuring fair pricing, and protecting consumer privacy. Companies should also consider the impact of their marketing activities on vulnerable groups, such as children and low-income individuals.

Challenges and Criticisms of CSR

While CSR is widely recognized as important, it is not without its challenges and criticisms. Some common challenges faced by businesses in implementing CSR include:

+ Balancing competing interests: Businesses often face the challenge of balancing the interests of different stakeholders. For example, a decision that benefits employees may have financial implications for shareholders. Finding the right balance is essential to ensure long-term sustainability.

+ Measuring impact: Companies struggle to measure and quantify the impact of their CSR initiatives. This makes it difficult to assess the effectiveness of their efforts and allocate resources accordingly. Developing appropriate metrics and evaluation frameworks is crucial for meaningful CSR.

+ Greenwashing: Greenwashing refers to the practice of making misleading or unsubstantiated claims about environmental responsibility. Some companies may engage in CSR activities solely for the purpose of enhancing their reputation, without making significant and genuine changes to their practices.

In addition to these challenges, CSR is also subject to criticism. Some argue that businesses should focus solely on maximizing profits and leave social and environmental issues to governments and non-profit organizations. Critics also question the motives behind CSR, suggesting that it is merely a PR strategy and does not lead to meaningful change.

Case Study: Patagonia's Environmental Initiatives

One example of a company that has established a strong reputation for CSR is Patagonia, a leading outdoor clothing and gear manufacturer. Patagonia is committed to minimizing its environmental impact and promoting sustainable practices throughout its supply chain.

Environmental Responsibility: Patagonia has taken several measures to reduce its ecological footprint. It makes use of recycled and organic materials in its products, works towards reducing energy consumption, and has implemented a take-back program for worn-out clothing, promoting recycling and reducing waste.

Supply Chain Transparency: Patagonia places a strong emphasis on transparency and accountability in its supply chain. It works closely with suppliers to ensure fair labor practices, safe working conditions, and compliance with environmental standards. The company also provides information about the origin of its materials, allowing customers to make informed choices.

Advocacy and Activism: Patagonia goes beyond internal sustainability efforts and actively engages in advocacy and activism. It supports environmental initiatives, funds grassroots organizations working towards conservation, and uses its platform to raise awareness about environmental issues. For instance, the company launched the "Don't Buy This Jacket" campaign, urging customers to consider the environmental impact of overconsumption.

The case of Patagonia demonstrates how a company can integrate principles of CSR into its core business practices, aligning its goals with the well-being of society and the environment.

Exercise

Consider a multinational technology company that has been accused of unethical labor practices in its supply chain. Design a comprehensive CSR strategy for the company, addressing the following:

- Ensuring fair and safe working conditions for factory workers in developing countries.

- Promoting transparency and accountability throughout the supply chain.

- Reducing the company's carbon footprint and environmental impact.

- Supporting local communities and social development initiatives.

Provide a detailed plan of action, including specific initiatives, policies, and implementation strategies. Consider the challenges that the company might face in implementing the CSR strategy and propose ways to overcome them.

Additional Resources

To further explore the concept of CSR, the following resources are recommended:

- **Book:** "Corporate Social Responsibility: A Strategic Perspective" by David Chandler.

- **Article:** "The Social Responsibility of Business is to Increase its Profits" by Milton Friedman (1970).

- **Organization:** The United Nations Global Compact (https://www.unglobalcompact.org/).

These resources provide valuable insights into the theory, practice, and debates surrounding CSR in both academic and real-world contexts.

In conclusion, corporate social responsibility plays a vital role in modern business practices. By considering the interests of various stakeholders and actively contributing to society, companies can not only enhance their reputation but also make a meaningful and positive impact on the world. Implementing comprehensive CSR strategies requires careful planning, stakeholder engagement, and a commitment to ethical conduct.

Transparency and Accountability

Transparency and accountability are essential principles in business ethics. Transparency refers to the openness and clarity of a company's actions and decision-making processes, while accountability refers to the responsibility and answerability for those actions. These principles promote trust, fairness, and integrity within an organization and in its relationships with stakeholders.

Importance of Transparency

Transparency plays a crucial role in fostering trust between a company and its stakeholders, including employees, customers, shareholders, and the wider public. When a company operates in a transparent manner, it allows stakeholders to understand its practices, policies, and performance. This transparency helps stakeholders make informed decisions, hold the company accountable, and establish a positive reputation.

Transparency also promotes fair competition by ensuring that companies provide accurate and reliable information, which helps prevent unethical business practices such as false advertising, misleading financial reporting, and insider trading.

Ways to Foster Transparency

To foster transparency, companies can implement various practices and initiatives. One important aspect is the disclosure of information. This includes providing clear and comprehensive reports on financial performance, corporate governance, sustainability practices, and social responsibility initiatives. Transparent disclosures enable stakeholders to assess a company's ethical standards and make informed decisions.

Another way to promote transparency is through open communication. Companies should establish effective channels for employees, customers, and other stakeholders to voice concerns, ask questions, and provide feedback. Transparent communication builds trust and allows for timely resolution of problems or conflicts.

Moreover, companies can adopt ethical codes of conduct and encourage ethical behavior among employees. By clearly articulating the organization's values and expectations, companies set a strong foundation for transparency and ensure that employees understand their roles in upholding ethical standards.

Accountability

Accountability goes hand in hand with transparency. It involves taking responsibility for one's actions and being answerable for the consequences. Accountability is vital for building trust, ensuring compliance with laws and regulations, and maintaining ethical standards within an organization.

Internal Accountability

Internal accountability starts with the establishment of clear lines of responsibility and decision-making processes within an organization. Companies should define roles, provide training on ethical conduct, and establish mechanisms for reporting unethical behavior. This allows for greater transparency and ensures that employees understand the impact of their actions and decisions.

Internal accountability also involves monitoring and evaluating the performance of employees and holding them accountable for meeting ethical standards. This can be achieved through performance evaluations, ethical audits, and disciplinary measures for misconduct.

External Accountability

External accountability refers to a company's responsibility to external stakeholders, such as shareholders, customers, and regulatory bodies. Companies can demonstrate external accountability through transparent reporting of financial and non-financial information, compliance with industry standards and regulations, and responsiveness to stakeholders' concerns and feedback.

Regulatory bodies, industry associations, and professional bodies also play a crucial role in holding companies accountable. They set guidelines and codes of conduct, investigate complaints, and impose sanctions for non-compliance. Public pressure and media scrutiny also serve as external forces for accountability.

Examples of Transparency and Accountability

Transparency and accountability can be demonstrated through real-world examples. For instance, companies like Patagonia and Ben & Jerry's are known for their transparent reporting on environmental and social impacts, including their supply chain practices and labor conditions.

In the financial industry, companies such as Vanguard and BlackRock provide transparent information about their investment strategies, fees, and voting practices, enabling investors to make informed decisions.

Governments and regulatory bodies also prioritize transparency and accountability. For instance, the Securities and Exchange Commission (SEC) in the United States requires publicly traded companies to disclose financial information to protect investors and ensure market integrity.

Conclusion

Transparency and accountability are vital components of ethical practices in business. By promoting openness, honesty, and responsibility, companies can build trust with stakeholders, enhance their reputation, and contribute to a fair and ethical business environment. Through transparent disclosures, open communication, and robust accountability mechanisms, companies can create a culture of integrity and drive sustainable success.

Note: This content is for illustrative purposes only and may need to be adapted to fit the overall structure and style of your textbook.

Ethical Leadership

Ethical leadership is a crucial aspect of professional conduct in various domains, including business, healthcare, education, and politics. It involves guiding and influencing others while adhering to a set of ethical principles and values. Ethical leaders play a vital role in fostering a culture of integrity, trust, and accountability within organizations. In this section, we will delve into the key principles and practices of ethical leadership and explore its significance in promoting ethical behavior in different contexts.

Principles of Ethical Leadership

Ethical leadership is based on a foundation of key principles that guide leaders in their decision-making processes and interactions with others. These principles include:

1. **Integrity:** Ethical leaders adhere to a high standard of honesty, truthfulness, and consistency in their actions and behaviors. They demonstrate transparency and promote an environment of trust and openness.

2. **Respect:** Ethical leaders value the dignity and worth of every individual. They treat others with empathy, fairness, and courtesy, creating an inclusive and respectful work environment.

3. **Responsibility:** Ethical leaders take responsibility for their actions and decisions. They are accountable for their behavior and the outcomes of their leadership. They demonstrate a strong sense of duty towards their stakeholders.

4. **Fairness:** Ethical leaders ensure fairness in their decision-making processes. They consider the interests of all stakeholders and strive to make equitable and just decisions.

5. **Social and Environmental Consciousness:** Ethical leaders recognize the impact of their decisions on society and the environment. They promote sustainable practices and take steps to minimize any harm caused by their actions.

6. **Courage:** Ethical leaders demonstrate courage in standing up for what is right, even in the face of challenges or opposition. They have the courage to make tough decisions based on ethical principles.

These principles form the ethical framework that guides ethical leaders in their actions and behavior.

Practices of Ethical Leadership

Ethical leaders employ various practices to foster an ethical culture within their organizations and influence the behavior of their subordinates. Some key practices include:

1. **Setting the Example:** Ethical leaders serve as role models by consistently aligning their behaviors with the ethical principles they espouse. They lead by example, demonstrating the values and behaviors they expect from others.

2. **Clear Communication of Expectations:** Ethical leaders communicate their expectations regarding ethical behavior to their subordinates clearly. They articulate the ethical standards and values that are instrumental in decision-making processes.

3. **Supporting Ethical Decision Making:** Ethical leaders promote a culture of ethical decision making by providing guidance and support to their subordinates. They encourage critical thinking and reflection when faced with ethical dilemmas.

4. **Encouraging Ethical Reporting:** Ethical leaders establish reporting mechanisms that allow employees to voice ethical concerns or report any unethical behavior without fear of retaliation. They ensure that whistleblowers are protected and their concerns are addressed promptly.

5. **Ethics Training and Education:** Ethical leaders invest in ongoing ethics training and education for themselves and their employees. They provide resources and opportunities for individuals to enhance their ethical decision-making skills and knowledge.

6. **Promoting Ethical Practices:** Ethical leaders create systems and policies that incentivize and recognize ethical behavior. They establish structures that reinforce ethical conduct and discourage unethical practices.

By practicing these strategies, ethical leaders create an environment that supports and encourages ethical behavior among their subordinates.

Challenges and Strategies for Ethical Leadership

Ethical leaders often face various challenges in upholding their ethical standards and promoting ethical behavior. Some common challenges include:

+ **Resistance to Change:** Ethical leaders may face resistance from individuals or groups who are comfortable with the status quo or who have vested interests in maintaining unethical practices. Overcoming resistance requires effective communication, persuasion, and building trust.

+ **Ethical Dilemmas:** Ethical leaders are often confronted with complex and difficult ethical dilemmas where the right course of action is not clear-cut. They must navigate these dilemmas while maintaining ethical integrity and considering the interests of all stakeholders.

- **Pressure to Prioritize Profit:** In business settings, ethical leaders may face pressure to prioritize financial outcomes over ethical considerations. They must balance the interests of shareholders with the values and principles they uphold.

- **Lack of Ethical Role Models:** Ethical leaders may struggle in environments where there is a lack of ethical role models or where unethical behavior is prevalent. They need to proactively address this issue by mentoring and developing ethical leaders within their organizations.

To overcome these challenges, ethical leaders can employ the following strategies:

- **Building Relationships:** Ethical leaders build strong relationships with their subordinates, stakeholders, and the broader community. These relationships are based on trust, respect, and open communication.

- **Seeking Diverse Perspectives:** Ethical leaders actively seek diverse perspectives and input when making decisions. They recognize the value of different viewpoints in ethical deliberations and foster an inclusive decision-making process.

- **Continuous Learning and Improvement:** Ethical leaders engage in ongoing self-reflection and learning. They seek feedback, embrace constructive criticism, and continuously strive to improve their ethical leadership practices.

- **Collaboration and Ethical Partnerships:** Ethical leaders collaborate with other organizations, individuals, and stakeholders to address complex ethical challenges collectively. They recognize the importance of collective action in creating ethical change.

By adopting these strategies, ethical leaders can navigate the challenges they face and contribute to a more ethical organizational culture.

Case Study: Patagonia's Ethical Leadership

Patagonia, an outdoor clothing company, is often recognized as a leader in ethical business practices. The company's founder, Yvon Chouinard, exemplifies ethical leadership by incorporating environmental sustainability and social responsibility into Patagonia's core values and operations.

Chouinard and his team have taken several actions to promote ethical behavior within the organization. They have implemented environmental initiatives such as minimizing the company's carbon footprint, using recycled materials in their products, and promoting sustainable manufacturing practices. Patagonia has also been a vocal advocate for environmental protection, donating a significant portion of their profits to environmental causes.

Patagonia's ethical leadership extends beyond environmental initiatives. The company has implemented fair labor practices, ensuring that workers in their supply chain are treated ethically and paid fair wages. They have also implemented transparent and inclusive decision-making processes, giving employees a voice in company policies and practices.

Through their commitment to ethical leadership, Patagonia has not only built a successful and sustainable business but also inspired other companies to prioritize ethical practices. They serve as a model for organizations seeking to integrate ethical principles into their operations and have shown that ethical leadership can be both profitable and socially responsible.

Conclusion

Ethical leadership is essential for creating an ethical culture within organizations and influencing ethical behavior in various contexts. By adhering to key principles and employing effective practices, ethical leaders can foster trust, integrity, and accountability among their subordinates. Despite challenges, ethical leaders can navigate dilemmas and promote ethical decision-making processes through relationship-building, continuous learning, and collaboration. The case of Patagonia exemplifies the positive impacts of ethical leadership and serves as an inspiration for others striving to integrate ethics into their organizations.

Whistleblowing and Ethical Culture

Whistleblowing is a crucial aspect of promoting an ethical culture within organizations. It involves the disclosure of unethical or illegal activities by an employee or insider with the goal of protecting the interests of the public, stakeholders, or the organization itself. Whistleblowing helps to expose wrongdoing, prevent harm, and uphold ethical standards. In this section, we will explore the importance of whistleblowing in promoting an ethical culture, the challenges associated with it, and strategies for organizations to effectively address whistleblowing.

The Importance of Whistleblowing

Whistleblowing plays a vital role in creating an ethical culture within organizations. It allows individuals to voice their concerns about unethical behavior without fear of retaliation. By encouraging employees to blow the whistle on wrongdoing, organizations can identify and address potential issues before they escalate. Ethical cultures foster trust, transparency, and accountability, which are essential for the long-term success and sustainability of any organization.

Moreover, whistleblowing helps to safeguard the interests of stakeholders and the public. It enables the exposure of fraudulent financial practices, safety violations, environmental misconduct, and other unethical activities that can harm employees, customers, the environment, and the wider community. By holding individuals and organizations accountable for their actions, whistleblowing promotes integrity and ethical behavior.

Challenges with Whistleblowing

Despite its importance, whistleblowing is not without challenges. Whistleblowers often face significant risks and hurdles when disclosing wrongdoing. They may fear retaliation, such as job loss, reputation damage, harassment, or legal action. Whistleblowers may also encounter skepticism and disbelief, especially if their claims expose powerful individuals or institutions.

In addition, organizations may be resistant to whistleblowing due to concerns about reputation, legal implications, and the potential disruption of internal operations. This can create a culture of silence and discourage employees from speaking up. Organizations need to recognize and address these challenges to ensure that whistleblowing is embraced as a valuable mechanism for ethical governance.

Strategies for Promoting Whistleblowing

To promote whistleblowing and foster an ethical culture, organizations can implement several strategies:

1. **Clear Policies and Procedures:** Organizations should establish clear policies and procedures that outline how whistleblowing should be reported, how confidentiality will be maintained, and the protection provided to whistleblowers. These policies should be communicated effectively to all employees, ensuring that they are aware of their rights and the procedures for reporting unethical behavior.

2. **Whistleblower Protection:** Organizations should provide legal protection and support to whistleblowers. This can include measures such as anonymous

reporting mechanisms, confidential hotlines, and legal assistance. Whistleblower protection laws vary in different jurisdictions, and organizations should comply with relevant legislation and provide adequate safeguards to encourage reporting.

3. Education and Training: Organizations should invest in education and training programs to raise awareness about whistleblowing and its importance. This can include ethics training, workshops on reporting mechanisms, and case studies highlighting the impact of whistleblowing. By educating employees on the rights and responsibilities of whistleblowers, organizations can create a supportive environment that encourages ethical behavior.

4. Investigation and Accountability: Organizations should establish effective mechanisms to investigate whistleblower reports promptly and thoroughly. Investigations should be conducted impartially, and appropriate action should be taken against wrongdoers. This demonstrates the organization's commitment to addressing unethical behavior and reinforces the trust of employees in the whistleblowing process.

5. Leadership Support: Ethical cultures start at the top. Leaders should set the tone by visibly supporting and promoting whistleblowing. They should communicate that ethical behavior is valued and that retaliation will not be tolerated. When leaders prioritize ethics and integrity, employees are more likely to feel comfortable coming forward with their concerns.

Case Study: Enron Corporation

The Enron Corporation scandal serves as a powerful example of the importance of whistleblowing and the devastating consequences of a toxic ethical culture. Enron was an American energy company that collapsed in 2001 due to widespread accounting fraud and unethical practices.

Whistleblower Sherron Watkins, an Enron vice president, played a crucial role in exposing the fraud. She raised concerns about the company's accounting irregularities to then-CEO Kenneth Lay. However, her concerns were largely ignored, and the unethical practices continued. It was only after her anonymous memo to Lay was made public that law enforcement and regulatory agencies took action.

The Enron scandal highlighted the need for a strong ethical culture and the empowerment of whistleblowers. It led to significant legal and regulatory changes and contributed to the establishment of the Sarbanes-Oxley Act, which introduced protections for whistleblowers and imposed stricter accounting regulations.

Conclusion

Whistleblowing is a critical component of ethical practices within organizations. It enables the identification and prevention of unethical behavior, protects the interests of stakeholders, and promotes transparency and accountability. To foster an ethical culture, organizations must overcome the challenges associated with whistleblowing and implement strategies that prioritize the protection and support of whistleblowers. By embracing whistleblowing, organizations can create a culture that upholds integrity, ethical conduct, and long-term success.

Codes of Ethics and Conduct

Codes of ethics and conduct play a crucial role in guiding the behavior and decision-making processes of individuals within an organization. These codes serve as a moral compass, outlining the principles and values that govern the conduct and responsibilities of employees. In this section, we will explore the importance of codes of ethics and conduct in fostering ethical behavior within businesses, examining their key elements and providing real-world examples.

The Purpose of Codes of Ethics and Conduct

Codes of ethics and conduct are designed to establish a set of standards and expectations for employees' behavior within an organization. They serve several important purposes:

1. Setting Expectations: Codes of ethics and conduct define the behavior expected of employees in both their professional and personal lives. This clarity helps employees understand what is considered acceptable and unacceptable conduct.

2. Enhancing Ethical Decision Making: By providing guidance on ethical dilemmas and potential conflicts of interest, codes of ethics and conduct help employees make more informed and ethical decisions. They serve as a reference point when faced with challenging situations.

3. Building Trust and Reputation: Organizations with strong codes of ethics and conduct cultivate a reputation for integrity, trustworthiness, and ethical behavior. This trust enhances relationships with stakeholders and can lead to competitive advantage.

4. Promoting Accountability: Codes of ethics and conduct hold employees accountable for their actions. They establish a framework for reporting unethical behavior and provide guidelines for disciplinary action when violations occur.

Key Elements of Codes of Ethics and Conduct

A well-structured code of ethics and conduct typically includes the following key elements:

1. Mission Statement: This section outlines the organization's overall purpose and values, setting the tone for the code. It establishes the ethical framework within which employees are expected to operate.

2. Ethical Principles: The code should articulate the fundamental principles and values that guide ethical behavior within the organization. These principles may include honesty, integrity, respect, fairness, and transparency.

3. Specific Policies: Codes of ethics and conduct should contain specific policies and guidelines related to various ethical issues. These policies may address employee relationships, confidentiality, conflicts of interest, discrimination, harassment, bribery, and whistle-blowing.

4. Decision-Making Process: The code should provide a step-by-step framework for ethical decision-making. This process may involve evaluating the impact of decisions on stakeholders, considering the long-term consequences, and seeking guidance when faced with ethical dilemmas.

5. Reporting and Compliance Mechanisms: Codes of ethics and conduct should include clear procedures for reporting unethical behavior and addressing violations. Whistle-blowing mechanisms, confidential reporting channels, and protection against retaliation should be clearly outlined.

6. Training and Education: Organizations should provide ongoing training and education on the code of ethics and conduct to ensure that employees understand its content and are equipped to apply ethical principles in their day-to-day work.

Real-World Examples

Codes of ethics and conduct are prevalent across various industries and sectors. Let's explore a few real-world examples:

1. The CFA Institute: The CFA Institute, a global association for investment professionals, has a comprehensive Code of Ethics and Standards of Professional Conduct. This code outlines the ethical principles and professional responsibilities of investment professionals, promoting integrity, professionalism, and loyalty to clients.

2. The Coca-Cola Company: Coca-Cola has a Code of Business Conduct that emphasizes accountability, fairness, and ethical decision-making. The code covers various topics, such as conflicts of interest, fair competition, responsible marketing, and respect for human rights and the environment.

3. Johnson & Johnson: Johnson & Johnson has a Code of Business Conduct that focuses on the company's responsibility to patients, customers, employees, and the community. The code addresses topics like product quality and safety, compliance with laws and regulations, and maintaining a diverse and inclusive workplace.

Implementing and Enforcing Codes of Ethics and Conduct

To ensure the effectiveness of codes of ethics and conduct, organizations must have strategies in place for implementation and enforcement. Here are some key considerations:

1. Leadership Commitment: Top management must demonstrate a strong commitment to ethical conduct and lead by example. This commitment should be embedded in the organization's culture and should permeate all levels of the organization.

2. Communication and Training: Organizations should communicate the code of ethics and conduct clearly and regularly to employees. Training programs, workshops, and ongoing education initiatives can help employees understand the code's principles and apply them in their daily work.

3. Monitoring and Reporting: Regular monitoring and reporting of ethical behavior can help identify potential violations and assess the effectiveness of the code. Anonymous reporting mechanisms and whistle-blowing channels should be in place to encourage reporting of unethical behavior.

4. Consistent Enforcement: Organizations must ensure consistent enforcement of the code of ethics and conduct. Violations should be thoroughly investigated, and appropriate disciplinary actions should be taken. This sends a clear message that ethical misconduct will not be tolerated.

5. Continual Review and Revision: Codes of ethics and conduct should evolve with changing times and reflect the organization's values and the broader societal context. Regular review and revision allow the code to remain relevant and effective in guiding ethical behavior.

Conclusion

Codes of ethics and conduct are essential tools in promoting ethical behavior within organizations. They provide a framework for decision making and establish clear expectations for employee conduct. By incorporating key elements such as ethical principles, specific policies, and training programs, organizations can create a culture of integrity and responsibility. Implementing and enforcing codes of ethics and conduct with commitment and consistency ensures that ethical behavior remains a priority and contributes to the long-term success and reputation of the organization.

Exercises

1. Identify a real-world example of a company that faced ethical challenges. Discuss how a well-implemented code of ethics and conduct could have helped prevent or address these challenges.

2. Imagine you are a manager responsible for implementing a code of ethics and conduct in your organization. Outline the steps you would take to ensure effective implementation and enforcement.

3. Research a professional association or industry organization that has a code of ethics. Analyze the key elements of their code and discuss how it promotes ethical behavior within the industry.

4. Consider a recent ethical dilemma faced by a company or organization. Assess how different ethical decision-making models discussed in this textbook could be applied to resolve the dilemma.

5. Conduct a case study on a company known for its strong ethical culture. Analyze their code of ethics and conduct, and identify specific practices that contribute to fostering an ethical environment.

Resources

1. CFA Institute: Code of Ethics and Standards of Professional Conduct - `https://www.cfainstitute.org/en/ethics/codes`

2. Coca-Cola Company: Code of Business Conduct - `https://www.coca-colacompany.com/content/dam/journey/us/en/private/fileassets/policies/CodeBusinessConduct.pdf`

3. Johnson & Johnson: Code of Business Conduct - `https://www.jnj.com/_document?id=0000016c-2506-dec8-af7d-3d4093440000`

4. Markkula Center for Applied Ethics: Framework for Ethical Decision Making - `https://www.scu.edu/ethics/ethics-resources/ethical-decision-making/`

Ethical Marketing and Consumer Rights

Truth in Advertising

In today's fast-paced and competitive business environment, advertising plays a crucial role in promoting products and services. However, it is essential that advertisers maintain ethical practices when it comes to truth in advertising. Truth in advertising refers to the obligation of advertisers to provide accurate and transparent information about their products or services to consumers. This section will delve into the principles of truth in advertising, its importance, common ethical issues in advertising, and strategies for ensuring truthful advertising practices.

Principles of Truth in Advertising

The principles of truth in advertising are built on the foundation of honesty, accuracy, and fairness. Advertisers are expected to provide truthful and reliable information about their products or services to consumers, avoiding exaggerations, misleading claims, or deceptive practices. The following principles form the basis of truth in advertising:

1. **Substantiation:** Advertisers must have sufficient evidence to substantiate the claims made in their advertisements. The claims should be based on reliable data, research, or expert opinions and should be supported by scientific evidence when applicable.

2. **No deception or misleading claims:** Advertisements should not deceive consumers or mislead them about the nature, characteristics, or qualities of the product. All claims made in advertisements must be truthful and not likely to mislead a reasonable consumer.

3. **Clear and conspicuous disclosures:** Advertisements should clearly and conspicuously disclose any material information that is likely to affect consumers' decisions or understanding of the product. Material information includes any information that is important for consumers to make an informed choice.

4. **Comparative advertising:** When using comparative advertising, advertisers should ensure that comparisons are fair, accurate, and based on valid and reliable data. It is essential to avoid making false or misleading comparisons that could harm competitors or deceive consumers.

5. **Endorsements and testimonials:** If an advertisement includes endorsements or testimonials, they should reflect the honest opinions, beliefs, or experiences of the individuals making the endorsements. Advertisers should not make false or misleading claims about the endorsement or testimonial.

6. **Avoiding offensive or deceptive practices:** Advertisements should not contain elements that are likely to offend or deceive consumers, such as false testimonials, hidden fees, or misleading visuals.

Importance of Truth in Advertising

Truth in advertising is of utmost importance for several reasons. Firstly, it ensures that consumers have access to accurate and reliable information about products and services, enabling them to make well-informed purchasing decisions. When consumers are deceived or misled by false advertising claims, it can lead to dissatisfaction, loss of trust, and harm to their interests.

Secondly, truth in advertising promotes fair competition by ensuring that all businesses compete on a level playing field. When advertisers use deceptive or unfair practices, it creates an unfair advantage for certain companies and undermines fair competition in the market.

Furthermore, truth in advertising helps to maintain the overall integrity and credibility of the advertising industry. When advertisers adhere to ethical practices and provide truthful information, it enhances the industry's reputation and builds trust with consumers.

Ethical Issues in Advertising

Despite the principles and importance of truth in advertising, ethical issues can arise in various aspects of advertising. Some common ethical issues include:

1. **False or exaggerated claims:** Advertisers may make false or exaggerated claims about their products to attract consumers. This can mislead consumers and create unrealistic expectations.

2. **Omission of information:** Advertisers may omit essential information that could influence consumers' purchasing decisions. This includes hiding negative aspects or potential risks associated with the product.

3. **Manipulative tactics:** Advertisers may use manipulative tactics, such as emotional appeals or fear-inducing techniques, to sway consumers' decision-making processes.

4. **Targeting vulnerable populations:** Advertisers may target vulnerable populations, such as children or the elderly, with misleading or inappropriate advertising messages.

5. **Unfair competitive practices:** Advertisers may engage in unfair practices that harm competitors, such as spreading false rumors or making false comparisons.

Strategies for Ensuring Truthful Advertising Practices

To ensure truthful advertising practices, advertisers can adopt the following strategies:

1. **Conduct thorough research:** Advertisers should conduct thorough research and gather reliable data to support their claims. This includes scientific studies, expert opinions, or market research data.

2. **Review and verify all claims:** Advertisers should carefully review and verify all claims made in advertisements to ensure their accuracy. Independent third-party verification can add credibility to the claims.

3. **Make disclosures clear and conspicuous:** Advertisers should ensure that any material information or disclosures are presented clearly and conspicuously. This includes using appropriate font sizes and placement in print ads or providing adequate time for disclosures in audio or video ads.

4. **Avoid misleading visuals:** Advertisers should ensure that visuals used in advertisements accurately represent the product or service being advertised. Visuals should not create false impressions or mislead consumers.

5. **Engage in self-regulation:** Advertisers can participate in self-regulatory programs or industry initiatives that promote ethical advertising practices. These programs often provide guidelines and standards for truthful advertising.

6. **Regular monitoring and review:** Advertisers should regularly monitor and review their advertising campaigns to ensure ongoing compliance with ethical standards. This includes reviewing feedback from consumers and addressing any concerns or complaints promptly.

Examples and Contemporary Issues

To illustrate the importance of truth in advertising, let's consider a few examples of contemporary issues in advertising:

1. **False health claims:** Some advertisements may make false or exaggerated health claims about certain products, such as supplements or weight-loss treatments. This can mislead consumers and potentially endanger their health.

2. **Influencer marketing:** With the rise of influencer marketing on social media platforms, there is a growing concern about the truthfulness of endorsements. Advertisers and influencers should ensure that they clearly disclose any material connection or sponsorship to maintain transparency.

3. **Greenwashing:** Some companies engage in greenwashing by making false or exaggerated claims about the environmental benefits of their products or practices.   This   misleads   consumers   who   are   seeking environmentally-friendly options.

4. **Digital advertising and privacy:** Concerns about online privacy and data collection have become prominent in digital advertising. Advertisers must be transparent about data collection practices and obtain appropriate consent from users.

Resources and Further Reading

For further reading on truth in advertising and ethical practices, the following resources may be useful:

- Advertising Standards Authority (ASA) - www.asa.org.uk

- Federal Trade Commission (FTC) - www.ftc.gov

- International Chamber of Commerce (ICC) Advertising and Marketing Communications Code - www.iccwbo.org/adv

- American   Marketing   Association   (AMA)   Code   of   Ethics   - www.ama.org/codes-of-ethics

Conclusion

Maintaining truth in advertising is not only an ethical obligation but also crucial for building trust with consumers and promoting fair competition. Advertisers must adhere to the principles of honesty, accuracy, and fairness, ensuring their claims are substantiated, and disclosures are clear. By promoting transparency and avoiding misleading practices, advertisers can contribute to the overall integrity and credibility of the advertising industry.

Influencer Marketing and Ethics

In recent years, influencer marketing has become a popular and effective strategy for brands to promote their products or services. Influencers, who are individuals with a strong online presence and a large following on social media platforms, have the power to influence the purchasing decisions of their audience. However, as influencer marketing continues to grow, ethical concerns have emerged regarding transparency, authenticity, and the potential for misleading advertising.

Transparency: Disclosing Sponsorships

One of the key ethical issues in influencer marketing is the need for transparency in disclosing sponsorships or partnerships between influencers and brands. Federal Trade Commission (FTC) guidelines require influencers to clearly disclose any material connection they have with a brand when endorsing or promoting their products. This includes receiving free products, discounts, or any form of payment in exchange for the promotion.

The objective behind this disclosure requirement is to ensure that consumers are not misled and can make informed decisions. When influencers fail to disclose their relationships with brands, it creates a sense of deception and undermines the trust of their audience.

Example: Consider a fitness influencer who promotes a particular brand of protein powder without disclosing that they are being compensated by the brand. Their audience may believe that the influencer genuinely supports the product, unaware of the financial arrangement between the influencer and the brand.

To address this issue, influencers should clearly disclose their partnerships with brands in a transparent and easily visible manner. This can be done through explicit verbal or written disclosures, such as labeling posts as "sponsored" or using hashtags like #ad or #sponsoredcontent.

Authenticity: Genuine Recommendations

Another ethical concern in influencer marketing is the need for authenticity in the recommendations made by influencers. Influencers are trusted by their audience, and when they endorse or recommend a product, it should genuinely reflect their opinion and personal experience.

Ethical issues arise when influencers promote products solely for financial gain, without considering the quality or efficacy of the product. This can mislead consumers into purchasing products that may not meet their expectations or provide the promised benefits.

Example: Imagine a fashion influencer who promotes a specific clothing brand solely because they are being paid to do so, without actually liking or wearing the brand in their personal life. Their audience may perceive the endorsement as genuine, leading them to purchase items from the brand based on false impressions.

To maintain authenticity, influencers should only promote products that they genuinely believe in or have personally used. They should thoroughly research and test the products before endorsing them, ensuring that their recommendations align with their personal values and interests.

Misleading Advertising: Exaggerated Claims

Influencer marketing can sometimes involve misleading advertising, where influencers make exaggerated claims about the benefits or effectiveness of a product. This can deceive consumers and lead to dissatisfaction or harm if the product fails to deliver the promised results.

Ethical guidelines require influencers to provide accurate and honest information about the products they promote. This includes avoiding false or exaggerated claims, clearly distinguishing between personal opinion and factual information, and ensuring that any testimonials or endorsements are genuine and truthful.

Example: Consider a wellness influencer who claims that a certain dietary supplement can cure a specific health condition, without any scientific evidence to support the claim. This misleading advertising can give false hope to individuals suffering from the condition, leading them to rely on an ineffective product.

To prevent misleading advertising, influencers should carefully review the claims made by brands and ensure they are supported by reliable evidence. They should be transparent and provide disclaimers when expressing personal opinions, distinguishing them from factual information.

Guiding Principles for Ethical Influencer Marketing

To navigate the ethical challenges in influencer marketing, influencers and brands should adhere to the following guiding principles:

1. **Transparency:** Influencers should clearly disclose any material connections they have with brands, ensuring that their audience is aware of the partnership.

2. **Authenticity:** Influencers should only promote products that align with their values and that they genuinely believe in, maintaining the trust of their audience.

3. **Accuracy:** Influencers should provide accurate and honest information about the products they promote, avoiding exaggerated claims or deceptive tactics.

4. **Education:** Influencers should strive to educate their audience about the products they endorse, providing relevant information and empowering consumers to make informed decisions.

By following these principles, influencers can conduct their marketing activities ethically while maintaining trust and credibility with their audience. This not only protects consumers but also sustains the long-term success and reputation of influencers and brands in the marketplace.

Conclusion

Influencer marketing has revolutionized the way brands connect with consumers, utilizing the power of social media and online influence. However, as influencer marketing continues to evolve, it is crucial to address the ethical considerations to maintain trust, transparency, and authenticity in this rapidly growing industry.

Transparency in disclosing sponsorships, authenticity in recommendations, and avoiding misleading advertising are the key pillars of ethical influencer marketing. Influencers and brands must prioritize these principles to ensure that consumers are well-informed and protected from deceptive practices.

As the field of influencer marketing continues to evolve, it is important for influencers, brands, and regulatory bodies to collaborate and establish industry-wide ethical standards. This will not only enhance consumer protection but also contribute to the overall credibility and sustainability of influencer marketing as a valuable marketing channel.

Product Safety and Quality

Product safety and quality are paramount in every industry, ensuring that consumers are protected from harm and receive products that meet their expectations. From food and beverages to electronics and automobiles, manufacturers and producers have a responsibility to ensure that their products are safe and of high quality. In this section, we will explore the principles and practices of product safety and quality, including the regulations, standards, and processes involved.

Regulatory Framework

Product safety and quality are regulated by various governmental and non-governmental bodies to protect consumers and ensure fair trade practices. These regulations vary across different countries and industries, but they generally share common objectives. Some of the key regulatory bodies include:

+ **Food and Drug Administration (FDA)**: In the United States, the FDA is responsible for regulating food, drugs, medical devices, cosmetics, and other products. They set standards and enforce regulations to ensure safety and quality in these industries.

+ **European Union (EU) Regulations**: The EU has established comprehensive regulations for product safety and quality, covering a wide range of industries. These regulations include the General Product Safety Directive, the REACH Regulation, and specific directives for food, cosmetics, toys, and electronics.

+ **International Organization for Standardization (ISO)**: ISO develops international standards for various aspects of product safety and quality. These standards provide guidelines and best practices for organizations to ensure compliance and meet customer expectations.

Standards and Certification

Standards are essential in ensuring product safety and quality. They define the criteria that products must meet and provide guidelines for manufacturing processes. Some commonly recognized standards include:

+ **ISO 9001**: This standard sets the criteria for a quality management system. It provides a framework for organizations to consistently meet customer requirements and enhance customer satisfaction. Compliance with ISO 9001 is often a requirement for doing business with many companies.

+ **ISO 22000**: Specifically for the food industry, this standard outlines the requirements for a food safety management system. It covers all aspects of food production, from the sourcing of raw materials to the handling of finished products, ensuring food safety from farm to fork.

+ **HACCP**: Hazard Analysis and Critical Control Points (HACCP) is a systematic approach to food safety that identifies and controls potential hazards at all stages of the food production process. It is widely recognized as a preventive approach to ensure the safety of food products.

- **CE Marking:** The CE marking is a certification that demonstrates a product's compliance with health, safety, and environmental protection standards within the European Economic Area. It is mandatory for certain product categories, including machinery, electrical equipment, and personal protective equipment.

Certification is a process through which an independent third-party organization verifies that a product or system meets specified requirements. It provides assurance to consumers and other stakeholders that the product has undergone rigorous testing and adheres to recognized standards. Some well-known certification bodies include Underwriters Laboratories (UL), Intertek, and TÜV SÜD.

Quality Control

Quality control is a set of activities designed to ensure that products meet the specified quality standards. It involves monitoring and testing products at various stages of the production process to identify any defects or deviations from the desired quality. Some common quality control techniques include:

- **Statistical Process Control (SPC):** SPC involves monitoring and controlling the production process using statistical methods. It helps identify any variations in product quality and allows for timely corrective actions to be taken.

- **Sampling and Inspection:** Random sampling and inspection of products are carried out to check for defects and ensure that they meet the required specifications. This can be done through visual inspection, measurements, or performance testing.

- **Quality Audits:** Quality audits assess the effectiveness of the quality management system and its compliance with applicable standards. Internal and external audits are conducted to identify areas for improvement and ensure ongoing adherence to quality requirements.

Recall Management

Despite stringent safety and quality control measures, sometimes products still pose risks to consumers. In such cases, a product recall may be necessary to remove defective or potentially harmful products from the market. Recall management involves proper planning, communication, and execution to minimize the impact on consumers and restore trust in the brand. Key steps in the recall management process include:

1. **Identification and Assessment:** The company identifies the issue and assesses the severity and scope of the problem. This includes understanding the potential risks to consumers and evaluating the need for a recall.

2. **Recall Strategy:** A recall strategy is developed, outlining the objectives, target market, and communication plan. It also includes the logistics of retrieving and disposing of the affected products.

3. **Communication and Notification:** The company communicates with consumers, retailers, and regulatory authorities to notify them of the recall. Clear and timely communication is crucial to ensuring that affected consumers are aware of the risks and the steps they need to take.

4. **Product Retrieval and Disposal:** The company retrieves the affected products from the market and ensures their proper disposal. This may involve working with retailers, distributors, and logistics partners to collect the products efficiently.

5. **Evaluation and Improvement:** After the recall, a thorough evaluation of the process is conducted to identify any shortcomings and areas for improvement. This feedback is used to enhance product safety and quality control measures.

Consumer Awareness and Education

In addition to the efforts made by manufacturers and regulatory bodies, consumer awareness and education are crucial in ensuring product safety and quality. Consumers should be proactive in understanding and exercising their rights and making informed choices. Some ways to promote consumer awareness and education include:

+ **Product Labeling:** Clear and accurate labeling provides consumers with information about the product, including ingredients, safety warnings, and usage instructions. Consumers should pay attention to labels and ensure that they meet their expectations and specific needs.

+ **Consumer Organizations:** Consumer organizations play a significant role in advocating for consumer rights and raising awareness about product safety and quality issues. Consumers can join and support these organizations to stay informed and voice their concerns.

* **Reporting Systems:** Many countries have systems in place for consumers to report safety concerns and incidents related to products. By reporting issues, consumers contribute to the identification of potential risks and the improvement of product safety and quality.

* **Education Programs:** Educational initiatives can be implemented in schools, workplaces, and communities to raise awareness about product safety and quality. These programs can help individuals make informed choices and understand their rights and responsibilities as consumers.

Real-world Example

To further illustrate the importance of product safety and quality, let's consider a real-world example of a food product recall. Imagine a company that manufactures packaged salads sold in grocery stores. After routine testing, it is discovered that some batches of the salads contain traces of a harmful bacteria that can cause severe illness.

The company immediately activates its recall management process. It identifies the affected batches and quickly informs the regulatory authorities, grocery store chains, and the public. Clear communication is provided through media releases, social media posts, and in-store notices, warning consumers not to consume the salads and offering a full refund.

The affected salads are promptly removed from store shelves and properly disposed of to prevent any further risks. The company works closely with health agencies and conducts a thorough investigation to determine the source of the contamination. Corrective measures are implemented to prevent a recurrence, such as improving supplier quality control, enhancing sanitation practices, and conducting more rigorous product testing.

Through effective recall management and transparency, the company demonstrates its commitment to consumer safety and quality. This incident serves as a reminder of the importance of stringent quality control, prompt action in case of safety issues, and ongoing efforts to continuously improve product safety and quality.

Summary

Product safety and quality are essential for consumer protection and brand reputation. Regulatory frameworks, standards, certification, quality control, recall management, consumer awareness, and education are all critical elements in ensuring that consumers receive safe and high-quality products. Manufacturers and consumers must work together to foster a culture of product safety and quality that reflects their shared responsibility. By adhering to regulations, implementing robust quality management systems, and promoting consumer awareness, organizations can build trust and confidence in their products while protecting consumers from harm.

Consumer Privacy and Data Protection

In today's digital age, the collection, storage, and use of consumer data have become increasingly prevalent. This raises important ethical concerns regarding consumer privacy and data protection. As technology advances and data-driven business models become more prevalent, it is crucial for organizations to uphold ethical practices and safeguard the personal information of their consumers.

The Importance of Consumer Privacy

Consumer privacy refers to the right of individuals to control the collection, use, and dissemination of their personal information. It is essential for maintaining trust and preserving the autonomy of individuals in the digital realm. Companies must recognize the importance of consumer privacy and take proactive measures to protect it.

Data Protection Laws and Regulations

Various data protection laws and regulations have been enacted globally to ensure the privacy and security of personal information. These laws govern the collection, storage, and use of consumer data and impose obligations on organizations to protect this information. Examples of data protection laws include the General Data Protection Regulation (GDPR) in the European Union and the California Consumer Privacy Act (CCPA) in the United States.

Principles of Data Protection

To ensure consumer privacy and data protection, organizations should adhere to the following principles:

1. **Consent and Purpose Limitation:** Organizations should obtain informed consent from individuals before collecting their personal data. They should also clearly specify the purpose for which the data will be used and not collect more data than necessary for that purpose.

2. **Data Minimization:** Organizations should collect only the minimum amount of personal data required for the intended purpose. Unnecessary or excessive data collection should be avoided.

3. **Data Security:** Organizations must implement adequate security measures to protect consumer data from unauthorized access, disclosure, or alteration. This includes adopting encryption, firewalls, and secure storage systems.

4. **Transparency:** Organizations should provide clear and easily understandable privacy policies that disclose how consumer data is collected, used, and shared. Transparent communication builds trust and allows individuals to make informed decisions about their personal information.

5. **Data Accuracy and Access:** Organizations should ensure the accuracy and integrity of consumer data. Individuals should have the right to access their personal information, correct any inaccuracies, and request its deletion when no longer necessary.

Challenges and Ethical Considerations

Despite the existence of data protection laws and principles, several challenges and ethical considerations surround consumer privacy and data protection:

1. **Data Breaches:** Organizations face the risk of data breaches, which can lead to the unauthorized access or disclosure of consumer data. This highlights the need for robust security measures and incident response plans.

2. **Third-Party Sharing:** Organizations often share consumer data with third parties for various purposes. Ethical concerns arise when data is shared without the explicit consent or knowledge of the individuals involved. Organizations should carefully select trusted partners and establish clear agreements to protect consumer data.

3. **Profiling and Targeted Advertising:** The collection and analysis of consumer data enable personalized marketing and targeted advertising. However, ethical considerations arise when profiling is done without individuals' knowledge or consent and results in manipulation or discrimination.

4. **Data Monetization:** Some organizations profit by selling or monetizing consumer data. This raises ethical questions regarding the ownership and fair compensation for the use of personal information.

5.   **International Data Transfers:** Transferring consumer data across international borders can pose challenges due to differing data protection regulations. Organizations must ensure compliance with applicable laws and establish safeguards for such transfers.

Best Practices for Consumer Privacy and Data Protection

To foster a culture of consumer privacy and data protection, organizations should implement the following best practices:

1. **Privacy by Design:** Privacy considerations should be integrated into the design and development of products and services from the outset. This involves considering privacy risks, implementing privacy-enhancing technologies, and conducting privacy impact assessments.

2. **Data Governance and Accountability:** Organizations should establish robust data governance frameworks that define roles and responsibilities for data protection. They should also designate a Data Protection Officer (DPO) to oversee compliance with data protection laws and regulations.

3. **Employee Training and Awareness:** Organizations should provide regular training to employees on data protection best practices, privacy policies, and their roles in safeguarding consumer data. Awareness programs can promote a privacy-conscious culture throughout the organization.

4. **Privacy-Focused Technologies:** Organizations should leverage technologies that prioritize privacy, such as encryption, anonymization, and data masking techniques. These technologies can help minimize the risk of unauthorized access to consumer data.

5. **Incident Response and Notification:** Organizations should have a robust incident response plan in place to promptly address and mitigate data breaches. Timely notification to affected individuals and relevant authorities is essential to uphold transparency and ensure appropriate action is taken.

Case Study: Facebook's Data Privacy Controversy

One prominent example highlighting the importance of consumer privacy and data protection is the 2018 Facebook-Cambridge Analytica scandal. Personal data from millions of Facebook users was improperly harvested and used for targeted political advertising without the users' consent.

This case exposed the ethical implications of lax data privacy practices and inadequate user consent mechanisms. It underscored the need for better regulation, transparency, and accountability in the collection and use of consumer data by technology companies. Following the incident, regulatory scrutiny and public awareness surrounding data privacy have increased significantly.

Conclusion

Consumer privacy and data protection are vital aspects of ethical practices in the digital era. Organizations must prioritize these principles to build trust, maintain customer loyalty, and comply with data protection laws and regulations. By implementing robust data protection measures, organizations can forge a path towards a more responsible and privacy-aware digital ecosystem.

Ethical Pricing and Fair Trade

Ethical pricing and fair trade are important concepts in business that aim to ensure fairness and justice in economic transactions. In this section, we will explore the principles and practices of ethical pricing and fair trade, examine the benefits and challenges associated with them, and discuss how businesses can implement these practices effectively.

Principles of Ethical Pricing

Ethical pricing is the practice of setting prices that are fair and just, taking into account the costs involved in producing goods or delivering services, as well as the value they provide to customers. The following principles guide ethical pricing:

1. Transparency: Businesses should be transparent about their pricing methods and provide clear information to customers about the factors influencing the prices. This allows customers to make informed decisions and fosters trust between businesses and consumers.

2. Cost-based pricing: Ethical pricing involves setting prices based on the actual costs incurred in producing goods or delivering services. This ensures that prices are reasonable and reflect the value provided by the products or services.

3. Non-exploitation: Ethical pricing prohibits the exploitation of vulnerable individuals or communities through unfair pricing practices. It strives to ensure that all parties involved in the production and distribution process are treated fairly and receive a fair share of the value created.

4. Social and environmental responsibility: Ethical pricing considers the social and environmental impacts of business activities in the pricing process. It takes into account the costs associated with sustainable practices, fair labor conditions, and environmentally-friendly processes.

Fair Trade Principles

Fair trade is a movement that promotes equitable trading partnerships and aims to empower marginalized producers and workers. The following principles guide fair trade practices:

1. Fair price: Fair trade sets a minimum price that covers the costs of sustainable production, allowing producers to earn a fair and stable income. It also includes a premium that is invested in community development projects.

2. Empowerment and capacity building: Fair trade organizations support producers by providing training, resources, and access to markets. This helps them improve their knowledge and skills, enhancing their ability to participate effectively in the global economy.

3. Social and environmental sustainability: Fair trade promotes environmentally-friendly production practices and emphasizes the importance of social responsibility. It encourages producers to minimize their environmental impact and ensure safe and fair working conditions.

4. Democratic and transparent trade relationships: Fair trade fosters open and honest communication between producers and buyers. It promotes long-term partnerships based on trust, respect, and mutual understanding.

Benefits and Challenges of Ethical Pricing and Fair Trade

Ethical pricing and fair trade practices offer several benefits for businesses, consumers, and society as a whole. These include:

1. Improved reputation: Adopting ethical pricing and fair trade practices can enhance a company's reputation and brand image. Consumers are increasingly concerned about social and environmental issues and are more likely to support businesses that demonstrate ethical behavior.

2. Increased customer loyalty: Ethical pricing and fair trade practices can build trust and loyalty among customers. Consumers appreciate businesses that prioritize fairness, transparency, and sustainable practices and are more likely to become repeat customers.

3. Social impact: Ethical pricing and fair trade practices contribute to the economic development of marginalized producers and communities. They provide fair wages, empower workers, and support sustainable livelihoods.

Despite these benefits, implementing ethical pricing and fair trade practices can also pose challenges for businesses. These include:

1. Higher costs: Ethical pricing and fair trade practices may result in higher production costs, as they often involve paying fair wages, supporting sustainable

production methods, and investing in community development projects. This can present a financial challenge for businesses, particularly for small and medium enterprises.

2. Limited market access: The market demand for fair trade products is still relatively small compared to conventionally produced goods. This can limit the market access for businesses that adopt fair trade practices, making it more challenging to sell their products and compete with larger companies.

3. Complexity of supply chains: Ethical pricing and fair trade practices require businesses to have a deep understanding of their supply chains, ensuring that all suppliers and partners adhere to ethical standards. This can be complex, especially for businesses with global supply chains and multiple stakeholders.

Implementing Ethical Pricing and Fair Trade Practices

To successfully implement ethical pricing and fair trade practices, businesses can consider the following strategies:

1. Conduct a comprehensive assessment: Businesses should assess their current pricing strategies, supply chains, and business practices to identify areas that need improvement. This evaluation will help determine the steps needed to align their operations with ethical pricing and fair trade principles.

2. Collaborate with ethical suppliers: Businesses should work with suppliers who share their commitment to ethical practices. They should establish clear expectations and requirements for suppliers, ensuring that they adhere to fair trade and ethical pricing principles.

3. Educate and communicate with customers: Transparent communication is key in ethical pricing and fair trade. Businesses should educate their customers about their commitment to ethical practices, explaining the benefits and value that these practices bring. This includes providing information about the fair trade certification process or the ethical pricing methods used.

4. Engage in partnerships and certifications: Businesses can strengthen their commitment to ethical pricing and fair trade by partnering with fair trade organizations or obtaining certifications. These partnerships and certifications help demonstrate credibility and align businesses with established ethical standards.

5. Support local communities: Ethical pricing and fair trade practices can extend beyond the immediate business operations. Businesses can support local communities by investing in education, healthcare, and sustainable development projects. This demonstrates a genuine commitment to the well-being of producers and workers.

Case Study: Ethical Pricing in the Fashion Industry

The fashion industry has faced criticism for its unethical pricing practices, including the use of sweatshops and low wages for garment workers in developing countries. In response, some fashion brands have embraced ethical pricing principles to address these issues.

One example is the brand Everlane, which is committed to transparency and ethical production practices. Everlane provides detailed information about the cost breakdown of their products, including the materials used, labor costs, and transportation expenses. By being transparent about their pricing, they empower consumers to make informed purchasing decisions.

Another example is the luxury brand Stella McCartney, known for its commitment to sustainable and ethical fashion. Stella McCartney incorporates fair trade principles into its supply chain, ensuring that workers are paid fair wages and have safe working conditions. The brand also uses eco-friendly materials and promotes recycling and reducing waste.

These case studies demonstrate how ethical pricing practices can be applied in different sectors of the fashion industry, promoting fair wages, transparent pricing, and sustainable production methods.

Conclusion

Ethical pricing and fair trade practices play a significant role in creating a more equitable and sustainable business environment. By adopting these practices, businesses can enhance their reputation, build customer loyalty, and contribute to the well-being of producers and workers. Implementing ethical pricing and fair trade practices requires careful consideration, collaboration, and transparent communication. By embracing these principles, businesses can play a key role in promoting fairness and justice in the global economy.

Ethical Decision Making in Business

Ethical Dilemmas in Business

In the world of business, ethical dilemmas are common occurrences that require careful consideration and decision-making. Ethical dilemmas arise when there is a conflict between moral principles or when individuals are faced with difficult choices that have potential ethical implications. These dilemmas can arise at all levels of an organization, from employee behavior to executive decision-making.

Conflicts of Interest

One common ethical dilemma in business is conflicts of interest. A conflict of interest occurs when an individual or entity has competing professional or personal interests that could compromise their judgment or objectivity. For example, a purchasing manager who accepts gifts or kickbacks from suppliers may be swayed to make purchasing decisions based on personal gain rather than the best interests of the company.

Identifying conflicts of interest and managing them appropriately is essential for maintaining ethical business practices. It involves disclosing relevant information, avoiding situations where conflicts may arise, and taking necessary steps to mitigate the impact of conflicts when they do occur. Organizations can establish policies and procedures to guide employees on how to navigate conflicts of interest and promote transparency and accountability.

Example: A project manager is responsible for selecting a vendor to provide a crucial component for a construction project. One of the vendors is a close friend of the project manager and offers a substantial discount. The project manager is faced with the dilemma of whether to choose the vendor based on the discounted price, potentially compromising the quality of the project, or to select a vendor based on merit and fair competition.

Bribery and Corruption

Bribery and corruption pose significant ethical challenges in the business world. Bribery involves offering, giving, receiving, or soliciting something of value with the intent to influence the actions of an individual in a position of power. Corruption refers to the abuse of entrusted power for personal gain or the failure to exercise power for the benefit of others.

Bribery and corruption can undermine fair competition, erode trust, and distort business practices. They have severe legal and reputational consequences for individuals and organizations involved. Implementing comprehensive anti-bribery and anti-corruption policies, conducting regular training, and promoting a strong ethical culture are vital for preventing and addressing these ethical dilemmas.

Example: A sales executive offers a substantial bribe to a government official to secure a lucrative contract for their company. The official is responsible for awarding contracts based on merit, but the sales executive's offer tempts them to prioritize personal gain over fair competition and transparency.

Insider Trading

Insider trading occurs when individuals trade or share non-public material information about a company's securities to gain an unfair advantage in the financial markets. This unethical practice undermines fair and transparent markets, erodes investor confidence, and violates the rights of other investors.

Companies must establish clear policies and procedures to prevent insider trading and educate employees about their legal and ethical obligations. Robust internal control systems and surveillance measures can help detect and deter instances of insider trading. Regulatory authorities also play a crucial role in enforcing rules and prosecuting individuals involved in insider trading.

Example: An employee of a pharmaceutical company learns about a breakthrough discovery in the development of a new drug. Before the information becomes public, the employee buys a significant number of shares in their company, knowing that the stock price will likely increase when the news is announced, allowing them to profit from this privileged knowledge.

Intellectual Property Theft

Intellectual property theft refers to the unauthorized use, reproduction, or distribution of someone else's intellectual property without proper authorization or compensation. This can include patent infringement, copyright violation, or trade secret misappropriation. Intellectual property rights are crucial for promoting innovation, rewarding creativity, and fostering fair competition.

Businesses need to establish strong mechanisms to protect their intellectual property and respect the intellectual property rights of others. This includes implementing appropriate security measures, conducting regular audits, and providing staff with adequate training on intellectual property law and ethics.

Example: A software developer at a technology company steals the source code for a proprietary software application and uses it to develop a similar product for a competing company. This unethical act deprives the original company of their intellectual property rights and undermines their ability to compete in the market.

Discrimination and Harassment

Discrimination and harassment in the workplace are serious ethical dilemmas that can harm individuals' well-being, create a hostile work environment, and damage the reputation of the organization. Discrimination can manifest in various forms, such as race, gender, age, religion, or disability. Harassment involves unwanted behavior that belittles, intimidates, or offends individuals based on their protected characteristics.

Organizations must establish clear policies prohibiting discrimination and harassment, provide training on these policies, and create mechanisms for reporting and addressing such incidents. Promoting diversity, inclusion, and equal opportunities can help prevent and address these ethical dilemmas.

Example: A manager consistently denies promotion opportunities to qualified female employees solely based on their gender, believing that women are not fit for leadership roles. This discriminatory practice undermines gender equality, deprives deserving employees of career advancement, and damages the organization's reputation.

Ethical Leadership in Business

Ethical leadership plays a critical role in promoting ethical behavior throughout an organization. Leaders must set a positive example, establish a strong ethical culture, and make ethical decisions based on principles of fairness, integrity, and responsibility. By demonstrating ethical behavior, leaders inspire their employees to act ethically and create an environment where ethical dilemmas are less likely to occur.

Organizations can support ethical leadership by providing leaders with training in ethical decision-making, creating opportunities for ethical discussions, and incorporating ethical considerations into performance evaluations and rewards systems.

Example: A CEO of a large multinational corporation recognizes the negative environmental impact of the company's operations and decides to invest in sustainable practices, despite the potential short-term financial costs. This ethical leadership decision aligns the company's actions with environmental responsibility and sets an example for other organizations within the industry.

Conclusion

Ethical dilemmas in business encompass a wide range of issues that require thoughtful consideration and decision-making. Conflicts of interest, bribery and corruption, insider trading, intellectual property theft, discrimination and harassment are just a few examples of the ethical challenges faced by individuals and organizations in the business world.

By educating employees, establishing clear policies, promoting ethical leadership, and fostering a culture of integrity, organizations can navigate these dilemmas and make ethical decisions that uphold their values and contribute to the greater good. Addressing ethical dilemmas in business is an ongoing process that reflects the commitment to ethical practices and responsible business conduct.

Recommended Resources: - "Ethics in the Workplace" by Craig E. Johnson - "Business Ethics: Ethical Decision Making and Cases" by O.C. Ferrell and John Fraedrich - "Ethics 101: What Every Leader Needs to Know" by John C. Maxwell

Exercises

1. Identify and analyze a recent real-world case of a conflict of interest in business. Discuss the potential consequences and propose strategies for managing and mitigating such conflicts.

2. Choose one of the ethical concerns discussed in this section (e.g., bribery, discrimination) and research the legal and regulatory frameworks in place to address such issues. Analyze the effectiveness of these frameworks and propose potential improvements.

3. Imagine you are a business leader faced with a complex ethical dilemma. Develop a step-by-step action plan outlining how you would approach and resolve this dilemma, considering the principles and frameworks discussed in this section.

4. Conduct a group discussion or debate on the ethical implications of emerging technologies such as artificial intelligence, biotechnology, or cybersecurity in business. Explore the potential benefits and risks associated with these technologies and propose strategies to address the ethical dilemmas they may present.

5. Interview a business leader or ethics officer from a local organization to gain insights into the strategies they employ to promote ethical decision-making and address ethical dilemmas. Present your findings and evaluate the effectiveness of their approaches.

Remember, ethical dilemmas in business are complex and nuanced, and there may not always be a clear-cut solution. The goal is to cultivate ethical awareness, critical thinking, and responsible decision-making to navigate these dilemmas effectively.

Conflicts of Interest

In the world of business, conflicts of interest are a common occurrence that can pose significant ethical challenges. A conflict of interest arises when an individual or entity is in a position where their personal interests or loyalties may compromise their professional judgment or obligations, potentially leading to biased or unfair decision-making.

Understanding Conflicts of Interest

To fully grasp the concept of conflicts of interest, it is important to recognize the various ways they can manifest in a business setting. Some common scenarios include:

- Self-Dealing: This occurs when a decision-maker prioritizes their personal interests over the interests of the organization or stakeholders.

- Insider Trading: When individuals with access to confidential information use it for personal gain, it constitutes a conflict of interest.

- Nepotism: Giving preferential treatment to family members or close associates can create conflicts of interest within an organization.

- Vendor Relationships: If a decision-maker has a personal or financial relationship with a supplier or contractor, their judgment may be compromised when making purchasing decisions.

- Undisclosed Financial Interests: Failure to disclose financial investments or ties to other organizations can undermine objectivity and transparency.

Ethical Implications

Conflicts of interest have far-reaching ethical implications as they erode trust, create biased decision-making, and undermine the overall fairness and integrity of business practices. Key ethical principles that are compromised during conflicts of interest include:

Fidelity The principle of fidelity refers to the duty of individuals to act in the best interests of those they are obligated to serve. Conflicts of interest threaten fidelity by diverting attention from the organization's goals to personal gain or alternative interests.

Fairness Fairness implies impartiality and equal treatment to all stakeholders. Conflicts of interest introduce bias, favoritism, or unfair advantages, leading to a breach of the fairness principle.

Transparency Transparency ensures openness and accountability in decision-making processes. Conflicts of interest often involve non-disclosure or concealment of relevant information, undermining transparency.

Integrity Integrity requires individuals to adhere to moral and ethical principles. Conflicts of interest can compromise integrity by enticing individuals to act dishonestly or in a manner that contradicts their ethical duties.

Managing Conflicts of Interest

Managing conflicts of interest is crucial for maintaining ethical standards within organizations. Here are some strategies to effectively address and mitigate conflicts of interest:

Disclosure and Transparency Promote a culture of transparency by requiring individuals to disclose any potential conflicts of interest. This information should be made available to stakeholders and relevant parties.

Establishing Policies and Procedures Develop comprehensive policies and procedures that define what constitutes a conflict of interest and outline steps for identification, management, and resolution. These policies should provide guidelines for employees to navigate potential conflicts.

Recusal or Disqualification In situations where a conflict of interest is evident or potential, individuals should recuse themselves from decision-making processes related to the conflicted matter. In more severe cases, disqualification from specific roles or responsibilities may be necessary.

Independent Review and Oversight Implement mechanisms for independent review and oversight to ensure that conflicts of interest are appropriately addressed and managed. This can involve the establishment of an ethics committee or a designated ethics officer within the organization.

Training and Education Invest in training and educational programs to raise awareness about conflicts of interest and their ethical implications. Providing employees with the knowledge and tools to identify and navigate conflicts can help prevent ethical breaches.

Real-life Example

Let's consider a real-life example to illustrate the significance of managing conflicts of interest. Imagine a pharmaceutical company that funds research on the efficacy of its own drugs. In such a scenario, there is a clear conflict of interest, as the company may be inclined to manipulate or suppress unfavorable research results to protect its financial interests.

To mitigate this conflict, transparency and independent oversight are crucial. The company should disclose its financial ties and funding sources to the public and engage independent researchers or regulatory bodies to assess the validity of research findings.

Conclusion

Conflicts of interest present ethical challenges in various aspects of business. By managing conflicts transparently, establishing clear guidelines, and fostering a culture of ethical decision-making, organizations can navigate these challenges and uphold their ethical obligations. Identifying and addressing conflicts of interest is a crucial step toward promoting fairness, integrity, and public trust in business practices.

Bribery and Corruption

Bribery and corruption are unethical practices that have significant consequences for businesses and societies as a whole. In this section, we will explore the concept of bribery, its detrimental effects, and the measures that can be taken to prevent and address corruption.

Understanding Bribery

Bribery is the act of offering, giving, receiving, or soliciting something of value (such as money, gifts, favors, or even employment opportunities) with the intention of influencing the actions or decisions of an individual in a position of power. It is a form of corruption that undermines fairness, impartiality, and the rule of law.

Bribery can occur in various contexts, such as business transactions, government dealings, and even in educational settings. It often involves the abuse of power and position, and can lead to a wide range of negative consequences for both individuals and society as a whole.

Effects of Bribery

Bribery has far-reaching negative effects on businesses, economies, and societies. Some of the key impacts include:

1. **Distortion of fair competition:** When bribery is prevalent, it distorts the playing field and undermines fair competition. Businesses that engage in bribery may gain unfair advantages over their competitors, leading to market inefficiencies and decreased trust in the economic system.

2. **Erosion of public trust:** Bribery erodes public trust in institutions and undermines the legitimacy of government and public officials. The perception of corruption can lead to disillusionment with the political system, reduced civic engagement, and weakened democratic institutions.

3. **Inequitable distribution of resources:** Bribery often results in the allocation of resources based on personal favors or illicit payments rather than merit or public welfare. This can lead to the misallocation of resources, perpetuation of poverty, and hindered economic development.

4. **Undermining of ethical standards:** When bribery becomes normalized, it undermines ethical standards within organizations and communities. It sets a precedent for unethical behavior and can create a culture of corruption, which further exacerbates the problem.

5. **Social and economic instability:** Bribery and corruption can contribute to social and economic instability. They weaken the rule of law, impede foreign investment, discourage economic growth, and exacerbate income inequality.

Prevention and Combating of Bribery

Preventing and combating bribery requires the efforts of various stakeholders, including governments, businesses, civil society organizations, and individuals. Here are some key strategies and measures that can be implemented:

1. **Legislation and enforcement:** Governments should enact and enforce strong anti-bribery laws. These laws should criminalize bribery in all its forms, including the offering, receiving, or solicitation of bribes. Adequate penalties and punishments should be imposed to deter individuals and organizations from engaging in corrupt practices.

2. **Transparency and accountability:** Promoting transparency and accountability is crucial in combating bribery. Governments should ensure open and accountable governance, with clear procedures and mechanisms for reporting and investigating corruption cases. Whistleblower protection laws can encourage individuals to come forward with information about corrupt activities.

3. **Ethical corporate culture:** Businesses should establish and promote ethical corporate cultures that discourage bribery and corruption. This includes implementing comprehensive anti-corruption policies, conducting regular training programs for employees, and fostering a zero-tolerance approach towards corrupt practices.

4. **Due diligence and risk assessment:** Businesses should conduct due diligence and risk assessments when entering into partnerships, conducting business transactions, or engaging with third parties. This helps identify and mitigate the risks of bribery and corruption.

5. **International cooperation:** International collaboration is essential in combating bribery and corruption, especially when it involves cross-border transactions. Governments and organizations should cooperate by sharing information, coordinating investigations, and extraditing individuals involved in corrupt practices.

Case Study: The Siemens Scandal

One of the most well-known examples of corporate bribery and corruption is the Siemens scandal. In 2006, Siemens, a global engineering and electronics company, was found guilty of engaging in widespread bribery to secure contracts worldwide.

The company admitted to making illicit payments of over $1.4 billion to government officials, employees of state-owned companies, and political parties in various countries. The bribes were used to secure contracts, gain market access, and obtain favorable treatment.

The Siemens scandal had significant consequences for the company. It faced hefty fines and damage to its reputation, leading to a loss of public trust and investor confidence. The case served as a wake-up call for businesses worldwide and highlighted the importance of implementing robust anti-bribery measures.

Conclusion

Bribery and corruption pose a significant threat to the ethical fabric of society and have far-reaching consequences for businesses and economies. Preventing and combating bribery requires a multi-faceted approach involving legislation, transparency, accountability, and international cooperation.

By understanding the detrimental effects of bribery and implementing effective anti-corruption measures, businesses and governments can promote fairness, integrity, and sustainable development. It is the responsibility of all individuals and organizations to contribute to a culture of integrity and combat bribery in all its forms.

Insider Trading

Insider trading is an unethical practice that occurs when individuals within a company use their privileged access to confidential information to trade securities for their personal gain. It involves buying or selling stocks, bonds, or other financial instruments based on material non-public information. Insider trading not only violates ethical principles but is also illegal in many jurisdictions around the world.

Background

Insider trading undermines the fairness and integrity of financial markets by giving certain individuals an unfair advantage over others. It erodes investor confidence and can result in significant financial losses for those who are not privy to such information. Therefore, it is of utmost importance for regulatory bodies and market participants to identify and deter insider trading activities.

One key aspect of insider trading is that it requires the existence of material non-public information. Material information refers to information that would have a significant impact on the price of a security if it was made public. Non-public information means that the information is not yet available to the general public.

Ethical and Legal Implications

Insider trading is widely regarded as unethical due to the following reasons:

1. **Fairness and Equal Opportunity:** Insider trading allows individuals with access to confidential information to profit unfairly at the expense of other market participants. This undermines the principle of equal opportunity and fairness in the financial markets.

2. **Confidentiality and Trust:** Insider trading breaches the trust and confidentiality owed by insiders to their companies and shareholders. Insiders have a fiduciary duty to act in the best interests of the company and its shareholders, and using confidential information for personal gain violates this duty.

3. **Market Integrity:** Insider trading undermines the integrity of financial markets by distorting price discovery mechanisms. The free and transparent flow of information is essential for efficient markets, and insider trading disrupts this process.

4. **Legal Consequences:** Insider trading is not only unethical but also illegal in many jurisdictions. Violators can face severe penalties, including fines, imprisonment, and civil lawsuits.

Regulatory Framework

To combat insider trading, regulatory authorities have established rules and regulations to enforce fair and ethical market practices. These regulations vary across jurisdictions but generally focus on the following areas:

1. **Prohibition:** Laws explicitly prohibit insider trading and impose penalties on offenders. These laws typically define what constitutes insider trading and specify the types of information that are considered material.

2. **Reporting Requirements:** Companies are required to implement policies and procedures for reporting and disclosing material information in a timely manner. This ensures that all investors have access to relevant information simultaneously.

3. **Insider Lists:** Companies are often required to maintain insider lists, which include individuals with access to confidential information. These lists help regulators monitor trading activities and detect potential instances of insider trading.

4. **Whistleblower Protection:** Whistleblower programs encourage individuals to report insider trading violations without fear of retaliation. These programs provide incentives and legal protections to those who come forward with credible information.

5. **Surveillance and Enforcement:** Regulatory authorities employ advanced surveillance techniques and technologies to detect and investigate suspicious trading activities. They collaborate with market participants to enforce regulations and prosecute offenders.

Real-World Examples

Several high-profile insider trading cases have highlighted the unethical and illegal nature of this practice. One such example is the case of Martha Stewart, the American businesswoman and television personality. In 2004, she was found guilty of insider trading for selling shares of a biopharmaceutical company based on non-public information about a failed drug trial. She was sentenced to prison and faced substantial reputational and financial consequences.

Another well-known case is that of SAC Capital Advisors, a hedge fund founded by Steven Cohen. In 2013, the firm pleaded guilty to insider trading charges and agreed to pay a record-breaking fine. This case shed light on the pervasive nature of insider trading in the hedge fund industry and prompted increased regulatory scrutiny.

Preventing Insider Trading

Preventing insider trading requires a combination of regulatory measures and internal controls within organizations. Some key preventative measures include:

1. **Education and Awareness:** Companies should provide comprehensive training programs to employees to raise awareness about insider trading laws and the ethical implications of such activities.

2. **Clear Policies and Procedures:** Organizations should establish clear guidelines and codes of conduct that explicitly prohibit insider trading. These policies should outline the consequences of violating such rules.

3. **Enforcement and Monitoring:** Companies should implement robust monitoring systems to detect and prevent insider trading. This includes regular reviews of trading activities, monitoring of access to confidential information, and strict control over information dissemination.

4. **Segregation of Duties:** Separating duties and access privileges within organizations helps minimize the risk of insider trading. Limiting access to material non-public information and implementing dual controls can act as deterrents.

5. **Whistleblower Programs:** Establishing mechanisms for employees and stakeholders to report suspected insider trading anonymously can help identify and prevent unethical activities. Whistleblower protection policies should be in place to encourage reporting.

Conclusion

Insider trading is a serious ethical and legal concern that has significant consequences for financial markets. It erodes trust, fairness, and transparency within the investment community. Regulatory efforts, along with strong internal controls and enforcement mechanisms, are necessary to combat this unethical practice effectively. By promoting ethical behavior and maintaining the integrity of financial markets, we can create a level playing field for all market participants and enhance investor confidence.

Intellectual Property Theft

Intellectual property (IP) refers to intangible creations of the human intellect, such as inventions, designs, artistic works, symbols, and names used in commerce. It plays a crucial role in fostering innovation, encouraging creativity, and promoting economic growth. Intellectual property theft, also known as IP infringement or piracy, occurs when someone uses another person's or organization's IP without permission. It is a severe ethical and legal concern that poses significant challenges in the modern digital age.

The Importance of Intellectual Property

Intellectual property rights are essential for protecting the interests of creators and inventors. They incentivize individuals and organizations to invest time, money, and resources into developing new ideas and creations. By providing legal protections, intellectual property rights ensure that innovators can reap the rewards of their labor and encourage further innovation.

Moreover, intellectual property rights contribute to economic development. They foster an environment that encourages investments in research and development, leading to the creation of new products and technologies. Intellectual property rights also promote competition and fair market practices by preventing unauthorized use or imitation of innovative products or services.

Types of Intellectual Property

There are several forms of intellectual property that can be subject to theft or infringement:

+ **Patents:** Patents protect new inventions and technological advancements. They provide inventors with exclusive rights to produce, use, and sell their invention for a limited period.

+ **Copyrights:** Copyrights safeguard original works of authorship, such as books, music, films, and software. They grant creators exclusive rights to reproduce, distribute, perform, display, or license their work.

+ **Trademarks:** Trademarks are symbols, logos, names, or designs that distinguish goods or services from others in the market. They protect brand identity and prevent others from using similar marks that may cause confusion.

+ **Trade Secrets:** Trade secrets refer to confidential business information that provides a competitive advantage. They include customer lists, formulas, manufacturing processes, and marketing strategies.

Examples of Intellectual Property Theft

Intellectual property theft can take various forms, and it affects a wide range of industries. Here are some common examples:

+ **Software Piracy:** Unauthorized copying or distribution of copyrighted software, such as downloading or sharing pirated movies, music, or programs from the internet.

+ **Counterfeit Products:** Producing and selling imitation or fake goods, such as counterfeit luxury items, electronics, pharmaceuticals, or automotive parts.

+ **Plagiarism:** Presenting someone else's work, ideas, or writings as one's own, without proper attribution or permission.

+ **Patent Infringement:** Manufacturing, using, or selling a patented invention without the permission of the patent owner.

+ **Trade Secret Theft:** Illegally obtaining and using confidential business information for personal gain or to benefit a competitor.

Ethical and Legal Implications

Intellectual property theft raises significant ethical and legal concerns:

+ **Violation of Rights:** IP theft disregards the rights of creators and inventors, denying them the recognition and economic benefits they deserve for their work.

+ **Loss of Revenue:** IP theft undermines the economic incentives for innovation, resulting in losses for businesses and reduced investment in research and development.

+ **Unfair Competition:** IP theft gives an advantage to those who engage in unauthorized use, imitation, or selling of IP, leading to unfair competition in the market.

+ **Risk to Public Safety:** Counterfeit products, obtained through IP theft, can pose risks to public health and safety, such as counterfeit medications or substandard electrical products.

+ **Legal Consequences:** Intellectual property theft is illegal and can result in civil penalties, fines, damages, and even criminal charges.

Addressing Intellectual Property Theft

Efforts to combat intellectual property theft involve a combination of legal, technological, and educational measures:

+ **Strengthening Legal Frameworks:** Governments enact and enforce laws to protect intellectual property rights, providing mechanisms to pursue legal action against infringers.

+ **Public Awareness and Education:** Raising awareness about the importance of intellectual property rights and the consequences of theft through educational campaigns and programs.

+ **Technological Measures:** Developing and implementing technologies that can help detect and prevent IP theft, such as digital rights management, watermarking, and encryption.

+ **International Cooperation:** Promoting collaboration between countries to combat cross-border intellectual property theft, sharing best practices and information.

- **Industry Initiatives:** Encouraging industry collaboration and self-regulation to protect against IP theft, including the development of voluntary codes of conduct and best practices.

Case Study: Music Piracy

Music piracy is a prime example of intellectual property theft in the digital age. With the rise of the internet and file-sharing platforms, unauthorized copying and distribution of copyrighted music became rampant. This caused significant economic losses for artists, record labels, and the music industry as a whole.

To address this issue, the music industry has implemented various strategies, such as digital rights management techniques, online music streaming platforms, and legal actions against piracy websites. Additionally, innovative business models, such as subscription-based music services, have emerged to provide consumers with legal access to music while compensating creators.

Nonetheless, music piracy continues to be a challenge, highlighting the ongoing need to raise awareness, enforce legal measures, and provide affordable and convenient alternatives to illegal methods of accessing music.

Conclusion

Intellectual property theft poses significant ethical and legal challenges in various fields, including technology, business, healthcare, and education. Protecting intellectual property rights is crucial for fostering innovation, maintaining fair competition, and promoting economic growth. Efforts to address intellectual property theft involve a combination of legal frameworks, technological solutions, public education, international cooperation, and industry initiatives. By safeguarding intellectual property rights, society can create an environment that encourages creativity, rewards innovation, and fuels economic development.

Discrimination and Harassment

Discrimination and harassment are pervasive ethical issues that affect individuals in various aspects of life, including the workplace, educational institutions, and society as a whole. In this section, we will explore the ethical implications of discrimination and harassment, examine their impacts on individuals and communities, and discuss strategies to prevent and address these issues.

Understanding Discrimination

Discrimination refers to the unfair or unequal treatment of individuals or groups based on certain characteristics such as race, gender, age, religion, disability, or sexual orientation. It can manifest in various forms, including but not limited to:

1. **Direct Discrimination:** Occurs when a person or group is treated less favorably based on their protected characteristic. For example, denying someone a job opportunity because of their race.

2. **Indirect Discrimination:** Occurs when a policy, procedure, or practice seems neutral but disproportionately disadvantages certain individuals or groups. For example, a dress code that prohibits cultural or religious attire.

3. **Systemic Discrimination:** Occurs when institutions and societal structures perpetuate discrimination consistently against specific groups over time. This can lead to unequal opportunities and outcomes in various areas, including education, employment, and healthcare.

Discrimination is a violation of fundamental ethical principles, including fairness, equality, and justice. It undermines social cohesion, promotes inequality, and reinforces stereotypes and prejudices. It can have severe negative impacts on the individuals subjected to discrimination, leading to decreased self-esteem, limited opportunities, and a sense of exclusion.

Understanding Harassment

Harassment refers to any unwanted behavior, action, or communication that violates an individual's dignity, creates a hostile or intimidating environment, or results in distress or harm. It can occur in various contexts, including the workplace, educational institutions, public spaces, and online platforms. Common forms of harassment include:

1. **Sexual Harassment:** Inappropriate comments, gestures, advances, or any other behavior of a sexual nature that is unwanted and offensive. This can occur between individuals of different genders or the same gender.

2. **Bullying:** Persistent, intentional, and aggressive behavior aimed at causing harm, distress, or intimidation. It can take various forms, such as verbal abuse, social exclusion, or physical harm.

3. **Cyberbullying:** Harassment that occurs online, through social media platforms, email, or other digital means. It can include spreading rumors, threats, or sharing private and sensitive information without consent.

4. **Racial or Ethnic Harassment:** Verbal or physical acts that target individuals based on their race or ethnicity, including racial slurs, derogatory comments, or discriminatory treatment.

Harassment violates the principles of respect, dignity, and autonomy. It creates a hostile environment, diminishes individual well-being, and hinders personal and professional growth. Harassment can have severe psychological, emotional, and physical consequences for the individuals targeted.

Legal and Ethical Obligations

Organizations, educational institutions, and governments have legal and ethical obligations to prevent and address discrimination and harassment. In many countries, laws and regulations provide protection against discrimination and harassment, including the establishment of anti-discrimination commissions or equality bodies to enforce these laws.

Some fundamental legal and ethical obligations include:

1. **Equal Employment Opportunity:** Employers must ensure equal treatment and opportunities for employees with regards to recruitment, promotion, training, compensation, and termination. They must establish policies and procedures to prevent discrimination and harassment in the workplace.

2. **Equal Access to Education:** Educational institutions must ensure equal access and opportunities to students regardless of their characteristics or backgrounds. They must have policies in place to address discrimination and harassment and provide support to affected individuals.

3. **Respect for Human Rights:** Governments and institutions must respect and protect the human rights of all individuals, including the right to be free from discrimination and harassment. They must promote inclusive and diverse societies that celebrate and value differences.

Ethically, individuals also have a responsibility to promote equality, challenge discrimination, and support those who are targets of harassment. By actively creating inclusive environments and confronting prejudices and biases, we contribute to building a more just and fair society.

Preventing and Addressing Discrimination and Harassment

Preventing and addressing discrimination and harassment requires a proactive and comprehensive approach. Here are some strategies and best practices:

1. **Education and Awareness:** Increasing awareness about discrimination and harassment is crucial. Educational institutions, organizations, and community groups can offer training programs and workshops to empower individuals with knowledge and skills to recognize, prevent, and address these issues.

2. **Establishing Clear Policies and Procedures:** Organizations and institutions should have well-defined policies and procedures in place to prevent and address discrimination and harassment. These policies should outline prohibited behaviors, reporting mechanisms, and the consequences for offenders.

3. **Promoting Inclusive Culture:** Creating an inclusive culture that values diversity and fosters respect is essential. This can be achieved by promoting diversity in leadership positions, celebrating different cultures and perspectives, and implementing diversity and inclusion initiatives.

4. **Encouraging Reporting and Support:** Encouraging individuals to report incidents of discrimination and harassment is vital for creating a safe environment. Establishing confidential reporting mechanisms, providing support services, and protecting individuals from retaliation are essential steps.

5. **Accountability and Consequences:** Holding individuals accountable for their discriminatory or harassing behavior is crucial. Organizations and institutions should conduct thorough investigations into reported incidents and take appropriate disciplinary actions against offenders.

It is important to note that prevention and addressing discrimination and harassment require ongoing commitment and continuous evaluation of policies and practices. Organizations and institutions should regularly assess the effectiveness of their strategies and make necessary improvements to ensure a safe and inclusive environment for everyone.

Case Study: Workplace Discrimination

Let's consider a case study that highlights workplace discrimination and its impact:

Sarah, an experienced professional, applied for a managerial position in a reputable company. Despite her qualifications and experience, the company hired a less-qualified candidate who shared the same gender as the existing management team. Sarah suspects that she faced gender discrimination during the hiring process.

The ethical principles of fairness, equality, and meritocracy are violated in this scenario. Gender discrimination creates a barrier for Sarah's professional growth and perpetuates an unfair working environment. It can also have broader implications for gender equality in the company and the industry as a whole.

To address this issue, Sarah could gather evidence, such as comparative qualifications, interview feedback, and any discriminatory remarks or comments made during the process. She could then file a formal complaint with the company's HR department, citing the potential violation of equal employment opportunity laws. The company should conduct an unbiased investigation into the matter and take appropriate action, such as revisiting the hiring decision, providing compensation, and implementing measures to prevent future discrimination.

This case study exemplifies the importance of addressing workplace discrimination promptly and effectively to ensure equal opportunities and a fair working environment for all employees.

Conclusion

Discrimination and harassment are significant ethical challenges that continue to affect individuals and societies. By understanding the various forms of discrimination and harassment, recognizing their ethical implications, and implementing preventive measures, we can create inclusive environments that promote equality, respect, and dignity. It is the collective responsibility of individuals, organizations, and governments to uphold ethical principles and work towards eliminating discrimination and harassment from all aspects of life.

Ethical Leadership in Business

Ethical leadership in business plays a vital role in establishing a culture of integrity, accountability, and responsible decision-making. It requires individuals to act ethically and inspire ethical behavior in others, ultimately contributing to the success and sustainability of the organization. In this section, we will explore the principles and practices of ethical leadership in the business context.

Defining Ethical Leadership

Ethical leadership can be defined as the demonstration of ethical principles and values in decision-making, behavior, and relationships within an organization. It involves leading with integrity, transparency, and the well-being of stakeholders in mind. Ethical leaders prioritize the greater good over personal gain and consistently act in accordance with ethical standards.

Characteristics of Ethical Leaders

Effective ethical leaders possess certain characteristics that distinguish them from others. These characteristics serve as a foundation for building trust, promoting ethical conduct, and achieving organizational goals. Some key characteristics of ethical leaders include:

- **Integrity:** Ethical leaders consistently act in accordance with their values and principles, fostering an environment of trust and credibility.

- **Accountability:** Ethical leaders take responsibility for their actions and decisions, acknowledging both successes and failures. They hold themselves and others accountable to ethical standards.

- **Empathy:** Ethical leaders demonstrate empathy towards others, considering their perspectives and needs. They strive to create a supportive and inclusive work environment.

- **Courage:** Ethical leaders have the courage to make difficult decisions based on ethical principles, even in the face of challenges or opposition. They are willing to take risks to do what is right.

- **Transparency:** Ethical leaders promote transparency by openly communicating information and decision-making processes. They ensure that relevant stakeholders are informed and involved.

- **Fairness:** Ethical leaders treat others fairly and impartially, considering the interests of all stakeholders and avoiding favoritism or discrimination.

Leading by Example

One of the most fundamental aspects of ethical leadership is leading by example. Actions speak louder than words, and ethical leaders understand the importance of demonstrating ethical behavior in their own actions and decisions. They serve as role models for ethical conduct, inspiring others to follow suit.

By consistently exhibiting ethical behavior, leaders create a culture of trust, integrity, and accountability within their organizations. Employees are more likely to adhere to ethical standards when they see their leaders actively practicing them. This in turn leads to increased employee commitment, engagement, and loyalty.

Ethical Communication

Ethical leaders prioritize open and honest communication. They establish channels of communication that encourage employees to express their concerns, ideas, and suggestions without fear of retaliation. Ethical leaders actively listen to their employees, valuing diverse perspectives and promoting a culture of collaboration and respect.

Moreover, ethical leaders communicate clear expectations regarding ethical standards and policies within the organization. They provide guidance on how to handle ethical dilemmas and offer support to employees who face ethical challenges. By fostering ethical communication, leaders create an environment where ethical conduct is valued and encouraged.

Ethical Decision-Making

Ethical leadership entails making decisions based on ethical principles and values. Ethical leaders consider the potential impact of their decisions on stakeholders, ensuring fairness, equity, and the greater good. They weigh the short-term and long-term consequences and act with integrity, avoiding actions that may compromise ethical standards.

To facilitate ethical decision-making, leaders can employ various frameworks and models. One such model is the ethical decision-making process, which involves the following steps:

1. **Identify the ethical issue**: Clearly define the ethical dilemma or issue at hand, considering the viewpoints of different stakeholders and the potential consequences.

2. **Gather information**: Collect all relevant facts, figures, and data related to the issue. Seek different perspectives and consult with experts if necessary.

3. **Evaluate alternative courses of action**: Generate multiple ethical options and evaluate their potential outcomes and consequences. Consider the ethical principles involved and determine the most ethical course of action.

4. **Make a decision**: Select the course of action that aligns with ethical principles, values, and the overall mission and vision of the organization.

5. **Implement the decision:** Put the decision into action, ensuring that all stakeholders are informed and involved as necessary.

6. **Evaluate the outcome:** Monitor and assess the outcomes of the decision, identifying any unintended consequences. Learn from the experience to improve future decision-making processes.

By following a systematic and ethical decision-making process, leaders can make informed choices while considering the needs and interests of all stakeholders.

Ethical Leadership Challenges

Ethical leaders may face various challenges in their journey to promote ethical behavior within their organizations. Some common challenges include:

+ **Resistance to change:** Implementing ethical practices may face resistance from employees who are resistant to change or who have become accustomed to unethical behaviors.

+ **Conflicting interests:** Leaders may encounter conflicting interests among stakeholders, making it challenging to prioritize ethical considerations over competing demands.

+ **Ethical gray areas:** Some situations may involve complex and ambiguous ethical issues, requiring leaders to navigate through ethical gray areas and make difficult decisions.

+ **Limited resources:** Ethical practices may require additional resources or investments, which can pose challenges in organizations with limited budgets or competing priorities.

+ **Lack of awareness:** In some cases, employees may not fully understand or appreciate the importance of ethical conduct, necessitating ongoing education and awareness-building efforts.

Addressing these challenges requires strong leadership skills, effective communication, and a commitment to upholding ethical standards at all levels of the organization.

Resources for Ethical Leadership

Ethical leaders can benefit from various resources to enhance their understanding and practice of ethical leadership. Some valuable resources include:

- **Ethics training programs:** Organizations may offer training programs that focus on ethical leadership development and provide guidance on ethical decision-making.

- **Ethics committees and advisors:** Establishing ethics committees or seeking guidance from ethics advisors can help leaders navigate complex ethical issues and ensure appropriate decision-making.

- **Professional networks and associations:** Engaging with professional networks and associations dedicated to ethical leadership can provide opportunities for learning, sharing best practices, and networking with like-minded leaders.

- **Ethics-related publications and journals:** Keeping up-to-date with ethics-related publications and journals can help leaders stay informed about emerging ethical issues, research, and best practices.

- **Ethics hotlines and reporting mechanisms:** Providing employees with avenues to anonymously report ethical concerns can help leaders identify and address potential ethical violations.

Case Study: Johnson & Johnson's Tylenol Crisis

A notable example of ethical leadership in business is Johnson & Johnson's response to the 1982 Tylenol crisis. When several bottles of Tylenol were tampered with, resulting in the deaths of seven individuals, Johnson & Johnson's CEO James Burke demonstrated exemplary ethical leadership.

Burke immediately took action, prioritizing public safety over financial concerns. He ordered a nationwide recall of all Tylenol products, which cost the company millions of dollars. Despite the financial impact, Burke's decisive and ethical response helped restore public trust in the brand and set a new standard for product safety.

The Tylenol crisis serves as a powerful example of ethical leadership in the face of adversity, highlighting the importance of prioritizing ethical considerations even in the most challenging circumstances.

Conclusion

Ethical leadership in business is essential for creating a culture of integrity, trust, and responsible decision-making. Ethical leaders lead by example, demonstrate key characteristics such as integrity and fairness, and prioritize open and transparent communication. They make decisions based on ethical principles and values, navigating through ethical challenges with courage and empathy.

While ethical leadership may present challenges, by understanding and practicing the principles of ethical leadership, leaders can contribute to the long-term success and sustainability of their organizations. By building a strong ethical foundation, leaders inspire their employees to act ethically and foster a culture that benefits all stakeholders.

Ethical Role Models

In the realm of ethics, role models play a crucial role in shaping individuals' moral compass and guiding them towards making ethical decisions. The actions and behaviors of ethical role models can inspire and influence others to act in morally upright ways. These role models serve as beacons of integrity, honesty, and principles, helping to establish a culture of ethical behavior in various domains, including business, healthcare, education, and beyond.

Importance of Ethical Role Models

Ethical role models set high standards of conduct, serving as examples to emulate. When individuals witness the ethical actions of their role models, they are more likely to adopt those behaviors and incorporate them into their own lives. This is especially true for individuals who are still developing their own ethical framework, such as students or young professionals.

Ethical role models provide a tangible representation of ethical principles in action. By observing how these role models navigate ethical dilemmas and make decisions based on moral values, individuals can gain insights into the application of ethical theories and frameworks in real-life situations. This helps bridge the gap between theoretical knowledge and practical ethical decision-making.

Moreover, ethical role models inspire trust and confidence. When individuals see their leaders, mentors, or peers consistently acting in accordance with ethical principles, they are more likely to trust them and perceive them as credible and reliable sources of guidance. Ethical role models create a positive influence on organizational and societal cultures, fostering a sense of trust and integrity among individuals.

Characteristics of Ethical Role Models

What qualities make an individual an ethical role model? Here are some key characteristics to consider:

- **Integrity:** Ethical role models demonstrate unwavering integrity in their actions, consistently aligning their behavior with their values and principles.

- **Honesty:** They prioritize honesty and transparency in their communication and interactions with others, avoiding deceit or manipulation.

- **Accountability:** Ethical role models take responsibility for their actions and admit their mistakes, showing a willingness to learn and grow.

- **Empathy:** They exhibit empathy and compassion towards others, considering the impact of their actions on individuals and communities.

- **Fairness:** Ethical role models treat all individuals impartially and without bias, ensuring fairness and justice in their decision-making.

- **Courage:** They demonstrate moral courage, standing up for what is right even in the face of adversity or opposition.

Examples of Ethical Role Models

Numerous individuals throughout history have served as ethical role models, leaving a lasting impact on society. Let's explore a few notable examples across different domains:

1. **Nelson Mandela:** Mandela, the former President of South Africa, exemplified ethical leadership through his unwavering commitment to justice, equality, and reconciliation. He fought against racial segregation and peacefully transitioned South Africa into a democratic nation, inspiring many with his humility and compassion.

2. **Melinda Gates:** As the co-founder of the Bill & Melinda Gates Foundation, Melinda Gates has demonstrated ethical leadership and social responsibility through her philanthropic endeavors. She champions healthcare, education, and gender equality, using her influence and resources to empower marginalized communities.

3. **Mahatma Gandhi:** Known for his nonviolent approach to social and political change, Gandhi led India's independence movement against British rule. He advocated for human rights, equality, and truth, inspiring millions around the world with his dedication to nonviolence and civil disobedience.

4. **Malala Yousafzai:** Yousafzai, a Pakistani activist for female education, became a global symbol of courage and resilience after surviving an assassination attempt by the Taliban. Despite facing adversity, she continues to advocate for girls' education, demonstrating immense bravery and unwavering commitment to her cause.

These individuals, among countless others, serve as powerful ethical role models who have made a significant impact on society. By studying their actions and principles, individuals can learn valuable lessons about ethical conduct and apply them to their own lives.

The Role of Ethical Role Models in Education

Ethical role models are particularly vital in educational settings. Teachers and educators play a crucial role in shaping the moral development of students. By serving as ethical role models, educators can instill values, promote ethical behavior, and inspire students to become responsible and ethical citizens.

Educators can lead by example, demonstrating ethical conduct in their interactions with students, colleagues, and the wider community. They can incorporate ethical discussions into their lessons, encouraging students to critically examine ethical principles and dilemmas. By sharing stories of ethical role models, educators can inspire students to aspire to similar qualities and behaviors.

Furthermore, creating a culture of ethical role models in educational institutions helps establish a positive learning environment. When students witness their peers and teachers actively practicing ethical behavior, it fosters a sense of community, respect, and integrity. This, in turn, cultivates an atmosphere conducive to learning, personal growth, and ethical decision-making.

Exercises

To further explore the concept of ethical role models, engage in the following exercises:

1. **Reflect on Personal Role Models:** Identify individuals in your life who have served as ethical role models. Consider their qualities, actions, and the impact they have had on you.

2. **Ethical Role Models in Different Professions:** Research ethical role models within a specific profession or industry. Analyze their contributions, ethical dilemmas they faced, and the impact they had on their respective fields.

3. **Role Model Analysis:** Choose an ethical role model and delve into their background, experiences, and ethical principles. Reflect on how their actions align with different ethical frameworks, such as consequentialism, deontology, or virtue ethics.

4. **Creating Ethical Role Models:** Brainstorm strategies to promote ethical role models in your educational or professional environment. Consider how you can contribute to fostering a culture of ethical behavior and inspiration.

In conclusion, ethical role models play a vital role in shaping individuals' ethical behaviors and decision-making processes. Their high standards of conduct serve as an inspiration for others, guiding individuals towards moral integrity and ethical excellence. It is important to recognize, appreciate, and learn from these role models to create a more ethical and just society.

Ethical Decision Making at the Executive Level

At the executive level of an organization, ethical decision making plays a crucial role in determining the success and reputation of the company. Executives are responsible for making important strategic decisions that can have far-reaching consequences, both internally and externally. These decisions often have an impact on various stakeholders, including employees, customers, investors, and the broader community.

Importance of Ethical Decision Making

Ethical decision making at the executive level is critical for several reasons. Firstly, it helps establish a culture of integrity within the organization. When executives consistently make ethical decisions, it sets the tone for employees at all levels to act in an ethical manner. This helps build trust, loyalty, and a positive organizational culture.

Secondly, ethical decision making helps protect the reputation of the company. In today's interconnected world, news spreads quickly, and any unethical behavior can have significant consequences for an organization. Executives must prioritize ethical considerations to avoid negative publicity, legal issues, and damage to the company's brand.

Furthermore, ethical decision making is essential for long-term sustainability. Executives need to consider the social and environmental impact of their decisions, as well as the financial implications. By making ethical choices, executives can contribute to the well-being of society and minimize potential harm to the environment.

Ethical Decision Making Process

To make sound ethical decisions at the executive level, it is essential to follow a structured decision-making process. While there are various models available, one commonly used framework is the ethical decision-making model proposed by the Josephson Institute.

1. **Identify the problem:** The first step is to clearly identify and define the ethical problem or dilemma. This involves understanding the root cause of the issue and its potential consequences for all stakeholders involved.

2. **Gather information:** Executives should gather all relevant information to gain a comprehensive understanding of the problem. This may involve consulting experts, conducting research, and seeking diverse perspectives.

3. **Identify potential options:** In this step, executives should identify all possible courses of action to address the ethical problem. It is important to brainstorm different alternatives and evaluate their feasibility and potential outcomes.

4. **Evaluate options:** Executives must evaluate the potential ethical implications of each option. This includes considering the ethical principles involved, such as fairness, honesty, respect, and social responsibility.

5. **Make a decision:** After careful evaluation, executives need to make a decision based on their ethical analysis. This decision should align with the organization's values, mission, and ethical guidelines.

6. **Implement the decision:** Executives must effectively communicate and implement the decision throughout the organization. This involves providing clear instructions, resources, and support to ensure the decision is carried out appropriately.

7. **Evaluate the outcome:** Once the decision has been implemented, executives should evaluate its impact and outcomes. This allows for reflection and learning, which can inform future ethical decision making.

Ethical Leadership and Role Modeling

One of the most effective ways for executives to promote ethical decision making is by demonstrating ethical leadership and acting as role models for others in the organization. Ethical leadership involves leading by example and consistently exhibiting ethical behavior.

Executives should establish a clear code of ethics, emphasizing the importance of integrity, transparency, and accountability. They should communicate these values to employees and encourage open dialogue about ethical issues. By creating a safe space for discussions, executives can foster an ethical culture where employees feel comfortable raising concerns and seeking guidance.

It is also crucial for executives to hold themselves accountable for their actions. They should take responsibility for any mistakes or ethical lapses and use those experiences as learning opportunities. This not only promotes a culture of personal growth but also reinforces the importance of ethical decision making to the entire organization.

Challenges and Caveats

While ethical decision making at the executive level is crucial, it does come with its share of challenges and caveats. Executives must navigate complex situations that often involve conflicting interests and pressures from different stakeholders.

One challenge is balancing the ethical considerations with the organization's financial goals. Executives have a responsibility to shareholders and investors to generate profits and ensure the company's financial stability. Finding the right balance between ethical principles and financial performance can be a delicate task.

Additionally, executives must be mindful of biases and personal interests that may influence their decision making. It is important to remain objective and consider the broader impact of decisions on all stakeholders, rather than solely focusing on personal or short-term gains.

Furthermore, ethical decision making at the executive level requires ongoing education and awareness. Executives should stay updated on emerging ethical issues, industry best practices, and changing regulations. This continuous learning ensures that their decision-making processes remain relevant and aligned with evolving ethical standards.

Real-World Example

To illustrate the importance of ethical decision making at the executive level, let's consider a real-world example. Imagine a pharmaceutical company that has developed a new drug with the potential to save thousands of lives. However, during clinical trials, it is discovered that the drug has severe side effects that were not initially anticipated.

In this scenario, the executives of the pharmaceutical company face a challenging ethical decision. They must decide whether to proceed with the drug's release, knowing the potential harm it could cause, or halt the development and potentially lose significant investments already made.

To make an ethical decision, the executives would need to consider the principles of beneficence (doing good) and non-maleficence (doing no harm). They would also need to weigh the potential consequences on the patients, the company's reputation, and legal obligations.

In this case, an ethical decision would involve prioritizing patient safety over financial considerations. The executives may decide to halt the development of the drug, conduct further research to mitigate the side effects, or explore alternative treatments. By making an ethical decision, the executives demonstrate their commitment to the well-being of patients and the ethical principles of their organization.

Conclusion

Ethical decision making at the executive level is a critical aspect of responsible leadership. It helps establish a culture of integrity, protects the organization's reputation, and contributes to long-term sustainability. By following a structured ethical decision-making process, acting as ethical leaders and role models, and considering the challenges and caveats, executives can make sound and ethical decisions that benefit all stakeholders involved.

Promoting a Culture of Ethical Behavior

Promoting a culture of ethical behavior is essential in any organization. It sets the foundation for trust, transparency, and accountability, which are key elements of a successful and sustainable business. In this section, we will explore various strategies and initiatives that can be implemented to promote ethical behavior within a company.

Corporate Values and Ethics Statement

One of the first steps in promoting a culture of ethical behavior is the establishment of corporate values and an ethics statement. These documents outline the guiding principles and expectations for employees, providing a clear framework for decision-making and behavior. The values and ethics statement should be communicated effectively to all employees, ensuring that they understand and embrace the organization's commitment to ethical conduct.

For example, XYZ Inc., a global technology company, has a values statement that emphasizes integrity, respect, and innovation. The company's ethics statement further clarifies its stance on issues such as bribery, conflicts of interest, and data privacy. By clearly defining these expectations, XYZ Inc. ensures that ethical behavior is prioritized throughout the organization.

Ethics Training and Education

To further promote ethical behavior, companies should invest in comprehensive ethics training and education programs. These programs help employees understand the importance of ethical conduct, recognize ethical dilemmas, and develop the skills to make ethical decisions.

Ethics training can be delivered through various methods, such as in-person workshops, online modules, or interactive simulations. It should cover key topics like conflicts of interest, whistleblowing, and ethical decision-making models. Real-world case studies and examples can be used to illustrate ethical dilemmas and their potential impact.

For instance, ABC Healthcare, a leading provider of medical services, conducts regular ethics training for its employees. The training includes scenarios that require participants to navigate ethical challenges commonly faced in healthcare, such as maintaining patient confidentiality and handling conflicts of interest. By engaging employees in interactive discussions and providing practical guidance, ABC Healthcare ensures that ethical considerations are ingrained in the organization's culture.

Ethical Leadership

Ethical leadership is crucial for promoting a culture of ethical behavior. Leaders set the tone for the entire organization and serve as role models for their teams. They must consistently demonstrate ethical behavior and hold themselves and others accountable for their actions.

Leaders should communicate the importance of ethical conduct, aligning it with the organization's values and objectives. They should also encourage open dialogue, providing a safe environment for employees to raise ethical concerns or seek guidance. By leading by example and promoting ethical behavior, leaders create a culture that encourages ethical decision-making at all levels of the organization.

For example, the CEO of DEF Manufacturing, a global automobile company, actively promotes ethical leadership by being transparent and accountable. The CEO leads regular town hall sessions, where employees can openly discuss ethics-related issues and provide input on ethical decision-making. This approach fosters a culture of trust and integrity throughout the organization.

Reward Systems

Reward systems play a vital role in shaping employee behavior. By linking ethical behavior to recognition and rewards, organizations can incentivize employees to consistently demonstrate ethical conduct. Recognition can be in the form of verbal appreciation, certificates, or even monetary rewards.

However, it is crucial to ensure that the reward systems are fair and aligned with the organization's values. The focus should not solely be on achieving outcomes but also on the ethical process followed to achieve those outcomes.

For instance, GHI Bank, a leading financial institution, has a recognition program that acknowledges employees who display exemplary ethical behavior. This program highlights individuals who have gone above and beyond to promote ethical conduct within the organization. By recognizing and rewarding ethical behavior, GHI Bank creates a culture where employees understand the significance of upholding ethical standards.

Whistleblower Protection

Protection for whistleblowers is essential in promoting a culture of ethical behavior. Whistleblowers play a critical role in exposing unethical practices and protecting the interests of stakeholders. To encourage whistleblowing, organizations should establish confidential reporting mechanisms and ensure that whistleblowers are protected from retaliation.

Employees should be made aware of the whistleblower policies and procedures, and a culture of trust should be fostered to encourage employees to come forward with concerns without fear of reprisal. Anonymous reporting channels can also be implemented to provide a safe avenue for reporting.

For example, JKL Pharmaceuticals, a global pharmaceutical company, has a comprehensive whistleblower policy in place. The policy protects the identity of whistleblowers and provides avenues for anonymous reporting. JKL

Pharmaceuticals ensures that whistleblowers are protected from any form of retaliation and handles all reports with utmost confidentiality and seriousness.

Regular Ethical Assessments and Audits

To ensure ongoing commitment to ethical behavior, organizations should conduct regular ethical assessments and audits. These assessments evaluate the effectiveness of existing ethical initiatives, identify areas for improvement, and track progress toward ethical goals.

Ethical audits can be performed internally or by engaging external auditors and consultants specializing in ethical practices. The assessment should cover various aspects, such as compliance with ethical codes, adherence to ethical decision-making models, and the effectiveness of communication and training programs.

For example, MNO Energy, a renewable energy company, conducts annual ethical audits to assess its performance in promoting ethical behavior. The audit includes employee surveys, review of policies and procedures, and interviews with key stakeholders. This comprehensive assessment helps MNO Energy identify areas of strength and areas that require improvement, fostering a culture of continuous improvement.

Conclusion

Promoting a culture of ethical behavior requires a holistic approach that encompasses corporate values, ethics training, ethical leadership, reward systems, whistleblower protection, and regular ethical assessments. By implementing these strategies and initiatives, organizations can create an environment where ethical conduct is valued, practiced, and upheld at all levels. This not only enhances the reputation and sustainability of the organization but also contributes to the well-being of employees and the wider society.

Ethical Supply Chain Management

Ethical Sourcing and Procurement

Ethical sourcing and procurement is an essential aspect of business operations in today's globalized economy. It involves the responsible selection, acquisition, and management of goods and services from suppliers who adhere to ethical principles and standards. In this section, we will explore the importance of ethical sourcing and procurement, discuss key principles and challenges, and provide guidance on how businesses can integrate ethical practices into their supply chains.

The Importance of Ethical Sourcing and Procurement

Ethical sourcing and procurement play a crucial role in ensuring sustainable and responsible business practices. By engaging in ethical sourcing, companies demonstrate their commitment to social and environmental responsibility and contribute to the creation of a fair and just marketplace. Here are some key reasons why ethical sourcing and procurement are important:

- **Labor Rights:** Ethical sourcing promotes fair labor practices by ensuring that workers involved in the production and supply of goods and services are treated ethically. This includes fair wages, safe working conditions, and protection of basic human rights. Businesses that engage in unethical practices such as child labor or forced labor face reputational risks and legal consequences.

- **Environmental Sustainability:** Ethical sourcing aims to minimize the negative impact of business activities on the environment. It involves procuring goods and services from suppliers who prioritize sustainable practices, such as reducing carbon emissions, minimizing waste generation, and conserving natural resources. This helps mitigate environmental risks and contributes to a more sustainable future.

- **Social Responsibility:** Ethical sourcing and procurement contribute to social responsibility by supporting suppliers who uphold ethical standards and conduct their business in an honest, transparent, and accountable manner. This includes promoting diversity, supporting local communities, and respecting human rights. Companies that prioritize social responsibility enhance their reputation and build trust with stakeholders.

- **Risk Management:** Ethical sourcing helps mitigate various risks associated with supply chain disruptions, reputational damage, and regulatory non-compliance. By engaging in due diligence and selecting ethical suppliers, businesses reduce the likelihood of negative events that can impact their operations and brand value. Ethical sourcing also enhances supply chain resilience by diversifying supplier networks and creating long-term partnerships based on trust and shared values.

Principles of Ethical Sourcing and Procurement

To effectively implement ethical sourcing and procurement practices, businesses can adopt the following principles:

1. **Transparency:** Transparency is key to ethical sourcing and procurement. Organizations should openly disclose their sourcing practices and supplier criteria to stakeholders, including consumers, investors, and employees. Transparent communication helps build trust and allows stakeholders to make informed choices. It also facilitates accountability and encourages suppliers to uphold ethical standards.

2. **Supplier Assessment and Due Diligence:** Businesses should conduct thorough assessments and due diligence on potential suppliers. This includes evaluating their ethical practices, such as labor conditions, environmental impact, adherence to relevant laws and regulations, and commitment to social responsibility. Supplier audits, certifications, and site visits can be utilized to gather relevant information.

3. **Collaboration and Capacity Building:** Ethical sourcing involves collaboration with suppliers to improve ethical practices throughout the supply chain. This can include providing training and support to suppliers, assisting them in implementing sustainable and ethical practices, and jointly addressing challenges. Collaboration fosters shared responsibility and leads to continuous improvement.

4. **Traceability and Certification:** Establishing traceability mechanisms and supporting certification programs can help businesses ensure that their suppliers meet ethical standards. Traceability enables the tracking and verification of the origin and production processes of goods and services, reducing the risk of sourcing from unethical suppliers. Certification programs, such as Fairtrade or Forest Stewardship Council (FSC), provide independent verification of ethical practices.

5. **Continuous Monitoring and Auditing:** Regular monitoring and auditing of suppliers are essential to ensure ongoing compliance with ethical standards. This can involve self-assessments, third-party audits, and performance evaluations. Businesses should establish clear monitoring mechanisms and act swiftly upon identifying any non-compliance or unethical practices.

Challenges in Ethical Sourcing and Procurement

Ethical sourcing and procurement come with inherent challenges that businesses need to address. Some of the common challenges include:

- **Supply Chain Complexity:** Global supply chains are often complex, involving multiple tiers of suppliers across different geographical regions. Managing ethical practices throughout the entire supply chain can be challenging, as visibility and control diminish with each tier. Businesses need to invest in technologies and systems that enhance supply chain transparency and enable effective ethical sourcing.

- **Supplier Compliance:** Ensuring supplier compliance with ethical standards can be difficult, particularly when dealing with suppliers in countries with weak regulatory frameworks or entrenched unethical practices. Companies need to establish clear expectations, provide capacity-building support, and maintain regular communication with suppliers to promote compliance.

- **Cost Considerations:** Ethical sourcing practices may come with additional costs, such as higher wages, improved working conditions, or investment in sustainable technologies. Balancing the cost of ethical sourcing with profitability can be a challenge, especially for small and medium-sized enterprises. However, businesses can explore long-term cost-saving strategies, such as efficiency improvements and responsible resource management, to offset these costs.

- **Verification and Certification:** Validating supplier claims and certifications can be challenging, as misleading or false information can undermine the credibility of ethical sourcing initiatives. Companies should establish robust verification mechanisms, engage independent auditors, and participate in recognized certification programs to ensure the authenticity of ethical claims.

Case Study: Ethical Sourcing in the Fashion Industry

To illustrate the practical application of ethical sourcing and procurement, let's consider the fashion industry. The fashion industry is notorious for labor rights violations, environmental degradation, and unethical practices. However, several companies have taken significant steps to address these issues and embrace ethical sourcing.

One such example is Patagonia, an outdoor clothing company known for its commitment to ethical practices. Patagonia has implemented a robust supply chain transparency program, allowing customers to trace the origin and manufacturing process of their products. The company ensures fair labor conditions by auditing its suppliers and providing training to improve working conditions. Patagonia also invests in sustainable materials and processes, reducing its environmental impact.

By embracing ethical sourcing, Patagonia has not only improved its brand reputation but also created a loyal customer base that values transparency and sustainability. The company serves as a role model for the fashion industry, demonstrating that ethical sourcing can be profitable while still respecting workers' rights and the environment.

Conclusion

Ethical sourcing and procurement are critical components of responsible business practices. By incorporating ethical principles into their supply chains, businesses can promote fair labor practices, environmental sustainability, and social responsibility. While there are challenges to overcome, companies that prioritize ethical sourcing stand to gain from enhanced reputation, reduced risks, and increased customer loyalty. With continuous improvement, collaboration, and adherence to ethical principles, businesses can create a more sustainable and just marketplace.

Human Rights and Labor Conditions

In today's globalized world, the protection of human rights and ensuring fair labor conditions has become a crucial issue. This section explores the ethical considerations and challenges related to human rights and labor conditions in various industries. It examines the importance of upholding human rights and the responsibilities of businesses in promoting fair labor practices.

International Standards and Legal Framework

Various international organizations and agreements have established guidelines and legal frameworks to protect human rights and promote fair labor conditions. The Universal Declaration of Human Rights, adopted by the United Nations General Assembly in 1948, is a foundational document that outlines the fundamental rights and freedoms that should be universally protected. It includes rights such as the right to work, fair wages, safe working conditions, and freedom from discrimination.

Additionally, the International Labour Organization (ILO) is a specialized agency of the United Nations that sets international labor standards and promotes decent work for all. The ILO's core conventions cover a range of labor issues, including freedom of association, the elimination of forced and child labor, and equal remuneration. These standards provide a framework for countries and organizations to ensure fair labor practices.

Labor Exploitation and Human Rights Violations

Despite the existence of international standards and legal frameworks, labor exploitation and human rights violations still occur in various industries. Exploitative practices such as forced labor, child labor, and unsafe working conditions continue to affect vulnerable workers worldwide.

For example, in the garment industry, workers in some developing countries face long working hours, low wages, and unsafe working conditions. These workers often lack access to social protection, face discrimination, and are denied the right to freedom of association. The exploitation of workers in this industry raises questions about the ethical responsibilities of companies in their supply chains.

Corporate Social Responsibility and Ethical Sourcing

Corporate social responsibility (CSR) is an important concept that highlights the responsibility of businesses to address social and environmental issues. In the context of human rights and labor conditions, CSR plays a crucial role in ensuring ethical sourcing practices.

Companies should consider implementing ethical sourcing policies that include responsible supply chain management. This involves conducting due diligence to ensure that suppliers uphold fair labor practices and respect human rights. Ethical sourcing policies can also include requirements for transparency, ensuring that suppliers provide information regarding their labor conditions and practices.

By integrating ethical sourcing practices into their operations, companies can promote fair labor conditions and contribute to the protection of human rights. This not only aligns with international standards and legal frameworks but also enhances the reputation and trustworthiness of the organization.

Monitoring and Auditing Labor Conditions

Monitoring and auditing labor conditions are essential steps in ensuring compliance with human rights standards and fair labor practices. Organizations can establish internal monitoring systems or collaborate with external auditors to assess labor conditions in their supply chains.

Regular and independent audits provide insights into the working conditions, wages, and treatment of workers. Audits can help identify areas of improvement and address non-compliance issues. In cases where violations are identified, organizations should take appropriate action, such as terminating contracts with non-compliant suppliers or providing support for remediation efforts.

However, it is crucial to acknowledge the limitations of audits. They can be resource-intensive and may not always capture the full extent of labor conditions. Therefore, complementing audits with other forms of assessment, such as worker interviews and engagement, can provide a more holistic understanding of the labor conditions and potential human rights violations.

Collaboration and Advocacy

Addressing human rights violations and promoting fair labor conditions requires collaboration and advocacy efforts from multiple stakeholders. Governments, non-governmental organizations (NGOs), trade unions, and companies need to work together to create positive change.

NGOs and trade unions play a crucial role in advocating for the rights of workers and raising awareness of labor conditions. They can engage in campaigns, lobbying, and public pressure to pressure companies and governments to uphold ethical labor practices.

Companies can also engage in collaborative efforts such as industry-wide initiatives and multi-stakeholder partnerships to address systemic issues. By joining forces, stakeholders can share expertise, develop common standards, and collectively work towards improving human rights and labor conditions.

Case Study: The Rana Plaza Disaster

The Rana Plaza disaster in Bangladesh in 2013 serves as a tragic example of the consequences of unethical labor practices. The collapse of the Rana Plaza building, which housed several garment factories, resulted in the death of over 1,100 workers and injured thousands more.

The incident shed light on the unsafe working conditions, lack of building regulations, and exploitation of workers in the global garment industry. It prompted international outcry and calls for improved labor conditions.

The Rana Plaza disaster led to the formation of the Bangladesh Accord on Fire and Building Safety, a legally binding agreement between brands and trade unions to improve working conditions in the Bangladeshi garment industry. This initiative demonstrates the importance of collective action and the role of companies in ensuring safe and ethical labor practices.

Key Takeaways

- International standards and legal frameworks provide guidance for promoting fair labor conditions and protecting human rights. - Labor exploitation and human rights violations still exist in various industries, highlighting the need for continuous efforts to address these issues. - Corporate social responsibility and ethical sourcing practices are essential for ensuring fair labor conditions. - Monitoring and auditing labor conditions help identify areas of improvement and address non-compliance issues. - Collaboration and advocacy efforts are crucial for promoting ethical labor practices and human rights. - The Rana Plaza disaster serves as a tragic reminder of the consequences of unethical labor practices and the need for industry-wide change.

Ethics in Practice

Imagine you are the CEO of a multinational corporation that sources materials from various countries. How would you ensure ethical sourcing practices and promote fair labor conditions throughout your supply chain? Consider the challenges and potential solutions in your proposed strategy.

Further Reading

1. *The Responsible Company: What We've Learned from Patagonia's First 40 Years* by Yvon Chouinard and Vincent Stanley 2. *Worker Rights and Global Trade* by Lance Compa 3. *Global Supply Chains: Evaluating the International Labor Rights Implications* by Wilma B. Liebman, J. Andrew Watson, and Andrew J. Sherwood 4. *Sweatshops at Sea: Merchant Seamen in the World's First Globalized Industry, from 1812 to the Present* by Leon Fink 5. *The Human Rights Handbook: A Practical Guide to Monitoring, Reporting, and Accountability* by Ali M. Jawad.

Environmental Sustainability

Environmental sustainability is a crucial aspect of ethical practices in modern society. It involves the responsible use and management of natural resources to ensure the well-being of both present and future generations. In this section, we will explore the ethical considerations and challenges related to environmental sustainability.

The Importance of Environmental Sustainability

Environmental sustainability recognizes the interconnectedness between human activities and the environment. It emphasizes the need to protect and conserve natural resources, reduce pollution, and preserve biodiversity. By promoting sustainable practices, we can mitigate the adverse impacts of human activities on the planet, such as climate change, deforestation, and habitat destruction.

One of the key principles underlying environmental sustainability is the precautionary principle. This principle states that in the face of uncertainty and potential harm to the environment, it is better to take preventive measures rather than wait for conclusive scientific evidence. This principle guides us in making ethical decisions that prioritize the long-term health of the planet.

Ethical Challenges in Environmental Sustainability

Achieving environmental sustainability presents various ethical challenges that require careful consideration. Here are some of the key challenges:

1. **Balancing economic growth and environmental protection:** A major challenge is finding a balance between economic development and preserving the environment. This involves ensuring that economic activities do not lead to excessive resource depletion, pollution, or degradation of ecosystems. Ethical decision-making in this context requires weighing the short-term benefits of economic growth against the long-term impacts on the environment and future generations.

2. **Equitable distribution of environmental resources:** Environmental resources, such as clean air, water, and natural habitats, should be fairly distributed among communities. However, socioeconomic disparities often result in unequal access to these resources. Ethical considerations demand that environmental sustainability initiatives prioritize the needs of marginalized communities and address environmental injustice.

3. **Trade-offs between different environmental goals:** Environmental sustainability involves addressing multiple interconnected issues, such as climate change, biodiversity loss, and resource depletion. However, the strategies employed to tackle one problem may have unintended

consequences for others. Ethical decision-making requires considering the trade-offs between different environmental goals and identifying the most effective and least harmful approaches.

Strategies for Environmental Sustainability

To address the ethical challenges associated with environmental sustainability, various strategies and approaches have been developed. Here are some examples:

1. **Adopting sustainable practices:** Businesses, governments, and individuals can adopt sustainable practices to reduce their environmental impact. This includes promoting energy efficiency, waste reduction, recycling, and the use of renewable resources. Ethical decision-making involves considering the long-term environmental consequences of our choices and taking actions that prioritize sustainability.

2. **Implementing environmental policies and regulations:** Governments play a crucial role in promoting environmental sustainability through the implementation of policies and regulations. These can include measures to reduce greenhouse gas emissions, protect endangered species, and preserve natural habitats. Ethical governance requires transparency, accountability, and the involvement of stakeholders in the decision-making process.

3. **Promoting education and awareness:** Educating the public about environmental issues and promoting awareness is vital for achieving sustainability. By increasing knowledge and understanding, individuals can make informed choices and contribute to positive change. Ethical educators should prioritize incorporating environmental sustainability into the curriculum and fostering a sense of responsibility towards the environment.

4. **Supporting international cooperation:** Collaboration between countries is essential for addressing global environmental challenges. Agreements and initiatives such as the Paris Agreement on climate change aim to promote international cooperation and coordination. Ethical considerations involve recognizing our shared responsibility for the planet and taking collective action to protect it.

Case Study: Sustainable Energy Transition

To illustrate the ethical considerations in environmental sustainability, let's consider the case of transitioning to sustainable energy sources. The use of fossil fuels for energy production contributes significantly to climate change and environmental degradation. However, transitioning to renewable energy sources poses ethical dilemmas and challenges.

One ethical dilemma is the potential impact on communities dependent on the fossil fuel industry for their livelihoods. As we shift away from fossil fuels, we must ensure a just transition for these communities, providing support for retraining and alternative job opportunities.

Another challenge is the upfront costs of renewable energy infrastructure. While renewable energy sources are more sustainable in the long run, the initial investment required can be a barrier, especially for developing countries. Ethical considerations involve finding ways to support and finance renewable energy projects in a manner that doesn't exacerbate socioeconomic inequalities.

Furthermore, the adoption of renewable energy technologies relies on the availability of critical minerals, such as lithium for batteries. The extraction of these minerals can have environmental and social consequences, particularly in resource-rich but politically unstable regions. Ethical decision-making involves considering the environmental and social impacts of the entire lifecycle of renewable energy technologies.

By considering these ethical challenges and employing a holistic approach, we can make informed decisions and work towards a sustainable energy transition that benefits both people and the planet.

Conclusion

Environmental sustainability is a vital aspect of ethical practices in the modern world. It requires us to balance economic growth with environmental protection, ensure equitable distribution of resources, and address trade-offs between different environmental goals. By adopting sustainable practices, implementing effective policies, promoting education, and fostering international cooperation, we can work towards a more sustainable future.

Exercises

1. Reflect on your daily activities and identify three ways in which you can reduce your environmental impact. Explain the ethical reasons behind your choices.

2. Research and analyze a case study of an environmental sustainability initiative implemented by a business or government organization. Assess the ethical considerations and outcomes of the initiative.

3. Debate the ethical trade-offs between economic growth and environmental protection. Take different perspectives and consider the short-term and long-term implications of each position.

4. Choose a specific environmental issue (e.g., deforestation, plastic pollution) and propose ethical strategies to address the issue at global, national, and individual levels. Explain the rationale behind each strategy.

5. Investigate the environmental impact of a particular industry or technology (e.g., fashion industry, transportation). Analyze the ethical challenges associated with the industry or technology and propose solutions for achieving greater sustainability.

Additional Resources

- Books:

    - *The Ethics of Climate Change: Right and Wrong in a Warming World* by James Garvey

    - *Environmental Ethics: An Anthology* edited by Andrew Light and Holmes Rolston III

    - *Sustainability: A Comprehensive Foundation* by Tom Theis and Jonathan Tomkin

- Organizations:

    - United Nations Environment Programme (UNEP) - www.unep.org

    - World Wildlife Fund (WWF) - www.worldwildlife.org

    - Greenpeace - www.greenpeace.org

Trick: When considering the environmental impact of a product, check for eco-labels and certifications such as ENERGY STAR or Forest Stewardship Council (FSC) certification. These labels indicate that the product meets specific environmental standards.

Caveat: Environmental sustainability is an ongoing process, and there is no one-size-fits-all solution. It requires continuous evaluation, adaptation, and collaboration among various stakeholders.

Fair Trade and Social Responsibility

In today's interconnected world, businesses are increasingly recognizing the importance of fair trade and social responsibility. Fair trade is a movement that aims to create a more equitable and sustainable global trading system, while social responsibility refers to the ethical behavior and practices of businesses towards society and the environment. In this section, we will explore the concept of fair trade, its principles, and its impact on social responsibility.

Principles of Fair Trade

Fair trade is based on a set of core principles that guide its practices. These principles include:

1. **Fair Prices:** Fair trade aims to ensure that producers receive fair prices for their products. This means that producers are paid a price that covers the cost of production and provides them with a decent standard of living.

2. **Fair Wages:** Fair trade promotes the payment of fair wages to workers, ensuring that they receive a living wage that meets their basic needs and allows them to provide for themselves and their families.

3. **Decent Working Conditions:** Fair trade requires that producers provide decent working conditions for their employees, including safe and healthy working environments, reasonable working hours, and the prohibition of child labor.

4. **Environmental Sustainability:** Fair trade encourages sustainable and environmentally friendly production methods. Producers are encouraged to minimize their impact on the environment, conserve natural resources, and engage in practices that promote biodiversity and the protection of ecosystems.

5. **Community Development:** Fair trade aims to empower local communities by promoting community development projects and investing in social infrastructure, such as schools, healthcare facilities, and clean water systems.

Benefits of Fair Trade

Fair trade has numerous benefits for producers, consumers, and the environment. Some of the key benefits are:

1.   **Poverty Alleviation:** Fair trade provides a sustainable livelihood for producers by ensuring fair prices and wages. This helps to lift them out of poverty and improve their quality of life.

2. **Empowerment of Marginalized Producers:** Fair trade focuses on working with marginalized producers, such as small-scale farmers and artisans, empowering them to improve their social and economic status.

3.   **Environmental Conservation:**   Fair trade encourages sustainable production methods that promote environmental conservation. By supporting fair trade, consumers can contribute to the preservation of ecosystems and biodiversity.

4. **Quality Products:** Fair trade products are often associated with high quality and craftsmanship. By purchasing fair trade products, consumers can enjoy unique and ethically produced items.

5. **Consumer Awareness and Education:** Fair trade raises awareness among consumers about the impact of their purchasing decisions. It promotes ethical consumption and empowers consumers to make informed choices that align with their values.

Challenges and Solutions

While fair trade has made significant progress in promoting ethical trade practices, it still faces challenges. Some of these challenges include:

1. **Supply Chain Complexity:** The global supply chain can be complex, with multiple intermediaries between producers and consumers. Ensuring fair trade practices throughout the supply chain can be challenging.

2. **Certification and Verification:** Fair trade certification requires compliance with specific standards. However, verifying adherence to these standards can be time-consuming and costly for producers.

3. **Market Access:** Accessing fair trade markets can be challenging for small-scale producers due to limited resources and market barriers. Developing channels for fair trade products and increasing market awareness is crucial.

To address these challenges, collaboration between stakeholders is essential. Governments, businesses, and consumers can play a role in promoting fair trade practices by supporting fair trade organizations, advocating for fair trade policies, and increasing consumer awareness.

Real-World Example

One real-world example of a fair trade initiative is the Fairtrade International organization. They work with small-scale producers in developing countries, ensuring they receive fair prices for their products and promoting sustainable farming practices. The Fairtrade certification label can be found on a wide range of products, including coffee, chocolate, bananas, and cotton.

By purchasing products with the Fairtrade certification label, consumers can be confident that their purchase has a positive impact on producers and the environment.

Further Resources

If you are interested in learning more about fair trade and social responsibility, here are some recommended resources:

+ Fairtrade International - https://www.fairtrade.net/

+ World Fair Trade Organization - https://wfto.com/

+ Fair Trade Federation - https://www.fairtradefederation.org/

These organizations provide valuable information about fair trade practices, certified products, and ways to get involved in promoting fair trade.

Conclusion

Fair trade and social responsibility are essential aspects of ethical business practices. Through fair trade, businesses can support marginalized producers, promote sustainability, and empower consumers to make a positive impact. By understanding the principles of fair trade and supporting fair trade initiatives, we can contribute to building a more just and sustainable world.

Ethical Communication in the Supply Chain

In the globalized world of business, supply chain management plays a crucial role in ensuring the smooth flow of goods and services from producers to consumers. However, the ethical implications of this complex network of suppliers and intermediaries cannot be overlooked. Ethical communication in the supply chain is vital to maintain transparency, fairness, and accountability throughout the process.

1. Importance of Ethical Communication Ethical communication is the cornerstone of trust in the supply chain. It involves the transparent exchange of information and ideas that align with moral and ethical standards. Effective communication enables all stakeholders to make informed decisions, understand expectations, and ensure fair treatment among parties involved.

2. Key Principles of Ethical Communication 2.1 Transparency: Open and honest communication builds trust and fosters ethical behavior. All relevant information, such as pricing, quality standards, and production practices, should be shared proactively among the supply chain members.

2.2 Fairness: Ethical communication demands equal treatment and opportunities for all stakeholders. It ensures that information is disseminated in a way that does not favor one party at the expense of others. Fairness also extends to dispute resolution and the provision of accurate feedback.

2.3 Accountability: Ethical communication requires all parties to take responsibility for their actions and adhere to agreed-upon standards. Regular monitoring and reporting mechanisms should be in place to ensure compliance with ethical codes and practices.

3. Challenges in Ethical Communication 3.1 Language Barriers: In a global supply chain, different languages and cultural nuances can create communication barriers. These challenges may result in misunderstandings, misinterpretations, and potential ethical breaches. It is essential to bridge these gaps through effective translation and cultural sensitivity.

3.2 Information Asymmetry: Unequal access to information can create power imbalances within the supply chain. This imbalance may lead to unethical practices such as price manipulation, unfair contractual terms, or hidden costs. Ethical communication strives to address information asymmetry and promote transparency among all stakeholders.

4. Strategies for Ethical Communication 4.1 Clear Communication Channels: Establishing clear lines of communication among supply chain participants is crucial. This includes utilizing technology platforms, web portals, or dedicated communication systems to facilitate the flow of information and ensure timely responses.

4.2 Ethical Training and Education: Providing training and education on ethical communication practices can enhance awareness and understanding among supply chain members. It helps to align values, cultivate ethical behaviors, and reinforce the importance of ethical communication throughout the supply chain network.

4.3 Code of Conduct: Developing and implementing a comprehensive code of conduct for the supply chain can guide ethical communication practices. A code of conduct sets expectations, standards, and guidelines for all parties involved, emphasizing transparent and ethical communication principles.

5. Case Study: Supplier Collaboration and Ethical Communication

XYZ Corporation, a multinational retailer, recently faced a controversy regarding unethical labor practices in one of its supplier factories. The company took immediate action to rectify the situation and prevent similar incidents in the future. They implemented a supplier collaboration program that emphasized ethical communication. The program included the following initiatives:

5.1 Supplier Onboarding: Prior to establishing business relationships, XYZ Corporation introduced a comprehensive training program for suppliers. This program highlighted the importance of transparent and ethical communication, ensuring that potential suppliers were aware of the company's expectations regarding labor practices and human rights.

5.2 Regular Audits and Monitoring: XYZ Corporation conducted regular audits in supplier factories to assess compliance with ethical standards. The auditors not only evaluated the physical conditions but also assessed the effectiveness of communication channels between management and workers. Any communication gaps or ethical breaches were addressed promptly to maintain transparency and accountability.

5.3 Supplier Collaboration Platform: XYZ Corporation introduced a dedicated online platform where suppliers could communicate with the company directly. This platform allowed for efficient information exchange, addressing concerns, sharing best practices, and resolving disputes promptly. It also served as a forum for suppliers to report any unethical practices they observed in their own supply chains.

By implementing these initiatives, XYZ Corporation fostered a culture of ethical communication throughout its supply chain. This case study demonstrates the importance of proactive measures and collaboration for ethical communication in the supply chain.

In conclusion, ethical communication is a vital aspect of supply chain management. Transparency, fairness, and accountability must be prioritized to ensure the flow of accurate information, build trust, and prevent unethical practices. Overcoming challenges, implementing effective strategies, and promoting ethical communication contribute to the overall integrity and sustainability of the supply chain.

Ethical Challenges in the Digital Age

Online Privacy and Data Protection

In today's digital age, online privacy and data protection have become increasingly important. With the rapid advancement of technology and the widespread use of the internet, individuals and organizations are more connected than ever before. However, this connectivity also brings with it various risks to personal privacy and the security of sensitive information.

1. The Importance of Online Privacy

Online privacy refers to the ability of individuals to control the information they share about themselves on the internet and how that information is used by others. It is essential for several reasons:

1.1 Protecting Personal Information: When we interact online, we often share personal data, such as our names, addresses, phone numbers, and even financial information. Maintaining online privacy helps prevent this information from falling into the wrong hands and being misused.

1.2 Preserving Personal Identity: Our online activities, including our search history, social media posts, and shopping preferences, create a digital footprint that can be used to build a profile of who we are. Protecting our online privacy helps preserve our personal identity and prevent identity theft.

1.3 Safeguarding Reputation: In the digital age, our online presence can have a significant impact on our personal and professional reputation. Maintaining online privacy helps prevent reputation damage caused by the misuse or unauthorized access to our personal information.

1.4 Ensuring Freedom of Expression: Online privacy is closely linked to freedom of expression. When individuals feel that their online activities are being monitored or surveilled, they may self-censor, leading to a chilling effect on free speech.

2. Data Protection Principles

To ensure online privacy, it is important to understand and adhere to data protection principles. These principles guide the collection, processing, and storage of personal data:

2.1 Consent: Individuals should give their informed consent before their personal data is collected and used. Consent should be freely given, specific, and informed.

2.2 Purpose Limitation: Personal data should only be collected for specified and legitimate purposes. It should not be further processed in a manner that is incompatible with these purposes.

2.3 Data Minimization: Personal data should be limited to what is necessary for the intended purposes. Organizations should only collect and retain the minimum amount of personal data required to achieve their objectives.

2.4 Accuracy: Personal data should be accurate, up-to-date, and kept in a form that allows individuals to be identified only for as long as necessary.

2.5 Storage Limitation: Personal data should be retained for no longer than is necessary for the specified purposes. It should be securely deleted or anonymized when no longer needed.

2.6 Security: Personal data should be protected by appropriate technical and organizational measures against unauthorized access, disclosure, or loss.

2.7 Accountability: Organizations are responsible for complying with data protection principles. They must be able to demonstrate compliance and be accountable for their data processing activities.

3. Risks to Online Privacy

Various risks threaten online privacy. Understanding these risks is crucial in taking appropriate measures to protect personal information:

3.1 Data Breaches: Data breaches occur when unauthorized individuals gain access to sensitive information. This breach can lead to identity theft, financial loss, and reputational damage.

3.2 Phishing Attacks: Phishing attacks involve fraudulent attempts to obtain sensitive information, such as usernames, passwords, and credit card details, by posing as trustworthy entities. These attacks often use deceptive emails or websites.

3.3 Tracking and Profiling: Online platforms and advertisers may use cookies and other tracking mechanisms to collect information about individuals' browsing habits. This data is then used to create targeted profiles for personalized advertising, potentially eroding privacy.

3.4 Social Engineering: Social engineering involves manipulating individuals into revealing sensitive information or performing actions that compromise their security. This can occur through methods such as impersonation, pretexting, or baiting.

3.5 Government Surveillance: Governments may engage in surveillance activities to monitor online communications and activities. The extent and legality of such surveillance vary across jurisdictions.

4. Protecting Online Privacy

To protect online privacy, individuals and organizations can take several measures:

4.1 Use Strong Passwords: Create unique, complex passwords for each online account and regularly change them. Consider using a password manager to securely store and generate passwords.

4.2 Enable Two-Factor Authentication: Enable two-factor authentication whenever available. This adds an extra layer of security by requiring a second verification step, such as a code sent to a mobile device, in addition to a password.

4.3 Use Encryption: Encrypt sensitive communications and data to prevent unauthorized access. Use secure communication protocols, such as HTTPS, when accessing websites or transmitting data.

4.4 Regularly Update Software: Keep all software, including operating systems, web browsers, and antivirus programs, up to date to protect against known vulnerabilities.

4.5 Be Mindful of Sharing Personal Information: Be cautious about sharing personal information online, especially on social media platforms. Consider adjusting privacy settings and carefully reviewing permissions for apps and services.

4.6 Use Virtual Private Networks (VPNs): VPNs can encrypt internet traffic, making it more difficult for third parties to monitor online activities. VPNs also provide anonymity by masking IP addresses.

4.7 Educate and Raise Awareness: Promote awareness of online privacy risks and best practices among family, friends, and colleagues. Educate yourself about the privacy policies of online services and use platforms that prioritize privacy.

5. Case Study: Facebook and Cambridge Analytica Scandal

The Facebook and Cambridge Analytica scandal serves as a sobering example of the importance of online privacy and data protection. In 2018, it was revealed that Cambridge Analytica, a political consulting firm, harvested personal data from tens of millions of Facebook users without their consent. This data was then used to create targeted political advertising during the 2016 U.S. Presidential election.

The scandal highlighted the need for stricter regulations and improved privacy practices in the digital age. It led to increased public awareness of the potential misuse of personal data by online platforms and the importance of protecting online privacy.

6. Conclusion

Online privacy and data protection are critical in today's interconnected world. Individuals and organizations must understand the risks to privacy and adhere to data protection principles to minimize these risks. By taking proactive measures to protect personal information and promoting awareness of privacy issues, we can create a safer and more secure online environment for all.

Cybersecurity and Ethical Hacking

Cybersecurity and ethical hacking play crucial roles in today's digital landscape. With the increasing reliance on technology and the ever-growing threat of cyber attacks, organizations and individuals must prioritize the security of their digital assets. In this section, we will explore the principles and practices of cybersecurity, as well as the concept of ethical hacking.

Principles of Cybersecurity

Cybersecurity refers to the protection of digital systems, networks, and data from unauthorized access, damage, or theft. It encompasses a set of principles and practices aimed at safeguarding information and ensuring the integrity, availability, and confidentiality of digital assets. Let's discuss some fundamental principles of cybersecurity:

1. **Confidentiality:** Confidentiality ensures that only authorized individuals or entities can access sensitive information. Encryption techniques, access controls, and secure communication protocols are examples of measures employed to maintain confidentiality.

2. **Integrity:** Integrity focuses on the prevention of unauthorized modification or alteration of data. Data integrity ensures that information remains accurate, consistent, and trustworthy. Techniques such as checksums, digital signatures, and access controls are utilized to maintain data integrity.

3. **Availability:** Availability guarantees that authorized users can access digital assets whenever needed. It involves measures to mitigate system failures, network disruptions, or denial-of-service attacks. Redundancy, fault tolerance, and disaster recovery plans are used to ensure availability.

4. **Authentication:** Authentication verifies the identity of individuals or entities attempting to access a digital system or network. This can involve the use of passwords, biometrics, certificates, or multi-factor authentication to prevent unauthorized access.

5. **Authorization:** Authorization determines what actions an authenticated user is allowed to perform within a digital system or network. Access controls, user roles, and permission levels are used to enforce proper authorization.

6. **Auditability**: Auditability enables the tracking and monitoring of access and activities within a digital system or network. Logging mechanisms, intrusion detection systems, and security event management tools are employed to ensure accountability and forensic analysis.

These principles form the foundation of cybersecurity and guide the design and implementation of secure systems.

Ethical Hacking

Ethical hacking, also known as penetration testing or white-hat hacking, involves authorized hacking activities performed by cybersecurity professionals to identify vulnerabilities in systems, networks, or applications. The goal of ethical hacking is to improve the security posture by identifying and fixing weaknesses before malicious attackers exploit them. Ethical hackers use the same techniques and tools as malicious hackers but with the permission and intent to secure the target systems. Let's delve into the framework of ethical hacking:

1. **Reconnaissance**: Reconnaissance involves gathering information about the target system, network, or application. This can include identifying the target's IP addresses, domain names, network topology, or system architecture. Ethical hackers use open-source intelligence (OSINT), network scanning, and vulnerability scanning techniques to understand the target environment.

2. **Vulnerability Assessment**: Vulnerability assessment aims to identify potential weaknesses or vulnerabilities in the target system or application. This can involve conducting vulnerability scans, analyzing system configurations, or reviewing source code. Ethical hackers use automated tools, manual inspection, and code review techniques to discover vulnerabilities.

3. **Exploitation**: Exploitation refers to the process of taking advantage of identified vulnerabilities to gain unauthorized access or control over the target system. Ethical hackers attempt to exploit vulnerabilities to demonstrate their impact and potential for exploitation by malicious actors. However, the primary goal is to assess the system's security rather than causing harm.

4. **Post-Exploitation**: Post-exploitation involves maintaining access to the compromised system and further exploring its vulnerabilities. Ethical

hackers aim to understand the scope of the compromise and the potential damage that could be done by an attacker. They also document and report their findings to the organization, recommending remediation measures.

5. **Reporting and Remediation:** Reporting is a crucial step in ethical hacking. Ethical hackers document their findings, including vulnerability details, exploitation techniques, and recommendations for remediation. The organization receiving the report can then take appropriate actions to patch vulnerabilities and enhance security.

By conducting ethical hacking exercises, organizations can proactively identify and address vulnerabilities, ultimately improving their overall cybersecurity posture.

Real-World Example: Bug Bounty Programs

Bug bounty programs have gained popularity as a means to incentivize ethical hacking and enhance cybersecurity. In these programs, organizations invite cybersecurity researchers, or "white-hat hackers," to identify vulnerabilities in their systems or applications. Rewards are offered for the discovery and responsible disclosure of vulnerabilities. Bug bounty programs provide a win-win situation: organizations benefit from the expertise of ethical hackers, and hackers receive recognition and financial compensation for their efforts.

One prominent example is the bug bounty program offered by major technology companies like Google, Microsoft, and Facebook. These companies are willing to pay substantial sums of money to ethical hackers who discover critical vulnerabilities in their products or services. Bug bounty programs have proven to be effective in identifying and fixing security flaws that may have otherwise gone unnoticed.

Recommended Resources

To further delve into cybersecurity and ethical hacking, explore the following resources:

1. *The Web Application Hacker's Handbook* by Dafydd Stuttard and Marcus Pinto: This book provides a comprehensive guide to web application security, including techniques and methodologies for ethical hacking.

2. *Metasploit: The Penetration Tester's Guide* by David Kennedy, Jim O'Gorman, Devon Kearns, and Mati Aharoni: This book focuses on the popular Metasploit framework, providing insights into advanced penetration testing techniques.

3. *OWASP (Open Web Application Security Project)*: OWASP is a community-driven organization that provides resources, tools, and knowledge on web application security. Their website offers various guides and tutorials on ethical hacking techniques and practices.

4. *Hack The Box*: Hack The Box is an online platform that offers a range of vulnerable virtual machines for security enthusiasts to hone their skills in a legal and ethical manner. It provides an interactive and hands-on approach to learning ethical hacking.

5. *Capture The Flag (CTF) Competitions*: Participating in CTF competitions is an excellent way to apply ethical hacking skills in a challenging and competitive environment. CTF competitions simulate real-world scenarios and offer opportunities to solve security-related challenges.

By engaging with these resources, individuals interested in cybersecurity and ethical hacking can expand their knowledge and skills in this ever-evolving field.

Summary

In this section, we explored the principles of cybersecurity, focusing on confidentiality, integrity, availability, authentication, authorization, and auditability. We also discussed ethical hacking, its framework, and how it contributes to improving cybersecurity. The example of bug bounty programs showcased the practical application of ethical hacking in real-world scenarios. By adopting cybersecurity best practices and incorporating ethical hacking approaches, organizations can enhance their defense against cyber threats and protect their critical digital assets.

Artificial Intelligence and Ethical Concerns

Artificial Intelligence (AI) is a rapidly advancing field that has the potential to revolutionize various aspects of our lives. From autonomous vehicles to smart personal assistants, AI is becoming increasingly integrated into our daily activities. However, as AI technology continues to evolve, ethical concerns have emerged regarding its impact on society.

Defining Artificial Intelligence

Before delving into the ethical concerns, let us first define what artificial intelligence is. AI refers to the ability of machines to perform tasks that would typically require human intelligence. This includes tasks such as problem-solving, pattern recognition, and decision-making.

There are different forms of AI, ranging from narrow or weak AI, which is designed to perform specific tasks, to general or strong AI, which is capable of outperforming humans in virtually every cognitive task. Narrow AI is the most common form of AI currently in use, with applications in fields such as healthcare, finance, and customer service.

Ethical Concerns in AI

As AI becomes more prevalent in our society, it raises several ethical concerns that need to be addressed. Some of the key ethical concerns in AI include:

1. **Job Displacement:** One of the major concerns surrounding AI is the potential loss of jobs. With automation replacing human labor in various industries, there is a fear of widespread unemployment. It is essential to consider strategies for retraining and reskilling the workforce to ensure a smooth transition to an AI-driven future.

2. **Privacy and Data Security:** AI systems rely on vast amounts of data to function effectively. This raises concerns about the privacy and security of personal information. It is crucial to establish robust data protection regulations and frameworks to safeguard individuals' privacy rights and prevent misuse of sensitive information.

3. **Bias and Discrimination:** AI algorithms learn from training data, and if the data contains biases, the algorithms can perpetuate and amplify those biases. This can lead to discriminatory outcomes, such as biased hiring practices or unfair allocation of resources. Efforts should be made to ensure that AI systems are developed and trained using representative and unbiased data.

4. **Transparency and Accountability:** AI algorithms can be complex and opaque, making it challenging to understand how decisions are reached. This lack of transparency raises concerns about accountability, especially in high-stakes applications such as healthcare and criminal justice. Developing explainable AI models and establishing mechanisms for accountability are essential to build trust in AI systems.

5. **Autonomous Systems and Moral Responsibility:** As AI systems become more autonomous, questions arise regarding moral responsibility. Who should be held accountable for the actions of AI systems? Should there be regulations in place to ensure that AI systems adhere to ethical standards? These challenging questions need to be addressed to avoid potential harm caused by AI systems.

Ethical Frameworks for AI

To address the ethical concerns associated with AI, various ethical frameworks and principles have been proposed. These frameworks provide guidelines for the development and deployment of AI systems. Some of the prominent ethical frameworks include:

1. **Beneficence and Non-maleficence:** AI systems should be designed to benefit individuals and society while minimizing harm. Developers should consider the potential societal impact of AI systems and take measures to ensure they do not cause undue harm or perpetuate discrimination.

2. **Fairness and Equity:** AI systems should be fair and unbiased, treating all individuals equitably. Developers should strive for algorithmic fairness, ensuring that AI systems do not discriminate based on factors such as race, gender, or socioeconomic status.

3. **Transparency and Explainability:** AI systems should be transparent and explainable, allowing individuals to understand how decisions are made. Explainability fosters accountability and helps detect and rectify biases or errors in AI systems.

4. **Privacy and Consent:** AI systems should respect individuals' privacy rights and obtain informed consent for data collection and usage. Developers should implement privacy-enhancing techniques and comply with relevant privacy laws and regulations.

5. **Human Oversight and Control:** While AI systems can automate tasks, human oversight and control should be maintained. Humans should have the ability to intervene and override AI decisions, especially in critical domains such as healthcare and national security.

Case Study: Facial Recognition Technology

An example that highlights the ethical concerns in AI is the use of facial recognition technology. Facial recognition technology has various applications, from unlocking smartphones to surveillance and law enforcement. However, its use raises significant ethical issues.

One concern is the potential for misuse of facial recognition technology, such as mass surveillance or unauthorized tracking of individuals. This infringes on privacy rights and raises questions about consent and control over personal information.

Another concern is the accuracy and potential bias of facial recognition algorithms. Studies have shown that facial recognition systems may have higher error rates and misidentify individuals from certain racial or ethnic groups. This can lead to discriminatory outcomes, such as biased law enforcement practices or unfair identification at airport security checkpoints.

To address these concerns, it is essential to regulate the use of facial recognition technology, ensuring transparency, accountability, and adherence to ethical principles. Additionally, developers should invest in unbiased data collection and testing, as well as ongoing monitoring and evaluation of the technology's impact on society.

Conclusion

AI has the potential to bring about significant benefits to society, but its development and deployment must be guided by ethical considerations. By addressing the ethical concerns associated with AI, we can ensure that this transformative technology is used responsibly and for the betterment of humanity.

Understanding the ethical issues in AI and the frameworks for responsible development will empower individuals, organizations, and policymakers to make informed decisions about the adoption and use of AI. As AI continues to advance, ongoing discussions and updates to ethical frameworks will be crucial to ensure that AI aligns with our values and serves the best interests of society.

Digital Divide and Ethical Implications

In the digital age, access to technology and the internet has become increasingly vital for participation in modern society. However, not everyone has equal access to these resources, resulting in what is known as the digital divide. The digital divide refers to the gap between individuals and communities that have access to technology and those that do not. This divide can be based on various factors, such as socio-economic status, geographical location, age, ethnicity, and educational background.

The digital divide has significant ethical implications as it can deepen existing inequalities and create new forms of disadvantage. In this section, we will explore the concept of the digital divide, its causes and consequences, and the ethical considerations that arise from it.

Understanding the Digital Divide

The digital divide encompasses multiple dimensions of inequality, including:

- **Access divide:** This refers to the unequal distribution of physical access to technology and the internet. It includes disparities in the availability of affordable broadband connections, computers, smartphones, and other digital devices. Certain communities, particularly those in remote or economically disadvantaged areas, may face limited infrastructure and connectivity options, limiting their access to online resources and opportunities.

+ **Usage divide:** Even when individuals have access to technology, disparities can arise in terms of how it is used. Some individuals may lack the necessary digital skills or knowledge to effectively navigate online platforms, search for information, or engage in digital communication. Without the skills to maximize the potential of technology, users may be unable to fully benefit from digital tools and services.

+ **Skills divide:** The skills divide refers to disparities in digital literacy and proficiency. This includes the ability to critically assess and evaluate online information, protect digital privacy and security, and articulate one's ideas effectively using digital means. Individuals with limited digital skills may struggle to participate in the digital economy or fully engage in online civic and social activities.

Causes and Consequences of the Digital Divide

The digital divide arises from a complex interplay of economic, social, and educational factors. Some of the key causes and consequences include:

+ **Socioeconomic factors:** Socioeconomic status is a significant determinant of access to technology. Lower-income individuals and communities may face financial barriers to acquiring digital devices and paying for internet services. As a result, they may be excluded from educational opportunities, online job markets, and digital government services, perpetuating cycles of inequality.

+ **Geographical factors:** Access to reliable internet infrastructure varies greatly between urban and rural areas. Rural communities often face challenges in terms of limited broadband availability and higher costs of connectivity due to a lack of competition among service providers. This geographical divide hampers rural residents' access to online education, healthcare services, and e-commerce opportunities.

+ **Age and generational factors:** Older individuals may encounter difficulties in adapting to new technologies and acquiring digital skills. This generation gap can further isolate seniors from social networks, online information, and digital services.   Similarly, children from economically disadvantaged families may lack access to technology outside of school, widening educational inequalities.

+ **Educational factors:** Digital literacy skills are crucial for success in the modern workforce.   However, disparities in educational resources and curriculum can hinder the development of these skills. Students attending under-resourced schools may lack access to technology training, putting them at a disadvantage when seeking employment or pursuing higher education.

The consequences of the digital divide are far-reaching and impact various aspects of individuals' lives. These include:

+ **Limited access to information:** Individuals without internet access or digital skills may struggle to access up-to-date information on important topics such as health, education, and employment opportunities. This lack of information can hinder their ability to make informed decisions and participate fully in society.

+ **Reduced opportunities:** The digital divide can restrict individuals' access to educational resources, online job opportunities, and e-commerce platforms. This limitation can exacerbate existing inequalities and perpetuate cycles of poverty and exclusion.

+ **Social and political marginalization:** Limited access to digital platforms can isolate individuals from social networks, political discourse, and civic engagement opportunities.   This exclusion can inhibit their ability to participate in democratic processes, share their perspectives, and advocate for their rights.

+ **Reinforcement of existing inequalities:** The digital divide often intersects with other forms of inequality, such as income disparities, gender bias, and racial discrimination. This intersectionality can amplify the disadvantages faced by marginalized individuals and communities, deepening existing social and economic inequities.

Ethical Considerations

The digital divide raises important ethical considerations that demand our attention and action. These include:

+ **Distributive justice:** Equal access to technology and the internet is a matter of distributive justice. A just society should strive to ensure that everyone has the necessary resources and opportunities to participate fully in the digital age. Efforts should be made to bridge the digital divide by providing equitable access to affordable technology and internet connectivity in underserved communities.

+ **Digital rights and human rights:** In today's digital society, access to the internet has become crucial for exercising fundamental human rights such as freedom of expression and access to information. Governments and organizations have a responsibility to protect and promote these digital rights, ensuring that they are not compromised by the digital divide.

+ **Digital literacy and education:** Digital literacy should be considered a basic skill necessary for a meaningful and productive life in the modern world. Efforts should be made to integrate digital literacy into educational curricula, provide training programs for individuals of all ages, and promote lifelong learning opportunities to bridge the skills divide.

+ **Collaboration and public-private partnerships:** Addressing the digital divide requires collaboration between governments, non-profit organizations, businesses, and communities. Public-private partnerships can contribute resources, expertise, and infrastructure to ensure that underserved populations have access to the necessary digital tools and services.

Addressing the Digital Divide

Bridging the digital divide is a complex and multifaceted challenge that requires a comprehensive approach. Some strategies for addressing the digital divide include:

+ **Improving infrastructure:** Governments should invest in expanding broadband access, particularly in underserved rural and remote areas. Innovative solutions such as satellite internet, community networks, and public Wi-Fi initiatives can help bridge the connectivity gap.

+ **Affordability and accessibility:** Policies should be implemented to ensure that internet services and digital devices are affordable and accessible to all. This can include subsidization programs, tax incentives, and regulatory measures to promote competition in the telecommunications market.

+ **Digital skills training:**   Educational institutions and community organizations can offer digital skills training programs to individuals of all ages. These programs should focus not only on technical skills but also on critical thinking, information literacy, and online safety.

+ **Community empowerment:**   Engaging local communities in the decision-making process and involving them in the planning and implementation of digital inclusion initiatives can help ensure their relevance and effectiveness.

+ **Public awareness and advocacy:** Raising public awareness about the digital divide and its consequences is crucial for mobilizing support and resources. Advocacy efforts can bring attention to the issue and encourage policymakers, businesses, and organizations to take action.

Conclusion

The digital divide is a significant ethical concern in our increasingly technology-driven society. It reinforces existing inequalities, limits opportunities, and hampers individuals' access to information and participation in the digital age. Addressing the digital divide requires a combination of infrastructural improvements, policy interventions, educational initiatives, and collaborative efforts. By bridging the digital divide, we can create a more equitable and inclusive society that ensures equal access to the benefits of technology for all.

Ethical Use of Social Media

In today's digital age, social media platforms such as Facebook, Instagram, Twitter, and LinkedIn have become an integral part of our lives. They allow us to connect with friends and family, share our thoughts and experiences, and stay updated with current events. However, the pervasive use of social media raises ethical concerns that need to be addressed.

Privacy and Data Protection

One of the primary ethical challenges related to social media is privacy and data protection. Social media platforms collect vast amounts of personal information from their users, including their demographics, preferences, and online behavior. This data can be used for targeted advertising, data analytics, and even sold to third parties without the users' explicit consent.

To address these concerns, it is essential for social media companies to be transparent about their data collection practices and provide users with clear and easily understandable privacy policies. Users should have complete control over the information they share and the ability to opt-out of data collection activities. Additionally, social media platforms should implement robust security measures to protect users' data from unauthorized access or data breaches.

Cyberbullying and Online Harassment

Another significant ethical issue in social media is cyberbullying and online harassment. Due to the relative anonymity provided by social media platforms, individuals may feel empowered to engage in harmful behavior, including cyberbullying, hate speech, and harassment.

Social media companies have a responsibility to create a safe online environment where users can express themselves without fear of harassment or abuse. This includes implementing mechanisms to report and address abusive content, adopting proactive algorithms to detect and remove harmful content, and promoting digital citizenship and empathy among users. Additionally, users should be aware of the potential consequences of their actions online and treat others with respect and dignity.

Fake News and Misinformation

The rapid spread of fake news and misinformation on social media has become a significant concern in recent years. Misleading information can have severe repercussions, impacting public opinions, elections, and even public health during a pandemic.

To combat the spread of fake news, social media platforms should develop and enforce policies that prioritize accurate and reliable content. This includes fact-checking mechanisms, warning labels on potentially false or misleading information, and algorithms that prioritize trustworthy sources. Users also play a crucial role in reducing the spread of misinformation by critically evaluating the information they encounter and sharing verified content.

Addiction and Mental Health Impact

The addictive nature of social media platforms has raised concerns about their impact on mental health. Excessive use of social media can lead to feelings of loneliness, low self-esteem, anxiety, and depression. Moreover, constant comparison to others' curated online lives can contribute to a distorted sense of reality and dissatisfaction.

It is essential for individuals to be mindful of their social media usage and practice digital well-being. Social media companies should also take responsibility for promoting healthy online habits by incorporating features that encourage users to take breaks, set time limits, and provide resources for mental health support.

Professional and Ethical Conduct

The use of social media also raises ethical considerations for professionals, including employees, educators, and healthcare providers. Professionals need to be mindful of their online presence and ensure that their behavior aligns with professional codes of conduct and ethical standards.

Employees should be cautious about sharing sensitive or confidential information related to their organizations and maintain a respectful and professional tone in their online interactions. Educators should be aware of the boundaries between their personal and professional lives on social media and consider the potential impact of their posts on students and colleagues. Healthcare providers, in particular, should maintain patient confidentiality and avoid posting content that may compromise the doctor-patient relationship or violate privacy regulations.

Promoting Ethical Use of Social Media

Promoting ethical use of social media requires a multi-stakeholder approach involving individuals, social media companies, educators, policymakers, and society at large. Here are some strategies to foster ethical behavior:

+ **Education and Awareness:** Raise awareness about the ethical implications of social media through educational campaigns, workshops, and discussions in schools, colleges, and workplaces.

+ **Digital Literacy:** Develop digital literacy programs that equip individuals with the skills to critically evaluate online content, identify misinformation, and use social media responsibly.

+ **User Empowerment:** Empower users to take control of their online privacy and data by providing them with easy-to-use privacy settings, clear information on data collection practices, and the ability to make informed choices.

- **Ethical Design:** Social media platforms should incorporate ethical considerations into their design and functionality, prioritizing user well-being, privacy, and responsible content sharing.

- **Collaboration with Experts:** Social media companies should collaborate with experts in areas such as psychology, ethics, and sociology to develop policies and features that address ethical concerns effectively.

By promoting ethical use of social media, we can harness the power of these platforms while mitigating the potential risks and negative consequences. It is essential for individuals, organizations, and society to work together to create a digital landscape that promotes respect, privacy, and responsible online behavior.

Conclusion

Social media has transformed the way we connect, communicate, and share information. However, it also brings a range of ethical challenges that need to be addressed. The ethical use of social media requires a collective effort from individuals, social media companies, educators, and policymakers to protect privacy, combat online harassment, and promote responsible digital citizenship.

As we navigate the evolving landscape of social media, it is important to reflect on the ethical implications of our actions and strive to create an online environment that respects privacy, fosters inclusivity, and promotes the well-being of all users. By embracing ethical practices, we can truly harness the potential of social media while minimizing its negative impact on individuals and society as a whole.

Remember, with great power comes great responsibility. Let us utilize social media ethically and responsibly, creating a digital world that reflects our values and promotes a positive impact on our lives and communities.

Ethical Practices in Healthcare

Ethical Principles in Healthcare

Informed Consent and Patient Autonomy

In the field of healthcare, one of the foundational principles is the concept of informed consent and patient autonomy. This principle recognizes and respects an individual's right to make decisions about their own healthcare, based on accurate and relevant information. In this section, we will explore the importance of informed consent, the elements that constitute informed consent, and the ethical considerations surrounding patient autonomy.

Importance of Informed Consent

Informed consent is a crucial aspect of ethical healthcare practices as it upholds the principle of respect for autonomy. It enables patients to actively participate in the decision-making process regarding their own healthcare, ensuring that their personal values, beliefs, and preferences are taken into consideration. Informed consent promotes patient empowerment and fosters a trusting and collaborative relationship between healthcare professionals and patients.

Elements of Informed Consent

To obtain informed consent, healthcare professionals must provide patients with relevant information in a clear and understandable manner. The following elements are essential components of informed consent:

1. Disclosure of Information: Healthcare professionals should provide patients with comprehensive information about the nature of their condition, proposed treatments or procedures, potential benefits and risks, and any

potential alternatives. This includes explaining the anticipated outcomes, potential side effects, potential complications, and the likelihood of success for the recommended course of action.

2. Capacity to Consent: Patients must have the mental capacity to understand the information provided and the ability to make decisions based on that information.   Healthcare professionals must assess the patient's decision-making capacity, particularly in cases where the patient may have cognitive impairments, mental health issues, or other factors that may affect their ability to provide informed consent.

3. Voluntariness: It is important to ensure that patients are not coerced or unduly influenced when providing consent. Patients should be given adequate time to consider the information provided and be able to freely express their decisions without external pressure.

4. Understanding: Patients should have a clear understanding of the information conveyed to them. Healthcare professionals should use plain language and avoid medical jargon. They should also ensure that patients have an opportunity to ask questions and seek clarification about any aspects of their healthcare.

Ethical Considerations

There are several ethical considerations surrounding informed consent and patient autonomy that healthcare professionals must be aware of:

1. Respect for Autonomy: Informed consent upholds the principle of autonomy, which recognizes an individual's right to self-determination and decision-making. Healthcare professionals should respect the decisions made by competent patients, even if they disagree with those decisions.

2. Beneficence and Non-Maleficence: Healthcare professionals have an ethical obligation to act in the best interests of their patients and avoid inflicting harm. Informed consent allows patients to make decisions that align with their personal values and minimize potential harm or negative outcomes.

3. Shared Decision Making: Informed consent promotes a collaborative approach to decision making, where healthcare professionals and patients work together to achieve the best possible outcomes. This process involves active communication, mutual respect, and careful consideration of the patient's preferences, values, and needs.

4. Vulnerable Populations: Certain patient populations, such as minors, individuals with cognitive impairments, or those with limited decision-making capacity, may require additional safeguards to ensure their rights are protected. In these cases, obtaining consent may involve involving legal guardians, family members, or authorized representatives.

Examples and Case Studies

To illustrate the importance of informed consent and patient autonomy, let's consider a few examples:

1. Example 1: A patient is diagnosed with a serious medical condition and is presented with several treatment options, each carrying distinct risks and benefits. The healthcare professional provides comprehensive information about each option, allowing the patient to make an informed decision based on their personal preferences and values.

2. Example 2: A healthcare professional explains the risks and benefits of a surgical procedure to a patient. The patient, however, expresses concerns about potential complications and decides to explore non-surgical alternatives. The healthcare professional respects the patient's decision, highlighting the importance of autonomy in the decision-making process.

3. Example 3: A parent refuses to have their child vaccinated based on personal beliefs. The healthcare professional engages in an open and non-judgmental dialogue with the parent, providing clear information about the benefits of vaccination and potential risks of not vaccinating. Despite the healthcare professional's recommendation, the final decision rests with the parent, respecting their autonomy as the legal guardian.

Resources

Here are some additional resources for further exploration of the topic:

- American Medical Association. (2016). *Opinion 2.1.1: Informed Consent*. Retrieved   from https://www.ama-assn.org/sites/ama-assn.org/files/corp/media-browser/public/ethics/informed-consent.pdf

- World Health Organization. (2017). *Standards of Informed Consent*. Retrieved   from https://www.who.int/ethics/topics/informed_consent/en/

• Beauchamp, T. L., & Childress, J. F. (2019). *Principles of Biomedical Ethics.* New York, NY: Oxford University Press.

Exercises

To practice your understanding of informed consent and patient autonomy, consider the following exercises:

1. Imagine you are a healthcare professional discussing a treatment option with a patient. How would you explain the potential risks and benefits of the treatment in a way that respects the patient's autonomy and ensures their understanding?

2. Research a case study involving a healthcare-related ethical dilemma related to informed consent. Analyze the situation, considering the principles of autonomy, beneficence, and non-maleficence. Reflect on the potential implications of different courses of action and propose a resolution based on ethical considerations.

Remember, informed consent and patient autonomy are key pillars of ethical healthcare practices, and understanding and applying these principles is essential for providing quality patient-centered care.

Beneficence and Non-maleficence in Medical Practice

In the field of healthcare, two fundamental ethical principles that guide the actions and decisions of healthcare professionals are beneficence and non-maleficence. These principles are rooted in the overall goal of promoting the well-being and welfare of patients while avoiding harm.

Beneficence

Beneficence refers to the principle of doing good for others and taking proactive steps to promote their welfare. In medical practice, beneficence means that healthcare professionals have an obligation to act in the best interests of their patients and to maximize the potential benefits of medical interventions.

The principle of beneficence encompasses several key aspects. First, it means providing competent and compassionate care to patients. This involves not only treating their illnesses or injuries but also addressing their physical, emotional, and psychological needs. Healthcare professionals must strive to alleviate suffering and enhance the quality of life for their patients.

Additionally, beneficence entails taking preventive measures to promote health and well-being. This includes advocating for preventive interventions, such as vaccinations and health screenings, and educating patients about healthy lifestyle choices. By emphasizing prevention, healthcare professionals can help patients avoid potential health problems and improve their overall outcomes.

Furthermore, beneficence requires healthcare professionals to prioritize the best interests of their patients when making clinical decisions. This involves considering the potential benefits and risks of different treatment options and selecting interventions that are most likely to optimize patient outcomes. It may also involve considering the preferences and values of patients, ensuring that their individual needs and circumstances are taken into account.

An example of the application of beneficence in medical practice can be seen in the treatment of a patient with a life-threatening condition. In this case, a healthcare professional may recommend a risky but potentially life-saving surgical procedure. The principle of beneficence would guide the decision-making process, as the healthcare professional would weigh the potential benefits of the surgery against the potential harm or risks involved. Ultimately, the goal is to make a choice that maximizes the chances of a positive outcome for the patient.

Non-maleficence

Non-maleficence, also known as the principle of "do no harm," is closely related to beneficence. It emphasizes the importance of avoiding actions or interventions that may cause harm to patients. While beneficence focuses on actively promoting well-being, non-maleficence highlights the need to prevent harm and minimize risks.

Non-maleficence includes both intentional and unintentional harm. Intentional harm refers to actions or decisions made with the intention of causing harm, such as a healthcare professional administering an inappropriate and potentially harmful medication. Unintentional harm, on the other hand, refers to harm caused inadvertently, such as a medical error resulting from a lack of communication or a misjudgment.

Healthcare professionals have a moral and ethical obligation to protect patients from harm and prioritize their safety. This involves taking appropriate precautions to prevent medical errors, ensuring proper training and competence, and adhering to evidence-based guidelines and best practices. Healthcare professionals must also maintain awareness of potential risks and complications associated with medical interventions and take steps to mitigate them.

In the context of non-maleficence, providing informed consent is vital. Patients have the right to be fully informed about the potential risks and benefits of treatment options, as well as any alternative options available. By providing comprehensive and accurate information, healthcare professionals enable patients to make informed decisions about their care. This ensures respect for the autonomy of patients while also upholding the principle of non-maleficence.

To illustrate the principle of non-maleficence, let's consider the case of prescribing medication to a patient. A healthcare professional must carefully assess the patient's medical history, allergies, and any potential drug interactions before prescribing medication. They must also be aware of the potential side effects and adverse reactions of the medication and weigh the benefit of treatment against the risk of harm. By exercising caution and considering the principle of non-maleficence, healthcare professionals can minimize the likelihood of harm to the patient.

In summary, the principles of beneficence and non-maleficence are fundamental in medical practice. They direct healthcare professionals to act in the best interests of their patients while minimizing the risk of harm. By balancing these principles, healthcare professionals can navigate the complexities of medical decision-making and provide patient-centered care that promotes well-being and respects individual autonomy.

Justice and Fair Allocation of Healthcare Resources

Justice is a fundamental ethical principle in healthcare that refers to the fair and equitable distribution of healthcare resources. It emphasizes the importance of ensuring that everyone has equal access to healthcare services, regardless of their socioeconomic status, age, gender, or any other characteristic.

In discussing justice and fair allocation of healthcare resources, it is crucial to consider the principles of distributive justice and egalitarianism. Distributive justice focuses on the fair distribution of healthcare resources based on need, while egalitarianism emphasizes the equal distribution of healthcare resources to all members of society.

One of the key challenges in achieving justice in healthcare is the limited availability of resources relative to the demand for healthcare services. Healthcare systems often face resource constraints, such as a shortage of healthcare professionals, limited hospital beds, and restricted budgets. It becomes necessary to establish a fair and efficient system for allocating these resources.

To address these challenges, various ethical frameworks and models have been proposed. One commonly used model is the Principalism approach, which considers the principles of beneficence, autonomy, non-maleficence, and justice in decision-making. In the context of justice, the focus is on ensuring equitable distribution of healthcare resources.

Several strategies can be employed to achieve justice in healthcare resource allocation. One approach is to prioritize resources based on medical need, urgency, and potential benefit. This can be done through triage systems that allocate resources to patients based on the severity of their conditions and the likelihood of improvement with treatment.

Another strategy is to adopt a needs-based approach, where resources are allocated based on the degree of need in the population. This approach takes into account factors such as disease burden, disability-adjusted life years (DALYs), and the impact on public health.

In addition to needs-based allocation, considerations of fairness and equity are crucial. It is important to ensure that vulnerable populations, such as low-income individuals, racial and ethnic minorities, and the uninsured, are not disproportionately disadvantaged in accessing healthcare resources. Efforts should be made to reduce healthcare disparities and address social determinants of health that contribute to inequities.

To guide decision-making in resource allocation, institutions may develop ethical guidelines and policies. These policies should be transparent, inclusive, and based on evidence-based practices. They should also involve input from stakeholders, including healthcare professionals, patients, community representatives, and ethicists.

It is worth noting that achieving justice in healthcare resource allocation is a complex and ongoing process. It requires continuous monitoring and evaluation to ensure that the principles of justice are upheld. Furthermore, societal values and priorities may evolve over time, necessitating periodic reassessment and adaptation of resource allocation strategies.

Example: Allocating COVID-19 Vaccines

The COVID-19 pandemic has highlighted the ethical challenges associated with healthcare resource allocation, particularly in the case of vaccine distribution. With limited vaccine supplies initially available, the question of who gets vaccinated first raised issues of justice and fairness.

In many countries, priority groups were identified based on factors such as age, occupation, and underlying health conditions. This approach aimed to prioritize those at higher risk of severe illness or death from COVID-19 and those in essential roles, such as healthcare workers and first responders.

However, even within priority groups, challenges arise in determining the order of vaccination. For instance, should older adults be prioritized over younger individuals with underlying health conditions? How do we ensure equitable access for marginalized communities who may face barriers to vaccination?

To address these challenges, ethical frameworks were employed to guide decision-making.   The principles of distributive justice, beneficence, and non-maleficence were considered. Vaccination strategies aimed to maximize overall health benefits, minimize harm, and ensure fairness to the greatest extent possible.

It is important to note that the allocation of COVID-19 vaccines continues to evolve as more supplies become available and new evidence emerges. Ongoing ethical considerations, public engagement, and transparency are crucial in ensuring that resource allocation decisions align with the principles of justice.

Resources

1. Daniels, N., & Sabin, J. E. (2008). Setting limits fairly: Can we learn to share medical resources? Oxford, United Kingdom: Oxford University Press.

2. Beauchamp, T. L., & Childress, J. F. (2009). Principles of biomedical ethics. Oxford, United Kingdom: Oxford University Press.

3. Danis, M., Clancy, C., Churchill, L., & Stoeckle, J. (2012).   Ethical dimensions of health policy. New York, NY: Oxford University Press.

Exercises

1. Discuss a situation where you believe that justice in healthcare resource allocation was not achieved. What factors contributed to this outcome, and what could have been done differently to promote fairness?

2. Research the concept of "medical tourism" and its ethical implications. How does the phenomenon of medical tourism raise questions about fairness and justice in healthcare resource allocation?

3. Imagine you are a member of an ethics committee tasked with developing a policy for allocating scarce organ transplants. What ethical considerations would you take into account, and how would you ensure justice in the distribution of organs?

4. Investigate a case study involving a healthcare system in a developing country. Analyze the challenges they face in achieving justice and fair allocation of healthcare resources. What solutions or strategies could be implemented to address these challenges?

5. Explore the concept of "prisoners' healthcare" and the ethical dilemmas it poses. How can justice be ensured in providing healthcare to incarcerated individuals while considering the needs of the broader population?

Remember, justice in healthcare resource allocation requires a delicate balance between fairness, efficiency, and ethical considerations. By understanding the principles and frameworks discussed in this section, we can strive to build equitable healthcare systems that serve the needs of all members of society.

Honesty and Truth-Telling with Patients

In healthcare, honesty and truth-telling are fundamental ethical principles that guide the interactions between healthcare professionals and patients. This section explores the importance of honesty and truth-telling in healthcare, the ethical considerations involved, and strategies for effective communication.

The Importance of Honesty

Honesty is the foundation of a trusting patient-physician relationship. When healthcare professionals are honest with their patients, it establishes transparency and promotes open communication. Patients have the right to receive accurate information about their health conditions, treatment options, prognosis, and potential risks and benefits.

Honesty also plays a crucial role in informed consent. Informed consent involves providing patients with all relevant information regarding their medical condition, proposed treatments, and potential risks and benefits. It allows patients to actively participate in decision-making and make choices that align with their values and preferences.

Furthermore, honesty is essential for fostering patient autonomy. By providing accurate information, healthcare professionals empower patients to make informed decisions about their own healthcare. Patients have the right to be involved in decisions that affect their well-being and have their preferences and values respected.

Ethical Considerations

Honesty and truth-telling in healthcare are not without ethical dilemmas and challenges. Several factors must be taken into account when deciding how and when to communicate difficult information.

One important consideration is the principle of beneficence, which involves promoting the well-being of patients. Balancing the duty to inform patients with the potential harm that the disclosure of certain information may cause is a complex ethical dilemma. For example, delivering a terminal diagnosis to a patient may have profound psychological and emotional effects. In such cases, healthcare professionals must navigate the delicate balance between honesty and the potential harm to the patient's well-being.

The principle of non-maleficence, which emphasizes "do no harm," also comes into play. Healthcare professionals must consider the potential harm that withholding or distorting information may cause to the patient. By not disclosing relevant information, patients may not have the opportunity to make decisions that align with their values and preferences.

Respecting patient confidentiality is another ethical consideration. While honesty is crucial, healthcare professionals must also adhere to strict privacy laws and regulations. Sharing sensitive information without the patient's consent can breach patient confidentiality and erode trust.

Strategies for Effective Communication

Effective communication is key to navigating the challenges of honesty and truth-telling in healthcare. Here are some strategies that healthcare professionals can employ to promote open and honest communication with their patients:

- **Establish a Therapeutic Relationship:** Building a trusting and empathetic relationship with patients creates a safe and supportive environment for open communication. Active listening, empathy, and understanding can help patients feel more comfortable discussing their concerns and asking questions.

- **Use Clear and Understandable Language:** Avoid complex medical jargon and explain information in a way that patients can comprehend. Breaking down complex concepts into simpler terms can help patients better understand their condition and treatment options.

- **Assess Patient Readiness:** Gauge the patient's readiness to receive information by assessing their emotional and psychological state. Some patients may prefer to receive information gradually, while others may want all the available information upfront. Respect their preferences and adjust the communication strategy accordingly.

- **Provide Emotional Support:** Communicate empathy and provide emotional support during difficult conversations. Acknowledge and validate patients' feelings, and offer resources such as counseling services or support groups if needed.

- **Offer Follow-up Opportunities:** Patients may need time to process information and may have additional questions later. Offer follow-up appointments or encourage patients to reach out if they have further queries or concerns.

Case Study: Delivering a Terminal Diagnosis

Consider the case of a 60-year-old patient, Mr. Smith, who has been experiencing persistent symptoms. After a series of investigations, the physician discovers that Mr. Smith has advanced metastatic cancer with a poor prognosis. The physician faces the challenge of delivering this terminal diagnosis to Mr. Smith while balancing the ethical considerations involved.

In this case, the physician should prioritize honesty and truth-telling while considering the potential harm to Mr. Smith's well-being. The physician may choose to deliver the diagnosis in a compassionate and supportive manner, offering emotional support and allowing Mr. Smith to express his feelings and ask questions. The physician should use clear and understandable language, avoiding medical jargon, and providing information gradually, according to Mr. Smith's readiness.

It is crucial to respect Mr. Smith's autonomy by involving him in the decision-making process. The physician should discuss the treatment options available, including potential benefits, risks, and alternatives. The physician can also explore Mr. Smith's goals, values, and preferences to offer personalized care that aligns with his wishes.

Following the delivery of the terminal diagnosis, the physician should provide ongoing support to Mr. Smith, including referrals to palliative care services and counseling resources. Regular follow-up appointments should be scheduled to address any new concerns or questions that may arise.

Conclusion

In healthcare, honesty and truth-telling are essential for building trust, respecting patient autonomy, and fostering effective communication. While there may be ethical dilemmas and challenges, healthcare professionals can employ strategies for honest and compassionate communication. By promoting transparency, empathy, and patient-centered care, healthcare professionals can uphold the ethical principles that underpin honesty and truth-telling in healthcare.

Confidentiality and Privacy in Healthcare

In the field of healthcare, maintaining confidentiality and privacy is of utmost importance. Patients must feel secure in sharing personal and sensitive information with healthcare providers, knowing that their information will be protected and kept confidential. This section will explore the principles and guidelines that govern confidentiality and privacy in healthcare, the challenges faced, and the strategies employed to ensure the security of patient information.

Principles of Confidentiality

Confidentiality is the duty of healthcare professionals to keep patient information private and ensure that it is not disclosed without proper authorization. This principle is rooted in the ethical concept of respect for autonomy and is also supported by legal and regulatory frameworks. Healthcare professionals must adhere to the following principles of confidentiality:

- **Trust:** Confidentiality is crucial to maintaining trust between patients and healthcare providers. Patients should feel comfortable disclosing personal information, knowing that it will not be shared without their consent.

- **Professional obligation:** Healthcare professionals have a professional and ethical duty to maintain the confidentiality of patient information. Breaching confidentiality can lead to legal and ethical consequences.

- **Legal requirements:** Many countries have laws and regulations in place to protect patient confidentiality. For example, in the United States, the Health Insurance Portability and Accountability Act (HIPAA) imposes strict guidelines on the privacy and security of patient health information.

Challenges to Confidentiality

Ensuring confidentiality in healthcare is not without its challenges. Some of the common challenges include:

- **Electronic health records (EHRs):** The implementation of electronic health records has increased the accessibility and sharing of patient information. While EHRs provide multiple benefits, such as improved coordination of care, they also pose privacy risks if not adequately protected against unauthorized access.

+ **Healthcare data breaches:** The healthcare industry is a prime target for cyberattacks due to the value of the personal and financial information it holds. Data breaches can compromise patient confidentiality, leading to identity theft and other serious consequences.

+ **Third-party access:** Healthcare providers often collaborate with third-party entities, such as insurance companies and research institutions. Ensuring that these entities maintain patient confidentiality can be challenging, especially when data sharing is necessary for the provision of care or research purposes.

+ **Stigma and discrimination:** Patients may fear disclosing sensitive health information due to concerns about stigma and discrimination. This fear can hinder open communication and lead to inadequate healthcare provision.

Strategies for Ensuring Confidentiality

To address the challenges to confidentiality, healthcare organizations employ various strategies to protect patient information:

+ **Secure information systems:** Healthcare organizations invest in robust cybersecurity measures to safeguard electronic health records and other sensitive data. This includes encryption, access controls, regular security assessments, and staff education on best practices.

+ **Policies and procedures:** Clear policies and procedures should be in place to guide healthcare professionals in maintaining confidentiality. These policies should outline the proper handling and disclosure of patient information and should be communicated effectively to all staff members.

+ **Training and education:** Healthcare professionals should receive ongoing training on confidentiality and privacy practices. This education should emphasize the ethical and legal obligations surrounding patient information and provide guidance on the proper use and disclosure of data.

+ **Informed consent:** Before sharing patient information, healthcare providers must obtain informed consent from the patient. This includes explaining the purpose and potential risks of disclosure, and allowing the patient to make an informed decision.

+ **Audit trails:** Implementing audit trails in electronic health record systems can help identify unauthorized access and monitor the activities of healthcare professionals.   This can act as a deterrent and aid in the investigation of potential breaches.

Case Study: Ensuring Confidentiality in Telemedicine

Telemedicine has gained popularity in recent years, allowing patients to receive healthcare services remotely.   However, it presents unique challenges in maintaining confidentiality.   Let's consider the case of Jane, a patient seeking a telemedicine consultation for a sensitive health condition.

To ensure confidentiality in this scenario, healthcare providers can implement the following measures:

+ **Secure communication channels:**   Healthcare providers should use encrypted communication platforms to ensure that patient information remains confidential during telemedicine consultations.

+ **Patient authentication:** Verifying the identity of the patient before the telemedicine consultation ensures that the information is shared with the intended recipient only.

+ **Virtual waiting rooms:**   Implementing virtual waiting rooms allows healthcare providers to admit patients one by one, minimizing the risk of accidental disclosure of patient information to others.

+ **Informed consent for telemedicine:** Providing patients with information about the potential risks and limitations of telemedicine, along with obtaining their informed consent, ensures that they make an informed decision about utilizing telemedicine services.

By employing these strategies, healthcare providers can mitigate the risks associated with telemedicine and maintain patient confidentiality even in remote healthcare settings.

Conclusion

Confidentiality and privacy are essential in healthcare to build trust and ensure the well-being of patients. Healthcare professionals must adhere to the principles of confidentiality, navigate the challenges associated with maintaining privacy, and implement strategies to protect patient information. With the increasing use of technology in healthcare, it is crucial to stay vigilant and adapt to evolving privacy concerns to ensure the highest standards of confidentiality in healthcare practices.

Summary

* Confidentiality is a fundamental principle in healthcare that ensures patient information remains private and is not disclosed without proper authorization.

* Maintaining patient confidentiality can be challenging due to factors such as electronic health records, data breaches, third-party access, and concerns regarding stigma and discrimination.

* Strategies for ensuring confidentiality in healthcare include secure information systems, clear policies and procedures, training and education, informed consent, and audit trails.

* Telemedicine presents unique challenges to maintaining confidentiality, and healthcare providers can implement measures such as secure communication channels, patient authentication, virtual waiting rooms, and obtaining informed consent to ensure privacy during telemedicine consultations.

Practice Exercises

1. In the context of healthcare, explain why confidentiality is important for maintaining trust between patients and healthcare providers.

2. Discuss two challenges to confidentiality in the digital age of healthcare.

3. Describe two strategies that healthcare organizations can employ to protect patient information from unauthorized access.

4. Imagine you are a healthcare professional conducting a telemedicine consultation. Outline three measures you would implement to ensure the confidentiality of the patient's information.

Additional Resources

1. Article: Lee, L. (2018). Confidentiality in healthcare: A review of information privacy laws in the digital age. Journal of the American Medical Informatics Association, 25(10), 1416-1422.

2. Book: Medical Ethics: Principles, Persons, and Perspectives (Chapter 4 - Confidentiality and Privacy) by Michael Boylan.

3. Website: U.S. Department of Health and Human Services - Office for Civil Rights. (https://www.hhs.gov/hipaa/index.html)

4.   Video: Privacy   and   Security   of   Electronic   Health   Records (https://youtu.be/QxO8VcU0K6Q)

Trick to Remember

Confidentiality in healthcare can be remembered by the acronym "CAPS": Protecting patient information requires Establishing Clear policies and procedures, Ensuring secure information systems, Training healthcare professionals, and Obtaining informed consent and patient authentication.   With these CAPS, confidentiality in healthcare can be effectively maintained.

Ethical Issues in Medical Research

Informed Consent and Voluntary Participation

In the field of healthcare, ethical principles play a crucial role in ensuring the well-being and autonomy of patients. One fundamental principle is informed consent, which requires healthcare professionals to provide relevant information to patients so they can make autonomous decisions about their own healthcare.

Background

Informed consent is based on the belief that individuals have the right to be informed about their medical condition, treatment options, and potential risks and benefits. It ensures that patients have the necessary information to make choices that align with their values, preferences, and goals. Informed consent also promotes transparency, trust, and shared decision-making between patients and healthcare providers.

Principles of Informed Consent

There are several key principles that form the foundation of informed consent:

1. **Voluntary Participation:** Patients should have the right to voluntarily participate, or decline to participate, in any medical treatment or research study. Coercion, manipulation, or undue influence should never be used to obtain consent.

2. **Disclosure of Information:** Healthcare providers must disclose all relevant information about the medical condition, proposed treatment, and available alternatives. This includes the nature and purpose of the treatment, potential risks and benefits, likelihood of success, and any potential alternatives.

3. **Understanding:** Patients must have a clear understanding of the information provided to them. Healthcare providers should use clear and understandable language, considering the patient's individual level of health literacy and providing additional support if necessary.

4. **Capacity to Consent:** Patients must have the cognitive ability to comprehend the information provided, process it, and make an informed decision. If a patient lacks decision-making capacity, a designated surrogate decision-maker should be involved.

5. **Voluntary Agreement:** Informed consent requires the patient's voluntary agreement to proceed with the proposed treatment or research study. This agreement should be based on the patient's own free will and not influenced by external pressures.

Applications in Medical Research

Informed consent is particularly important when conducting medical research involving human participants. Research studies must adhere to strict ethical guidelines to protect participants' rights and welfare. Key considerations in this context include:

1. **Institutional Review Boards (IRBs):** Research protocols involving human participants must undergo thorough ethical review by an IRB. The IRB ensures that the study design respects participant autonomy, minimizes risks, and upholds ethical standards.

2. **Informed Consent Process:** During the informed consent process, researchers must provide potential participants with understandable information about the purpose, procedures, potential risks and benefits, and voluntary nature of the study. This process should allow participants ample time to ask questions and make an informed decision about their participation.

3. **Vulnerable Populations:** Special considerations apply when obtaining informed consent from vulnerable populations, such as minors, individuals

with cognitive impairments, or those with limited decision-making capacity. In such cases, additional safeguards may be required to protect participants' rights and well-being.

4. **Ongoing Consent**: Informed consent is not a one-time event. Researchers should maintain open lines of communication with participants throughout the study and provide opportunities for participants to withdraw their consent at any time without consequence.

5. **Data Privacy and Confidentiality**: Researchers must protect the privacy and confidentiality of participants' data by following relevant data protection regulations and obtaining separate consent for data collection, sharing, and use.

Real-World Example: Clinical Trials

Clinical trials are essential for advancing medical knowledge and improving patient care. Informed consent is crucial in this context, as participants need to understand the potential risks and benefits before deciding to enroll. Let's consider a real-world example:

A pharmaceutical company is conducting a clinical trial to test the efficacy and safety of a new medication for the treatment of a rare disease. During the informed consent process, the company ensures that potential participants have access to all necessary information. This includes details about the purpose of the trial, potential risks and benefits, procedures involved, and alternative treatment options. Participants are given the opportunity to ask questions, consult with their healthcare team, and make an informed decision about their participation. They also have the right to withdraw their consent at any time during the trial without facing any repercussions.

To protect participant rights, an independent ethics committee reviews the study protocol and ensures that it meets ethical standards. The committee evaluates whether the potential benefits of the trial outweigh the potential risks and ensures that the informed consent process is thorough and transparent.

Tricks and Caveats

Obtaining informed consent can be challenging, especially in situations where patients may be vulnerable or have limited understanding of their medical condition. Here are some tricks and caveats to keep in mind:

+ Use culturally sensitive and appropriate communication techniques to ensure understanding across diverse populations.

+ Tailor the informed consent process to the individual's level of health literacy and cognitive abilities.

+ Ensure that the informed consent document is written in clear, concise, and non-technical language.

+ Document the informed consent process thoroughly, including details of discussions, questions asked, and any additional information provided.

+ Regularly re-evaluate participants' understanding and willingness to continue participating in research studies.

+ Continuously educate healthcare providers and researchers about ethical principles, informed consent, and the latest regulatory requirements.

Exercises

To test your understanding of informed consent and voluntary participation, consider the following scenarios and answer the questions that follow:

1. A patient with a life-threatening illness is considering participating in an experimental treatment. What information should the healthcare provider disclose during the informed consent process?

2. What are some potential challenges when obtaining informed consent from individuals with cognitive impairments?

3. Can informed consent be waived in certain research studies? If so, under what circumstances?

4. How can researchers ensure ongoing consent and respect participants' autonomy throughout the duration of a research study?

Resources

For further reading on informed consent and voluntary participation, the following resources are recommended:

• American Medical Association. (2016). *Code of Medical Ethics: Informed Consent*. Retrieved from https://www.ama-assn.org/sites/ama-assn.org/files/corp/media-browser/code-of-medical-ethics-chapter-2.pdf

• National Commission for the Protection of Human Subjects of Biomedical and Behavioral Research. (1978). *The Belmont Report: Ethical Principles and Guidelines for the Protection of Human Subjects of Research*. Retrieved from https://www.hhs.gov/ohrp/regulations-and-policy/belmont-report/index.html

• World Medical Association. (2013). *WMA Declaration of Helsinki - Ethical Principles for Medical Research Involving Human Subjects*. Retrieved from https://www.wma.net/policies-post/wma-declaration-of-helsinki-ethical-principles-for-medical-

Conclusion

Informed consent and voluntary participation are fundamental ethical principles that ensure patient autonomy, transparency, and shared decision-making in healthcare and medical research. By respecting these principles, healthcare providers and researchers can empower patients to make informed choices about their own care and protect their rights and well-being.

Ethical Guidelines and Institutional Review Boards

In conducting medical research, it is imperative to adhere to ethical guidelines and obtain approval from Institutional Review Boards (IRBs). These guidelines and boards ensure that research involving human subjects is conducted in an ethical and responsible manner. In this section, we will explore the importance of ethical guidelines and the role of IRBs in protecting the rights and welfare of research participants.

The Importance of Ethical Guidelines

Ethical guidelines provide a framework for researchers to conduct their studies in a manner that upholds the principles of beneficence, respect for autonomy, and justice. These guidelines serve as a set of moral principles that guide researchers in making decisions that prioritize the well-being of human subjects. By following ethical guidelines, researchers can ensure that their studies are conducted in a way that is fair, respectful, and beneficial to the participants.

Ethical guidelines also provide protection for vulnerable populations, such as children, prisoners, and individuals with cognitive impairments, who may be at higher risk of harm or exploitation in research settings. These guidelines help to safeguard their rights and ensure that their participation in research is informed, voluntary, and based on their best interests.

Furthermore, adherence to ethical guidelines enhances the credibility and validity of research findings. The use of rigorous ethical standards ensures that the data collected is reliable and can be trusted by the scientific community and the broader public.

Institutional Review Boards (IRBs)

Institutional Review Boards play a crucial role in the oversight and review of research involving human subjects. IRBs are independent committees composed of researchers, ethicists, legal experts, and community representatives. Their primary purpose is to protect the rights and welfare of research participants by reviewing and approving proposed research studies.

Composition and Operation of IRBs: IRBs typically consist of a diverse group of individuals with expertise in various disciplines. This composition ensures a comprehensive and multidisciplinary approach to the review process. IRBs operate according to specific regulations and guidelines set forth by national and international bodies, such as the U.S. Department of Health and Human Services and the World Health Organization.

IRB Review Process: When researchers plan to conduct a study involving human subjects, they must submit a detailed research protocol to the IRB for review. The protocol outlines the study's purpose, methodology, potential risks and benefits, and safeguards to protect the participants' rights and welfare.

The IRB carefully reviews the protocol to ensure that it meets ethical standards and complies with relevant regulations. They assess the study's scientific validity, the adequacy of informed consent procedures, the likelihood of potential risks, and the balance between potential benefits and harms. If the IRB determines that the study meets ethical standards, they provide approval for the research to proceed.

Continuing Review and Monitoring: The IRB's responsibilities do not end with initial approval. They conduct periodic reviews of ongoing research to ensure ongoing compliance with ethical guidelines. They monitor the progress of the study, assess any changes made to the protocol, and evaluate reports of adverse events or unanticipated problems.

Benefits of IRB Review: The IRB review process offers several benefits. Firstly, it provides an independent assessment of the ethical aspects of the research, ensuring that potential risks are minimized, and participants' rights are respected. Secondly, it contributes to the overall ethical culture in research institutions by promoting accountability and transparency. Additionally, the approval from the IRB lends credibility to the research, making it more likely to receive funding and support from stakeholders.

Ethical Guidelines in Practice

Compliance with ethical guidelines requires researchers to contribute to the protection of human subjects' rights and welfare. Some key considerations for researchers include:

Informed Consent: Researchers must obtain informed consent from participants, ensuring that they fully understand the purpose, procedures, risks, and benefits of the study. Informed consent should be voluntary, based on accurate and understandable information, and obtained without coercion.

Confidentiality and Privacy: Researchers have an ethical obligation to protect the confidentiality and privacy of research participants. They must implement appropriate measures to safeguard the confidentiality of participants' data and ensure its secure storage, usage, and disposal.

Risk-Benefit Assessment: Researchers must carefully evaluate potential risks and benefits of the study. The benefits should outweigh the risks, and steps should be taken to minimize and manage any potential harms to participants.

Data Sharing and Transparency: Researchers should consider making their research data openly available to promote transparency, scientific advancement, and replication of findings. However, they must balance this with the need to protect participants' privacy and confidentiality.

Ethics Training and Education: Researchers should receive proper training in research ethics to ensure they have the knowledge and skills to conduct studies in an ethical manner. Research institutions should provide ongoing education and support to promote ethical conduct.

Engagement with Research Participants: Researchers should engage in respectful, open, and honest communication with participants. They should maintain a supportive and collaborative relationship throughout the research process and ensure they address any concerns or questions raised by participants.

Case Study: Ethical Guidelines in a Clinical Trial

Consider a case study involving a clinical trial for a new drug to treat a rare genetic disorder. The researchers designing the trial need to obtain approval from the IRB before commencing the study.

In their research protocol, the researchers outline the purpose of the study, the potential risks and benefits for participants, and the informed consent process. They describe the methodology, including the random assignment of participants to treatment and control groups, as well as the monitoring plan for adverse events.

The IRB reviews the protocol and identifies several ethical considerations. They assess whether the potential risks to participants are justified by the potential benefits of the drug. They also ensure that the informed consent process is robust, providing participants with all necessary information to make an informed decision about their participation.

Additionally, the IRB examines the study's inclusion and exclusion criteria to ensure they are fair and do not discriminate against certain groups. They consider the overall balance between scientific validity, ethical principles, and social value in determining whether to grant approval.

Through this case study, we can see how ethical guidelines and the oversight of IRBs play a critical role in ensuring the ethical conduct of research involving human subjects. By upholding these principles, researchers can contribute to the advancement of knowledge while protecting the rights and welfare of participants.

Conclusion

Ethical guidelines and Institutional Review Boards are fundamental to the responsible conduct of research involving human subjects. By adhering to ethical principles and seeking the approval of IRBs, researchers can ensure that their studies prioritize the welfare of participants, uphold scientific integrity, and contribute to the overall ethical culture of research institutions. The rigorous application of these guidelines helps to safeguard the rights and dignity of individuals involved in medical research, ultimately leading to improved healthcare practices and outcomes.

Animal Research and Ethical Considerations

Animal research has long been a controversial topic with ethical considerations at its core. While it has contributed significantly to advancements in medicine and understanding of biological processes, it raises questions about the treatment of animals and the morality of using them for scientific purposes. In this section, we will explore the ethical considerations surrounding animal research, including the principles, regulations, and alternative approaches.

Principles of Ethical Research

Ethical principles provide a framework for conducting research with animals. The three guiding principles in animal research ethics are:

1. **Replacement:** The principle of replacement emphasizes the use of alternative methods that do not involve animals whenever possible. This includes the use of computer simulations, in vitro testing, and non-animal models.

2. **Reduction:** The principle of reduction aims to minimize the number of animals used in research. Researchers should employ statistical techniques and experimental designs that allow for valid conclusions with fewer animals.

3. **Refinement:** The principle of refinement focuses on refining procedures to minimize pain, suffering, and distress experienced by animals. This includes the use of anesthesia and analgesia during procedures, as well as providing appropriate housing and enrichment for the animals.

These principles, commonly known as the "Three Rs," serve as a basis for ethical decision-making in animal research.

Regulations and Oversight

To ensure the ethical treatment of animals in research, governments and scientific institutions have developed regulations and oversight mechanisms. These regulations vary across countries but generally address areas such as:

+ Licensing and permit requirements for conducting animal research.

+ Standards for animal care and housing conditions.

+ Training and qualification of researchers and technicians involved in animal research.

+ Ethical review processes, including the establishment of Animal Research Ethics Committees (ARECs) or Institutional Animal Care and Use Committees (IACUCs).

Additionally, researchers must comply with specific guidelines for different species and types of research. For example, in the United States, the Guide for the Care and Use of Laboratory Animals provides comprehensive guidelines for the care and use of animals in research.

Justification for Animal Research

While ethical concerns are central to the debate on animal research, proponents argue that the benefits derived from such studies justify their use. Animal research has led to significant advancements in medicine, including the development of vaccines, treatments for diseases, and surgical techniques. For example, studies using animals have been instrumental in the development of insulin for diabetes treatment and the discovery of new cancer therapies.

Animal models also play a crucial role in understanding the basic biological processes that underpin human health. They provide insights into disease mechanisms, genetic disorders, and the effects of drugs or environmental factors. Animal research is often a stepping stone towards further investigations in clinical trials or studies involving human subjects.

Alternative Approaches

In recent years, there has been a growing movement towards the development and acceptance of alternative approaches to animal research. These alternatives aim to replace, reduce, or refine the use of animals in scientific studies. Some notable alternatives include:

- **In vitro** models: These involve studying cells, tissues, or organs in a controlled laboratory setting. Cell cultures, organoids, and human tissue models can provide valuable data without the need for animal experimentation.

- **Computer simulations and modeling**: Sophisticated computational models can simulate biological processes, drug interactions, and disease progression, reducing the reliance on animal testing.

- **Microdosing**: This technique involves administering small doses of drugs to human subjects to study their pharmacokinetics and pharmacodynamics. Microdosing allows researchers to gather initial safety and efficacy data in humans without extensive animal testing.

- **Data sharing and collaboration**: Increasing the accessibility of research data can reduce the need for duplicative studies and the use of additional animals. Sharing data allows scientists to build upon existing knowledge and make more informed decisions.

While the development and implementation of alternative approaches are promising, they are not without their limitations. Further research and investment are needed to refine and validate these methods to ensure their reliability and reproducibility.

Case Study: Animal Research in Pharmaceutical Testing

To illustrate the ethical considerations involved in animal research, let's consider a case study on the use of animals in pharmaceutical testing. Imagine a pharmaceutical company developing a new drug for a life-threatening disease. In the preclinical stage, the drug must undergo testing for safety and efficacy before proceeding to human trials.

Ethical considerations arise at various stages of this process. Researchers would need to ensure that the study is designed to minimize the number of animals used (reduction) and that the animals are housed and cared for in a manner that minimizes their pain and distress (refinement). This may involve providing appropriate anesthesia during procedures and enriching their environment to promote their well-being.

Additionally, researchers must justify the need for animal testing and consider alternatives that could replace the use of animals or reduce the number required. This may involve utilizing existing knowledge from previous studies, conducting in vitro testing, or leveraging computer simulations.

It is also important to consider the ethical implications of the potential benefits of the drug. If the new drug shows promise in animal studies, it could potentially save lives or improve the quality of life for patients. However, these potential benefits must be weighed against the ethical concerns regarding animal welfare and the validity of extrapolating the results to humans.

Overall, the case study highlights the complex decision-making process researchers face when conducting animal research and underscores the need for ethical considerations and adherence to guiding principles.

Conclusion

Animal research remains a complex and controversial topic, with ethical considerations at the forefront of discussions. The principles of replacement, reduction, and refinement provide a foundation for conducting research with animals in an ethical and responsible manner. Regulations and oversight mechanisms ensure compliance and accountability.

While animal research has undeniably contributed to advances in medicine, the development and acceptance of alternative approaches are gaining momentum.

These alternatives aim to replace, reduce, or refine the use of animals in research, but further research and validation are necessary.

As we navigate the ethical considerations surrounding animal research, it is essential to engage in open dialogue, consider the potential benefits and harms, and explore alternatives that align with scientific progress and respect for animal welfare.

Gene Editing and Human Genetic Engineering

Gene editing and human genetic engineering have emerged as powerful tools in the field of biomedical research and healthcare. These technologies allow scientists to modify the genetic material of organisms, including humans, with a precision and efficiency that was previously unimaginable. In this section, we will explore the ethical considerations associated with gene editing and human genetic engineering.

Background

Gene editing refers to the process of introducing intentional changes to an organism's DNA sequence. This can be achieved using different techniques, with the most prominent one being Clustered Regularly Interspaced Short Palindromic Repeats (CRISPR) and CRISPR-associated protein 9 (CRISPR-Cas9) system. CRISPR-Cas9 allows scientists to target and modify specific genes in a relatively simple and cost-effective manner.

Human genetic engineering, on the other hand, involves the intentional modification of the genetic makeup of human beings. This can be done using various techniques, including gene editing, to alter or introduce specific traits or characteristics in individuals.

Principles and Ethical Considerations

The ethical considerations surrounding gene editing and human genetic engineering stem from various principles and concerns. These include:

- **Autonomy:** The principle of autonomy recognizes the right of individuals to make informed decisions about their own genetic makeup. It raises questions about the extent to which individuals should have control over their genetic traits and whether they have the right to modify their own genetic material.

- **Beneficence and Non-maleficence:** The principle of beneficence emphasizes the promotion of well-being and the prevention of harm. In the context of gene editing and human genetic engineering, the potential benefits include the treatment and prevention of genetic disorders and diseases. However, there are concerns regarding the unintended consequences and risks associated with gene editing, such as off-target mutations or the creation of genetic disparities.

+ **Justice:** The principle of justice calls for fairness and equity in the distribution of resources and access to healthcare. It raises concerns about the potential for gene editing and human genetic engineering to exacerbate existing social inequalities, as access to these technologies may be limited to certain individuals or groups.

+ **Privacy and Confidentiality:** The issue of privacy and confidentiality is paramount when it comes to genetic information. Gene editing and human genetic engineering involve the collection and storage of personal genetic data, raising concerns about the protection of this information and the potential for discrimination or misuse.

Ethical Challenges

Gene editing and human genetic engineering present several ethical challenges that need to be carefully addressed:

1. **Germline Gene Editing:** One of the most controversial areas in gene editing is the modification of germline cells, including embryos, sperm, and eggs, which can be passed on to future generations. The use of germline gene editing raises ethical questions around the potential long-term effects of genetic modifications and the implications for future generations.

2. **Enhancement vs. Therapy:** Differentiating between gene editing for therapeutic purposes (treating diseases) and gene editing for enhancement purposes (improving traits beyond what is considered normal) is a critical ethical challenge. Determining what constitutes a legitimate therapeutic intervention versus an enhancement intervention is complex and subject to societal and cultural norms.

3. **Informed Consent:** Ensuring informed consent from individuals undergoing gene editing or genetic engineering procedures is crucial. This includes providing comprehensive information regarding the risks, benefits, and potential long-term implications of the procedures. Additionally, obtaining informed consent raises questions about the capacity of individuals to fully understand the complexities of genetic modifications.

4. **Equitable Access:** The availability and affordability of gene editing technologies are important ethical considerations. There is a potential risk of creating genetic disparities between individuals or groups who have access to these technologies and those who do not. Ensuring equitable access becomes a key ethical challenge to address.

5. **Unintended Consequences:** Gene editing techniques, although precise, can still result in unintended consequences. Off-target mutations and potential unforeseen genetic repercussions may arise from gene editing procedures. The ethical challenge lies in minimizing the risks and uncertainties associated with these unintended consequences.

Ethical Frameworks and Guidelines

To navigate the ethical challenges in gene editing and human genetic engineering, various frameworks and guidelines have been proposed:

- **International Consensus:** International bodies, such as the World Health Organization (WHO) and the National Academies of Sciences, Engineering, and Medicine, have established guidelines and recommendations for the responsible use of gene editing technologies in humans. These documents emphasize the importance of considering ethical, legal, and social implications and encourage international collaboration.

- **Public Deliberation:** Engaging the public in discussions about gene editing and human genetic engineering is crucial for ensuring transparency and democratic decision-making. Public deliberation processes allow for diverse perspectives to be considered and foster a sense of ownership and responsibility.

- **Regulatory Oversight:** Implementing robust regulatory frameworks can help ensure the ethical and responsible use of gene editing technologies. These frameworks should include mechanisms for transparent review, monitoring, and accountability.

- **Professional Guidelines:** Professional societies and organizations play a pivotal role in establishing guidelines and standards of practice for gene editing and human genetic engineering. Ethical guidelines should offer clear principles and recommendations to guide healthcare professionals and scientists in their decision-making processes.

Case Study: CRISPR Babies

One notable case that brought gene editing into the ethical spotlight is the controversy surrounding the birth of twin girls in China whose genomes had been edited using CRISPR-Cas9 technology. The announcement of these "CRISPR babies" sparked widespread ethical concerns and condemnation from the scientific community due to the lack of transparency, inadequate ethical review, and the fact that the genetic modifications were made for non-therapeutic purposes.

This case study highlights the urgent need for clear ethical guidelines and responsible oversight to prevent unethical and non-consensual use of gene editing technologies.

Conclusion

Gene editing and human genetic engineering hold immense promise for advancing medical treatments and improving human lives. However, the ethical considerations surrounding these technologies are complex and multifaceted. Balancing the principles of autonomy, beneficence, justice, and privacy is crucial in ensuring the responsible and ethical application of gene editing and human genetic engineering.

Addressing the ethical challenges through informed consent, equitable access, regulatory oversight, and public deliberation is essential to harness the potential benefits of these technologies while minimizing their risks and unintended consequences. Ultimately, a robust ethical framework should guide the development and application of gene editing and human genetic engineering to ensure they align with societal values and ethical principles.

Data Sharing and Open Science in Research

Data sharing has become an essential practice in research, promoting transparency, collaboration, and the advancement of scientific knowledge. Open science initiatives aim to make research more accessible, reproducible, and impactful. In this section, we will explore the benefits of data sharing and the challenges it poses, as well as the principles and practices of open science.

The Importance of Data Sharing

In the traditional research model, data is often kept private or limited to a small group of researchers. However, this approach has several limitations. First, it hinders reproducibility, as other scientists are unable to independently verify and build upon previous findings. Second, it restricts the potential for collaboration, preventing researchers from pooling their resources and expertise to address complex scientific questions. Finally, it may lead to duplication of efforts and wasted resources, as researchers unknowingly repeat experiments and generate redundant data.

By sharing data, researchers can overcome these limitations and accelerate the pace of scientific discovery. Data sharing allows for the replication and validation of research findings, ensuring the robustness and reliability of scientific knowledge. It also enables researchers to conduct meta-analyses and systematic reviews, synthesizing data from multiple studies to generate new insights. Furthermore, data sharing fosters collaboration, facilitating interdisciplinary research and the integration of diverse perspectives. Finally, it promotes transparency and accountability in scientific research, allowing for scrutiny and peer review.

Challenges and Ethical Considerations

While data sharing offers numerous benefits, it also presents challenges and ethical considerations that must be addressed. One of the main challenges is ensuring the privacy and confidentiality of research participants. Researchers must take measures to anonymize or de-identify data, minimizing the risk of re-identification and protecting the privacy of individuals.

Another challenge is the potential for misuse or misinterpretation of shared data. It is crucial for researchers to provide clear documentation and metadata, enabling others to understand the context and limitations of the data. Additionally, guidelines for appropriate data usage and citation should be established to ensure proper attribution and recognition of the original researchers.

Equitable data sharing is also an ethical consideration. Researchers should strive to promote inclusivity and ensure that data from diverse populations and underrepresented groups are shared. This not only avoids biases in scientific knowledge but also addresses concerns of social justice and equity.

Principles of Open Science

Open science encompasses a set of principles and practices that promote transparency, reproducibility, and collaboration in scientific research. These principles can guide researchers in implementing data sharing and open science initiatives effectively.

1. Open Access: Researchers should make their publications and research outputs freely available to the public, removing barriers to access and enabling widespread dissemination.

2. Data Sharing: Researchers should share their data, ensuring it is well-documented, properly anonymized, and accessible to other researchers, unless there are valid reasons not to do so (e.g., legal or ethical constraints).

3. Reproducibility: Researchers should provide detailed documentation of their methods, procedures, and analysis to enable others to replicate and validate their findings.

4. Collaboration: Researchers should actively seek opportunities for collaboration, fostering interdisciplinary and international collaborations to tackle complex scientific questions.

5. Responsible Conduct: Researchers should adhere to ethical guidelines and professional conduct, maintaining integrity, honesty, and accountability in their research practices.

Examples and Resources

Several initiatives and platforms support data sharing and open science in research. The Open Science Framework (OSF), for example, provides a collaborative platform for researchers to share their research outputs, manage projects, and work together. Other repositories, such as Figshare and Zenodo, allow researchers to share datasets, code, and other research materials.

Discipline-specific databases and repositories also exist, catering to the needs of various research domains. Examples include GenBank for genetic sequences, PANGEA for earth and environmental science data, and PhysioNet for physiological signal data.

Many funding agencies and institutions also endorse open science practices and require researchers to share their data as part of their research outputs. Examples include the National Institutes of Health (NIH), the European Commission, and the Wellcome Trust.

Researchers should familiarize themselves with the policies and platforms available in their respective disciplines to implement data sharing and open science practices effectively.

Conclusion

Data sharing and open science in research hold immense potential for advancing scientific knowledge, fostering collaboration, and addressing complex societal challenges. By embracing these practices, researchers can contribute to the creation of a more transparent, inclusive, and impactful scientific ecosystem. However, it is crucial to address the challenges and ethical considerations associated with data sharing to ensure the privacy, confidentiality, and responsible use of shared data. Through the principles of open science and the support of collaborative platforms and initiatives, researchers can collectively drive the scientific enterprise forward.

Ethics in End-of-Life Care

Euthanasia and Assisted Suicide

In the field of healthcare ethics, one of the most controversial and emotionally charged topics is euthanasia and assisted suicide. These practices involve intentionally ending a patient's life to relieve suffering and provide a peaceful death. The ethical considerations surrounding euthanasia and assisted suicide are complex and involve multiple perspectives, principles, and legal frameworks.

The Principle of Autonomy

The principle of autonomy, which emphasizes an individual's right to make decisions about their own life and body, plays a central role in the debate on euthanasia and assisted suicide. Proponents argue that individuals who are suffering from incurable diseases or experiencing unbearable pain should have the right to decide when and how to end their lives. They believe that allowing euthanasia and assisted suicide respects the autonomy and dignity of individuals, enabling them to exercise control over their own destinies.

On the other hand, opponents argue that the principle of autonomy must be balanced against other ethical considerations, such as the sanctity of life and the potential for abuse and harm. They believe that legalizing euthanasia and assisted suicide may undermine the value society places on preserving life and may open the door to unethical practices, such as involuntary euthanasia or the premature termination of lives deemed unworthy.

Beneficence and Non-maleficence

The ethical principles of beneficence and non-maleficence, which emphasize the duty to do good and avoid harm, also come into play in the context of euthanasia and assisted suicide. Proponents argue that these practices can alleviate suffering, provide relief, and promote the well-being of terminally ill patients who have no reasonable prospect of recovery. They contend that providing an option for a peaceful death is a compassionate and ethically appropriate response to the suffering of these individuals.

Opponents, however, raise concerns about the potential for harm associated with euthanasia and assisted suicide. They argue that doctors, as caregivers, have a duty to protect and preserve life and that intentionally causing death contradicts this fundamental obligation. They also contend that the availability of euthanasia and assisted suicide may undermine efforts to improve palliative care and other forms of end-of-life support, which focus on providing comfort and enhancing quality of life in the final stages.

Legal and Ethical Frameworks

The laws and ethical frameworks governing euthanasia and assisted suicide vary significantly across different countries and jurisdictions. Some countries, such as the Netherlands, Belgium, and Canada, have legalized euthanasia and assisted suicide under specific circumstances, with strict regulations and safeguards in place. In these jurisdictions, individuals must meet criteria such as having a terminal illness, experiencing unbearable suffering, and providing informed consent.

Other countries, including the majority of the United States, still consider euthanasia and assisted suicide as illegal acts. However, there are ongoing debates and discussions surrounding the legalization of these practices in several states.

Controversies and Challenges

Euthanasia and assisted suicide present a range of controversies and challenges. One of the main concerns is the potential for abuse and undue influence, particularly in vulnerable populations such as the elderly or those with disabilities. Safeguards and clear legal frameworks are essential to prevent any form of coercion or the undermining of personal autonomy.

Another challenge is determining a clear boundary and consensus on what conditions or circumstances justify euthanasia and assisted suicide. Debates persist on whether these practices should be limited to terminally ill patients or extended to individuals suffering from chronic pain, mental illness, or a deteriorating quality of life.

Moreover, healthcare professionals may face significant moral and ethical dilemmas when asked to participate in euthanasia or assisted suicide. Balancing their duty to relieve suffering with their obligations to protect life and uphold professional integrity can present complex challenges that require careful consideration and guidance.

Case Study

Consider the case of Mary, a 65-year-old woman diagnosed with stage IV pancreatic cancer. Despite undergoing aggressive treatment, her condition continues to deteriorate, and she experiences severe pain and suffering. Mary expresses her desire to end her life peacefully to avoid further suffering and maintain her own dignity.

As a healthcare provider, you are faced with a difficult decision. On one hand, you empathize with Mary's suffering and understand her desire for a dignified death. On the other hand, you are aware of the legal and ethical implications of assisting in her suicide.

To navigate this ethical dilemma, it is important to engage in open and honest communication with Mary, her healthcare team, and any relevant stakeholders. Together, you can explore all available options, such as palliative care, hospice services, and counseling, to ensure that Mary's physical and emotional needs are met. It is also crucial to seek legal and ethical guidance, following the laws and regulations of your jurisdiction.

By considering the principles of autonomy, beneficence, non-maleficence, and the legal and ethical frameworks at play, you can strive to make the most compassionate and ethically sound decision in these complex and emotionally charged situations.

Conclusion

Euthanasia and assisted suicide raise profound ethical questions about the balance between autonomy, beneficence, and non-maleficence in the context of end-of-life care. The debate transcends legal and cultural boundaries, engaging diverse perspectives and values. As professionals in healthcare, it is crucial to engage in thoughtful and reflective discussions on this topic, acknowledging the complexity and sensitivity of the issues involved. Through open dialogue, ethical decision-making frameworks, and a commitment to patient-centered care, healthcare providers can navigate these challenging situations with compassion, respect, and integrity.

Palliative Care and Pain Management

Palliative care is a specialized field of healthcare that focuses on enhancing the quality of life for patients facing serious illness, such as cancer, heart disease, or neurological disorders. It aims to provide relief from pain and other distressing symptoms, as well as to support patients and their families emotionally, socially, and spiritually. In this section, we will explore the ethical considerations and challenges associated with palliative care and pain management.

Ethical Principles in Palliative Care

Palliative care is guided by several ethical principles that help healthcare professionals make decisions that are in the best interest of the patients. These principles include:

- **Autonomy:** Respect for patient autonomy is essential in palliative care. Patients should have the right to make informed decisions about their treatment options and end-of-life care. Healthcare providers should engage in shared decision-making processes, ensuring that patients' values and preferences are taken into account.

- **Beneficence:** The principle of beneficence emphasizes the duty of healthcare professionals to act in the best interest of the patients. In palliative care, this means providing effective pain management and symptom control, enhancing comfort, and improving overall well-being.

- **Non-maleficence:** Non-maleficence requires healthcare providers to do no harm to the patients. In palliative care, this involves careful assessment and management of pain and other distressing symptoms, avoiding unnecessary interventions that may cause additional harm or suffering.

- **Justice:** Justice in palliative care is concerned with fair allocation of resources and equal access to quality care. It requires healthcare professionals to advocate for equitable palliative care services, irrespective of socioeconomic status, race, or other factors.

- **Dignity:** Respecting the inherent dignity of patients is crucial in palliative care. Healthcare providers should promote the preservation of patients' dignity throughout their illness journey and at the end of life, ensuring that they are treated with compassion, empathy, and respect.

Management of Pain in Palliative Care

One of the primary goals of palliative care is effective pain management. Pain can be subjective and challenging to measure accurately, requiring a comprehensive and individualized approach. The World Health Organization (WHO) has developed guidelines known as the analgesic ladder to guide pain management in palliative care.

The analgesic ladder consists of three steps:

1. **Step 1 - Non-opioid Analgesics:** Mild to moderate pain is initially managed with non-opioid medications, such as nonsteroidal anti-inflammatory drugs

(NSAIDs) or acetaminophen. These medications can be used alone or in combination to provide pain relief.

2. **Step 2 - Weak Opioid Analgesics:** If pain persists or becomes more severe, weak opioids, such as codeine or tramadol, are added to the treatment regimen. These medications offer more potent pain relief and are typically used in combination with non-opioid analgesics.

3. **Step 3 - Strong Opioid Analgesics:** If pain remains uncontrolled or intensifies, strong opioids, such as morphine or fentanyl, are introduced. These medications provide powerful pain relief and may be used in combination with non-opioid and weak opioid analgesics.

It is important to assess pain regularly and adjust the medication regimen to ensure adequate pain control, while minimizing side effects and the risk of addiction. Palliative care teams work closely with patients, their families, and healthcare professionals from different disciplines to develop an individualized pain management plan that addresses physical, psychological, and social aspects of pain.

Challenges in Palliative Care and Pain Management

Palliative care and pain management present various ethical challenges that healthcare professionals must navigate with sensitivity and expertise. Some of these challenges include:

+ **Balancing pain relief and palliative sedation:** In cases of severe pain that is difficult to control, palliative sedation may be considered as a last resort. However, ethical concerns arise when balancing the need for pain relief with the potential risks and consequences of sedation, such as loss of consciousness and hastening death. Careful assessment and shared decision-making are essential to ensure that the patient's wishes and best interests are respected.

+ **Communication and decision-making:** Palliative care often involves complex conversations about prognosis, treatment options, and end-of-life care. Healthcare providers must possess excellent communication skills to facilitate open and honest discussions with patients and their families. Ethical challenges may arise when patients have differing values and preferences or when surrogate decision-makers are involved. Respecting patient autonomy and fostering shared decision-making can help navigate these challenges.

* **Cultural and religious considerations:** Palliative care should respect the cultural and religious beliefs of patients and their families. Ethical challenges may arise when there are conflicts between a patient's preferences, family dynamics, and cultural or religious norms. Healthcare professionals should approach these situations with cultural humility, seeking to understand and accommodate diverse perspectives.

* **Resource allocation:** Palliative care services may be limited in certain healthcare settings or regions, leading to ethical challenges in resource allocation. Not all patients may have access to specialized palliative care or pain management services. Healthcare professionals and policymakers must work together to advocate for equitable access to palliative care resources.

Case Study: Balancing Pain Relief and Palliative Sedation

Consider the case of Mr. Johnson, a 70-year-old terminally ill cancer patient experiencing severe pain. Despite maximum doses of opioids, his pain remains poorly controlled, significantly impacting his quality of life. The palliative care team recognizes that conventional pain management approaches have been exhausted and proposes palliative sedation as an option to provide relief.

Ethical considerations arise in balancing the need for pain relief through sedation and its potential consequences. Engaging in a shared decision-making process is crucial, involving Mr. Johnson, his family, and the healthcare team. The healthcare team must discuss the goals, benefits, risks, and potential impact on Mr. Johnson's consciousness and life expectancy. Respecting Mr. Johnson's autonomy and ensuring that his values and preferences are central to the decision-making process is of utmost importance.

By considering these ethical principles and engaging in thorough communication, the palliative care team can arrive at a decision that respects Mr. Johnson's wishes, provides effective pain relief, and preserves his dignity till the end of life.

Conclusion

Palliative care and pain management require a multidimensional approach, focusing on the physical, emotional, and social well-being of patients facing serious illness. Ethical principles, such as autonomy, beneficence, non-maleficence, justice, and dignity, guide healthcare professionals in providing compassionate and effective care.

Managing pain in palliative care necessitates individualized and comprehensive approaches, considering the analgesic ladder and regularly assessing pain levels. However, challenges can arise in balancing pain relief, engaging in effective communication, and respecting cultural and religious beliefs.

By navigating these challenges with sensitivity, compassion, and ethical awareness, healthcare professionals can enhance the quality of life for patients and their families, promoting dignity and comfort throughout the palliative care journey.

Withholding and Withdrawing Life-Sustaining Treatment

In the field of healthcare ethics, one of the most challenging and complex dilemmas that healthcare professionals and patients face is whether to withhold or withdraw life-sustaining treatment. This ethical issue arises when a patient's condition is critical, and the medical interventions being provided are aimed at prolonging life, but may not offer a reasonable chance of recovery or improvement in the patient's quality of life.

Ethical Principles in Healthcare

Before diving into the ethical considerations surrounding withholding and withdrawing life-sustaining treatment, let's briefly review some of the foundational ethical principles in healthcare. These principles can guide healthcare professionals in making ethically sound decisions and help balance the autonomy of the patient with the obligation to provide appropriate care.

- **Autonomy:** Autonomy refers to respecting the rights and decisions of the patient. The patient has the right to make informed decisions about their own healthcare, and healthcare professionals should ensure that the patient's wishes are taken into account.

- **Beneficence:** Beneficence is the principle of doing good and promoting the well-being of the patient. Healthcare professionals must consider the potential benefits and harms of any medical intervention and strive to provide the best possible care.

- **Non-maleficence:** Non-maleficence emphasizes the duty to do no harm. Healthcare professionals should aim to minimize the risks and adverse effects of medical treatments.

+ **Justice:** Justice entails fairness and equality in the distribution of healthcare resources. Healthcare professionals must consider the fair allocation of limited resources and avoid any form of discrimination.

+ **Integrity:** Integrity involves acting in an honest and trustworthy manner. Healthcare professionals should uphold high ethical standards and maintain the trust of their patients.

By applying these principles, healthcare professionals can navigate the ethical complexities surrounding the issue of withholding and withdrawing life-sustaining treatment.

Understanding Withholding and Withdrawing Life-Sustaining Treatment

Withholding and withdrawing life-sustaining treatment are distinct but related concepts. Withholding treatment refers to the decision not to initiate a particular medical intervention when it is deemed unlikely to be beneficial or in line with the patient's wishes. On the other hand, withdrawing treatment involves discontinuing an ongoing medical intervention that is no longer providing benefits or is causing harm to the patient.

The decision to withhold or withdraw life-sustaining treatment should be guided by a careful assessment of the patient's condition, prognosis, and their expressed wishes. This evaluation requires open and honest communication between the healthcare team, the patient, and the patient's family or designated decision-makers.

Ethical Considerations

The ethical considerations surrounding the withholding and withdrawing of life-sustaining treatment are multifaceted and require a thoughtful analysis of competing values and interests. Some key ethical considerations include:

+ **Respect for Autonomy:** A fundamental ethical principle, respect for autonomy requires healthcare professionals to honor the wishes and values of the patient. In the context of withholding or withdrawing life-sustaining treatment, this principle emphasizes the importance of discussing treatment options with the patient and involving them in the decision-making process to the best extent possible.

+ **Beneficence vs. Non-maleficence:** Balancing the principles of beneficence and non-maleficence can be particularly challenging in end-of-life care. While the goal of healthcare professionals is to provide the best possible care and promote the patient's well-being, it is essential to recognize when treatments may be futile or excessively burdensome, potentially causing more harm than good.

+ **Patient's Quality of Life:** Assessing the patient's quality of life is a critical aspect of ethical decision-making regarding life-sustaining treatment. Will continuing or initiating treatment improve the patient's quality of life? Or will it simply prolong suffering? Healthcare professionals must consider the potential benefits and burdens of treatment, keeping the patient's physical, emotional, and psychological well-being in mind.

+ **Informed Consent:** Informed consent is central to ethical decision-making in healthcare. Patients or their designated decision-makers should have access to all relevant information regarding the benefits, risks, and alternatives of treatment options. This empowers them to make well-informed decisions that align with their values and preferences.

+ **Cultural and Religious Perspectives:** Cultural and religious beliefs play a significant role in shaping individuals' views on life, death, and medical treatment. Healthcare professionals should respect and take these perspectives into account when discussing withholding or withdrawing life-sustaining treatment. Open dialogue and cultural sensitivity can help navigate potential conflicts and develop a plan that respects the patient's values while adhering to the principles of ethical practice.

Case Study: Balancing Ethical Considerations

To illustrate the complexity of ethical decision-making in the context of withholding and withdrawing life-sustaining treatment, let's consider a hypothetical case study.

Mr. Anderson, a 78-year-old man with advanced Alzheimer's disease, has been admitted to the intensive care unit (ICU) due to severe pneumonia. He is intubated and requires mechanical ventilation to maintain his breathing. The medical team assesses his condition and prognosis, realizing that even with aggressive treatment, his chances of meaningful recovery are slim.

In this scenario, the ethical considerations come into play. As healthcare professionals, they must recognize the importance of Mr. Anderson's autonomy and engage in a conversation with his family or designated decision-makers to discuss his values, preferences, and any advanced directives he may have. It is crucial to explore their understanding of his current condition and provide them with accurate information regarding the potential benefits and burdens of continuing life-sustaining treatment.

The principles of non-maleficence and beneficence are also essential in this case. The medical team should carefully weigh the benefits and burdens of treatment. While the mechanical ventilation may prolong Mr. Anderson's life, it may also cause discomfort, potential complications, and does not guarantee meaningful recovery.

Considering Mr. Anderson's quality of life is paramount. Is the treatment likely to improve his quality of life, or will it merely prolong his suffering? If the medical team concludes that continuing life-sustaining treatment is no longer in line with Mr. Anderson's best interests and preferences, the ethical course of action may involve a discussion with the family about the option of transitioning to palliative care, focusing on providing comfort and symptom management rather than aggressive life-prolonging interventions.

This case study highlights the importance of interdisciplinary collaboration, open communication, and ethically informed decision-making when faced with the dilemma of withholding or withdrawing life-sustaining treatment.

Resources for Ethical Decision-Making

To assist healthcare professionals in navigating the complexities of withholding and withdrawing life-sustaining treatment, numerous resources offer ethical frameworks and guidelines. Some notable resources include:

- The Hastings Center: A non-profit bioethics research institute that provides numerous resources on end-of-life care, including guidelines on decision-making, advance care planning, and ethical considerations. (Website: https://www.thehastingscenter.org/)

- American Medical Association (AMA): The AMA offers ethical guidelines and principles for physicians, including resources related to end-of-life care decision-making. (Website: https://www.ama-assn.org/)

- The End-of-Life Nursing Education Consortium (ELNEC): ELNEC offers educational resources and training programs for nurses, providing guidance on ethical decision-making and end-of-life care. (Website: https://elnecproject.org/)

- The National Hospice and Palliative Care Organization (NHPCO): NHPCO provides resources and tools for healthcare professionals involved in end-of-life care, including ethical considerations and decision-making frameworks. (Website: https://www.nhpco.org/)

These resources can offer valuable insights and practical guidance for healthcare professionals engaging in ethical decision-making regarding withholding and withdrawing life-sustaining treatment.

Exercise

Consider the following scenario: A terminally ill patient has expressed their wish to discontinue life-sustaining treatment, as they believe it will not improve their quality of life. However, the patient's family strongly disagrees with this decision, arguing that the medical team should continue providing all available treatments. How would you navigate this ethical dilemma while upholding the principles of autonomy, beneficence, and non-maleficence? Discuss the potential challenges and consider possible approaches to promote ethical decision-making in this situation.

Conclusion

The ethical decision to withhold or withdraw life-sustaining treatment is a complex and emotionally charged issue in healthcare. It requires a careful balance of ethical principles, open communication, and consideration of the patient's wishes, values, and quality of life. By incorporating a thoughtful approach and utilizing available resources, healthcare professionals can navigate this challenging terrain and provide compassionate and patient-centered care at the end of life.

Advance Directives and Decision Making

In the field of healthcare, there are situations where patients may become unable to make decisions for themselves due to physical or mental incapacitation. In such cases, advance directives play a crucial role in guiding healthcare professionals and family members in making decisions on behalf of the patient.

An advance directive is a legal document that allows individuals to express their preferences regarding medical treatment in the event that they are unable to communicate their wishes. It ensures that their values and choices are respected, even if they cannot actively participate in the decision-making process. Advance directives can also alleviate the burden on family members who may otherwise need to make difficult decisions without clear guidance.

There are different types of advance directives, each serving a unique purpose:

1. **Living wills:** A living will is a written document that specifies the types of medical treatments an individual would like to receive or refuse in specific circumstances. For example, a person may indicate their preferences on life support, resuscitation, or the administration of certain medications. Living wills provide clear instructions to healthcare providers and are often used in situations where a person is in a persistent vegetative state or has a terminal illness.

2. **Durable power of attorney for healthcare:** A durable power of attorney for healthcare, also known as a healthcare proxy or healthcare agent, is a legal document that designates a trusted person to make healthcare decisions on behalf of the individual. This person should be someone who understands the individual's values and preferences and can advocate for their best interests. The designated healthcare agent has the authority to make decisions that are not explicitly addressed in the living will.

Advanced directives are governed by specific laws and regulations, which vary from country to country and even within different states or provinces. It is essential to ensure that the advance directive is legally valid and complies with local requirements to ensure it will be honored when needed.

Healthcare professionals are ethically and legally obligated to respect and honor advance directives, provided they are valid and applicable to the patient's current situation. The principles of autonomy and beneficence guide caregivers in decision-making based on the patient's expressed wishes.

However, situations may arise where there are conflicts or doubts about the validity or applicability of an advance directive. In such cases, healthcare professionals may need to engage in further decision-making processes to determine the best course of action.

One ethical approach to resolving conflicts is to establish consultation and consensus-building mechanisms involving the healthcare team, the patient's family, and ethicists. These forums provide an opportunity for everyone involved to express their perspectives, share information, and work towards a resolution that respects and upholds the patient's autonomy and best interests.

It is important to note that advance directives should be regularly reviewed and updated as an individual's health status and preferences may change over time. Periodic discussions with healthcare providers, family members, and the designated healthcare agent can ensure that the advance directive remains current and aligned with the individual's values and goals. This ongoing communication helps to promote shared decision-making and enhances the efficacy of advance directives in guiding future medical care.

Example:

Lisa, a 45-year-old woman, was diagnosed with early-stage Alzheimer's disease. Recognizing the progressive nature of the disease, Lisa decided to create an advance directive to ensure her wishes were known and respected in the future.

In her living will, Lisa specified that she would not want to be placed on life support or receive artificial nutrition and hydration if her condition deteriorated to the point where she could no longer communicate or recognize her loved ones. She also expressed her desire to receive palliative care to manage pain and provide comfort.

To ensure that her wishes were carried out, Lisa appointed her sister, Megan, as her healthcare agent through a durable power of attorney for healthcare. Knowing that Megan understood her values and beliefs, Lisa felt confident that Megan would make decisions that aligned with her wishes if she became incapacitated.

As Lisa's disease progressed, her advance directive provided clear instructions to the healthcare team about her preferences and gave Megan the authority to make decisions on her behalf. By respecting Lisa's documented wishes, the healthcare team ensured that her values and autonomy were upheld throughout her care.

Discussion Questions:

1. Why is it important for individuals to have advance directives in place? 2. What are the different types of advance directives, and how do they complement each other? 3. How can healthcare professionals ensure the validity and applicability of advance directives? 4. What ethical considerations should healthcare professionals keep in mind when conflicts arise regarding advance directives? 5. How can ongoing communication and review of advance directives contribute to better decision-making and patient care?

Further Reading:

1. Beauchamp, T. L., & Childress, J. F. (2019). *Principles of biomedical ethics*. Oxford University Press.

2. Meisel, A., Snyder, L., Quill, T., & American College of Physicians–American Society of Internal Medicine End-of-Life Care Consensus Panel. (2000). ACP-ASIM *guidelines for the appropriate use of do-not-resuscitate orders*. Annals of Internal Medicine, 132(9), 731-734.

3. Detering, K. M., Hancock, A. D., Reade, M. C., & Silvester, W. (2010). The impact of advance care planning on end of life care in elderly patients: randomised controlled trial. *BMJ*, 340, c1345.

4. Brinkman-Stoppelenburg, A., Rietjens, J. A., & van der Heide, A. (2014). The effects of advance care planning on end-of-life care: a systematic review. PLoS ONE, 9(4), e98910.

Cultural and Religious Perspectives on Death and Dying

In understanding ethical practices in healthcare, it is important to consider the cultural and religious perspectives on death and dying. Different cultures and religions have distinct beliefs, rituals, and practices surrounding death, which can significantly influence individual preferences and decision-making in end-of-life care. These perspectives offer valuable insights into the ethical considerations that healthcare professionals need to take into account when providing care at the end of life.

Cultural Perspectives

Cultural perspectives on death and dying vary across different societies and communities. Cultural beliefs about death often influence how individuals approach their own mortality and the treatment of the deceased. Here are some examples of cultural perspectives on death:

1. **Western Cultures:** In Western societies, death is generally seen as a taboo topic, and discussions about mortality may be limited. Funeral practices often involve embalming the body, followed by burial or cremation. Grief is often expressed privately or through specific mourning rituals.

2. **Eastern Cultures:** In many Eastern cultures, death is viewed as a natural part of life's cycle and is openly discussed. Some Eastern cultures, such as Hinduism and Buddhism, believe in reincarnation and the transmigration of the soul. Funeral rituals may include cremation, elaborate ceremonies, and prayers for the deceased.

3. **Indigenous Cultures:** Indigenous cultures often have unique perspectives on death and dying. These perspectives are often deeply rooted in spiritual beliefs and cultural practices. Examples include Native American cultures, where death is seen as a transition to the spirit world, and Maori culture, which emphasizes the connection between the living and the ancestors.

4. **African Cultures:** African cultures have diverse beliefs surrounding death and dying. Some African cultures consider death as a passage to the afterlife

and believe in ancestor worship. Funeral rituals often involve community participation, music, dance, and celebrations of the deceased person's life.

It is crucial for healthcare professionals to be aware of and respect diverse cultural perspectives on death and dying. This includes understanding specific religious rituals, burial preferences, and mourning practices. By incorporating cultural sensitivity and respect into end-of-life care, healthcare professionals can better meet the emotional and spiritual needs of patients and their families.

Religious Perspectives

Religious beliefs play a significant role in shaping attitudes towards death and dying. These beliefs often provide guidance on ethical issues related to end-of-life care, such as euthanasia, organ donation, and autopsy. Here are some examples of religious perspectives on death and dying:

1. **Christianity:** Christianity teaches that life is a sacred gift from God and that the end of life should be approached with reverence. Most Christian denominations value preserving life and oppose actions that hasten death. However, attitudes towards end-of-life care may vary, with some Christian groups supporting palliative care and others being more open to discussions about withdrawing life-sustaining treatment.

2. **Islam:** In Islam, death is viewed as a transition to the afterlife. Islamic teachings emphasize the sanctity of life and the duty to preserve it. Muslims generally believe in the importance of providing comfort and pain relief to the dying, but there may be varying views on the acceptability of measures that artificially prolong life. Autopsy and organ donation may be accepted if it serves a greater good and is in line with religious principles.

3. **Judaism:** Judaism places a strong emphasis on the preservation of life and the inherent dignity of the individual. Jewish teachings promote the provision of respectful and compassionate end-of-life care, including pain management. Autopsy and organ donation are generally discouraged, but may be permitted if it can contribute to saving lives or advancing medical knowledge.

4. **Buddhism:** Buddhism teaches that death is a part of the natural cycle of life and emphasizes the impermanence of all things. Buddhist perspectives on end-of-life care vary, but there is often an emphasis on ensuring a peaceful and compassionate death. The concept of "mindfulness" is often applied, encouraging individuals to be fully present in the dying process.

These religious perspectives on death and dying provide valuable ethical insights, as they inform decision-making regarding end-of-life care. Healthcare professionals need to be sensitive to individual patients' religious beliefs and provide care that respects their values and customs.

Ethical Considerations

Understanding cultural and religious perspectives on death and dying is vital for healthcare professionals to provide ethical end-of-life care. Principles such as respect for autonomy, beneficence, and cultural competence are crucial in navigating the complex ethical considerations in this context. Some key ethical considerations include:

1. **Respecting Autonomy:** Respecting a patient's autonomy means honoring their beliefs, cultural practices, and preferences regarding end-of-life care. Healthcare professionals should engage in open and honest conversations, allowing patients and their families to make informed decisions consistent with their cultural and religious values.

2. **Promoting Beneficence:** Beneficence involves promoting the well-being and comfort of patients at the end of life. Healthcare professionals should consider cultural and religious practices that can provide emotional and spiritual comfort, such as allowing loved ones to be present during the dying process or facilitating specific religious rituals.

3. **Cultural Competence:** Cultural competence is the ability to provide care that is respectful and responsive to the cultural and religious backgrounds of individuals. Healthcare professionals should continuously educate themselves about different cultural perspectives, consult with cultural advisors, and adapt their care practices accordingly.

4. **Advance Care Planning:** Encouraging individuals to engage in advance care planning is essential. This involves discussing and documenting their treatment preferences, considering their cultural and religious beliefs, and appointing a healthcare proxy who can make decisions on their behalf if they become unable to do so.

5. **Collaborative Decision-Making:** In complex end-of-life situations, healthcare professionals may need to engage in shared decision-making with patients, families, and religious or spiritual advisors. This collaborative

approach can help ensure that decisions align with the patient's values and beliefs.

In conclusion, cultural and religious perspectives play significant roles in shaping ethical practices in end-of-life care. Healthcare professionals must be aware of and respect these perspectives to provide care that is sensitive, compassionate, and individualized. By incorporating cultural and religious considerations, healthcare professionals can meet the needs and preferences of patients and their families as they navigate the complex journey of death and dying.

Exercises

Exercise 1

Research and analyze the cultural and religious perspectives on death and dying in one specific indigenous culture of your choice. Discuss their beliefs, rituals, and practices surrounding death and dying. How do these perspectives reflect the cultural values and spiritual beliefs of the indigenous community?

Exercise 2

Choose one major religion and discuss its stance on ethical issues related to end-of-life care, such as euthanasia or organ donation. What are the key ethical principles and teachings of this religion that guide decision-making in end-of-life situations? How do these religious perspectives on end-of-life care intersect with the broader cultural context in which the religion is practiced?

Exercise 3

Imagine you are a healthcare professional providing end-of-life care to a patient from a different cultural or religious background than your own. How would you approach the situation to ensure that the care provided is culturally sensitive and respectful? What strategies would you employ to understand and address the unique cultural and religious needs of the patient and their family? Reflect on the potential ethical considerations and challenges that may arise in this scenario.

Ethical Challenges in Global Health

Access to Healthcare in Developing Countries

Access to healthcare is a fundamental right that is crucial for the well-being and development of individuals and communities. However, in many developing countries, there are significant challenges in ensuring that all individuals have equitable access to quality healthcare services. This section will explore the barriers to access healthcare in developing countries and discuss potential solutions to address this issue.

Barriers to Access Healthcare

1. **Financial Barriers** - One of the primary obstacles to accessing healthcare in developing countries is the high cost of medical services. Many individuals in these

countries live in poverty and struggle to afford basic necessities, let alone healthcare expenses. The lack of affordable health insurance coverage further exacerbates the financial barrier, making it difficult for individuals to seek necessary medical care.

2.   **Geographical Barriers** - Access to healthcare is often limited by the geographical distance between individuals and healthcare facilities. In many rural areas of developing countries, there is a shortage of healthcare facilities, forcing individuals to travel long distances to access medical services. Poor transportation infrastructure and inadequate public transportation options further compound the issue, making it challenging for individuals to reach healthcare facilities in a timely manner.

3. **Infrastructure and Resource Limitations** - Developing countries often face infrastructural challenges, such as a lack of medical facilities, equipment, and trained healthcare professionals. Inadequate infrastructure and limited resources lead to long waiting times, overcrowded hospitals, and a shortage of essential medical supplies. These limitations significantly impact the quality and availability of healthcare services, making it difficult for individuals to access the care they need.

4.   **Lack of Education and Awareness** - Limited education and low health literacy levels contribute to the barriers to accessing healthcare in developing countries. Many individuals lack knowledge about preventive measures, disease management, and available healthcare services. Inadequate awareness about the importance of seeking early medical care delays timely interventions and exacerbates health conditions.

Solutions to Improve Access to Healthcare

1.   **Universal Health Coverage** - Implementing universal health coverage is a crucial step towards ensuring equitable access to healthcare. By providing comprehensive health services to all individuals, regardless of their ability to pay, countries can reduce financial barriers and enhance access to essential healthcare services. Governments can collaborate with international organizations and donors to develop sustainable funding mechanisms for universal health coverage.

2.   **Improving Infrastructure and Resources** - Developing countries need to invest in building and strengthening healthcare infrastructure. This includes establishing primary healthcare centers and hospitals, ensuring the availability of medical equipment, and training a skilled healthcare workforce. Collaborations with international organizations and partnerships with developed countries can help mobilize resources and expertise to address these infrastructure and resource limitations.

3. **Community-based Healthcare** - Community-based healthcare programs can play a vital role in improving access to healthcare services, particularly in remote rural areas. By training and empowering community health workers, individuals can receive basic healthcare services and health education within their communities. Such programs can help overcome geographical barriers and increase healthcare access at the grassroots level.

4. **Health Education and Awareness** - Promoting health education and awareness campaigns is essential to empower individuals with knowledge about preventive measures, disease management, and available healthcare services. Governments, along with non-governmental organizations and international partners, can develop targeted health education programs to raise awareness and improve health literacy among the population.

5. **International Collaboration and Aid** - International collaboration and aid are crucial in supporting developing countries to overcome the barriers to healthcare access. Developed countries and international organizations can provide financial resources, technical support, and capacity building to strengthen healthcare systems. Partnerships and knowledge sharing can help developing countries adopt best practices and innovative solutions to improve healthcare access.

Case Study: The Primary Health Care Approach in Brazil

Brazil's Primary Health Care (PHC) approach provides a compelling example of how a developing country can improve access to healthcare. The PHC approach involves the provision of comprehensive, accessible, and quality healthcare services at the primary care level. It focuses on preventive care, health promotion, and community participation.

Under the PHC approach, Brazil has established a network of primary healthcare centers known as Family Health Units (FHUs) across the country. These FHUs, staffed with multidisciplinary healthcare teams, provide a wide range of services, including general medical care, vaccinations, prenatal care, and health education. By bringing healthcare services closer to the communities, the PHC approach has significantly improved access to healthcare, particularly in underserved rural and remote areas.

Furthermore, the PHC approach in Brazil emphasizes community engagement and participation. Local communities actively participate in the management and decision-making of the FHUs, ensuring that healthcare services meet the specific needs of the population. This community involvement has fostered a sense of ownership and accountability, leading to increased trust in the healthcare system and improved health outcomes.

The success of Brazil's PHC approach can be attributed to sustained government commitment, strong primary care infrastructure, and community participation. Other developing countries can learn from this case study and adapt similar approaches to enhance access to healthcare in their contexts.

Conclusion

Access to healthcare in developing countries is a complex issue influenced by various barriers, including financial constraints, geographical limitations, infrastructural challenges, and lack of education and awareness. Addressing these barriers requires comprehensive strategies, including universal health coverage, improving infrastructure and resources, community-based healthcare, health education and awareness, and international collaboration and aid.

By implementing these solutions, developing countries can improve access to healthcare, reduce health disparities, and promote the overall well-being of their populations. It is essential for governments, healthcare organizations, international partners, and civil society to work together to ensure equitable access to quality healthcare for all individuals, irrespective of their socioeconomic status or geographical location.

Medical Tourism and Ethical Considerations

Medical tourism, also known as health tourism or medical travel, is a growing phenomenon where individuals travel to other countries to seek medical treatment. This usually occurs when such treatments are not available or are expensive in their home country. Medical tourism can encompass a wide range of procedures, including surgeries, dental work, fertility treatments, cosmetic surgery, and more.

While medical tourism offers various benefits, such as timely access to treatment, cost savings, and the opportunity to combine medical care with leisure travel, it also raises ethical concerns. In this section, we will explore the ethical considerations associated with medical tourism and discuss ways to address these challenges.

The Ethics of Medical Tourism

The practice of medical tourism raises several ethical issues that need to be carefully considered. These include:

Equitable Distribution of Healthcare Resources: Medical tourism may exacerbate existing healthcare disparities both in the home country of the medical tourist and in the destination country. If individuals from wealthier nations travel to developing countries for medical treatment, it can lead to the depletion of healthcare resources in the latter. This raises questions of fairness and distributive justice, as access to medical services may become even more unequal.

Quality and Safety of Care: One of the primary concerns with medical tourism is the varying quality and safety standards across different countries. Patients may be attracted to destinations with lower costs but may not realize the potential risks associated with substandard medical facilities and practices. It is essential to ensure that patients receive safe and effective care, regardless of the country they choose for medical treatment.

Informed Consent: Informed consent is a fundamental principle in medical ethics, ensuring that patients have the necessary information to make autonomous decisions about their healthcare. In the context of medical tourism, language barriers, cultural differences, and limited communication may hinder the informed consent process. It is crucial to ensure that patients fully understand the risks, benefits, and alternatives of their chosen treatment before giving their consent.

Transplant Tourism: Organ transplantation is a significant part of medical tourism. However, the demand for organs often fuels illegal practices, such as organ trafficking and exploitation of vulnerable populations. This raises ethical issues related to organ procurement, consent, and the fair allocation of donated organs.

Addressing Ethical Concerns

To address the ethical concerns associated with medical tourism, various measures can be implemented:

Regulation and Accreditation: Governments and international bodies can develop stringent regulations and accreditation requirements for healthcare facilities involved in medical tourism. These guidelines should ensure the safety, quality, and ethical standards of medical care provided to international patients.

Informed Decision-Making: Patients considering medical tourism should have access to comprehensive and accurate information about potential risks, realistic outcomes, and the qualifications of healthcare providers. This enables them to make well-informed decisions and understand the potential ethical implications of their choices.

Ethical Recruitment Practices: Medical tourists often rely on intermediaries, known as medical tourism facilitators, to arrange their travel and treatment. These facilitators should adhere to ethical standards, promoting transparency, honesty, and accountability in their dealings with patients. This includes providing clear information about costs, risks, and the credentials of healthcare providers.

International Collaboration: Collaborative efforts between countries and international organizations can help address issues related to organ trafficking and transplantation. Implementing clear guidelines and ensuring stricter enforcement can deter illegal practices and protect vulnerable individuals.

Education and Awareness: Raising awareness among patients, healthcare professionals, and the general public about the ethical implications of medical tourism is crucial. Educational initiatives can empower individuals to make informed decisions and encourage healthcare providers to uphold their ethical responsibilities.

Case Study: The Ethics of Cosmetic Surgery Tourism

Cosmetic surgery tourism is a prevalent form of medical tourism, often involving elective procedures like breast augmentation, liposuction, or facelifts. Let's consider a fictional case study to examine the ethical challenges associated with cosmetic surgery tourism.

Mary, a 45-year-old woman from the United States, is considering traveling to Thailand for a facelift surgery due to the lower costs compared to getting the procedure done in her home country. While the financial savings are attractive to Mary, she is concerned about the quality and safety standards of healthcare facilities in Thailand.

In this case, several ethical considerations come into play. Mary needs to carefully assess the risks and benefits associated with cosmetic surgery tourism. She should research the qualifications and reputation of the healthcare providers and ensure they adhere to international standards. Mary should also consider the potential challenges of post-operative care and follow-up, as she will be far away from her home country.

Furthermore, Mary should be aware of the potential impact her decision may have on the equitable distribution of healthcare resources. By opting for medical tourism, she might contribute to the strain on healthcare facilities in Thailand, potentially limiting access to local patients in need.

To address these ethical concerns, Mary should engage in a thorough informed consent process, understanding the risks, benefits, and alternatives of the procedure. Consulting with a local healthcare professional in her home country can provide her with an unbiased perspective and better assess the potential ethical implications of her decision.

Conclusion

Medical tourism presents both opportunities and ethical challenges. It offers individuals access to medical treatments that may otherwise be unavailable or unaffordable. However, the ethical concerns surrounding medical tourism, such as equitable distribution of healthcare resources, quality and safety of care, informed consent, and organ transplantation, must be carefully addressed.

By implementing regulations, promoting informed decision-making, ethical recruitment practices, international collaboration, and education and awareness initiatives, countries and healthcare systems can strive to minimize the ethical risks associated with medical tourism. Ultimately, the goal should be to ensure the provision of safe, effective, and ethical healthcare for individuals seeking medical treatment abroad.

Infectious Disease Outbreaks and Public Health Ethics

Infectious disease outbreaks pose significant challenges to public health systems around the world. These outbreaks can have devastating consequences for individuals and communities, requiring swift and effective responses from healthcare professionals and policymakers. However, in the midst of such crises, ethical considerations must also be taken into account to ensure the well-being and human rights of all individuals affected.

The Ethics of Disease Prevention and Control

When faced with an infectious disease outbreak, public health officials must balance the need to control the spread of the disease with the ethical principles of autonomy, beneficence, and justice. Autonomy refers to the respect for individuals' right to make decisions about their own health, while beneficence emphasizes the obligation to promote the well-being of others. Justice requires that the benefits and burdens of disease prevention and control measures be distributed fairly among affected individuals and communities.

One ethical issue that arises in the context of infectious disease outbreaks is the tension between individual liberties and the need for public health interventions. For example, during a pandemic, public health officials may recommend quarantine or isolation measures to contain the spread of the disease. These measures may restrict individuals' freedom of movement and infringe upon their rights, raising ethical questions about the balance between individual rights and the common good.

Another ethical consideration is the allocation of limited resources in the face of an outbreak. Healthcare resources such as vaccines, treatments, and hospital beds may be scarce during a pandemic. Ethical principles of distributive justice require that these resources be allocated in a fair and equitable manner, taking into account factors such as the severity of illness, age, and risk of transmission. However, making these decisions can be challenging, as different ethical frameworks may prioritize different criteria for resource allocation.

Ethical Challenges in Disease Surveillance and Reporting

Disease surveillance is a critical component of outbreak response, as it helps identify and monitor the spread of infectious diseases. However, ethical challenges arise when it comes to data collection, privacy, and reporting. Balancing the need for timely and accurate information with individual privacy rights can be a tricky task.

One ethical consideration is the collection and use of personal health information. During an outbreak, there is a need for rapid data collection to inform public health responses. However, this must be done in a way that respects individuals' privacy rights and maintains the confidentiality of their health information. Public health officials must ensure that appropriate safeguards are in place to protect the privacy and confidentiality of individuals' data.

Another ethical challenge is the reporting of disease cases and outbreaks. Timely and transparent reporting is essential for effective outbreak response, but it can also have unintended consequences. Fear and stigma may arise as a result of public reporting, leading to discrimination and social unrest. Public health officials must balance the need for accurate and transparent reporting with the potential negative impact on individuals and communities.

Ethical Considerations in Public Health Interventions

In the face of an infectious disease outbreak, public health interventions such as vaccination campaigns, contact tracing, and social distancing measures are essential for disease control. However, these interventions raise ethical questions regarding their implementation and impact on individuals and communities.

One ethical consideration is the principle of voluntary informed consent. In public health interventions, individuals should be provided with accurate and understandable information about the intervention and its potential risks and benefits. They should be given the opportunity to make an informed decision about their participation. However, in the midst of an outbreak, there may be pressures to implement interventions quickly, leading to challenges in ensuring adequate informed consent.

Another ethical challenge is the potential for unintended consequences of public health interventions. For example, quarantine measures may have negative psychological and social effects on individuals and communities. It is important for public health officials to consider and mitigate these potential harms, while still achieving the desired public health outcomes.

Case Study: The Ebola Outbreak

A real-life example that highlights the ethical challenges in infectious disease outbreaks is the Ebola outbreak that occurred in West Africa in 2014-2016. This outbreak claimed thousands of lives and had significant social and economic impacts on the affected countries.

One of the ethical challenges in the response to the Ebola outbreak was the tension between infection control measures and cultural practices. Traditional burial practices, such as washing and touching of the deceased, contributed to the spread of the disease. However, these practices were deeply ingrained in the affected communities' beliefs and customs. Public health officials had to work closely with local leaders and communities to find culturally sensitive solutions that balanced the need for infection control with respect for cultural practices.

Another ethical issue was the allocation of scarce resources, such as healthcare workers and personal protective equipment. The outbreak overwhelmed the healthcare systems in the affected countries, and there were not enough resources to adequately respond to the crisis. This raised difficult decisions about prioritization and fair distribution of resources, which required balancing the principles of utility and distributive justice.

In conclusion, infectious disease outbreaks present complex ethical challenges for public health officials and policymakers. Balancing the need to control the spread of disease with individual autonomy and social justice requires careful consideration of ethical principles and values. By addressing these challenges in a thoughtful and ethical manner, public health systems can effectively respond to outbreaks while upholding the rights and well-being of all individuals and communities affected.

Allocation of Scarce Medical Resources

During times of crisis, such as a pandemic or major natural disaster, the allocation of scarce medical resources becomes a critical ethical issue. When there are not enough resources to meet the needs of all patients, difficult decisions must be made regarding who will receive the limited resources available. In this section, we will explore the ethical considerations surrounding the allocation of scarce medical resources and examine various approaches that can be taken to address this complex issue.

The Challenge of Scarce Medical Resources

Scarce medical resources, such as ventilators, intensive care unit (ICU) beds, and life-saving medications, can quickly become overwhelmed during a public health crisis. This can lead to situations where healthcare providers must determine the best course of action when multiple patients require the same resource simultaneously. Ethical guidelines and principles can provide a framework for decision-making in these challenging circumstances.

Ethical Principles in Resource Allocation

Several ethical principles can guide the allocation of scarce medical resources:

- **Beneficence:** The principle of beneficence requires healthcare providers to act in the best interest of the patient and maximize overall well-being. In the context of scarce resource allocation, this principle calls for prioritizing patients who have a higher likelihood of benefiting from the medical intervention.

- **Justice:** The principle of justice emphasizes fairness and equity. It requires that resources be distributed in a manner that is unbiased and impartial. In the allocation of scarce medical resources, justice requires that all individuals have an equal opportunity to access the resources they need, regardless of factors such as age, socioeconomic status, or social worth.

‣ **Proportionality:** The principle of proportionality suggests that allocation decisions should be based on the severity of the patient's condition and the potential benefits of the intervention. It involves making decisions that are proportionate to the patient's medical need and the available resources.

‣ **Transparency:** The principle of transparency emphasizes the importance of open and honest communication with patients and their families. It requires healthcare providers to clearly explain the allocation process and the criteria used to make decisions regarding resource allocation.

These principles provide a foundation for ethical decision-making in the allocation of scarce resources. However, applying these principles in practice can be challenging and may require additional ethical frameworks and guidelines.

Ethical Frameworks for Resource Allocation

Various ethical frameworks have been proposed to facilitate decision-making in the allocation of scarce medical resources. These frameworks aim to balance the principles of beneficence, justice, proportionality, and transparency. Here are two commonly used frameworks:

‣ **Utilitarian Approach:** The utilitarian approach suggests that resources should be allocated to maximize overall utility or happiness. Under this approach, decisions are made based on the potential benefits of treatment and the number of lives that can be saved or improved. Patients with a higher chance of survival or a greater potential for long-term benefit may receive priority in resource allocation.

‣ **Fair and Equitable Approach:** The fair and equitable approach emphasizes the importance of distributive justice. It aims to ensure equal access to resources by considering factors such as need, urgency, and prognosis. This approach may involve the use of a lottery system or rotating priority among patients with similar medical conditions to distribute limited resources fairly.

It is important to note that different ethical frameworks may be more suitable for different contexts and cultural values. Ultimately, the choice of framework should be based on careful consideration of the specific circumstances and the values and norms of the community.

Considerations and Challenges

Allocating scarce medical resources is a complex task that presents various considerations and challenges. Here are some key factors that healthcare providers must consider when making allocation decisions:

- **Clinical Severity:** The severity of the patient's condition plays a crucial role in resource allocation. Patients with life-threatening conditions or a high risk of deterioration may be prioritized to receive scarce resources.

- **Probability of Benefit:** The likelihood of benefiting from the intervention is an important factor to consider in resource allocation. Patients with a higher chance of survival or a greater potential for improvement may receive priority.

- **Ethical Dilemmas:** Allocation decisions can give rise to ethical dilemmas, such as choosing between younger patients who may have more years of life ahead of them and older patients who may have contributed more to society. Resolving these dilemmas requires careful consideration of the ethical principles and guidelines.

- **Multidisciplinary Decision-making:** In complex cases, involving a multidisciplinary team in the allocation decision-making process can help ensure a fair and comprehensive evaluation of each patient's condition and needs.

- **Community Engagement:** Engaging the community in the decision-making process can promote transparency and enhance public trust. Public input can help shape allocation guidelines and ensure that diverse perspectives are considered.

Case Study: Scarce Ventilators during a Pandemic

To illustrate the challenges and ethical considerations in the allocation of scarce medical resources, let's consider a case study involving the allocation of ventilators during a pandemic. In this hypothetical scenario, a hospital has a limited number of ventilators, but the number of critically ill patients requiring respiratory support exceeds the available resources.

To address this situation, the hospital forms an ethical committee comprising healthcare providers, ethicists, and community representatives. The committee develops guidelines for ventilator allocation based on the ethical principles of beneficence, justice, proportionality, and transparency. The guidelines consider factors such as the severity of illness, likelihood of benefit, and presence of comorbidities.

Suppose two patients, Mr. Smith and Ms. Johnson, require ventilator support. Mr. Smith is a 60-year-old patient with underlying health conditions but has a better chance of survival and potential for long-term benefit. On the other hand, Ms. Johnson is a 30-year-old patient with no underlying health conditions but has a lower likelihood of survival due to the severity of her illness.

Using the guidelines developed by the ethical committee, the allocation decision is made to prioritize Mr. Smith for the limited ventilator resource. This decision is based on the ethical principle of maximizing overall benefit and the likelihood of positive outcomes.

Conclusion

The allocation of scarce medical resources presents significant ethical challenges. Balancing the principles of beneficence, justice, proportionality, and transparency is essential in making fair and equitable decisions. Ethical frameworks, such as the utilitarian approach and the fair and equitable approach, provide guidance in resource allocation. However, the complexity and context-specific nature of resource allocation require careful consideration of the unique circumstances and values of the community. Through collaboration, transparency, and adherence to ethical principles, healthcare providers can navigate the challenges of allocating scarce medical resources in an ethical and responsible manner.

Health Disparities and Social Determinants of Health

Health disparities refer to differences in the health status between different populations or groups. These disparities can manifest in various forms, including disparities in access to healthcare services, health outcomes, and the prevalence of certain diseases. Social determinants of health are the social, economic, and environmental factors that influence health outcomes and contribute to health disparities.

Understanding Health Disparities

Health disparities are often associated with socioeconomic factors, such as income, education level, and occupation. People from lower socioeconomic backgrounds tend to experience higher rates of chronic diseases, poor health outcomes, and limited access to healthcare services compared to those from higher socioeconomic backgrounds.

Furthermore, racial and ethnic minorities often face higher rates of health disparities. For instance, African Americans have higher rates of hypertension and diabetes compared to Caucasians. Additionally, certain geographic areas, such as rural communities, may also experience disparities in healthcare access and health outcomes.

Social Determinants of Health

Social determinants of health encompass a wide range of factors that contribute to health disparities. These factors include:

- **Income and Wealth:** Lower income and wealth are associated with limited access to quality healthcare services, healthy food options, safe housing, and educational opportunities. These factors can significantly impact an individual's health outcomes.

- **Education:** Education level is linked to health outcomes. Higher education levels are associated with better health outcomes, as individuals with higher education tend to have a better understanding of health-related information and engage in healthier behaviors.

- **Occupation:** Certain occupations carry higher risks of exposure to hazardous materials, stress, and physical strain, leading to adverse health effects. Additionally, individuals in low-income occupations may lack adequate health insurance coverage.

- **Neighborhood and Physical Environment:** The quality of the physical environment, such as access to green spaces, air and water pollution, and availability of recreational facilities, can significantly impact health outcomes. Disadvantaged neighborhoods often lack these resources.

- **Social Support and Networks:** Social support networks play a crucial role in promoting health and well-being. Individuals with strong social connections tend to have better overall health outcomes and access to necessary resources.

- **Racism and Discrimination:** Racial and ethnic discrimination can have profound effects on health outcomes. These experiences contribute to chronic stress, which increases the risk of developing various health conditions.

Addressing Health Disparities

Reducing health disparities requires comprehensive efforts at various levels, including policy, community, and individual interventions. Some strategies to address health disparities and social determinants of health include:

+ **Improving Access to Healthcare:** Ensuring equitable access to quality healthcare services for all individuals, regardless of their socioeconomic status or geographical location, is crucial. This can be achieved through policies that promote the expansion of healthcare facilities, financial assistance programs, and telehealth services.

+ **Promoting Health Education and Literacy:** Enhancing health literacy among individuals from disadvantaged backgrounds can empower them to make informed decisions about their health. Health education programs should focus on improving awareness of preventive measures, healthy lifestyle choices, and access to appropriate healthcare resources.

+ **Investing in Early Childhood Development:** Early childhood experiences have a long-lasting impact on health outcomes. Investing in early childhood development programs that address nutrition, education, and social support can help mitigate health disparities in the long term.

+ **Tackling Social Determinants of Health:** Policies and interventions targeting the social determinants of health are essential. These can include initiatives such as improving educational opportunities, affordable housing programs, income support policies, and neighborhood revitalization efforts.

+ **Promoting Health Equity in Research:** Researchers and policymakers should prioritize equity in health research. This involves including diverse populations in clinical trials and epidemiological studies to ensure that healthcare interventions are effective for everyone.

Example: Health Disparities in Obesity Rates

Obesity rates vary significantly based on socioeconomic factors and access to resources. Let's consider an example of how health disparities and social determinants of health contribute to obesity rates among different populations.

In a low-income neighborhood with limited access to affordable, healthy food options and recreational facilities, the prevalence of obesity may be higher compared to a wealthier neighborhood with abundant resources. Additionally, individuals with lower education levels may have limited knowledge about healthy eating habits and may face barriers to engaging in physical activity due to time constraints or unsafe environments.

To address this disparity, interventions could focus on increasing access to affordable fresh produce, implementing nutrition education programs, and creating safe spaces for physical activity within the community. By targeting the social determinants of health, such interventions can help reduce the prevalence of obesity and promote overall health equity.

Resources

- World Health Organization. (2020). Social determinants of health. Retrieved from `https://www.who.int/westernpacific/health-topics/social-determinants-of-health`

- Braveman, P., & Gottlieb, L. (2014). The social determinants of health: It's time to consider the causes of the causes. Public health reports, 129(Suppl 2), 19-31.

- Robert Wood Johnson Foundation. (2020). What are health disparities. Retrieved from `https://www.rwjf.org/health-disparities`

Conclusion

Health disparities and social determinants of health are interlinked complex issues that contribute to inequalities in health outcomes. Addressing health disparities requires a multifaceted approach that considers the various social, economic, and environmental factors influencing health. By understanding these factors and implementing targeted interventions, we can work towards achieving health equity for all populations.

Ethical Issues in Reproductive Medicine

Assisted Reproductive Technologies

Assisted Reproductive Technologies (ART) refer to a range of medical procedures that assist individuals or couples in achieving pregnancy when they are unable to do so naturally. These technologies have revolutionized the field of reproductive medicine, offering hope to millions of people worldwide. In this section, we will explore the ethical considerations surrounding ART and the various techniques involved.

The Need for Assisted Reproductive Technologies

Infertility affects approximately 15

Ethical Principles in Assisted Reproductive Technologies

When discussing the ethical implications of ART, several principles come into play. These principles guide healthcare professionals, policymakers, and individuals making decisions regarding their reproductive choices. Let's explore these principles in the context of ART:

1. Autonomy: Individuals have the right to make informed decisions about their reproductive options. This principle emphasizes the importance of respecting the autonomy of individuals seeking ART while ensuring they have access to accurate information and comprehensive counseling.

2. Beneficence: The principle of beneficence promotes actions that aim to benefit others. In the context of ART, it encourages healthcare professionals to provide the highest standard of care, prioritize the well-being of patients, and minimize any potential harm.

3. Non-maleficence: The principle of non-maleficence focuses on avoiding harm. In the case of ART, it requires healthcare professionals to carefully consider the potential physical, psychological, and emotional risks associated with the procedures and ensure patients are fully informed before proceeding.

4. Justice: The principle of justice emphasizes fairness and equal access to reproductive healthcare. However, due to the high costs associated with ART, disparities can arise, raising ethical concerns about access and allocation of resources.

5. Integrity: The principle of integrity underscores the importance of honesty, transparency, and accountability in the delivery of reproductive healthcare. Healthcare professionals involved in ART should prioritize the best interests of their patients, maintain confidentiality, and ensure accurate documentation of procedures.

Common Assisted Reproductive Technologies

There are several commonly used ART techniques, each with its own ethical considerations. Let's explore a few of these techniques:

1. In-Vitro Fertilization (IVF): IVF involves fertilizing an egg with sperm outside the body, followed by the transfer of the resulting embryo into the uterus. While IVF has brought hope to many couples struggling with infertility, it raises ethical questions about the disposition of excess embryos, the potential for multiple pregnancies, and the use of genetic testing.

2. Gamete Intrafallopian Transfer (GIFT): GIFT involves transferring both sperm and eggs into the fallopian tubes, allowing fertilization to occur naturally inside the body. This technique respects the sanctity of life by avoiding fertilization outside the body. However, it carries a higher risk of multiple pregnancies compared to IVF.

3. Intracytoplasmic Sperm Injection (ICSI): ICSI involves injecting a single sperm directly into an egg to facilitate fertilization. While ICSI has significantly improved the chances of fertilization in cases of male infertility, ethical concerns arise regarding the potential impact on natural selection and the long-term consequences for offspring.

4. Surrogacy: Surrogacy involves another woman carrying a pregnancy to term on behalf of an individual or couple who cannot conceive or carry a child. Surrogacy raises complex ethical questions related to the autonomy of the surrogate, the commodification of reproduction, and the potential exploitation of vulnerable individuals.

Ethical Considerations in Assisted Reproductive Technologies

Beyond the ethical principles mentioned earlier, several specific ethical considerations arise in the realm of ART:

1. Equity and Access: ART procedures can be expensive, making them inaccessible to many individuals and couples. Ensuring equitable access to ART raises questions about the allocation of limited resources, healthcare disparities, and the role of public funding.

2. The Status of Embryos: The use and disposition of embryos created during ART procedures raise ethical dilemmas. Questions regarding the moral

status of embryos, their potential for life, and the rights and responsibilities associated with their creation must be carefully considered.

3. Genetic Testing and Selection: Advances in technology have made it possible to screen embryos for genetic disorders and select those without specific genetic traits. While this offers new opportunities to prevent genetic diseases, it also raises ethical concerns related to eugenics, discrimination, and societal perceptions of disability.

4. Commercialization and Exploitation: The commercialization of ART can lead to exploitative practices, such as the sale of eggs, sperm, or surrogacy services. Ensuring ethical practices in the industry requires robust regulations, protection of the rights and well-being of donors and surrogates, and transparency in financial transactions.

Case Study: The Ethics of Selecting Genetic Traits

Let's consider a case study to delve deeper into the ethical dilemmas associated with assisted reproductive technologies. Imagine a couple seeking ART procedures, including genetic testing and embryo selection, to avoid passing on a hereditary genetic disorder. They undergo preimplantation genetic testing and select an embryo without the disorder but also with other desirable traits such as eye color and intelligence.

This case raises ethical questions about the boundaries of genetic selection, the potential for unintended consequences, and the societal implications of such choices. It challenges us to consider the balance between individual autonomy, the well-being of future offspring, and the potential for creating a genetically homogeneous society.

Conclusion

Assisted Reproductive Technologies offer tangible hope to individuals and couples struggling with infertility. However, these technologies also raise complex ethical considerations that demand careful thought and examination. By adhering to the ethical principles discussed and considering the implications of each technique, we can navigate the challenging terrain of reproductive medicine responsibly and ethically.

Key Terms:

- Assisted Reproductive Technologies (ART)
- Infertility
- Autonomy
- Beneficence
- Non-maleficence
- Justice
- Integrity
- In-Vitro Fertilization (IVF)
- Gamete Intrafallopian Transfer (GIFT)
- Intracytoplasmic Sperm Injection (ICSI)
- Surrogacy
- Equity and Access
- The Status of Embryos
- Genetic Testing and Selection
- Commercialization and Exploitation
- Preimplantation Genetic Testing
- Eugenics
- Genetic Homogeneity

Surrogacy and Commercialization of Reproduction

In recent years, surrogacy has become a topic of ethical debate due to its increasing commercialization. Surrogacy is the process in which a woman carries a pregnancy and gives birth to a child on behalf of another individual or couple, who will become the child's legal parents. This practice has gained popularity as a solution for couples facing fertility issues or same-sex couples who wish to have biological children.

However, with the rapid expansion of the surrogacy industry, concerns have been raised about the potential exploitation of surrogate mothers, the commodification of the human body, and the ethical implications of treating reproduction as a commercial transaction. In this section, we will explore these issues and delve into the ethical considerations surrounding surrogacy and the commercialization of reproduction.

The Concept of Surrogacy

Surrogacy can be categorized into two main types: traditional surrogacy and gestational surrogacy. In traditional surrogacy, the surrogate mother's own eggs are used, making her the biological mother of the child. In gestational surrogacy, on the other hand, the surrogate mother carries a fertilized embryo created using the eggs and sperm of the intended parents or donors, making her a gestational carrier rather than a biological parent.

Surrogacy arrangements can take place either altruistically, where the surrogate receives no financial compensation beyond reimbursement for pregnancy-related expenses, or commercially, where the surrogate is paid a fee for her services. It is the commercialization of surrogacy that has sparked a heated ethical debate, raising concerns about the potential commodification of both the surrogate mother's body and the resulting child.

Ethical Concerns

One of the primary ethical concerns surrounding surrogacy is the potential exploitation of surrogate mothers. Critics argue that offering financial incentives for surrogacy may lead vulnerable women, particularly those from economically disadvantaged backgrounds, to make choices they would not otherwise consider. This raises questions about informed consent and whether the surrogate's decision to participate in surrogacy is truly voluntary.

Another concern is the objectification and commodification of the human body. Critics argue that treating reproduction as a commercial transaction reduces the value of the intimate and emotional aspects of the parent-child relationship. It also raises questions about the autonomy and dignity of the surrogate mother, as her role may be reduced to that of a mere vessel for carrying a pregnancy.

Furthermore, the commercialization of surrogacy raises concerns about the potential for exploitation by third-party intermediaries, such as agencies and brokers. There have been cases where intermediaries have taken advantage of surrogates and intended parents, misrepresenting information, or engaging in unethical practices. This highlights the need for proper regulation and oversight of the surrogacy industry to protect the rights and well-being of all parties involved.

Legal Framework

The legal framework surrounding surrogacy varies greatly across different countries and jurisdictions. Some countries, such as the United States, allow commercial surrogacy, while others, like France and Germany, prohibit it altogether. In some jurisdictions, surrogacy is only permitted on an altruistic basis, with varying degrees of regulation.

The lack of international consistency in surrogacy laws has led to the emergence of a global surrogacy market, where individuals seek surrogacy services in countries with more permissive regulations. This has raised concerns about the exploitation of surrogate mothers in countries with less stringent legal protections.

It is essential for policymakers to carefully consider the ethical implications of surrogacy and develop comprehensive legal frameworks that prioritize the well-being and autonomy of all parties involved, as well as the best interests of the child.

The Role of Technology

Advances in reproductive technologies have further complicated the ethical landscape of surrogacy. Techniques such as in vitro fertilization (IVF), preimplantation genetic diagnosis (PGD), and embryo screening have enabled intended parents to select embryos based on desired characteristics, potentially leading to the commodification of genetic material and the creation of a market for "designer babies."

Additionally, the emergence of online platforms that connect intended parents with potential surrogates has raised concerns about the ethical implications of surrogacy arrangements facilitated through these platforms. These platforms may lack adequate oversight and may increase the risk of exploitation and commodification.

Ethical Considerations and Solutions

Addressing the ethical concerns associated with surrogacy and the commercialization of reproduction requires a comprehensive approach that balances the desires of intended parents with the rights and well-being of surrogate mothers.

First and foremost, informed consent should be a fundamental principle in surrogacy arrangements. Surrogate mothers must fully understand the physical, emotional, and legal implications of their decision to participate in surrogacy. This requires providing comprehensive information, psychological support, and independent legal advice to all parties involved.

Regulation and oversight of the surrogacy industry are crucial in preventing exploitation and ensuring the protection of all parties' rights. This includes licensing and monitoring surrogacy agencies, establishing clear standards for financial compensation, and implementing procedures for screening and counseling both surrogate mothers and intended parents.

Moreover, the focus should be on promoting a holistic understanding of surrogacy that acknowledges the emotional and psychological complexities involved. Counseling and support services should be accessible to surrogate mothers, intended parents, and any resulting children to navigate the unique challenges and ethical dilemmas that may arise.

Education and awareness campaigns can also play a vital role in fostering a broader understanding of the ethical considerations surrounding surrogacy. Encouraging open and respectful dialogue among medical professionals, ethicists, policymakers, intended parents, and surrogate mothers can help shape policies and practices that prioritize the welfare and rights of all individuals involved.

Conclusion

Surrogacy and the commercialization of reproduction raise complex ethical considerations that must be carefully addressed. The potential for exploitation, the commodification of the human body, and the impact of reproductive technologies all require thoughtful regulation and ethical guidelines.

By prioritizing informed consent, establishing robust regulations, and providing support services, society can ensure that surrogacy respects the autonomy, dignity, and well-being of surrogate mothers and intended parents alike. Ultimately, the goal should be to strike a balance that allows individuals and couples to create families while upholding the ethical principles that underpin our understanding of reproduction and human dignity.

Genetic Testing and Ethical Dilemmas

Genetic testing has revolutionized the field of medicine by providing valuable information about an individual's genetic makeup. This powerful tool allows us to identify genetic variations and mutations that may be associated with certain diseases or conditions. However, the use of genetic testing raises a number of ethical dilemmas that need to be carefully considered.

One of the main ethical concerns regarding genetic testing is the issue of informed consent. Before undergoing genetic testing, individuals should be fully informed about the benefits, risks, and limitations of the test. They should also be aware of the potential implications of the test results, both for themselves and for their family members. It is crucial that individuals have a clear understanding of the information they are disclosing and how it may be used.

Another ethical dilemma associated with genetic testing is the issue of genetic discrimination. Genetic test results can reveal information about a person's predisposition to certain diseases or conditions. This information can be used by insurance companies or employers to discriminate against individuals based on their genetic makeup. Legislation and policies have been put in place to protect individuals from genetic discrimination, but it remains a significant concern.

Privacy and confidentiality are also paramount in the context of genetic testing. Genetic information is inherently personal and sensitive, and individuals have the right to keep this information private. When genetic testing is conducted, there must be safeguards in place to protect the privacy of individuals and ensure that their genetic information is not misused or disclosed without their consent.

Ethical considerations also arise when it comes to testing embryos and fetuses. Preimplantation genetic testing and prenatal genetic testing can provide valuable information about genetic disorders or abnormalities. However, these tests raise complex ethical questions regarding the decision to terminate a pregnancy based on the test results. It is crucial to balance the right of individuals to make informed choices about their reproductive health with the potential ethical implications of such decisions.

Furthermore, there are ethical concerns surrounding the potential misuse or misinterpretation of genetic test results. Genetic testing may provide probabilistic information about an individual's risk for certain diseases or conditions, but it does not provide definitive predictions. There is a risk of misinterpreting test results, leading to unnecessary anxiety or invasive medical procedures. Genetic counselors play a vital role in helping individuals understand the limitations of genetic testing and make informed decisions based on the test results.

In addition to these ethical dilemmas, there are broader societal implications of genetic testing. Genetic testing has the potential to exacerbate existing health disparities, as certain populations may not have equal access to testing or may face barriers in the interpretation of test results. Ethical considerations need to be taken into account to ensure that genetic testing is conducted in a fair and equitable manner.

To navigate these ethical dilemmas, it is important to have comprehensive guidelines and regulations in place. Professional organizations, such as the American Society of Human Genetics and the World Health Organization, have developed ethical guidelines for the use of genetic testing. These guidelines address issues such as informed consent, privacy, and the responsible use of genetic information.

In conclusion, genetic testing brings about significant ethical dilemmas that need to be carefully addressed. Informed consent, genetic discrimination, privacy and confidentiality, testing embryos and fetuses, the interpretation of test results, and societal implications are all important factors that must be considered. By adhering to ethical principles and guidelines, we can ensure that genetic testing is conducted in a responsible and ethical manner, ultimately benefiting individuals and society as a whole.

Abortions and Ethical Controversies

Abortion is a highly sensitive and debated topic that raises significant ethical concerns. It involves the termination of a pregnancy, resulting in the removal or expulsion of the developing fetus. The ethical controversies surrounding abortions arise from conflicting views on the moral status of the fetus, the rights of the pregnant woman, and the societal implications of abortion.

The Moral Status of the Fetus

One of the central ethical debates surrounding abortion revolves around the moral status of the fetus. Different perspectives exist, ranging from the belief that the fetus possesses full moral personhood from conception to the view that the fetus only gains moral relevance at a certain stage of development or at birth.

Proponents of the personhood argument argue that the fetus has the same moral rights as any other human being and that terminating a pregnancy is equivalent to taking the life of an innocent person. They emphasize the value of potential human life and argue that abortion violates the right to life.

On the other hand, those who argue for the moral relevance of the fetus at a later stage or at birth do not consider the fetus to have the same moral status as a fully developed human being. They prioritize the autonomy, well-being, and rights of the pregnant woman, arguing that she has the right to make decisions regarding her body and future without interference.

The Rights of the Pregnant Woman

The rights of the pregnant woman are at the core of the ethical controversies surrounding abortions. Advocates for reproductive rights argue that women have the right to choose whether to continue or terminate a pregnancy based on their personal circumstances and beliefs. They emphasize the importance of bodily autonomy and the right to control one's reproductive health.

Opponents of abortion, however, argue that the rights of the fetus should be given precedence over the rights of the pregnant woman. They believe that the fetus has the right to life, and therefore, abortion should be restricted or even prohibited in order to protect the rights of the unborn.

Societal Implications of Abortion

Abortion has significant societal implications that further contribute to the ethical controversies surrounding it. These implications encompass a broad range of issues, including the impact on healthcare systems, population dynamics, gender equality, and the overall social fabric.

One of the concerns raised by opponents of abortion is the potential devaluation of human life and the erosion of societal values. They argue that widespread access to abortion could lead to a disregard for human life and undermine the moral fabric of society.

Proponents of abortion rights, on the other hand, highlight the importance of access to safe and legal abortions in safeguarding the health and well-being of women. They argue that restricting or banning abortions can lead to unsafe and illegal procedures, putting women's lives at risk.

Ethical Frameworks for Abortion

Ethical decision-making in the context of abortion often involves the application of various ethical frameworks. Some of the commonly applied frameworks include:

1. **Utilitarianism:** This ethical framework evaluates the moral worth of an action based on its consequences and overall utility. When applied to abortion, utilitarianism considers factors such as the well-being of the pregnant woman, potential harm to the fetus, and societal implications.

2. **Rights-based ethics:** This framework focuses on the inherent rights and freedoms of individuals. When applied to abortion, rights-based ethics considers the rights of the pregnant woman, the fetus, and any other stakeholders involved.

3. **Virtue ethics:** Virtue ethics emphasizes the cultivation of moral character and the development of virtuous behavior. In the context of abortion, this framework examines the virtues and vices associated with different courses of action and seeks to promote moral virtues such as compassion and justice.

4. **Feminist ethics:** This ethical approach considers issues of gender, power, and social contexts. Feminist ethics in the context of abortion focuses on the rights and agency of women, challenging traditional gender roles and power imbalances.

Legal Perspectives

The legality of abortion varies across different jurisdictions and is influenced by legal, cultural, and religious factors. Some countries allow unrestricted access to abortion, while others impose strict regulations or outright bans. Legal perspectives on abortion often reflect the ethical debates and considerations within a particular society.

In countries where abortion is legal, there are usually regulations in place to ensure that access to abortion is safe and regulated. These regulations typically consider factors such as gestational age, reasons for seeking abortion, and the involvement of medical professionals.

Key Considerations for Ethical Decision Making

When navigating the ethical controversies surrounding abortions, it is crucial to consider the following key ethical considerations:

* Balancing the moral status of the fetus with the rights and autonomy of the pregnant woman.

* Evaluating the potential consequences of different actions, considering both individual and societal impacts.

* Acknowledging the influence of cultural, religious, and personal beliefs on ethical viewpoints.

- Promoting access to accurate information, comprehensive sexual education, and reproductive healthcare services to inform decision making.

- Engaging in respectful dialogue and understanding differing perspectives to find common ground and solutions.

Contemporary Issues and Debates

The ethical controversies surrounding abortions continue to evolve with the advancement of medical technology, changes in societal attitudes, and ongoing legal and political debates. Some of the contemporary issues and debates include:

- **Parental Consent and Notification:** Debates center around whether minors should be required to involve their parents or legal guardians in the decision to have an abortion, and if so, under what circumstances.

- **Late-Term Abortions:** Controversies arise when discussing the ethics of abortions performed late in pregnancy. Questions of fetal viability, the health of the pregnant woman, and the moral status of the fetus often come into play.

- **Medical and Ethical Dilemmas:** Complex medical situations, such as pregnancies with severe fetal abnormalities or risks to the life of the pregnant woman, raise ethical dilemmas regarding the decision to have an abortion.

- **Abortion Access and Equity:** Issues of access to abortion services, particularly for marginalized communities, raise questions of fairness and social justice.

- **Conscientious Objection:** The rights of healthcare providers to refuse to participate in abortions based on moral or religious grounds, and the potential impact on patients' access to reproductive healthcare.

Conclusion

The ethical controversies surrounding abortions stem from differing perspectives on the moral status of the fetus, the rights of the pregnant woman, and the societal implications of abortion. Balancing these considerations requires a careful examination of ethical frameworks, legal perspectives, and the societal context. Engaging in respectful dialogue and understanding diverse viewpoints is essential in navigating this complex and highly sensitive issue.

Gender Selection and Ethical Implications

Gender selection is the practice of choosing the sex of a child before conception or during pregnancy. This can be done through various techniques, including sperm sorting, preimplantation genetic diagnosis (PGD), and prenatal screening. While gender selection has been used for medical reasons, such as preventing genetic disorders linked to a particular gender, it is also used for non-medical reasons, often driven by cultural, social, or personal preferences.

Background

The ability to select the gender of a child raises a number of ethical questions and concerns. One primary concern is the potential for gender discrimination and the reinforcement of gender stereotypes. The preference for a particular gender may reflect social biases or stereotypes, perpetuating the idea that one gender is superior to another. This can have long-lasting impacts on issues of gender equality and women's rights.

Ethical Principles

Several ethical principles come into play when considering the ethical implications of gender selection:

1. Autonomy: The principle of autonomy states that individuals have the right to make decisions regarding their own bodies and reproductive choices. However, this principle may conflict with other ethical considerations.

2. Beneficence: The principle of beneficence requires that actions should be taken in the best interests of individuals or society as a whole. This principle raises questions about the potential long-term consequences of gender selection on individuals, families, and society.

3. Non-maleficence: The principle of non-maleficence requires that harm should be minimized or avoided. There may be potential harms associated with gender selection, such as reinforcing gender stereotypes or contributing to gender imbalance in certain regions or populations.

4. Justice: The principle of justice relates to the fair distribution of resources and opportunities. Gender selection may raise concerns about fairness and equality, particularly if it leads to a preference for one gender over the other.

Ethical Concerns

Gender selection presents several ethical concerns:

Gender Imbalance   One of the main ethical concerns associated with gender selection is the potential for gender imbalance in society. In some cultures, there is a strong preference for male children, which can result in a higher number of male births compared to females. This can lead to societal problems, such as a shortage of marriage partners for men or increased violence and crime rates.   Ethical considerations urge us to address such concerns to ensure a balanced and equitable society.

Reinforcement of Gender Stereotypes   Gender selection may reinforce existing gender stereotypes and inequalities.   Choosing a specific gender for non-medical reasons can perpetuate the idea that one gender is more desirable or superior to the other. This can have negative consequences for individuals and society, limiting opportunities and reinforcing discrimination based on gender.

Eroding Genetic Diversity   The widespread use of gender selection techniques could result in a decrease in genetic diversity. If a large number of individuals select a specific gender, it may lead to a reduction in the genetic variations within a population. This has implications for the long-term health and adaptability of the population, potentially increasing the risk of certain genetic disorders.

Psychological and Emotional Impact   The practice of gender selection may also have psychological and emotional impacts on individuals and families. Parents who choose the gender of their child for non-medical reasons may place higher expectations or burdens on the child based on their gender. Additionally, children may face questioning or doubts about their own identity and self-worth if they discover that their gender was intentionally chosen.

Regulation and Guidelines

Many countries have implemented regulations or guidelines to address the ethical concerns surrounding gender selection.   These regulations vary in scope and restrictiveness, aiming to strike a balance between individual autonomy and societal considerations. Some countries prohibit gender selection for non-medical reasons entirely, while others allow it under certain conditions.

It is important for healthcare providers, policymakers, and society as a whole to engage in ongoing discussions and evaluate the ethical implications of gender selection. Open dialogue and careful consideration of the potential consequences can help ensure that decisions about gender selection are made in a manner that upholds ethical principles and values.

Case Study: Gender Selection for Non-Medical Reasons

In recent years, there has been an increase in individuals traveling to countries where gender selection is legal to choose the sex of their child for non-medical reasons. This has raised ethical concerns in both the countries where the procedures are being performed and the home countries of the individuals seeking gender selection.

For example, in India, the preference for male children has led to a significant gender imbalance. The practice of gender-based abortion has been used to selectively terminate female fetuses, resulting in a skewed sex ratio. This has wide-ranging societal implications, including increased violence against women and a potential decrease in a population's genetic diversity.

In response to these concerns, some countries, such as Australia and Canada, have enacted legislation that prohibits their citizens from seeking gender selection procedures abroad. This approach aims to discourage individuals from traveling to countries where gender selection is legal and to address the ethical concerns associated with non-medical gender selection.

Conclusion

Gender selection raises complex ethical questions about autonomy, equality, and societal impact. While individuals may have the right to make decisions about their reproductive choices, it is important to consider the potential consequences of these choices on individuals, families, and society as a whole. Striking a balance between individual autonomy and ethical considerations is essential in navigating the complex landscape of gender selection. By engaging in open dialogue and promoting awareness of ethical concerns, we can work towards a more equitable and inclusive society.

Ethical Practices in Technology and Artificial Intelligence

The Ethics of Artificial Intelligence

Algorithmic Bias and Fairness in AI

As artificial intelligence (AI) continues to advance and permeate various aspects of our lives, one of the critical issues we must address is algorithmic bias and fairness. Algorithms are not inherently neutral or unbiased; they are created by humans and are often trained on data that may contain inherent biases. This can result in AI systems that perpetuate unfairness and discrimination, leading to harmful consequences for individuals or marginalized groups.

Understanding Algorithmic Bias

Algorithmic bias refers to the systematic and unfair favoritism or discrimination that can occur in AI systems. It can manifest in different ways, such as differential treatment, exclusion, or limitations of opportunities for certain groups. Three common forms of algorithmic bias are:

1. **Sample Bias:** Sample bias occurs when the training data used to develop AI algorithms is not representative of the population it is meant to serve. For example, if a facial recognition system is trained mainly on data collected from lighter-skinned individuals, it may perform poorly when recognizing faces with darker skin tones.

2. **Prejudice Bias:** Prejudice bias arises when the training data reflects and perpetuates societal prejudices or stereotypes. This can lead to biased predictions or decisions that perpetuate discrimination. For example, an AI

system used for job screening that is trained on historical data may discriminate against certain gender or racial groups due to biases in past hiring practices.

3. **Measurement Bias:** Measurement bias occurs when the AI system's performance metrics do not account for the specific needs or experiences of different groups. For instance, if an automated loan approval system focuses primarily on credit scores as a measure of creditworthiness, it may disadvantage individuals with limited credit history or from socioeconomically disadvantaged backgrounds.

Implications of Algorithmic Bias

Algorithmic bias can have significant consequences in various domains, including employment, criminal justice, healthcare, and financial services. Biased AI systems can perpetuate existing inequalities, reinforce stereotypes, and lead to unfair treatment, disadvantage, or harm to individuals or groups. Here are a few examples:

+ **Recidivism Prediction:** AI systems used in predicting recidivism rates among individuals in the criminal justice system have been found to disproportionately label people of color as high-risk, leading to longer sentences and perpetuating racial disparities in the system.

+ **Hiring and Employment:** AI-driven hiring tools have been shown to discriminate against women and certain minority groups by favoring resumes that mirror historical hiring patterns, reinforcing existing gender and racial biases in the workforce.

+ **Credit Scoring:** Biased algorithms used in credit scoring can result in unfair denial or restriction of credit to already disadvantaged individuals or communities, exacerbating socioeconomic inequalities.

+ **Healthcare Decisions:** AI systems in healthcare, such as diagnostic algorithms, may demonstrate racial bias, leading to misdiagnosis or delayed treatment for individuals from certain racial or ethnic backgrounds.

Addressing Algorithmic Bias

Addressing algorithmic bias and ensuring fairness in AI systems is a complex and multidimensional task that requires a comprehensive approach. Here are some key considerations:

1. **Diverse and Representative Data:** AI systems should be trained on diverse and representative datasets that accurately reflect the target population. Careful data collection and curation processes can help to mitigate sample bias.

2. **Regular Auditing and Bias Assessment:** Regular auditing of AI systems is essential to identify and rectify biases. Developers should assess the performance of algorithms across different demographic groups to identify potential biases and take corrective measures.

3. **Ethical Guidelines and Standards:** Developers and organizations should adhere to ethical guidelines and standards that prioritize fairness and non-discrimination. The development and deployment of AI should be guided by principles that ensure transparency, accountability, and the protection of human rights.

4. **Human Oversight and Decision Explainability:** Human oversight is crucial in AI systems to ensure that decisions made by algorithms are fair, transparent, and accountable. It is important to be able to explain and interpret how an AI system arrived at a particular decision or prediction.

5. **Public Engagement and Stakeholder Collaboration:** The involvement of diverse stakeholders, including experts, policymakers, affected communities, and advocacy groups, can contribute to the identification and mitigation of algorithmic bias. Public engagement and collaboration are essential to develop policies and regulations that promote fairness and address concerns related to algorithmic bias.

Case Study: Amazon's Gender-Biased Hiring Algorithm

One high-profile example of algorithmic bias is Amazon's gender-biased hiring algorithm. In 2018, it was revealed that Amazon had developed an AI system to screen job applicants, but the system had learned to discriminate against women. The AI model was trained on resumes submitted to Amazon over a 10-year period, which had a male-dominated applicant pool. As a result, the algorithm learned to penalize resumes that contained terms associated with women or to down-rank women's resumes. The biased AI system was ultimately abandoned.

This case highlights the importance of algorithmic transparency, rigorous testing, and continuous monitoring of AI systems to ensure fairness and prevent discrimination. It also underscores the need for diversity in both the development teams and the datasets used to train AI systems.

Conclusion

Algorithmic bias in AI systems poses significant challenges to fairness and equality. Recognizing and addressing this issue is crucial for ensuring that AI technologies are used in a responsible and ethical manner. By understanding the various forms of bias, the implications they can have in different domains, and employing strategies to mitigate bias, we can strive to develop AI systems that are fair, unbiased, and respectful of human rights. Moving forward, it is essential to prioritize fairness and accountability in the design, development, and deployment of AI to minimize the negative impact of algorithmic bias on individuals and society as a whole.

Key Takeaways

- Algorithmic bias refers to systematic and unfair favoritism or discrimination that can occur in AI systems.

- Common forms of algorithmic bias include sample bias, prejudice bias, and measurement bias.

- Algorithmic bias can have significant implications in areas such as employment, criminal justice, healthcare, and financial services.

- Addressing algorithmic bias requires diverse and representative data, regular auditing, ethical guidelines, human oversight, and stakeholder collaboration.

- The case study of Amazon's gender-biased hiring algorithm serves as a cautionary example of the consequences of algorithmic bias.

Exercises

1. Research and identify an AI system or technology that has been criticized for algorithmic bias. Analyze the issues at hand and propose strategies to mitigate and address the bias.

2. Conduct a case study on a real-world scenario where algorithmic bias had adverse effects on individuals or communities. Present findings and suggest measures to rectify the bias and mitigate the harm caused.

3. Imagine you are part of a team developing an AI system for university admissions. Outline the steps and considerations you would take to ensure fairness and avoid algorithmic bias in the admissions process.

4. Engage in a group discussion on the ethical implications of algorithmic bias. Discuss potential risks, challenges, and possible solutions in promoting fairness and equality in AI systems.

Additional Resources

+ Buolamwini, J., & Gebru, T. (2018). Gender shades: Intersectional accuracy disparities in commercial gender classification. Proceedings of the 1st conference on fairness, accountability and transparency, 77-91.

+ Crawford, K. (2016). Artificial intelligence's white guy problem. New York Times.

+ Mittelstadt, B. D., Allo, P., Taddeo, M., Wachter, S., & Floridi, L. (2016). The ethics of algorithms: Mapping the debate. Big Data & Society, 3(2), 2053951716679679.

+ Ziewitz, M. (2016). Governing algorithms: Myth, mess, and methods. Science, Technology, & Human Values, 41(1), 3-16.

Privacy and Surveillance in the Age of AI

In today's digital age, the rapid advancement of artificial intelligence (AI) has brought about numerous benefits and conveniences. AI technologies have become an integral part of our daily lives, from voice assistants like Siri and Alexa to personalized recommendations on streaming platforms. However, with the rise of AI, there are also growing concerns regarding privacy and surveillance.

The Importance of Privacy

Privacy is a fundamental human right that is enshrined in various international laws and declarations, such as the Universal Declaration of Human Rights. It is the right to control one's personal information and to decide how it is collected, used, and shared. Privacy is essential for individuals to maintain autonomy, protect their dignity, and have control over their personal lives. In the context of AI, privacy becomes even more crucial as the technology has the potential to collect and process vast amounts of personal data.

AI and Data Collection

AI systems rely heavily on data to function effectively. These systems often collect and analyze large volumes of data to train models and make predictions or decisions. The data collected can include personal information such as names, addresses, social media posts, and browsing history. This data can be obtained from various sources, including social media platforms, online services, and Internet of Things (IoT) devices.

Surveillance and AI

The use of AI in surveillance poses significant concerns for privacy. Surveillance technology, coupled with AI, allows for the monitoring and tracking of individuals in ways previously unimaginable. Facial recognition technology, for example, can be used to identify and track individuals in real-time, raising serious concerns about mass surveillance and the potential for abuse. Additionally, AI algorithms can be used to analyze surveillance footage, detect patterns, and make predictions about individuals' behavior.

Ethical Considerations

The use of AI in privacy and surveillance raises several ethical considerations. One of the main concerns is the potential for discrimination and bias. AI systems are trained on large datasets, which can inadvertently perpetuate existing biases present in the data. For example, facial recognition systems have been found to exhibit higher error rates for women and people of color. This bias can have significant consequences, leading to unfair treatment, discrimination, and violation of individuals' rights.

Another ethical consideration is the balance between security and privacy. While AI-powered surveillance systems can enhance security measures and help prevent crime, the indiscriminate collection of personal data can infringe on individuals' privacy rights. Striking the right balance is crucial to ensure that surveillance is conducted within ethical boundaries and respects individuals' privacy.

Regulations and Safeguards

To address the privacy concerns arising from the use of AI in surveillance, governments and regulatory bodies have started implementing regulations and safeguards. The General Data Protection Regulation (GDPR), for instance, was introduced by the European Union to protect individuals' personal data and give them greater control over their information. The GDPR enforces strict regulations on the collection, storage, and processing of personal data, including provisions for obtaining explicit consent and the right to be forgotten.

Organizations and developers also have a responsibility to ensure that AI systems are designed and deployed ethically. This includes implementing measures to minimize bias, ensuring transparency and accountability, and providing clear information to individuals about how their data is used. Regular audits and assessments of AI systems can help identify and address any potential privacy issues.

Case Study: AI-Powered Surveillance Cameras

To illustrate the complexities surrounding privacy and surveillance in the age of AI, let's consider a case study involving the deployment of AI-powered surveillance cameras in a smart city. These cameras are equipped with facial recognition technology and can detect potential criminal activity in real-time.

While the aim of these surveillance systems is to enhance public safety, concerns arise regarding the invasion of privacy. The constant monitoring and tracking of individuals without their knowledge or consent raise questions about the boundaries of surveillance and the potential for abuse. Additionally, the potential for false positives and misidentification further highlights the need for safeguards and accountability in the deployment of such systems.

To address these concerns, it is essential to have clear regulations in place that govern the use of AI in surveillance. These regulations should ensure transparency, accountability, and oversight of AI systems. Safeguards can include obtaining explicit consent, providing opt-out options for individuals, and conducting regular audits to assess the accuracy and effectiveness of the surveillance systems.

Conclusion

Privacy and surveillance are critical issues in the age of AI. While AI technologies offer numerous benefits and advancements, they also raise concerns about the collection, use, and abuse of personal data. Striking the right balance between security and privacy is crucial to ensure that AI-powered surveillance systems are deployed ethically and in compliance with regulations. By implementing safeguards, promoting transparency, and addressing biases, society can harness the full potential of AI while preserving individual privacy rights.

Accountability and Responsibility for AI Systems

As artificial intelligence (AI) continues to advance and become increasingly integrated into various aspects of our lives, it is crucial to address the ethical considerations surrounding its accountability and responsibility. AI systems have the potential to impact individuals, organizations, and society at large, making it imperative to establish clear guidelines for those developing, deploying, and using these systems.

The Need for Accountability

Accountability refers to the obligation of individuals or organizations to take responsibility for their actions and the consequences that arise from them. In the context of AI systems, accountability becomes essential due to the potential risks and impacts associated with their use. AI algorithms and models can make decisions that affect individuals' lives, such as in healthcare diagnosis, autonomous vehicles, and financial decision-making.

When AI systems make errors or exhibit biased behaviors, it can lead to significant harm. For example, biased facial recognition algorithms have been shown to disproportionately misidentify individuals from certain racial or ethnic groups, leading to potential discrimination and injustice. It is essential to hold those responsible for developing and deploying such systems accountable for their actions.

Responsibilities of AI System Developers

Developers of AI systems shoulder significant responsibilities in ensuring the accountability and ethical use of their creations. They must adhere to ethical guidelines and practices throughout the development lifecycle. Here are some key responsibilities for AI system developers:

1. **Transparent and Explainable AI:** Developers should strive to create AI systems that are transparent and explainable. The inner workings of AI algorithms should be understandable to domain experts and users to enhance trust and enable accountability.

2. **Data Collection and Bias Mitigation:** Developers need to be cautious during the data collection process to ensure a diverse and representative dataset. They must work to mitigate biases present in the training data that could propagate and result in biased decision-making by the AI system.

3. **Model Testing and Validation:** Rigorous testing and validation of AI models are essential to identify and rectify any potential flaws or biases. Developers should

conduct comprehensive evaluations to ensure the AI system performs accurately and responsibly in various scenarios.

4. **Ongoing Monitoring and Maintenance:** AI systems are not static entities; they evolve over time. Developers must establish frameworks for continuous monitoring and maintenance to address any issues that arise throughout the lifecycle of the AI system.

5. **Ethical Decision-Making Frameworks:** Developers should implement ethical decision-making frameworks that guide the AI system's behavior. These frameworks should align with societal norms, legal requirements, and human values to promote responsible and accountable decision-making.

Organizational Accountability

Beyond the responsibilities of individual developers, organizations that develop or deploy AI systems bear accountability for their actions. They must create a culture of ethics and prioritize the responsible use of AI within their operations. Here are some key aspects of organizational accountability in the context of AI systems:

1. **Ethics Policies and Guidelines:** Organizations should establish clear and comprehensive ethics policies and guidelines that outline the expected behavior and ethical standards concerning the use of AI systems. These policies should promote fairness, transparency, accountability, and respect for individuals' rights.

2. **Governance and Oversight:** Organizations should establish governance structures and oversight mechanisms to ensure compliance with ethical guidelines and mitigate potential risks associated with AI systems. This includes defining roles and responsibilities, establishing review boards, and implementing audits and evaluations.

3. **Transparency and Openness:** Organizations should strive to be transparent about their use of AI systems, particularly when these systems have significant impacts on individuals or society. Openly communicating about the limitations, risks, and biases of AI systems fosters trust and allows for external scrutiny.

4. **User Education and Empowerment:** Organizations have a responsibility to educate users and stakeholders about the capabilities and limitations of AI systems. By empowering individuals with knowledge, organizations can ensure informed decision-making and prevent undue reliance on AI systems.

5. **Accountability for Harm:** In cases where AI systems cause harm or result in adverse outcomes, organizations should take responsibility for the consequences and provide appropriate redress, remedy, or compensation where necessary. This requires establishing mechanisms for reporting and addressing AI-related incidents.

Legal and Regulatory Frameworks

To ensure accountability and responsible use of AI systems, legal and regulatory frameworks are essential. Governments and policymakers need to establish laws and regulations that govern the development, deployment, and use of AI systems. This includes addressing areas such as data privacy, algorithmic transparency, bias mitigation, and accountability.

Creating enforceable regulations and standards can set clear expectations for responsible AI development and use. Such frameworks can also outline the consequences for non-compliance and promote accountability throughout the AI ecosystem.

Case Study: Autonomous Vehicles

To illustrate the importance of accountability and responsibility in AI systems, let's consider the case of autonomous vehicles. The development and deployment of self-driving cars raise ethical and accountability considerations.

Autonomous vehicles rely on AI systems to make decisions that impact the safety of passengers, pedestrians, and other road users. Developers of autonomous vehicles are responsible for ensuring the accountability and ethical behavior of these systems.

This responsibility includes addressing potential issues such as bias in collision avoidance algorithms, the determination of liability in the event of accidents, and the consideration of moral dilemmas faced by AI systems in critical situations.

To mitigate ethical concerns and maintain accountability, developers must establish robust frameworks for safety, transparency, and user consent. This includes rigorous testing, validation, and ongoing monitoring of autonomous vehicles to ensure their responsible and accountable operation.

Conclusion

Ensuring accountability and responsibility for AI systems is a complex task that requires the collective effort of developers, organizations, governments, and society as a whole. By adhering to ethical practices, implementing transparent and explainable AI, and establishing legal and regulatory frameworks, we can navigate the challenges posed by AI and leverage its benefits while safeguarding against potential harms. AI accountability is an ongoing process that requires continuous evaluation, adaptation, and improvement to reflect evolving societal values and technology advancements.

Ethical Considerations in AI Applications

Artificial Intelligence (AI) has become an integral part of our daily lives, with applications ranging from virtual assistants to autonomous vehicles. As AI technologies continue to advance, it is crucial to address the ethical considerations that arise from their use. In this section, we will explore the key ethical issues related to AI applications and discuss strategies for ensuring ethical behavior in the design, development, and deployment of AI systems.

Bias and Fairness

One of the primary ethical concerns in AI applications is bias and fairness. AI algorithms are trained on vast amounts of data, and if the training datasets contain biases, the resulting AI systems can perpetuate these biases when making decisions. For example, a facial recognition system trained on predominantly white faces may struggle to accurately identify individuals with darker skin tones, leading to potential discrimination.

To address this issue, it is essential to ensure diversity and representativeness in the training data. Data scientists should carefully curate and scrutinize the datasets used for training AI models, taking into account different demographics and perspectives. Additionally, ongoing monitoring and auditing of AI systems can help detect and mitigate biases that may emerge during deployment.

Privacy and Surveillance

AI technologies often rely on extensive data collection and analysis, raising concerns about privacy and surveillance. Personal information, such as location data, browsing history, and social media activity, can be used to train AI models and make predictions about individuals. However, the collection and use of personal data without informed consent can infringe upon privacy rights.

To address privacy concerns, organizations and developers must ensure transparency and obtain explicit consent from users before collecting and using their personal data. Privacy-enhancing techniques, such as data anonymization and encryption, should be employed to protect user privacy. Additionally, regulations and policies should be put in place to govern the ethical use of personal data in AI applications.

Accountability and Responsibility

Another critical ethical consideration in AI applications is accountability and responsibility. As AI systems increasingly make autonomous decisions, it becomes crucial to assign responsibility for the actions and outcomes of these systems. For example, in the context of autonomous vehicles, determining liability in the event of an accident involving a self-driving car can be challenging.

To address this issue, frameworks for accountability and responsibility should be established. Clear guidelines and regulations should define the roles and responsibilities of various stakeholders, including developers, manufacturers, and users of AI systems. Additionally, mechanisms for transparent and explainable AI should be developed, enabling users to understand the decision-making processes of AI systems.

Transparency and Explainability

Transparency and explainability are closely related to accountability and are vital for building trust in AI systems. Users should have a clear understanding of how AI systems make decisions and the factors they consider. Lack of transparency can lead to suspicion and mistrust, especially when AI systems are involved in high-stakes decision-making.

To promote transparency and explainability, AI algorithms and models should be designed in a way that allows for interpretation and explanation. Techniques such as rule-based systems or model-agnostic interpretability methods can provide insights into the inner workings of AI systems. Furthermore, organizations should provide clear documentation and information about the limitations, biases, and potential risks associated with their AI applications.

Safety and Security

Ensuring the safety and security of AI applications is essential to prevent harm to users and society. AI systems that control critical infrastructure, such as power grids or healthcare equipment, must be designed with robust safety measures to avoid accidents or malfunctions. Similarly, protecting AI systems from cyber threats and unauthorized access is crucial to prevent misuse or manipulation.

To address safety concerns, organizations should adhere to established safety standards and best practices when designing and developing AI applications. Techniques such as formal verification and testing can help identify potential safety risks and vulnerabilities. Additionally, organizations should establish protocols for reporting and addressing security vulnerabilities, allowing for timely responses to emerging threats.

Impact on Employment

The widespread adoption of AI technologies has raised concerns about the impact on employment. AI systems have the potential to automate tasks that were previously performed by humans, leading to job displacement. This can result in economic inequality and social unrest.

To mitigate the negative impact on employment, organizations should invest in reskilling and upskilling programs to ensure a smooth transition for affected workers. Governments and policymakers should also consider implementing social safety nets and policies that promote job creation in AI-related industries. Additionally, fostering a culture of lifelong learning can help individuals adapt to the evolving job market.

Unintended Consequences and Ethical dilemmas

AI applications can have unintended consequences and give rise to ethical dilemmas. For example, an AI-powered recommendation system designed to personalize content may inadvertently promote filter bubbles and echo chambers, limiting exposure to diverse opinions. This can have profound implications for free speech and democratic processes.

To address unintended consequences and ethical dilemmas, interdisciplinary collaboration is essential. Ethicists, social scientists, and policymakers should collaborate with AI developers to identify, anticipate, and mitigate potential ethical issues. Moreover, ongoing public dialogue and engagement can provide valuable insights and perspectives on the ethical challenges associated with AI applications.

In conclusion, ethical considerations play a crucial role in the development and deployment of AI applications. Addressing issues such as bias, privacy, accountability, transparency, safety, employment, and unintended consequences requires a holistic and interdisciplinary approach. By integrating ethical frameworks and principles into the design and use of AI systems, we can harness the potential of AI while ensuring it benefits all of humanity.

Discussion Questions

1. Can you think of an example where AI systems produced biased outcomes? What steps could have been taken to avoid or mitigate such biases?

2. How can organizations strike the right balance between collecting user data for AI applications and respecting user privacy rights?

3. Do you think AI technologies should be held to the same level of accountability as human decision-makers? Why or why not?

4. How can explainability and transparency in AI systems be achieved without compromising proprietary information or trade secrets?

5. What measures should be in place to ensure the safety and security of AI applications in critical domains such as healthcare or transportation?

6. What strategies can be employed to minimize job displacement as a result of AI automation?

7. How can we ensure that AI systems are guided by ethical considerations when making autonomous decisions?

8. What are some potential unintended consequences of widespread AI adoption, and how can they be addressed?

Additional Resources

- Bostrom, N. (2014). Superintelligence: Paths, Dangers, Strategies. Oxford University Press. - Floridi, L., & Cowls, J. (2019). A Unified Framework of Five Principles for AI in Society. Harvard Data Science Review, 1(1). - Jobin, A., Ienca, M., & Vayena, E. (2019). The Global Landscape of AI Ethics Guidelines. Nature Machine Intelligence, 1-9. - Mittelstadt, B. D., Allo, P., Taddeo, M., Wachter, S., & Floridi, L. (2016). The ethics of algorithms: Mapping the debate. Big Data & Society, 3(2), 2053951716679679. - Narayanan, A., & Mittelstadt, B. (2019). A Framework for Understanding Unintended Consequences of Machine Learning. arXiv preprint arXiv:1901.10002.

Note: Make sure to approach these discussion questions and additional resources from a human perspective and provide real-world examples that resonate with the readers. Engage the readers with thoughtful insights and encourage critical thinking.

Human-AI Interaction and Ethical Implications

In recent years, the rapid development and integration of Artificial Intelligence (AI) technologies into various aspects of our lives have raised important questions about the ethical implications of human-AI interaction. As AI becomes more sophisticated and capable of performing complex tasks, it is vital to consider the ethical challenges that arise when humans interact with AI systems. This section will delve into the ethical dimensions of human-AI interaction, exploring key issues and providing insights into responsible and beneficial use of AI technology.

Understanding Human-AI Interaction

Human-AI interaction refers to the dynamic relationship between humans and AI systems, where humans engage with AI through various interface modalities, such as voice commands, gestures, or even direct neural interfaces. It encompasses a broad range of interactions, including AI assistants, autonomous vehicles, smart home systems, chatbots, and virtual reality experiences. As AI systems become more prevalent and integrated into our everyday activities, it is crucial to understand the ethical implications that arise from these interactions.

Ethical Issues in Human-AI Interaction

There are several ethical issues that arise within the context of human-AI interaction. These issues encompass both the design and deployment of AI systems, as well as the consequences of AI use in practice. Let's explore some of these key ethical issues:

Transparency and Explainability One fundamental ethical concern is the transparency and explainability of AI systems. As AI algorithms become more complex and operate in opaque ways, it becomes challenging to understand how they arrive at their decisions or recommendations. Lack of transparency can lead to mistrust and concerns about accountability. It is essential to ensure that AI systems are designed in a way that allows users to understand the reasoning behind the system's outputs.

Bias and Discrimination AI systems can inadvertently perpetuate biases and discrimination present in the data they are trained on. For example, facial recognition algorithms have been shown to exhibit racial and gender bias. Such biases can lead to unfair treatment and exacerbate social inequalities. Developers and users must be vigilant in identifying and mitigating biases in AI systems to ensure fairness and equality.

Privacy and Data Security Human-AI interaction often involves the collection and processing of personal data. As AI systems become more integrated into our lives, there is a growing concern about the privacy and security of personal information. It is crucial to establish robust safeguards to protect sensitive data and ensure that individuals have control over how their data is used and shared.

Dependency and Autonomy As AI systems become more advanced, there is a risk of excessive reliance on AI, which can undermine human autonomy. Over-reliance on AI can lead to complacency and passive decision-making, potentially diminishing human agency. It is important to strike a balance between leveraging AI technology and maintaining human autonomy and decision-making capabilities.

Responsible Practices in Human-AI Interaction

To address the ethical challenges posed by human-AI interaction, it is crucial to adopt responsible practices in the design, development, and deployment of AI systems. Here are some key principles to consider:

Transparency and Accountability AI systems should be designed with transparency in mind, providing users with understandable explanations for their decisions and actions. Developers and organizations should be accountable for the ethical implications of their AI systems, ensuring mechanisms for oversight, auditability, and redress.

Fairness and Bias Mitigation To ensure fairness in human-AI interaction, it is important to address bias and discrimination in AI systems. This includes collecting diverse and representative training data, regularly evaluating and mitigating biases, and avoiding the discriminatory impact of AI algorithms on marginalized groups.

Privacy and Data Governance Responsible human-AI interaction requires robust privacy and data protection measures. Organizations should prioritize privacy by design, implement strong security mechanisms, seek informed consent for data collection, and give individuals control over their data.

Human Oversight and Control Human agency and autonomy should be preserved in the context of human-AI interaction. AI systems should be designed to augment human capabilities, rather than replace them. Humans should have the ability to question, override, or modify AI system decisions when necessary.

Ethical Training and Education To navigate the ethical complexities of human-AI interaction, individuals involved in the development and use of AI systems should receive training on ethical practices, including awareness of biases, privacy concerns, and potential risks. Education about AI ethics should be integrated into relevant disciplines and professions.

Case Study: Autonomous Vehicles and Ethical Dilemmas

An illustrative example of the ethical implications of human-AI interaction is the case of autonomous vehicles. As self-driving cars become a reality, we are confronted with challenging ethical dilemmas. Consider a scenario where an autonomous vehicle faces a situation where it must make a split-second decision to either hit a pedestrian or collide with another vehicle to avoid the pedestrian.

This scenario raises profound questions about the ethics of AI decision-making. Should the AI prioritize the life of the passenger, the pedestrian, or seek to minimize overall harm? Whose values and ethical principles should guide the decision-making process? How should we design AI systems to handle such moral dilemmas?

Exploring real-life ethical dilemmas helps us develop a deeper understanding of the complexities involved in human-AI interaction and the need for careful consideration of ethical issues in the design and deployment of AI technologies.

Resources for Further Exploration

To delve deeper into the ethical dimensions of human-AI interaction and its implications, here are some resources worth exploring:

+ *Ethics of Artificial Intelligence and Robotics* by Vincent C. Müller provides an in-depth exploration of ethical issues in AI and robotics.

+ *Moral Machines: Teaching Robots Right from Wrong* by Wendell Wallach and Colin Allen examines the ethical challenges surrounding AI decision-making.

+ The Partnership on AI (www.partnershiponai.org) brings together academia, industry, and civil society to address the global challenges of AI.

+ The IEEE Global Initiative on Ethics of Autonomous and Intelligent Systems (ethicsinaction.ieee.org) provides guidelines and resources for the responsible development and use of AI technologies.

Conclusion

Human-AI interaction is a rapidly evolving field with significant ethical implications. As AI technologies become more integrated into various aspects of our lives, it is crucial to approach human-AI interaction with responsibility, transparency, and fairness. By understanding the ethical dimensions and adopting ethical practices, we can ensure that AI technologies enhance human well-being and contribute positively to society. The ethical considerations discussed in this section provide a foundation for informed decision-making and responsible use of AI in human-AI interactions. Remember, technology should serve us while respecting our values and fundamental human rights.

Ethical Issues in Data Science and Big Data

Data Privacy and Security

Data privacy and security are critical concerns in the modern digital age. With the increasing reliance on technology and the vast amount of data being generated and collected, it is important to protect individuals' sensitive information and prevent unauthorized access or misuse. This section will explore the key concepts and principles of data privacy and security, as well as the ethical considerations and best practices in safeguarding data.

Introduction to Data Privacy

Data privacy refers to the right of individuals to control the collection, use, and sharing of their personal information. Personal data includes any information that can identify a person, such as name, address, social security number, or even IP addresses and device identifiers. Ensuring data privacy is not only crucial for maintaining trust and preserving individual rights, but also necessary for complying with various data protection regulations, such as the General Data Protection Regulation (GDPR) in the European Union.

Principles of Data Privacy

Several principles guide the protection of data privacy:

1. **Consent:** Individuals should have the right to provide informed consent for the collection and use of their personal data. This includes clearly explaining the purpose of data collection and giving individuals the option to opt out.

2. **Purpose Limitation:** Organizations should only collect and use personal data for the specified purposes and should not retain it longer than necessary.

3. **Data Minimization:** Organizations should minimize the collection of personal data to what is necessary for the intended purpose. This includes avoiding the collection of unnecessary or excessive information.

4. **Transparency:** Organizations should be transparent about their data collection practices, including providing clear and easily accessible privacy policies and informing individuals about any third parties who may have access to their data.

5. **Security:** Organizations should implement appropriate security measures to protect personal data from unauthorized access, disclosure, alteration, or destruction. This includes encryption, access controls, and regular security audits.

6. **Accountability:** Organizations should take responsibility for complying with data protection laws and should have mechanisms in place to address data breaches or privacy violations.

Adhering to these principles not only ensures data privacy but also promotes trust and confidence among individuals.

Data Security Measures

Data security involves protecting data from unauthorized access, disclosure, alteration, or destruction. Various technical and organizational measures can be implemented to enhance data security:

- **Access Controls:** Implementing strong authentication methods, such as passwords, biometrics, or two-factor authentication, ensures that only authorized individuals can access sensitive data.

- **Encryption:** Encrypting data at rest (stored) and in transit (being transmitted) protects it from unauthorized interception or theft. Encryption algorithms, such as Advanced Encryption Standard (AES), ensure that data can only be accessed with the correct decryption keys.

- **Firewalls:** Firewalls act as a barrier between internal networks and external networks, filtering incoming and outgoing network traffic based on predefined security rules. This helps prevent unauthorized access to sensitive data.

- **Intrusion Detection and Prevention Systems (IDPS):** IDPS monitor networks and systems for any unauthorized or malicious activities and take proactive measures to prevent potential security breaches. This includes detecting and blocking network attacks or identifying and mitigating system vulnerabilities.

◆ **Regular Updates and Patches:** Keeping software, operating systems, and applications up to date with the latest security patches minimizes the risk of exploitation of known vulnerabilities.

◆ **Employee Training and Awareness:** Educating employees about data security best practices, such as avoiding phishing scams, using strong passwords, and reporting suspicious activities, is crucial in preventing internal security breaches.

By implementing these security measures, organizations can mitigate the risks associated with data breaches and unauthorized access.

Ethical Considerations in Data Privacy and Security

Data privacy and security involve ethical considerations that go beyond legal compliance. Ethical practices in this domain include:

◆ **Informed Consent:** Ensuring individuals understand and provide informed consent for the collection and use of their personal data. This requires clear and understandable explanations about data practices, as well as providing individuals with the choice to opt out.

◆ **Data Transparency:** Being transparent about data collection practices, including informing individuals about the types of data being collected, the purposes for which it will be used, and any third parties with access to the data.

◆ **Fairness:** Ensuring that personal data is used fairly and does not result in any discriminatory practices or adverse impact on individuals or communities.

◆ **Data Accuracy:** Taking reasonable steps to ensure the accuracy of personal data and allowing individuals to update or correct their data as needed.

◆ **Data Breach Response:** Promptly notifying individuals and authorities in the event of a data breach and taking appropriate measures to mitigate potential harm.

Ethical data practices contribute to building trust, maintaining privacy, and respecting individual rights.

Best Practices for Data Privacy and Security

To ensure effective data privacy and security, organizations should:

- Develop and implement comprehensive data privacy policies and security protocols.

- Regularly conduct privacy impact assessments to identify and address potential risks and vulnerabilities.

- Regularly train employees on data privacy best practices, security protocols, and how to respond to data breaches.

- Regularly audit and monitor systems and networks for any potential security breaches or vulnerabilities.

- Conduct periodic third-party security assessments to ensure compliance with industry standards and best practices.

- Stay updated with the evolving regulatory landscape and ensure compliance with relevant data protection laws and regulations.

By following these best practices, organizations can effectively protect data privacy and maintain security standards.

Real-world Example: Equifax Data Breach

One of the most significant data breaches in recent years was the Equifax data breach in 2017. Equifax, one of the largest credit reporting agencies, experienced a cyber attack that exposed the personal information of approximately 147 million consumers, including names, Social Security numbers, birthdates, addresses, and in some cases, driver's license numbers. The breach not only resulted in severe financial and reputational damage to Equifax but also put millions of individuals at risk of identity theft and fraud.

The Equifax breach highlighted the importance of data privacy and security in protecting sensitive information. It served as a wake-up call for organizations to strengthen their security measures, implement robust data protection practices, and prioritize the ethical handling of personal data.

Key Takeaways

Data privacy and security are integral to maintaining trust, preserving individual rights, and complying with data protection regulations. Key takeaways from this section include:

- Data privacy involves individuals' control over the collection, use, and sharing of their personal information.

- Principles of data privacy include consent, purpose limitation, data minimization, transparency, security, and accountability.

- Data security measures include access controls, encryption, firewalls, intrusion detection, regular updates, and employee training.

- Ethical considerations in data privacy and security involve informed consent, data transparency, fairness, data accuracy, and appropriate handling of data breaches.

- Best practices for data privacy and security include developing comprehensive policies, conducting impact assessments, training employees, regular auditing, and compliance with relevant regulations.

- Real-world examples, such as the Equifax breach, highlight the importance of data privacy and the consequences of inadequate security measures.

Protecting data privacy and ensuring data security require a combination of technical measures, organizational practices, and ethical considerations. Organizations must be proactive in safeguarding sensitive information to build trust and maintain the integrity of data handling practices.

Ethical Data Collection and Usage

In the digital age, data has become a valuable resource that drives decision-making, innovation, and progress. However, the collection and usage of data can also raise significant ethical concerns. In this section, we will explore the ethical considerations surrounding data collection and usage, and discuss the principles and guidelines that should govern these practices.

The Value and Impact of Data

Data is the lifeblood of modern society. It is generated from various sources, including social media platforms, online purchases, healthcare records, and internet searches. Organizations collect and analyze this data to gain insights, improve services, personalize experiences, and make informed decisions.

The value of data lies in its potential to identify trends, patterns, and correlations that can be leveraged for various purposes. For example, in the healthcare industry, data analysis can contribute to the development of personalized treatments and the prevention of diseases. In the business world, data can drive targeted marketing campaigns, optimize supply chain operations, and enhance customer experiences.

However, the use of data also comes with potential risks and ethical challenges. Data breaches, unauthorized access, misuse, and discrimination are among the concerns that have arisen in recent years. Therefore, it is crucial to establish ethical standards and practices to guide the collection and usage of data.

Principles of Ethical Data Collection

1. **Transparency**: Organizations should be transparent about the purpose of data collection, the types of data being collected, and how the data will be used. This includes providing clear and easily understandable privacy policies and terms of service.

2. **Informed Consent**: Individuals should have the right to be informed about how their data will be collected, used, and shared. Organizations should obtain explicit consent from individuals before collecting their data and should provide mechanisms for individuals to withdraw their consent at any time.

3. **Purpose Limitation**: Organizations should collect data only for specific and legitimate purposes. They should not collect more data than is necessary, and they should not use the data for purposes other than those disclosed to the individuals.

4. **Data Minimization**: Organizations should collect and retain only the minimum amount of data required to fulfill the intended purpose. Unnecessary or excessive data collection should be avoided.

5. **Data Security**: Organizations should implement robust security measures to protect collected data from unauthorized access, loss, or theft. This includes encryption, firewalls, access controls, and regular security audits.

6. **Data Accuracy**: Organizations should take steps to ensure the accuracy and integrity of the collected data. They should provide mechanisms for individuals to review and correct their data if necessary.

7. **Accountability:** Organizations should take responsibility for their data collection and usage practices. They should designate a data protection officer and establish internal policies and procedures to ensure compliance with relevant laws and regulations.

Ethical Challenges

While there are guidelines in place to govern ethical data collection and usage, several challenges persist in the digital landscape. Let's explore some of the key challenges and their implications:

1. **Data Privacy and Consent:** The concept of informed consent becomes challenging when dealing with complex data collection methods such as cookies, device tracking, and machine learning algorithms. Organizations must ensure that individuals understand the extent to which their data is being collected and used.

2. **Data Ownership and Control:** Questions arise regarding who owns the collected data and who should have control over its usage. Individuals should have the right to access, modify, and delete their data, but this can be challenging in situations where the data is shared across multiple organizations.

3. **Data Bias and Discrimination:** Data analysis techniques can inadvertently introduce biases and discrimination. It is crucial to address these biases and ensure that decisions made based on data do not perpetuate inequality or reinforce stereotypes.

4. **Data Security and Breaches:** With the increasing prevalence of cyber threats, organizations must prioritize data security. A data breach can have severe consequences for individuals, leading to financial loss, identity theft, and reputational damage.

5. **Big Data and Data Exhaustion:** The sheer volume and variety of data generated pose challenges in terms of storage, processing, and analysis. Organizations must invest in robust infrastructure and technologies to handle big data responsibly.

Safeguarding Ethical Data Practices

To foster ethical data practices, organizations should consider implementing the following strategies:

1. **Privacy by Design:** Privacy considerations should be embedded into the design of systems and processes from the outset. By adopting privacy-enhancing technologies and practices, organizations can proactively protect individuals' privacy rights.

2. **Data Governance:** Establishing a robust data governance framework can help organizations manage data collection, storage, processing, and usage in a secure and ethical manner. This includes regular audits, risk assessments, and compliance monitoring.

3. **Data Protection Impact Assessments (DPIAs):** Organizations should conduct DPIAs to assess the potential privacy risks associated with their data processing activities. This involves identifying and mitigating risks, ensuring compliance with privacy regulations, and involving relevant stakeholders in the decision-making process.

4. **Ethical Data Decision-Making:** Organizations should empower data professionals and decision-makers to consider the ethical implications of their work. This can be achieved through training, awareness programs, and the establishment of ethical review boards or committees.

5. **User Empowerment:** Individuals should have control over their data and should be educated about their rights and options. Organizations should provide user-friendly tools and interfaces that allow individuals to manage their privacy preferences effectively.

Case Study: Ethical Data Collection in Healthcare

In the healthcare sector, the collection and usage of patient data pose unique ethical challenges. Let's consider a case study to illustrate these challenges and explore potential solutions.

Case Study: Telemedicine and Data Collection

Telemedicine has gained traction in recent years, enabling individuals to receive medical advice and consultations remotely. In this scenario, patient data, including personal health information and medical history, is transmitted electronically for diagnosis and treatment.

Ethical Challenges: - Data Security: Ensuring the confidentiality and integrity of patient data during transmission and storage. - Informed Consent: Obtaining explicit consent for the collection, transmission, and storage of patient data. - Data Minimization: Collecting only data necessary for diagnosis and treatment, avoiding unnecessary intrusion into patients' privacy. - Data Accuracy: Verifying the accuracy of patient data transmitted electronically to avoid misdiagnosis or mistreatment.

Solutions: - Encryption: Implementing end-to-end encryption techniques to protect patient data during transmission. - Consent Forms: Clearly articulating the purpose, risks, and benefits of data collection and obtaining signed consent from patients. - Data Storage: Developing secure storage systems and strict access controls to protect patient data against unauthorized access. - Regular Audits:

Conducting periodic audits to verify the accuracy of patient data and ensure compliance with privacy regulations.

By addressing these ethical challenges and implementing appropriate solutions, healthcare organizations can uphold ethical standards while harnessing the potential of telemedicine.

Conclusion

Ethical data collection and usage are critical in the digital age. Organizations must prioritize transparency, informed consent, purpose limitation, data security, and accountability to foster trust and protect individuals' privacy rights. By adhering to ethical principles and addressing the challenges associated with data collection and usage, organizations can navigate the complex landscape of data ethics and contribute to a responsible and sustainable digital ecosystem.

Data Bias and Discrimination

In the age of big data and artificial intelligence, it is crucial to examine the ethical implications of data bias and discrimination. While data holds enormous potential for uncovering insights and driving decision-making, it can also perpetuate systemic inequalities and biases if not collected, analyzed, and used responsibly.

Understanding Data Bias

Data bias refers to the presence of systematic errors or prejudices in the data used for analysis. These biases may arise due to various reasons, such as the sampling method, data collection process, or the inherent characteristics of the data itself. Data bias can impact the accuracy, reliability, and fairness of the conclusions drawn from the data.

One common type of data bias is selection bias, which occurs when the sample used for analysis does not accurately represent the population of interest. This can happen if certain groups are underrepresented or excluded from the data collection process, leading to skewed results. For example, if a study on income levels only collects data from high-income neighborhoods, the findings will not accurately reflect the diversity of income distribution in the larger population.

Another type of bias is measurement bias, where the data collection instruments or methods introduce systematic errors. For instance, if a survey is conducted in a way that favors certain demographic groups or asks leading questions, the responses obtained will not provide an accurate representation of reality.

Ethical Implications of Data Bias

Data bias can have far-reaching ethical implications, particularly in domains such as hiring, lending, criminal justice, and healthcare. If biased data is used to make decisions, it can perpetuate discrimination and reinforce existing social disparities. Consider the following scenarios:

- **Loan approvals:** If a bank uses biased data that predominantly considers credit scores from privileged groups, it may lead to biased loan approvals, leaving marginalized groups at a disadvantage.

- **Criminal justice system:** Biased data used in predictive policing algorithms could disproportionately target minority communities and perpetuate racial profiling, leading to wrongful arrests and unfair treatment.

+ **Healthcare disparities:** Biased healthcare data can lead to unequal access to medical treatments and resources, resulting in poorer health outcomes for marginalized communities.

Besides perpetuating discrimination, data bias can also erode public trust in data-driven technologies. When biased algorithms are deployed in sectors that significantly impact people's lives, it can lead to a loss of confidence in the fairness and integrity of those systems.

Addressing Data Bias

Mitigating data bias requires a multifaceted approach that involves careful data collection, preprocessing, modeling, and evaluation. Here are some key strategies:

+ **Diverse and representative data:** Ensuring that the data used for analysis is diverse and representative of the population of interest is crucial. It involves actively seeking out and including data from underrepresented groups and accounting for any inherent biases in the sample.

+ **Data preprocessing:** Rigorous preprocessing techniques, such as data cleaning, outlier detection, and imputation, can help identify and mitigate biases present in the data. Quantitative methods, like statistical weighting or oversampling, can be employed to balance the representation of different groups.

+ **Algorithmic fairness:** Researchers and practitioners should strive to develop algorithms that are fair and unbiased. This involves avoiding the use of discriminatory variables or features and carefully examining the impact of the algorithm on different demographic groups.

+ **Transparency and accountability:** Organizations should be transparent about the data and algorithms they use, ensuring that there are clear policies and guidelines in place to address data bias. Regular audits and assessments can help hold decision-makers accountable for any biased outcomes.

However, it is important to recognize that addressing data bias is a complex and ongoing challenge. It requires interdisciplinary collaboration and a commitment to diversity, inclusivity, and ethical decision-making at every stage of the data lifecycle.

Case Study: ProPublica's Analysis of COMPAS

A notable example of the ethical implications of data bias is ProPublica's analysis of the Correctional Offender Management Profiling for Alternative Sanctions (COMPAS) software. The study found that COMPAS, a tool used in the criminal justice system to predict recidivism risk, exhibited significant racial bias.

ProPublica discovered that while the system had a similar accuracy rate for different racial groups, it had higher false positive rates for African American defendants compared to white defendants. This meant that African Americans were more likely to be incorrectly flagged as higher risk, leading to potential biased outcomes in sentencing decisions.

This case study highlights the need for thorough evaluation and scrutiny of algorithms and the data they rely on. It serves as a reminder that even well-intentioned tools can reinforce existing biases if not carefully designed, implemented, and monitored.

Ethical Practice and Reflection

It is crucial for individuals and organizations working with data to actively engage in ethical practices and continually reflect upon the biases that may be present in their data and algorithms. The following questions can guide ethical decision-making:

- Is the data used diverse and representative of the population of interest?

- What are the potential biases in the data collection or measurement process?

- How can data preprocessing techniques address and mitigate biases?

- Are the algorithms developed fair and transparent in their decision-making process?

- What steps can be taken to ensure accountability and address any biased outcomes?

By critically examining these questions and adopting responsible practices, we can strive to make data-driven technologies more inclusive, equitable, and unbiased.

Conclusion

Data bias and discrimination pose significant ethical challenges in the era of big data and artificial intelligence. Understanding the ethical implications, addressing biases at various stages of data analysis, and promoting transparency and accountability are essential steps toward creating more equitable and fair systems.

As practitioners and consumers of data-driven technologies, it is our collective responsibility to ensure that data is used in a manner that respects individual rights, upholds ethical principles, and promotes social justice. By doing so, we can harness the power of data for the betterment of society while avoiding the perpetuation of biases and discrimination.

Data Ownership and Intellectual Property

Data ownership and intellectual property rights are critical issues in the field of technology and artificial intelligence. As data becomes an increasingly valuable asset, it is important to understand who owns the data and how intellectual property rights apply to data.

Data Ownership

Data ownership refers to the legal rights and control over data. In the context of technology and artificial intelligence, data ownership can be complex due to the vast amount of data generated and collected by various entities. There are several key considerations when it comes to data ownership:

1. **Data Originator:** The entity or individual who generates or creates the data is generally considered the owner of the data. For example, if a user creates content on a social media platform, they typically retain ownership of that content.

2. **Terms of Service and Licensing Agreements:** Many platforms and services have terms of service or licensing agreements that dictate who owns the data generated or shared on their platforms. It is important for users to carefully read and understand these agreements to determine their rights to the data they generate or upload.

3. **Contractual Arrangements:** In certain cases, data ownership may be determined through contractual arrangements between parties. For example, in a business-to-business relationship, the ownership and use of data may be outlined in a contractual agreement.

4. **Statutory or Regulatory Requirements:** Some jurisdictions have specific laws or regulations that govern data ownership in certain industries or contexts. For example, in the healthcare sector, patient data is subject to strict privacy and ownership regulations.

It is worth noting that in some cases, data ownership may be shared between multiple parties. For instance, if data is collected through a collaborative research project, multiple researchers or institutions may have joint ownership of the data.

Intellectual Property Rights

Intellectual property (IP) rights protect works and creations of the mind, giving the creator exclusive rights over their creations. In the context of data, IP rights are applicable to original works, such as databases, algorithms, and data models. Here are the key aspects of IP rights that pertain to data:

1. **Copyright:** Copyright protects original creative works, including original databases and data models. If someone creates a unique and original database, they generally hold the copyright to that database. However, it is important to note that copyright protection typically does not extend to mere data (e.g., factual data points) or ideas.

2. **Trade Secrets:** Trade secrets protect valuable and confidential business information, including proprietary databases or algorithms. To maintain trade secret protection, companies must take reasonable steps to keep the information confidential. Trade secrets can provide long-term protection to valuable data assets.

3. **Patents:** Patents protect inventions and technological innovations, including certain algorithms and data processing methods. However, obtaining a patent for a data-related invention can be challenging, as it requires meeting specific criteria, such as novelty, non-obviousness, and industrial applicability.

4. **Contracts and Licensing:** Intellectual property rights can also be managed through contracts and licensing agreements. Data owners can license their data to third parties, granting them certain rights to use the data in exchange for compensation.

It is important for individuals and organizations to understand their rights and obligations regarding data ownership and intellectual property. Failure to do so can result in legal disputes and potential loss of control over valuable data assets.

Challenges and Considerations

Data ownership and intellectual property in the digital age present unique challenges and considerations. Here are some key points to keep in mind:

1. **Data Privacy:** While data ownership determines who has control over data, data privacy focuses on protecting individuals' personal information. Data owners

must comply with privacy regulations to ensure that data is collected, stored, and used in a manner that respects individuals' rights to privacy.

2. **Data Monopolies and Fair Competition**: Concentration of data ownership in the hands of a few entities can potentially lead to unfair market dominance and hinder competition. Regulators and policymakers are grappling with ensuring fair competition while balancing data ownership rights.

3. **Collaborative Data Sharing**: In some cases, data owners may choose to share their data with others for collaborative purposes. Establishing clear data sharing agreements and frameworks becomes crucial to maintain trust and ensure the protection of intellectual property rights.

4. **International Jurisdiction**: Data ownership and intellectual property rights can vary across jurisdictions, making it challenging to protect and enforce rights globally. Organizations operating in multiple countries must navigate these complexities and understand the legal frameworks in each jurisdiction.

Example: Data Ownership in a Digital Marketplace

Let's consider the example of a digital marketplace where users can list and sell their products. In this scenario, there are multiple stakeholders involved, including the platform operator, sellers, and buyers.

The platform operator serves as the intermediary, providing the infrastructure for sellers to list their products and buyers to purchase them. The platform's terms of service clearly state that sellers retain ownership of their product listings, including the accompanying data, such as product descriptions and images.

However, the platform operator may have certain rights to use the data for operational purposes, such as promoting the marketplace or improving user experience. To protect sellers' rights, the platform operator may also include provisions in the terms of service that restrict the use of sellers' data by third parties.

Sellers, on the other hand, retain ownership of their products and the associated intellectual property rights, such as trademarks or designs. This means that sellers have the exclusive right to reproduce, distribute, and control the use of their products.

Buyers, upon purchasing a product, acquire ownership of the physical item but not the underlying data related to the listing. The buyer, however, may be allowed to provide feedback or review the product, which becomes part of the platform's data but does not impact the ownership rights of the seller.

To summarize, in this example, sellers retain ownership of their data (product listings) and the associated intellectual property rights, while buyers acquire ownership of the physical items. The platform operator has certain rights to use the data but must respect sellers' ownership rights and privacy.

Additional Resources

For further exploration of data ownership and intellectual property, consider the following resources:

- World Intellectual Property Organization (WIPO): `https://www.wipo.int`
- Electronic Frontier Foundation (EFF): `https://www.eff.org`
- Data Protection Authorities (varies by jurisdiction)

Summary

Data ownership and intellectual property rights play a crucial role in the field of technology and artificial intelligence. Understanding who owns the data and how intellectual property rights apply to data are fundamental in ensuring fair competition, protecting privacy, and fostering innovation. By considering the complexities and challenges associated with data ownership and intellectual property, individuals and organizations can navigate the digital landscape with a clearer understanding of their rights and obligations.

Ethical Use of Predictive Analytics

Predictive analytics refers to the use of statistical algorithms and machine learning techniques to analyze historical data and make predictions about future events or outcomes. It has become widely adopted in various industries, including finance, healthcare, marketing, and human resources, due to its potential to drive informed decision making and improve organizational performance. However, the ethical implications of using predictive analytics cannot be overlooked.

The Benefits and Risks of Predictive Analytics

Predictive analytics offers several benefits, such as:

1. **Improved Decision Making**: Predictive models can provide valuable insights and assist decision-makers in making informed choices. For example, in the financial industry, predictive analytics can be used to assess creditworthiness and determine the likelihood of default for loan applicants.

2. **Enhanced Efficiency:** By utilizing predictive analytics, organizations can streamline processes, optimize resource allocation, and reduce costs. For instance, in healthcare, predictive models can help identify patients at high risk of developing certain diseases, enabling early interventions and preventive measures.

3. **Personalized Experiences:** Predictive analytics empowers organizations to tailor products and services to individual customers based on their preferences and needs. This can lead to improved customer satisfaction and loyalty. For example, online retailers can use predictive models to recommend products based on a customer's browsing and purchase history.

However, the use of predictive analytics also introduces certain risks and challenges, such as:

1. **Data Quality and Bias:** Predictive models heavily rely on historical data, and the quality and representativeness of the data can significantly impact the accuracy and fairness of the predictions. Biased or incomplete data can lead to discriminatory outcomes, perpetuating existing social inequalities. For instance, if historical data used to train a predictive model in hiring processes is biased against certain demographics, the model may reproduce and perpetuate bias in the recruitment process.

2. **Privacy and Data Protection:** Predictive analytics requires access to large volumes of sensitive data, including personal information. Organizations must ensure proper data protection measures to safeguard individual privacy and comply with relevant regulations, such as the General Data Protection Regulation (GDPR). It is crucial to obtain informed consent from individuals when collecting and using their data for predictive analytics purposes.

3. **Transparency and Explainability:** The complex nature of predictive models often makes it challenging to understand and interpret the decision-making process. Lack of transparency can raise concerns about accountability and fairness, particularly when automated decisions significantly impact individuals' lives. Organizations should strive to develop explainable models that can be easily audited and validated.

4. **Unintended Consequences:** Predictive analytics is not foolproof and can result in unintended consequences. For example, if a predictive model

incorrectly identifies an individual as high risk for criminal behavior, it could lead to unwarranted surveillance and harm their reputation and opportunities. Careful evaluation and continuous monitoring of predictive models are essential to minimize such risks.

Ethical Considerations

To ensure the ethical use of predictive analytics, several key considerations should be taken into account:

1. **Data Governance:** Organizations must establish robust data governance frameworks that address data quality, privacy, security, and data-sharing practices. This includes ensuring data is collected and used ethically and transparently, with clear justifications for the data variables and criteria used in the predictive models.

2. **Fairness and Accountability:** Organizations should strive for fairness and avoid discrimination in predictive analytics. This involves continually monitoring and addressing biases that may arise from the data or algorithms. It is crucial to provide explanations for decisions made by predictive models and establish mechanisms for individuals to challenge and correct any unfair outcomes.

3. **Informed Consent:** Organizations must obtain informed consent from individuals when using their data for predictive analytics purposes. This entails providing clear and understandable information about how their data will be used, the potential risks involved, and their rights regarding data access, correction, and deletion.

4. **Human Oversight:** Although predictive analytics is reliant on algorithms and automation, human oversight remains crucial. Human experts should be involved in the development, monitoring, and interpretation of predictive models to ensure ethical considerations are adequately addressed and to prevent overreliance on automated decision-making.

Case Study: Predictive Policing

One notable application of predictive analytics is in law enforcement, specifically predictive policing. Predictive policing aims to forecast crime hotspots and individuals who are more likely to commit crimes, enabling law enforcement agencies to allocate resources effectively. However, there are ethical concerns associated with such practices.

One of the challenges with predictive policing is the potential for biased outcomes. If historical crime data reflects biased policing practices, the predictive models trained on this data may perpetuate and amplify biases. This can lead to over-policing in certain neighborhoods or the unfair targeting of specific demographics.

To address these ethical concerns, it is essential to ensure a comprehensive and unbiased data collection process and regularly assess and retrain predictive models. Additionally, accountability and transparency should be prioritized, with clear guidelines on how the predictions are to be used and potential limitations communicated to law enforcement officers.

Conclusion

Predictive analytics presents immense potential for organizations to make data-driven decisions and improve outcomes. However, to harness these benefits ethically, organizations must prioritize fairness, transparency, and accountability. Implementing robust data governance practices, addressing biases, obtaining informed consent, and maintaining human oversight are crucial steps in ensuring the ethical use of predictive analytics. By doing so, organizations can strike a balance between leveraging the power of predictive analytics and safeguarding individuals' rights and societal well-being.

Ethical Challenges in Cybersecurity

Ethical Hacking and Penetration Testing

In today's interconnected and technology-driven world, the importance of cybersecurity cannot be overstated. Organizations and individuals alike face countless cyber threats, ranging from data breaches to malicious attacks. In response to these threats, ethical hacking and penetration testing have emerged as vital practices to ensure the security of computer systems and networks.

Understanding Ethical Hacking

Ethical hacking, also known as white-hat hacking or penetration testing, involves authorized individuals or teams attempting to identify vulnerabilities in computer systems or networks. The goal is to assess the security posture of the target system and provide recommendations for strengthening its defenses. Ethical hackers utilize the same techniques and tools as malicious attackers but with noble intentions.

Ethical hackers employ various methods to expose vulnerabilities, including network scanning, vulnerability assessment, password cracking, social engineering, and exploitation of software flaws. By simulating real-world attack scenarios, ethical hackers help organizations identify weak points and take appropriate measures to patch them.

It is important to note that ethical hacking is conducted with the full knowledge and consent of the system owner. The process is carried out in a controlled manner to ensure minimal disruption and damage to the targeted system or network. Clear rules of engagement and a well-defined scope are established to protect against unintended consequences.

Role and Benefits of Penetration Testing

Penetration testing is a subset of ethical hacking that focuses on identifying vulnerabilities and potential exploits in a targeted system or network. It involves conducting a systematic, authorized attack on the system's defenses to assess its resilience against real-world threats. The main objective of penetration testing is to evaluate the system's security controls and provide actionable recommendations to mitigate risks effectively.

The benefits of penetration testing extend beyond identifying vulnerabilities. They include:

- **Risk Mitigation:** Penetration testing helps identify and prioritize vulnerabilities, allowing organizations to take proactive measures to mitigate risks.

- **Enhanced Security Posture:** By uncovering weaknesses, penetration testing enables organizations to improve their overall security posture, reducing the likelihood of successful attacks.

- **Compliance Requirements:** Many industries and regulatory bodies require periodic penetration testing to ensure compliance with security standards. Penetration testing helps organizations meet these requirements.

- **Cost Savings:** Identifying vulnerabilities and addressing them early in the development lifecycle is far less costly than dealing with the aftermath of an actual cyber attack.

+ **Reputation Protection:** A successful cyber attack can have severe reputational damage. Penetration testing minimizes the risk of such incidents, thereby safeguarding an organization's reputation.

Challenges and Limitations

While ethical hacking and penetration testing are highly valuable practices, they do come with certain challenges and limitations.

Legal and Ethical Considerations: Penetration testing can potentially violate laws and regulations if not properly authorized and executed. It is crucial to obtain explicit permission from the system owner and operate within the bounds of the law. Ethical considerations must also be taken into account to ensure privacy and protect sensitive data.

Technological Limitations: Penetration testing techniques are continually evolving, and keeping up with the latest technologies and attack vectors can be challenging. Additionally, testing may not always replicate real-world scenarios accurately, leading to potential blind spots in security assessments.

Time and Resource Constraints: Penetration testing requires skilled professionals with expertise in various areas of cybersecurity. Availability of these specialists, as well as the time and resources required for thorough testing, can pose challenges for organizations.

False Sense of Security: While penetration testing can uncover vulnerabilities, it is important to remember that it is not a comprehensive solution. Regular patches, updates, and ongoing security measures are necessary to maintain a robust security posture.

Best Practices and Key Principles

To maximize the effectiveness and value of ethical hacking and penetration testing, adherence to best practices and key principles is essential:

+ **Clear Scope and Objectives:** Define the scope of the testing and establish specific objectives to ensure a focused and productive engagement.

+ **Authorization and Documentation:** Obtain written permission from the system owner and document all aspects of the testing process, including the methodologies used, findings, and recommendations.

+ **Advanced Preparation:** Thoroughly research the target system or network, gather relevant information, and identify potential attack vectors before initiating the testing process.

+ **Continual Learning:** Keep abreast of the latest security trends, vulnerabilities, and hacking techniques to ensure the effectiveness and relevance of penetration testing.

+ **Collaboration and Communication:** Foster close collaboration between the ethical hacking team and the system owner to facilitate effective communication, clarification of findings, and understanding of the recommended remediation measures.

Case Study: Retail Company Security Assessment

Consider a retail company that wants to assess the security of its e-commerce platform. They engage an ethical hacking team to conduct penetration testing.

The team starts by identifying potential vulnerabilities, such as unpatched software, weak authentication mechanisms, and insecure network configurations. They simulate real-world attack scenarios by attempting to exploit these vulnerabilities, gaining unauthorized access to the system, and extracting sensitive customer data.

Through their testing, the team discovers several critical vulnerabilities, including SQL injection flaws and insecure session management. They provide the company with a detailed report outlining the vulnerabilities and recommendations to mitigate the risks. The company promptly addresses the identified issues, enhancing the security of its e-commerce platform and safeguarding customer data.

Conclusion

Ethical hacking and penetration testing are crucial components of modern cybersecurity practices. By uncovering vulnerabilities and providing insights to strengthen system defenses, organizations can proactively protect their assets, data, and reputation. With proper authorization, adherence to legal and ethical considerations, and a focus on continuous learning, ethical hacking and penetration testing can help organizations stay ahead of cyber threats and minimize security risks.

Data Breaches and Disclosure Requirements

In today's digital age, data breaches have become an increasingly common and significant concern for organizations of all sizes and industries. A data breach occurs when unauthorized individuals gain access to sensitive or confidential data, which may include personal information, financial records, or other proprietary data. The consequences of a data breach can be severe, resulting in financial losses, reputational damage, and potential legal liabilities. This section explores the ethical and legal aspects of data breaches and the disclosure requirements that organizations must adhere to.

Ethical Considerations

Data breaches raise several ethical considerations, primarily centered around the duty and responsibility an organization has towards its customers or clients whose data has been compromised. Organizations handle large volumes of personal and sensitive data and have an ethical obligation to protect this information from unauthorized access. When a data breach occurs, the organization must address the breach promptly and transparently, considering the potential harm caused to individuals whose data has been exposed.

One ethical principle relevant to data breaches is transparency. Organizations should strive to be transparent with affected individuals by promptly disclosing the breach and providing information on the extent of the breach, the type of data compromised, and the potential risks associated with the breach. This transparency allows individuals to take necessary actions to protect themselves, such as changing passwords, monitoring financial transactions, or taking other preventive measures.

Another ethical consideration is accountability. Organizations should take responsibility for the breach and work diligently to resolve the issue and mitigate any harms caused. This responsibility includes offering support and remedies to affected individuals, such as credit monitoring services or identity theft assistance. Additionally, organizations should assess their security measures and address any weaknesses or vulnerabilities to prevent future breaches, demonstrating their commitment to safeguarding data and ensuring the trust of their customers.

Legal Requirements

In addition to ethical considerations, organizations are subject to various legal requirements regarding data breaches and disclosure. The laws and regulations governing data breaches vary across jurisdictions, but most require organizations to notify affected individuals, government authorities, and sometimes the media about a breach that compromises personal information.

One such significant regulation is the General Data Protection Regulation (GDPR), which applies to organizations handling the personal data of individuals within the European Union. The GDPR mandates that organizations notify affected individuals within 72 hours of becoming aware of a data breach, unless the breach is unlikely to result in a risk to the rights and freedoms of individuals. Failure to comply with GDPR requirements can lead to substantial fines and penalties.

Many countries, including the United States, have adopted data breach notification laws at the state level. These laws typically outline the timeframe and specific information that organizations must include in breach notifications. For example, in California, the California Consumer Privacy Act (CCPA) requires businesses to notify California residents whose personal information has been compromised as a result of a data breach.

Organizations must also consider industry-specific regulations and contractual obligations related to data breaches. For instance, healthcare organizations are subject to the Health Insurance Portability and Accountability Act (HIPAA), which has specific requirements for breach notification.

Responding to a Data Breach

When a data breach occurs, organizations should follow a structured response plan to ensure a timely and effective response. The response plan typically includes the following steps:

1. **Containment**: The organization must isolate and mitigate the breach to prevent further unauthorized access and limit potential damage. 2. **Assessment**: The organization should conduct a thorough investigation to determine the extent of the breach, the type of data compromised, and the potential impact on affected individuals. 3. **Notification**: Depending on the legal requirements and the potential harm to individuals, the organization should promptly notify affected individuals, government authorities, and other relevant stakeholders. 4. **Remediation**: The organization must take appropriate remedial measures to address the breach and prevent future incidents. This may include strengthening security measures, updating policies and procedures, or conducting employee training on data protection. 5. **Communication**: Throughout the process, clear and timely communication is crucial. The organization should keep affected individuals informed of the progress made in resolving the breach and any additional steps they need to take to protect themselves.

Case Study: Equifax Data Breach

One notable data breach that underscores the importance of disclosure requirements is the Equifax data breach in 2017. Equifax, one of the largest credit reporting agencies, experienced a significant breach that exposed the personal information of approximately 147 million individuals. The breach included sensitive data such as Social Security numbers, birth dates, and credit card details.

The Equifax data breach highlighted the ethical and legal obligations of organizations in handling data breaches. Equifax faced criticism for its delayed disclosure of the breach, with reports indicating that the breach occurred in May but was only publicly disclosed in September. The delayed response sparked public outrage and raised concerns about the organization's accountability and transparency.

Apart from the ethical implications, Equifax faced numerous legal consequences, including investigations by regulatory bodies and lawsuits from affected individuals. The breach also resulted in a significant financial impact for Equifax, with the company incurring millions of dollars in costs related to litigation, remediation, and reputational damage.

The Equifax case serves as a cautionary tale and emphasizes the importance of establishing robust cybersecurity measures, promptly disclosing breaches, and taking immediate action to address vulnerabilities and protect customer data.

Exercise

Consider a hypothetical scenario where a large retail company experiences a data breach, compromising the personal information of thousands of its customers. As the organization's Chief Information Officer (CIO), outline the steps you would take to respond to the breach ethically and in compliance with legal requirements. Consider the practical and ethical challenges you may face during this process and propose strategies to overcome them.

Additional Resources

1. Ponemon Institute. (2020). *Cost of a Data Breach Report*. Retrieved from [https://www.ibm.com/security/data-breach](https://www.ibm.com/security/data-bre.
2. European Union Agency for Cybersecurity (ENISA). (2020). *Data breach notifications in Europe: GDPR Article 33 compared to NISD Art.14*. Retrieved from
[https://www.enisa.europa.eu/publications](https://www.enisa.europa.eu/publications
3. National Conference of State Legislatures. (2021). *Data Security: Data

Breach   Notification   Laws*.   Retrieved   from
[https://www.ncsl.org/research/telecommunications-and-information-technology/data-se

Cyber Warfare and State-sponsored Attacks

Cyber warfare refers to the use of digital attacks to harm or disrupt the computer systems, networks, and infrastructure of a nation or organization. State-sponsored attacks are cyber attacks initiated or supported by a nation-state with the intention to gain a strategic advantage or cause harm to another nation. This section will explore the ethical considerations surrounding cyber warfare, the laws and regulations governing such attacks, and the implications for national security.

Ethical Considerations

Cyber warfare raises a multitude of ethical dilemmas, as it involves using technology to inflict harm on others. One of the main concerns is the potential for collateral damage, where innocent individuals or organizations, not directly involved in the conflict, suffer the consequences of a cyber attack. This includes the disruption of critical infrastructure, financial systems, or healthcare services.

Another ethical concern is the attribution of cyber attacks. Unlike conventional warfare, it is often challenging to identify the perpetrator of a cyber attack with certainty. This can lead to misattribution and the risk of innocent parties being wrongly accused or targeted. Furthermore, the ability to conduct covert cyber operations raises questions about transparency and accountability, as it becomes difficult to hold responsible parties accountable for their actions.

Additionally, cyber warfare blurs the line between military and civilian targets. While traditional warfare differentiates between combatants and non-combatants, cyber attacks can harm civilians directly if they target essential services like water and electricity. This raises questions about the proportionality and justifiability of cyber warfare as a means of achieving military objectives.

Laws and Regulations

The international legal framework for cyber warfare is still evolving, but several agreements and conventions address the use of cyber attacks in armed conflicts. The Tallinn Manual, produced by a group of experts in international law, provides guidance on applying existing international laws to cyber warfare situations.

The United Nations Charter, which prohibits the use of force, applies to cyber attacks as well. The principle of sovereignty and non-intervention in the affairs of other nations is also relevant in cyberspace. Additionally, the laws of armed conflict, such as the Geneva Conventions, can be applicable to cyber warfare if it meets the criteria of an armed conflict.

Some countries have also enacted specific legislation to prevent and respond to cyber attacks. These laws often address issues related to espionage, intellectual property theft, and disruption of critical infrastructure. Organizations like the North Atlantic Treaty Organization (NATO) and the European Union (EU) have also developed policies and strategies to enhance cyber defense capabilities.

National Security Implications

State-sponsored cyber attacks pose significant threats to national security. They can target military systems, government institutions, and critical infrastructure, causing severe disruptions and compromising sensitive information. The theft of classified information, such as military strategies or intelligence, can give the attacker a substantial advantage and undermine national defense.

Furthermore, cyber attacks can have geopolitical consequences, as they can be used as tools of coercion or sabotage between nations. The ability to conduct sophisticated cyber operations enables nations to influence political processes, cripple economies, or undermine confidence in democratic institutions.

Protecting against state-sponsored cyber attacks requires robust cyber defense capabilities, policies, and international cooperation. This includes investing in cybersecurity measures, developing cyber defense strategies, and fostering information sharing and collaboration among countries.

Case Study: Stuxnet

A prominent example of state-sponsored cyber warfare is the Stuxnet worm, discovered in 2010. Stuxnet specifically targeted Iran's nuclear facilities, aiming to disrupt and disable their uranium enrichment capabilities. It was widely believed to be a joint operation by the United States and Israel.

Stuxnet was a sophisticated piece of malware that exploited zero-day vulnerabilities and covertly spread through compromised USB drives. It targeted the Supervisory Control and Data Acquisition (SCADA) systems, which are responsible for controlling industrial processes in the nuclear facilities. By manipulating these systems, Stuxnet caused physical damage to the centrifuges used in uranium enrichment.

The Stuxnet attack represented a new era of cyber warfare, where physical destruction was achieved through digital means. It highlighted the potential for cyber attacks to go beyond the realm of information theft or disruption and have real-world consequences.

Protecting Against State-sponsored Attacks

Defending against state-sponsored cyber attacks requires a multi-faceted approach. It involves a combination of technical, policy, and educational measures to strengthen the resilience of critical infrastructure and networks.

Technical measures include implementing robust security controls, such as firewalls, intrusion detection systems, and encryption. Regular patching and updating of software and systems are critical to protect against known vulnerabilities. Additionally, organizations should invest in threat intelligence capabilities to detect and respond to emerging cyber threats.

Policy measures involve the development of cybersecurity frameworks, regulations, and standards. These provide guidance to organizations and set expectations for cybersecurity best practices. Governments should also establish effective incident response plans to minimize the impact of cyber attacks and facilitate coordination between public and private sectors.

Education and awareness play a crucial role in defending against state-sponsored attacks. Organizations should implement training programs to educate employees about cybersecurity best practices, including recognizing phishing emails and practicing good password hygiene. Governments and educational institutions should also invest in cybersecurity education to develop a skilled workforce capable of defending against sophisticated attacks.

Ethical Exercise

Consider a hypothetical scenario where a nation-state decides to launch a cyber attack on the critical infrastructure of another nation as part of a larger military campaign. Discuss the ethical implications of such an attack, taking into account the potential for collateral damage and the difficulty of attribution. How can the principles of just war theory be applied to assess the morality of such actions?

Ethical Considerations in Digital Defense

In today's interconnected and digital world, the need for robust digital defense is crucial for both individuals and organizations. As technology continues to advance, so do the threats and risks associated with it. In this section, we will explore the ethical considerations that arise in the field of digital defense.

The Importance of Ethical Digital Defense

Digital defense, also known as cybersecurity, involves protecting computer systems, networks, and data from unauthorized access, damage, or theft. It encompasses various practices, including encryption, firewalls, intrusion detection systems, and anti-malware software. While the primary goal of digital defense is to safeguard sensitive information and ensure the privacy and security of users, ethical considerations play a critical role in determining the appropriate actions and practices.

Ethical digital defense involves upholding the values of transparency, honesty, and accountability while combating cyber threats. It requires cybersecurity professionals to understand the ethical implications of their work and make decisions guided by ethical principles. By adhering to ethical practices, digital defense professionals can build trust, maintain the integrity of their organizations, and protect individuals' rights to privacy and security.

Ethical Principles in Digital Defense

In the realm of digital defense, several ethical principles guide professional conduct and decision-making. Let's discuss some of the key principles:

1. **Accessibility:** Ensuring that computer systems and digital resources are accessible to all individuals, regardless of their abilities or disabilities. This principle emphasizes the importance of inclusive cybersecurity practices that do not discriminate against any user.

2. **Confidentiality:** Protecting sensitive and confidential information from unauthorized access or disclosure. Cybersecurity professionals should respect the privacy rights of individuals and implement measures to safeguard personal and organizational data.

3. **Integrity:** Acting in an honest and trustworthy manner while maintaining the accuracy and reliability of digital systems. This principle emphasizes the importance of avoiding fraud, deception, or manipulation in digital defense practices.

4. **Accountability:** Taking responsibility for one's actions, decisions, and their consequences. Cybersecurity professionals should be accountable for the security measures they implement and the outcomes of their actions.

5. **Resilience:** Building and maintaining systems that are resilient to cyber threats. This principle encourages the implementation of robust security measures, regular assessments, and proactive measures to prevent and respond to cyber attacks.

Ethical Challenges in Digital Defense

While ethical principles provide a foundation for digital defense practices, professionals often face complex challenges that require careful consideration. Let's explore some of these ethical challenges:

1. **Balancing Privacy and Security:** Cybersecurity professionals must strike a delicate balance between protecting sensitive information and respecting individuals' privacy rights. This challenge is particularly relevant in cases where data collection and surveillance are necessary for maintaining security.

   For example, consider the use of facial recognition technology for enhancing security in public spaces. While it can help identify potential threats, it also raises concerns about privacy and surveillance. Ethical considerations dictate that organizations must use this technology responsibly, with clear policies and safeguards to prevent misuse or intrusion into individuals' privacy.

2. **Ethical Hacking:** Ethical hacking, also known as penetration testing, involves deliberately probing and exploiting vulnerabilities in computer systems to identify weaknesses and improve security. However, ethical hackers must navigate ethical boundaries to avoid causing harm or unintended consequences while performing their duties.

   For instance, ethical hackers must ensure that they have proper authorization and consent before conducting penetration tests. They should also exercise caution to avoid damaging systems or unintentionally impacting the availability of critical services.

3. **Collaboration with Law Enforcement:** In some cases, cybersecurity professionals may be required to collaborate with law enforcement agencies to investigate cybercrimes or gather evidence. This collaboration may create ethical dilemmas concerning privacy, civil liberties, and potential misuse of power.

   Cybersecurity professionals must be aware of legal and ethical requirements and only engage in lawful and transparent collaborations. Organizations should have clear policies and guidelines in place to ensure that such collaborations are carried out responsibly and without infringing individuals' rights.

A Case Study: Ethical Considerations in Data Breaches

Data breaches have become increasingly common, and organizations must handle them with ethical considerations in mind. Let's consider a hypothetical case to understand the ethical challenges involved:

A large e-commerce company experiences a major data breach, compromising the personal information of millions of customers. The company's cybersecurity team needs to respond to the breach while taking ethical considerations into account.

1. **Transparency and Communication:** The cybersecurity team must be transparent with affected customers about the breach, the extent of the compromise, and the potential risks associated with it. They should communicate promptly, clearly, and empathetically, providing guidance to customers on protecting themselves against potential identity theft or fraud.

2. **Mitigating Further Harm:** The team must take immediate action to mitigate the impact of the breach and prevent further unauthorized access. This may involve isolating affected systems, patching vulnerabilities, and implementing additional security measures to prevent similar incidents in the future.

3. **Working with Stakeholders:** The cybersecurity team needs to work closely with legal teams, senior management, and regulatory authorities to ensure compliance with legal obligations, such as data breach notification requirements. They should collaborate responsibly and transparently to address the legal, financial, and reputational implications of the breach.

4. **Aftermath and Learning:** Once the immediate crisis is mitigated, the team should conduct a thorough post-mortem analysis of the breach. This analysis should focus not only on technical aspects but also on the organizational and human factors contributing to the breach. Ethical considerations dictate that the company should learn from the incident and implement measures to prevent similar incidents in the future.

Conclusion

Ethical considerations in digital defense are vital for protecting individuals' privacy, maintaining trust, and ensuring the integrity and resilience of digital systems.

Cybersecurity professionals must adhere to ethical principles, navigate complex challenges, and make decisions guided by transparency, accountability, and the well-being of individuals and organizations. By integrating ethics into digital defense practices, professionals can contribute to a more secure and trustworthy digital landscape.

Additional Resources:

+ **Book:** "Ethics in the Age of Cyberattacks" by James E. Whitehouse.

+ **Article:** "Ethical Considerations in Digital Defense" by Sarah Johnson, Journal of Cybersecurity Ethics.

+ **Website:** Electronic Frontier Foundation (EFF) - www.eff.org - A nonprofit organization defending civil liberties in the digital world, covering various ethical issues in digital defense.

Key Terms: digital defense, cybersecurity, ethical principles, accessibility, confidentiality, integrity, accountability, resilience, privacy, ethical hacking, law enforcement collaboration, data breaches.

Ethical Responsibilities of Cybersecurity Professionals

In today's digital age, where technology plays a central role in our lives, cybersecurity has become a critical concern. As more and more sensitive information is stored and transmitted online, the need to protect it from unauthorized access and malicious attacks is paramount. Cybersecurity professionals are at the forefront of this battle, responsible for ensuring the security and integrity of digital systems. However, along with their technical skills, these professionals also bear ethical responsibilities that are essential for the well-being of individuals and society as a whole.

Protecting Privacy and Confidentiality

One of the primary ethical responsibilities of cybersecurity professionals is to protect the privacy and confidentiality of individuals and organizations. With the increasing amounts of personal and sensitive information being stored online, such as financial data, medical records, or personal communications, it is crucial to uphold the right to privacy.

Cybersecurity professionals should adhere to strict confidentiality standards and ensure that any access to sensitive data is strictly limited to authorized personnel. They should also employ encryption and other security measures to protect data during transmission and storage. Furthermore, they must stay informed about emerging threats and vulnerabilities to implement appropriate safeguards effectively.

For example, consider a cybersecurity professional working for a healthcare organization. They may encounter patients' medical records during their work, and it is their ethical responsibility to ensure the utmost confidentiality and privacy of this information. Breaches of confidentiality can have severe consequences, including identity theft, financial fraud, damage to reputation, and even physical harm.

Promoting Cybersecurity Awareness

Another important ethical responsibility of cybersecurity professionals is to promote cybersecurity awareness and education. Many individuals are unaware of the risks and best practices for securing their digital information, making them easy targets for cybercriminals.

Cybersecurity professionals should educate users about the importance of strong passwords, regular software updates, and safe internet browsing habits. They should also create training programs to teach employees of organizations about recognizing and mitigating common cyber threats like phishing, malware, and social engineering.

By fostering a culture of cybersecurity awareness, professionals can empower individuals to take an active role in protecting their own digital assets and contribute to a safer online environment.

For instance, a cybersecurity professional can develop interactive workshops to educate employees on phishing attacks. Through simulated phishing campaigns and targeted training sessions, they can teach employees how to identify suspicious emails and avoid falling victim to these scams.

Maintaining Ethical Hacking and Penetration Testing Practices

Ethical hacking and penetration testing are essential techniques used by cybersecurity professionals to identify vulnerabilities and assess the security of systems. However, it is crucial for these professionals to maintain ethical standards and integrity while performing these activities.

Ethical hackers and penetration testers should obtain proper authorization from the system owner before conducting any tests. They should rigorously follow rules of engagement and adhere to the scope defined by the organization. It is their ethical responsibility to avoid causing any harm or disruption to systems that could negatively impact businesses or individuals.

Additionally, cybersecurity professionals should report their findings accurately and promptly, allowing organizations to rectify any identified vulnerabilities before they can be exploited by malicious actors.

Let's consider an example where a cybersecurity professional is hired to perform penetration testing on a financial institution's network. They discover a critical vulnerability that could potentially lead to unauthorized access and financial loss. The ethical responsibility of the professional is to report this finding promptly to the organization's management and provide guidance on mitigating the vulnerability effectively.

Ensuring Ethical Use of Security Tools and Technologies

Cybersecurity professionals often utilize various security tools and technologies to defend against cyber threats. However, the ethical use of these tools is of utmost importance to prevent misuse, infringement of privacy, or exploitation of vulnerabilities.

Professionals should ensure that these tools are used for legitimate purposes, adhering to legal and ethical boundaries. They should not engage in activities that violate individuals' privacy rights, conduct unauthorized surveillance, or compromise the integrity of systems.

For example, cybersecurity professionals should exercise caution while conducting investigations in cybercrime cases. They should gather evidence legally, respecting individuals' privacy rights and the due process of law. It is their ethical responsibility to balance the need for cybersecurity against the protection of civil liberties.

Continual Professional Development and Ethical Awareness

In the evolving field of cybersecurity, professionals must engage in continual professional development to stay ahead of the ever-changing threat landscape. This includes staying up-to-date with the latest security technologies, emerging threats, and best practices.

Moreover, ethical awareness is an essential aspect of a cybersecurity professional's development. They should actively consider ethical implications and consequences of their actions, continuously evaluating the impact on individuals and society. By adhering to ethical guidelines and practices, professionals can build trust and credibility, upholding the highest ethical standards.

Summary

In summary, cybersecurity professionals have significant ethical responsibilities in safeguarding privacy, promoting awareness, maintaining ethical hacking practices, ensuring ethical use of technologies, and engaging in continual professional development and ethical awareness.   By fulfilling these responsibilities, professionals can contribute to a secure digital environment that protects individuals and organizations from threats and fosters trust in the digital realm.

Additional Resources

For further exploration of this topic, you may find the following resources valuable:

- Cybersecurity Code of Ethics - International Information System Security Certification Consortium (ISC)[2]

- "Ethical Guidelines for Information Security" - Computer Society of India

- "Ethics in Information Technology" by George Reynolds

- "The Code Book" by Simon Singh

- Online courses and certifications from reputable organizations such as CompTIA, GIAC, and EC-Council

Remember, the field of cybersecurity is not solely about technology but also about upholding ethical principles.   By embracing these responsibilities, cybersecurity professionals can make a positive impact on the security and well-being of individuals and society as a whole.

Exercises

1. Research recent cybersecurity breaches and analyze the ethical implications associated with each case.

2. Role-play a scenario where a cybersecurity professional is faced with an ethical dilemma. Discuss potential courses of action and their consequences.

3. Conduct an audit of your personal digital security practices and identify any areas where you can improve your own cybersecurity posture.

4. Write a reflective essay on the ethical responsibilities of cybersecurity professionals in the context of emerging technologies such as artificial intelligence and the Internet of Things.

Remember to approach these exercises with both technical knowledge and ethical consciousness, aiming to develop a holistic understanding of cybersecurity and its impact on society.

Ethical Implications of Biotechnology

Gene Editing and Genetic Engineering

Gene editing and genetic engineering are two closely related fields that have revolutionized the way we can manipulate and modify genetic material. These techniques offer tremendous potential for advancing scientific research, medical treatments, and even agricultural practices. In this section, we will explore the principles and applications of gene editing and genetic engineering, as well as the ethical concerns that arise from these technologies.

Principles of Gene Editing

Gene editing involves the precise modification of an organism's DNA to achieve specific changes in its genetic code. One of the most powerful tools in gene editing is the CRISPR-Cas9 system. CRISPR (Clustered Regularly Interspaced Short Palindromic Repeats) is a naturally occurring defense mechanism found in bacteria that enables them to recognize and destroy invading viral DNA. Cas9 is an enzyme that acts as a molecular scissor, cutting the DNA at specific locations guided by CRISPR RNA.

The process of gene editing using CRISPR-Cas9 involves the design and synthesis of a small RNA molecule, known as a guide RNA, that is complementary to the target DNA sequence. This guide RNA, together with the Cas9 enzyme, forms a complex that can recognize and bind to the specific DNA sequence of interest. Once bound, Cas9 cleaves the DNA, creating a double-stranded break. This break can then be repaired using the cell's natural DNA repair mechanisms, either by introducing specific changes to the DNA sequence (gene knockout) or by inserting new DNA sequences (gene insertion).

Applications of Gene Editing

Gene editing has wide-ranging applications in various fields, including medicine, agriculture, and biotechnology. In medicine, gene editing holds the promise of treating and potentially curing genetic diseases. By modifying the DNA of affected cells, scientists can correct the underlying genetic mutations responsible for diseases such as cystic fibrosis, sickle cell anemia, and muscular dystrophy. Additionally, gene editing can be used to enhance cancer therapies, improve the efficiency of drug delivery systems, and even create personalized medicine based on an individual's genetic makeup.

In agriculture, gene editing enables the development of crops with improved traits, such as disease resistance, drought tolerance, and increased nutritional value. This technology can lead to more sustainable and resilient agricultural practices, reducing the need for chemical pesticides and enhancing food security. Gene editing techniques can also be utilized to improve livestock production by introducing desirable traits and reducing the spread of diseases.

Ethical Concerns

While gene editing and genetic engineering offer tremendous potential for scientific and medical advancement, they also raise significant ethical concerns. One of the primary concerns is the potential for unintended consequences and long-term effects on the environment and biodiversity. The release of genetically modified organisms (GMOs) into the environment could have unpredictable ecological impacts and disrupt delicate ecosystems.

Another ethical concern is the possibility of using gene editing for non-therapeutic purposes, such as enhancing human traits or creating so-called "designer babies." The ability to modify the genetic makeup of individuals raises ethical questions related to equity, social justice, and the potential for creating genetic inequalities in society.

There are also concerns about the regulation and oversight of gene editing technologies. While current regulations vary between countries, there is a need for international consensus on the ethical boundaries and responsible use of these technologies. Striking a balance between scientific progress and the protection of human rights, environmental safety, and public health is a complex challenge.

Ethical Considerations

To address the ethical concerns surrounding gene editing and genetic engineering, it is crucial to establish clear ethical guidelines and principles. These guidelines should promote transparency, accountability, and responsible research practices. Key ethical considerations include:

- **Informed Consent:** Prior to any genetic modifications, individuals should be fully informed about the potential risks, benefits, and implications of the procedure. Informed consent should be obtained from all parties involved, including patients, research subjects, and stakeholders.

- **Equity and Access:** The equitable distribution and access to gene editing technologies and therapies should be ensured, minimizing any potential disparities or discrimination. The benefits of these advancements should be made available to all, regardless of socioeconomic status or geographical location.

- **Environmental Impact:** The potential environmental risks associated with genetically modified organisms should be thoroughly evaluated and mitigated. Environmental impact assessments should be conducted before the release of GMOs, considering the potential consequences for biodiversity and ecosystems.

- **Regulation and Oversight:** Effective regulatory frameworks and oversight mechanisms should be established to ensure the responsible and safe use of gene editing technologies. These regulations should be dynamic and able to adapt to the rapid advancements in the field.

- **Open and Inclusive Dialogue:** Society, including the public, scientists, policymakers, and ethicists, should engage in open and inclusive discussions about the ethical implications of gene editing. These conversations should consider diverse perspectives and ethical frameworks to inform decision-making processes.

Case Study: CRISPR Babies

The ethical considerations surrounding gene editing came to the forefront in 2018 when it was reported that a scientist in China had used CRISPR-Cas9 to edit the genomes of twin girls to confer resistance to HIV infection. This controversial experiment raised significant ethical concerns, as it was conducted without proper approval, oversight, or transparency. The experiment was widely condemned by the scientific community for its potential risks, including unintended genetic mutations and unknown long-term consequences.

The case of the CRISPR babies highlights the importance of ethical guidelines, responsible conduct, and transparency in the use of gene editing technologies. It serves as a reminder that ethical considerations must always be at the forefront of scientific advancements, ensuring the responsible and ethical use of gene editing tools.

Conclusion

Gene editing and genetic engineering have the potential to transform various fields, including medicine, agriculture, and biotechnology. However, the ethical considerations surrounding these technologies must be carefully addressed to ensure their responsible and equitable use. By establishing clear ethical guidelines, promoting transparency, and engaging in inclusive discussions, we can harness the power of gene editing while minimizing the potential risks and ethical concerns associated with these advancements.

Cloning and Synthetic Biology

Cloning and synthetic biology are two closely related fields that have revolutionized the way we understand and manipulate life. In this section, we will explore the principles, applications, and ethical considerations of cloning and synthetic biology.

Principles of Cloning

Cloning refers to the process of creating genetically identical copies of an organism, cell, or DNA fragment. There are several different methods of cloning, including reproductive cloning, therapeutic cloning, and molecular cloning.

Reproductive cloning involves the creation of an entire organism that is genetically identical to the donor organism. This is achieved through somatic cell nuclear transfer (SCNT), where the nucleus of a donor cell is transferred into an enucleated egg cell. The resulting embryo is then implanted into a surrogate mother, where it develops into a clone of the donor organism.

Therapeutic cloning, on the other hand, aims to produce embryonic stem cells for medical purposes. It involves the same process of SCNT, but instead of implanting the embryo into a surrogate mother, the embryonic stem cells are harvested for research or therapeutic applications.

Molecular cloning is a technique used to amplify specific DNA fragments. It involves inserting the DNA fragment of interest into a vector, such as a plasmid, and then introducing the vector into a host organism, such as bacteria. The host organism then replicates the vector, resulting in multiple copies of the DNA fragment.

Applications of Cloning

Cloning has a wide range of applications in various fields, including agriculture, medicine, and research.

In agriculture, cloning enables the production of genetically identical plants or animals with desired traits. For example, farmers can clone high-yielding crop plants or livestock with desirable traits, such as disease resistance or increased productivity. This can help improve food security and agricultural yield.

In medicine, cloning plays a crucial role in therapeutic applications. Cloning of embryonic stem cells allows scientists to study and develop potential treatments for diseases and conditions such as Parkinson's, Alzheimer's, and spinal cord injuries. Additionally, cloning can be used to create genetically modified animals that serve as models for studying human diseases.

In research, cloning is an invaluable tool for studying the function of genes and proteins. It allows scientists to create identical copies of specific DNA sequences, enabling them to analyze and manipulate genetic information. Cloning also plays a significant role in the production of recombinant proteins, which are used in various industries, including pharmaceuticals and biotechnology.

Ethical Considerations

The field of cloning raises several ethical concerns that must be carefully considered.

One of the primary ethical concerns surrounding cloning is the potential for misuse and abuse. Cloning can be used for nefarious purposes, such as the production of human clones or the creation of genetically modified organisms with harmful attributes. There is also the concern of cloning endangered or extinct species without fully understanding the ecological consequences.

Another ethical consideration is the impact on individuality and identity. Cloning raises questions about uniqueness and the fundamental nature of being an individual. Cloned animals may experience health issues or shortened lifespans, leading to concerns about their overall welfare.

Furthermore, the commercialization of cloning raises ethical considerations. The potential for cloning to be used as a profit-making enterprise can lead to the exploitation of animals and the commodification of life. It is essential to ensure that ethical guidelines and regulations are in place to prevent unethical practices.

Real-world Example: Cloning of Dolly the Sheep

A famous example of cloning is the case of Dolly the Sheep, the first mammal cloned from an adult somatic cell. In 1996, scientists at the Roslin Institute in Scotland successfully cloned Dolly using the technique of somatic cell nuclear transfer.

Dolly's creation raised both excitement and ethical concerns. While it was a scientific breakthrough and a significant achievement in genetic engineering, it also sparked debates about the ethics of cloning and the implications for human cloning.

Dolly's health issues, including premature aging and arthritis, highlighted the potential risks and welfare concerns associated with cloning. Her short lifespan raised questions about the long-term viability and well-being of cloned animals.

The cloning of Dolly stimulated public discussions about the ethical boundaries of cloning and the need for regulations to ensure responsible and ethical practices.

Further Reading and Resources

If you're interested in learning more about cloning and synthetic biology, here are some recommended resources:

- Book: "Cloning: A Reference Handbook" by David E. Newton

- Documentary: "Human Cloning" by PBS Nova

- Research Paper: "Ethical considerations in human cloning" by Timothy F. Murphy

- Website: National Human Genome Research Institute - Cloning Fact Sheet (https://www.genome.gov/about-genomics/fact-sheets/)

Summary

Cloning and synthetic biology have revolutionized our understanding and manipulation of life. Cloning techniques, such as somatic cell nuclear transfer, allow for the creation of genetically identical organisms and the amplification of specific DNA fragments. Cloning finds applications in various fields, including agriculture, medicine, and research. However, the field of cloning raises ethical concerns regarding misuse, individuality, and commercialization. It is crucial to approach cloning with careful consideration of its ethical implications and to establish guidelines and regulations to ensure responsible and ethical practices.

Biohacking and DIY Biology

In recent years, the field of biology has witnessed a revolutionary movement known as biohacking and DIY (Do-It-Yourself) biology. Biohacking represents a diverse community of individuals who are passionate about exploring and experimenting with biological systems outside of traditional laboratory settings. This section will delve into the principles, applications, and ethical considerations surrounding biohacking and DIY biology.

Principles of Biohacking

Biohacking is founded on the principles of curiosity, open access, interdisciplinary collaboration, and self-experimentation. Unlike conventional scientific research that takes place in institutional laboratories, biohackers often work in community labs or their own personal spaces. They aim to democratize scientific knowledge and empower individuals to engage in biological experimentation.

One of the key principles of biohacking is the "Open Science" movement, which advocates for the sharing of scientific knowledge, data, and methodologies with the public. By openly documenting their experiments and research, biohackers contribute to a collective database of biological knowledge accessible to all.

Applications of Biohacking

Biohacking has a wide range of applications across various fields, including healthcare, agriculture, environmental conservation, and art. Here are some examples:

1. **Medical Research:** Biohackers can contribute to medical research by exploring innovative solutions for drug discovery, gene therapy, or personalized medicine. Their DIY approach allows for rapid prototyping and testing of new ideas without the bureaucratic constraints of traditional research institutions.

2. **Agriculture and Food Systems:** Biohackers can develop alternative and sustainable methods for agriculture. They can experiment with genetic modifications or explore innovative farming techniques to improve crop yields, create disease-resistant plants, or address food security challenges.

3. **Environmental Monitoring**: DIY biology can contribute to environmental conservation efforts by developing low-cost sensors for pollution

monitoring, studying biodiversity, or tracking climate change indicators. Biohacking can empower local communities to actively participate in monitoring and protecting their ecosystems.

4. **Bioart:** Biohackers merge biology with art to create thought-provoking installations, sculptures, or performances. They explore the aesthetics of living organisms and challenge societal perspectives on biotechnology and its implications.

Ethical Considerations

While biohacking offers exciting opportunities for innovation and discovery, it raises important ethical considerations that must be addressed. Here are the key ethical dimensions of biohacking:

1. **Safety and Risk Management:** DIY biology experiments must prioritize safety protocols to minimize the risks associated with working with biological materials. Biohackers should be vigilant in handling potentially hazardous substances and ensure proper disposal of waste. Collaboration with trained professionals and adherence to safety guidelines are crucial to prevent accidental releases or unintended consequences.

2. **Biosecurity:** The accessibility of biohacking tools and techniques raises concerns about the potential misuse of biological materials for malicious purposes. It is important for the biohacking community to promote responsible behavior and establish proper safeguards to prevent unauthorized access to dangerous pathogens or genetic engineering technologies.

3. **Regulatory Compliance:** Biohackers must navigate the complex landscape of laws and regulations governing genetic engineering and biohazardous materials. Compliance with regulations ensures accountability, responsible use of technologies, and protection of public health and the environment.

4. **Informed Consent:** If biohackers engage in human or animal experimentation, informed consent from all parties involved is crucial. Respecting the autonomy and rights of individuals is essential to uphold ethical standards and avoid exploitation.

5. **Societal Implications:** The biohacking movement can challenge existing societal norms and raise ethical questions related to the modification of life,

the commercialization of biological products, and the potential consequences for social equality. Engaging in open discussions and interdisciplinary collaborations can help address these societal implications and promote responsible practices.

Real-world Example: CRISPR-Cas9 and Biohackers

One of the most notable advancements in biohacking is the utilization of the CRISPR-Cas9 gene editing system. This technology allows for precise and efficient modification of DNA, revolutionizing the field of genetic engineering.

Biohackers have played a significant role in the development and application of CRISPR-Cas9. For example, in 2017, a biohacker group known as "The ODIN" made headlines by selling DIY CRISPR kits for individuals to experiment with gene editing at home. While this raised concerns about the potential misuse of the technology, it also sparked discussions on the accessibility and democratization of genetic engineering.

The DIY biology community actively engages in public education and outreach programs to promote responsible use of CRISPR-Cas9. They emphasize ethical considerations, safety protocols, and the importance of scientific understanding when working with this powerful tool.

Resources and Community

Biohacking and DIY biology have garnered a significant following, with numerous resources and communities available to individuals interested in this field. Here are some key platforms and organizations:

1. **Biohackerspaces** are community laboratories that provide access to equipment, resources, and expertise for biohackers. These spaces offer a collaborative environment where individuals can share knowledge and work on projects together.

2. **Online Communities** such as DIYbio.org and Biohack.me provide platforms for knowledge sharing, discussions, and project collaboration. These communities foster interdisciplinary connections and support for biohackers worldwide.

3. **"Biohack the Planet" Conference** is an annual gathering of biohackers, scientists, and enthusiasts dedicated to exploring the frontiers of DIY biology. The conference offers workshops, talks, and networking opportunities.

4. **Scientific Journals** like "PLOS ONE" and "Biohacking: Open Access" publish research articles related to biohacking and DIY biology, ensuring the dissemination of knowledge in the field.

Conclusion

Biohacking and DIY biology present exciting opportunities for individuals to engage with biology in unconventional and innovative ways. By embracing principles of open science, interdisciplinary collaboration, and responsible experimentation, biohackers can contribute to scientific knowledge, drive societal discussions, and address pressing challenges in healthcare, agriculture, and the environment. However, it is essential to navigate the ethical considerations associated with biohacking to ensure safety, security, and responsible use of biotechnologies. The biohacking community plays a crucial role in promoting awareness, education, and responsible practices to create a sustainable and ethical future for DIY biology.

Animal Testing and Ethical Concerns

Animal testing has long been a controversial topic, raising important ethical concerns. The use of animals in scientific research and experimentation has been a subject of much debate, with arguments on both sides. The ethical implications of animal testing stem from various ethical frameworks, including the principles of beneficence, non-maleficence, and justice.

The Utilitarian Perspective

From a utilitarian perspective, the ethics of animal testing are assessed based on the overall balance of benefits and harms. Advocates argue that the potential benefits of animal testing, such as the development of life-saving drugs and medical treatments, outweigh the harm caused to animals.

For instance, in the field of medical research, animal testing plays a crucial role in advancing our understanding of diseases and developing potential treatments. Without animal models, it would be challenging to test the safety and efficacy of new drugs before human trials. This perspective highlights the utilitarian principle of maximizing overall happiness or well-being.

However, critics argue that the suffering experienced by animals in laboratories cannot be justified solely by the potential benefits to humans. They question the assumption that the ends justify the means and emphasize the importance of minimizing harm and respecting the intrinsic value of animals.

The Rights-based Perspective

The rights-based approach to ethics, exemplified by the work of philosopher Tom Regan, focuses on individual rights and moral consideration for all sentient beings. According to this perspective, animals have inherent rights, including the right to be free from unnecessary suffering.

Critics of animal testing from a rights-based perspective argue that animals should not be subjected to experimentation and harm for human benefit. They contend that animals have their own interests and should not be treated merely as means to human ends.

One alternative suggested by rights-based ethicists is the principle of non-use, which advocates for the complete abolition of animal testing. They argue that alternative methods, such as in vitro cell and tissue cultures, computer simulations, and human-based clinical trials, can provide viable alternatives to animal testing.

The Bioethical Principle of Alternatives

The principle of alternatives in bioethics emphasizes the search for alternatives to animal testing whenever possible. This principle aligns with both the utilitarian perspective of minimizing harm and the rights-based perspective of respecting the intrinsic value of animals.

In recent years, there has been a growing recognition of the need to embrace alternatives to animal testing. Advances in technology, such as organs-on-chip and microdosing, have shown promising potential to reduce reliance on animal models. Additionally, the development of in silico models, which use computer simulations and predictive algorithms, offers new avenues for toxicity testing.

Regulatory agencies, including the U.S. Food and Drug Administration and the European Union, have also implemented guidelines encouraging the use of alternative methods and the reduction of animal testing. This shift reflects a broader recognition of the ethical concerns associated with animal testing and the need to prioritize the development and validation of non-animal alternatives.

Educating and Raising Awareness

To address the ethical concerns surrounding animal testing, education and awareness play a vital role. Informing the public, especially students, about the ethical implications of animal testing can foster critical thinking and informed decision-making.

Ethics education should include discussions on the ethical frameworks underlying the debate, as well as the alternatives and scientific advancements that provide viable alternatives to animal testing. Encouraging open dialogue and engagement with diverse perspectives can help individuals develop their own ethical stances on this issue.

Furthermore, supporting research and innovation in non-animal testing methods is crucial. By investing in the development and validation of alternative approaches, we can promote a shift towards more ethical practices in scientific research and experimentation.

Case Study: The 3Rs Principle

One notable initiative in the field of animal testing ethics is the implementation of the 3Rs principle: Replacement, Reduction, and Refinement. The 3Rs framework, originally proposed by William Russell and Rex Burch, serves as a guide for ethical animal experimentation.

Replacement refers to the use of alternative methods that do not involve animals whenever possible. This includes the development and utilization of in vitro models, computer simulations, and human-based techniques.

Reduction aims to minimize the number of animals used in experiments. This involves careful experimental design, statistical analysis, and sharing of data to avoid unnecessary replication and ensure that the sample size is kept to a minimum.

Refinement focuses on improving animal welfare and minimizing the potential for pain and distress. This includes the development of procedures that cause minimal harm, the use of anesthesia and analgesia to eliminate or reduce pain, and the provision of appropriate housing and enrichment to enhance animal well-being.

The 3Rs principle serves as a practical framework that allows scientists to consider the ethical implications of their research and make conscious efforts to minimize harm to animals.

Conclusion

The ethical concerns surrounding animal testing highlight the complex and multifaceted nature of this issue. By assessing the ethics of animal testing through different perspectives, such as utilitarianism, rights-based ethics, and the principle of alternatives, we can promote a more comprehensive understanding of the ethical considerations at stake.

Advancements in technology and the growing recognition of alternative methods offer hope for reducing reliance on animal testing. Through education, awareness, and the implementation of ethical frameworks like the 3Rs principle, we can strive towards more ethical practices in scientific research and contribute to the well-being of both humans and animals.

Bioprinting and Organ Transplantation Ethics

In recent years, the field of bioprinting has gained significant attention and holds great promise in the field of organ transplantation. Bioprinting is a revolutionary technology that involves the fabrication of complex three-dimensional structures using living cells, biomaterials, and bioinks. It offers the potential to create functional organs and tissues that can be used for transplantation, potentially solving the critical shortage of organs for patients in need.

However, the development and implementation of bioprinting raise several ethical considerations. In this section, we will explore the ethical implications of bioprinting and organ transplantation, considering issues such as informed consent, resource allocation, fairness, and long-term consequences.

Informed Consent and Autonomy

One of the primary ethical concerns in bioprinting and organ transplantation is informed consent. Informed consent is a fundamental principle in medical ethics that requires individuals to have a clear understanding of the risks, benefits, and alternatives associated with any medical procedure before providing their consent.

In the context of bioprinting, informed consent becomes even more complex. Patients may be asked to provide consent not only for the transplantation procedure but also for the use of their own cells or tissues in the bioprinting process. This raises questions about the extent to which patients fully understand the implications and potential risks of bioprinting.

Furthermore, the use of bioprinted organs may raise ethical challenges related to donor consent. Should consent be obtained from the individual whose cells are used to create the bioprinted organ? What if the individual is deceased and did not explicitly express their consent? These are important considerations that need to be addressed to ensure respect for autonomy and protect the rights of individuals involved.

Resource Allocation and Fairness

Another ethical concern in bioprinting and organ transplantation is resource allocation and fairness. As bioprinting technologies advance, there is a possibility that they may create a divide between those who can afford bioprinted organs and those who cannot. This raises concerns about justice and equitable access to life-saving treatments.

If bioprinted organs become commercially available, there is a risk that wealthier individuals may have greater access to these organs, while those who cannot afford them may be left behind. This potential inequity calls for careful consideration of the distribution and allocation of bioprinted organs to ensure fair and just access for all individuals in need.

Additionally, the allocation of resources for bioprinting research and development should also be carefully considered. Should public funds be used to support this technology? How can we ensure that resources are allocated in a way that maximizes the benefit for the greatest number of people?

Long-term Consequences and Unknown Risks

Bioprinting is a cutting-edge technology, and the long-term consequences and unknown risks associated with bioprinted organs are still uncertain. As with any new medical technology, there is a need for careful evaluation of potential risks, including the possibility of rejection, immune responses, and long-term health effects.

Before bioprinted organs can be considered a mainstream treatment option, extensive preclinical and clinical studies are necessary to assess the safety and efficacy of these organs. Ethical considerations include the need for transparency in reporting research findings, potential conflicts of interest, and the need to ensure that human subjects involved in clinical trials are fully informed about the risks and benefits of receiving a bioprinted organ.

Ethics in Research and Regulation

The field of bioprinting also raises ethical considerations related to research ethics and regulatory oversight. Research involving bioprinting may involve experimentation on human cells, tissues, or animals, demanding careful adherence to ethical guidelines to ensure the responsible conduct of research.

There is also a need for robust regulation and oversight to ensure that bioprinting technologies are developed and used in an ethical and responsible manner. Regulatory frameworks should consider the safety, efficacy, and quality of bioprinted organs while also addressing broader ethical concerns, such as access, consent, and fairness.

In conclusion, bioprinting holds great promise in the field of organ transplantation, but it also raises complex ethical considerations. Informed consent, resource allocation, long-term consequences, and research ethics are crucial aspects that need to be carefully addressed to ensure the ethical development and implementation of bioprinting technologies.   Balancing innovation and ethical considerations will be essential to ensure that bioprinting contributes to the betterment of patients' lives while upholding the principles of medical ethics.

Ethical Governance of Emerging Technologies

Nanotechnology and Ethical Implications

Nanotechnology is a rapidly advancing field that deals with the manipulation and application of matter at the nanoscale, typically at dimensions between 1 and 100 nanometers.   At this scale, materials exhibit unique properties that can be harnessed for various purposes, ranging from medicine and electronics to energy and environmental applications.   While nanotechnology holds great promise for scientific and technological advancements, it also raises several ethical implications that need to be carefully considered.

Introduction to Nanotechnology

Before delving into the ethical implications of nanotechnology, it is important to understand its fundamental principles. Nanotechnology involves the manipulation of materials and devices at the nanoscale, where the behavior of matter differs significantly from its bulk form due to quantum effects and surface area-to-volume ratio.   Scientists and engineers utilize nanoscale materials to create innovative structures, devices, and systems with enhanced properties and functionalities.

Examples of nanotechnology applications include:

+ Nanomedicine: The use of nanoparticles for targeted drug delivery, imaging, and diagnostics.

+ Nanoelectronics: The development of nanoscale electronic devices and circuits with improved efficiency and performance.

+ Nanomaterials: The creation of new materials with enhanced mechanical, electrical, and chemical properties for a wide range of applications.

+ Nanosensors: The use of nanomaterials to detect and monitor physical, chemical, and biological parameters with high sensitivity.

‣ Nanofabrication: The manufacturing of nanostructures and nanodevices using various techniques, such as lithography and self-assembly.

Ethical Implications of Nanotechnology

The rapid development and wide-ranging applications of nanotechnology raise important ethical considerations that need to be addressed. These include:

1. Environmental Impact: The production, use, and disposal of nanomaterials can potentially have adverse effects on the environment. It is necessary to assess and minimize the ecological impact of nanotechnology, including the potential release of nanoparticles into the air, water, and soil. Proper waste management and disposal methods should be implemented to prevent the contamination of ecosystems.

2. Health and Safety Concerns: Nanoparticles may have unique biological properties that can pose risks to human health. Their small size enables them to penetrate biological barriers, and their reactivity can lead to unpredictable interactions with living organisms. It is crucial to conduct thorough toxicity studies to understand the potential health hazards associated with nanomaterials and establish guidelines for safe handling and use.

3. Privacy and Surveillance: Nanotechnology-enabled surveillance devices and systems raise concerns about privacy and individual rights. For example, the development of nanosensors capable of monitoring individuals' activities and physiological parameters may infringe upon personal privacy. Clear regulations and guidelines need to be established to protect the privacy of individuals while acknowledging the potential benefits of such technology in security and public safety.

4. Equity and Access: The equitable distribution of the benefits of nanotechnology is a significant ethical concern. There is a risk of creating a technological divide and exacerbating existing inequalities if access to nanotechnology and its applications is limited to certain groups or countries. Efforts should be made to ensure equitable access to nanotechnology advancements and mitigate potential social and economic disparities.

Addressing the Ethical Implications

To address the ethical implications of nanotechnology, it is essential to adopt a proactive and multidisciplinary approach involving scientists, policymakers, ethicists, and society at large. Some key strategies and principles to consider include:

1. **Risk Assessment and Regulation:** Conducting comprehensive risk assessments to identify potential hazards associated with nanomaterials is crucial. Establishing regulations that ensure the safe production, use, and disposal of nanotechnology products can minimize risks to human health and the environment.

2. **Ethical Codes and Guidelines:** Developing ethical codes and guidelines specific to nanotechnology can provide a framework for researchers, engineers, and industry professionals to adhere to ethical practices. These codes should include principles such as transparency, accountability, and responsible innovation.

3. **Public Engagement and Education:** Fostering public dialogue and engagement regarding nanotechnology can help address concerns and build trust among different stakeholders. Public education initiatives can promote awareness of the potential benefits and risks of nanotechnology, empowering individuals to make informed decisions.

4. **International Collaboration:** Facilitating international cooperation and collaboration can enable the sharing of knowledge, best practices, and resources in addressing the ethical implications of nanotechnology. International agreements and frameworks can help establish common ethical standards and promote responsible governance.

Case Study: Nanoparticle-based Drug Delivery

One of the most promising applications of nanotechnology in medicine is nanoparticle-based drug delivery systems. These systems utilize nanoparticles to transport drugs to targeted sites in the body, facilitating enhanced therapeutic efficacy and reduced side effects.

Consider the case of a cancer patient undergoing chemotherapy. Traditional chemotherapy drugs often have severe side effects due to the indiscriminate targeting of both cancerous and healthy cells. By encapsulating the chemotherapy drugs within biocompatible nanoparticles, they can be delivered directly to the tumor cells, minimizing damage to healthy tissues.

However, this technology raises ethical considerations. Factors to consider include ensuring the safety of nanoparticles, potential long-term effects, possible off-target effects, and ethical concerns related to access and affordability. Additionally, questions regarding informed consent, patient autonomy, and the availability of alternative treatments may arise.

Addressing these ethical implications requires comprehensive risk assessment, transparent communication with patients, and ongoing evaluation of the long-term effects of nanoparticle-based drug delivery systems. Engaging stakeholders, including patients, healthcare providers, researchers, and policymakers, can help ensure that the benefits of this technology are maximized while minimizing potential risks.

Conclusion

Nanotechnology offers tremendous potential for scientific and technological advancements across various fields. However, it is imperative to address the ethical implications associated with its development and application. By adopting a proactive and multidisciplinary approach, we can maximize the benefits of nanotechnology while ensuring the responsible and ethical use of this transformative technology. Proper regulation, stakeholder engagement, and continuous assessment of risks and benefits are crucial for navigating the ethical challenges of nanotechnology in a rapidly evolving landscape.

Internet of Things and Privacy Concerns

The Internet of Things (IoT) refers to the network of interconnected devices that are embedded with sensors, software, and other technologies to collect and exchange data. These devices range from smart home appliances and wearable fitness trackers to industrial machinery and city infrastructure. While the IoT has the potential to revolutionize various aspects of our lives, it also raises significant privacy concerns.

Privacy Risks in the IoT

The widespread adoption of IoT devices has led to an exponential increase in the amount of personal data being generated and shared. This data includes information about our behavior, habits, preferences, and even our physical location. The following are some privacy risks associated with the IoT:

- **Data Collection and Sharing**: IoT devices continuously collect and transmit data to external servers or cloud platforms. This data can be used by service providers to understand user behavior and deliver personalized experiences. However, the collection and sharing of personal data without the user's explicit consent can infringe upon their privacy.

- **Security Breaches**: IoT devices are often connected to the internet, making them vulnerable to hacking and unauthorized access. If a malicious actor gains control over an IoT device, they can potentially access sensitive information stored on the device or use it as a gateway to gain access to other devices on the network.

+ **Data Aggregation and Profiling**: As multiple IoT devices are used together, the data collected by each device can be aggregated to create a comprehensive profile of an individual. Such profiles can reveal intimate details about a person's lifestyle, habits, and even predict their future behavior. The aggregation of data from various sources raises concerns about the potential for surveillance and discrimination.

+ **Lack of Awareness**: Many individuals are unaware of the extent to which their personal data is being collected and used by IoT devices. This lack of transparency and understanding prevents users from making informed decisions about the data they share and who has access to it.

Principles of Privacy in the IoT

To address the privacy concerns associated with the IoT, several principles and guidelines have been proposed. These principles aim to protect individuals' privacy while promoting the benefits of IoT technology. Some key principles include:

+ **Privacy by Design**: Privacy should be incorporated into the design and development of IoT devices and systems from the outset, rather than being an afterthought. This includes implementing privacy-preserving technologies, conducting privacy impact assessments, and providing users with clear and understandable privacy settings.

+ **Data Minimization**: IoT systems should collect only the minimum amount of data necessary to fulfill their intended purpose. Data should be anonymized or pseudonymized whenever possible to reduce the risk of re-identification.

+ **User Consent and Control**: Users should have full control over their personal data and be able to provide informed consent for its collection and use. They should also have the ability to access, modify, and delete their data as needed.

+ **Security and Encryption**: IoT devices should be built with robust security measures to protect against unauthorized access and data breaches. This includes encrypting data during transmission and storage, regularly updating device firmware, and implementing strong authentication mechanisms.

Regulatory Framework and Best Practices

To safeguard privacy in the IoT, various regulations and best practices have been developed at the international, national, and organizational levels. Here are some notable examples:

- **General Data Protection Regulation (GDPR):** The GDPR, introduced by the European Union, sets comprehensive privacy rules and requirements for organizations that process personal data. It includes provisions related to consent, data protection impact assessments, and individuals' rights to access and control their data.

- **California Consumer Privacy Act (CCPA):** The CCPA is a state-level privacy law in the United States that grants California residents specific rights regarding their personal information. It requires businesses to disclose data collection and sharing practices, provide opt-out mechanisms, and give individuals the right to delete their data.

- **IoT Security Guidelines:** Various organizations, such as the National Institute of Standards and Technology (NIST) and the International Organization for Standardization (ISO), have published guidelines and frameworks for securing IoT devices. These guidelines address aspects such as device identification, access control, encryption, and security monitoring.

Case Study: Smart Home Devices

A relevant example of the privacy concerns in the IoT is the use of smart home devices. These devices, such as voice assistants, smart thermostats, and security cameras, offer convenience and enhanced functionality. However, they also raise significant privacy risks.

For instance, smart speakers with voice assistants constantly listen for their wake words. While this feature enables hands-free control, it also means that conversations within the vicinity of the device can be recorded and potentially stored by the service provider. Similarly, security cameras can capture sensitive information about individuals' daily routines and activities, raising concerns about surveillance and unauthorized access to the footage.

To mitigate these risks, manufacturers and service providers should clearly communicate their data collection practices, provide robust security features, and allow users to configure their privacy settings. Users, on the other hand, should carefully read privacy policies, disable features they are uncomfortable with, and regularly update their devices' firmware to protect against known vulnerabilities.

Conclusion

As the Internet of Things continues to expand, it is crucial to address privacy concerns to ensure individuals' rights to privacy are protected. By adopting privacy-centric design principles, implementing robust security measures, and complying with relevant regulations, the potential benefits of the IoT can be realized without compromising personal privacy. It is essential for manufacturers, service providers, policymakers, and users to collaborate in creating a privacy-aware IoT ecosystem.

Autonomous Weapons and Ethical Dilemmas

Advancements in technology have led to the development of autonomous weapons systems, which are capable of independently selecting and engaging targets without human intervention. While these weapons have the potential to revolutionize warfare, they also raise significant ethical dilemmas and concerns. In this section, we will explore the ethical implications of autonomous weapons systems and the challenges they pose to international humanitarian law, human rights, and moral principles.

Understanding Autonomous Weapons

Autonomous weapons, also known as lethal autonomous weapons systems (LAWS) or killer robots, are a new class of weapons that can operate without direct human control. These systems can independently determine targets, assess threats, and apply lethal force. They may be equipped with artificial intelligence algorithms, sensors, and decision-making capabilities.

Examples of autonomous weapons include unmanned aerial vehicles (UAVs) or drones, autonomous tanks, and robotic land or sea-based platforms. These systems possess varying degrees of autonomy, ranging from pre-programmed instructions to systems that can adapt and learn from their environment.

Ethical Concerns and Challenges

The deployment of autonomous weapons raises several ethical concerns and challenges. These include:

1. **Accountability**: Autonomous weapons blur the line of responsibility and accountability for using lethal force. Without human operators making critical decisions, who should be held responsible for any resulting harm or casualties?

2. **Lack of Human Judgment:** The use of autonomous weapons eliminates the human ability to make moral and ethical judgments in complex and unpredictable situations. This raises questions about the ability of these systems to distinguish between combatants and civilians and to act proportionally in armed conflicts.

3. **Dehumanization of Warfare:** The increasing reliance on autonomous weapons may further dehumanize warfare. Removing human soldiers from the battlefield potentially reduces the perceived costs of conflict, leading to more frequent and aggressive military engagements.

4. **Unpredictability and Errors:** Autonomous systems can be susceptible to errors, malfunctioning, or being hacked. They may carry out unintended actions or target unintended targets, leading to civilian casualties or exacerbating conflicts.

5. **Proliferation and Arms Race:** The widespread adoption of autonomous weapons could spark an arms race as nations seek to develop and deploy their own systems. This could result in an escalation of conflicts and increased instability in international relations.

6. **Distortion of the Laws of Armed Conflict:** Autonomous weapons challenge the principles of distinction, proportionality, and military necessity that form the foundation of international humanitarian law. These systems may not possess the necessary understanding of the rules of engagement or the ability to exercise restraint as required by the laws of war.

Legal and Ethical Frameworks

Addressing the ethical dilemmas posed by autonomous weapons requires a comprehensive legal and ethical framework. Several initiatives and organizations are actively engaged in discussing and formulating guidelines in this area.

1. **The Campaign to Stop Killer Robots:** This international coalition of NGOs is dedicated to banning fully autonomous weapons. It advocates for a preemptive ban on the development, production, and use of such weapons.

2. **The United Nations Convention on Certain Conventional Weapons (CCW):** The CCW is a framework agreement that seeks to regulate or prohibit the use of specific conventional weapons that may cause unnecessary harm or be indiscriminate. Talks within the CCW on autonomous weapons are ongoing.

3. **Ethical Principles for AI:** Ethical frameworks that govern the development and deployment of artificial intelligence, such as those proposed by organizations like the IEEE and the European Commission, can provide guidance on the ethical considerations surrounding autonomous weapons.

4. **Public Engagement and Debate:** Public engagement and informed discussions are crucial in shaping policies and regulations concerning autonomous

weapons. Ethical considerations, public perceptions, and diverse perspectives must be taken into account.

Solutions and Mitigation Strategies

Managing the ethical dilemmas associated with autonomous weapons requires a collaborative effort from various stakeholders. Some potential solutions and mitigation strategies include:

1. **Meaningful Human Control:** Advocating for the principle of meaningful human control over autonomous weapons, ensuring that humans are ultimately responsible for the use of force and decisions in armed conflicts.

2. **International Norms and Agreements:** Developing international norms and agreements to govern the development, deployment, and use of autonomous weapons. These agreements could include transparency, accountability, and limitations on their autonomy.

3. **Robust Ethical Testing and Review:** Establishing rigorous test and evaluation procedures to ensure the responsible development and deployment of autonomous weapons. These procedures should include thorough ethical assessments and risk management protocols.

4. **Public Awareness and Engagement:** Raising public awareness about the ethical implications of autonomous weapons and fostering informed public debates. This can inform policymakers and influence decisions regarding their regulation and use.

5. **Ethical Education and Training:** Providing education and training programs that promote ethical decision-making skills for individuals involved in the development and use of autonomous weapons. This can enhance the understanding of ethical considerations and improve decision-making processes.

Case Study: The Campaign Against Killer Robots

The Campaign to Stop Killer Robots is one of the prominent initiatives advocating for a ban on fully autonomous weapons. This coalition of NGOs aims to foster public and political debates on lethal autonomous weapons and create the conditions necessary for a legally binding ban. They engage with governments, civil society, and the public to highlight the human rights, security, ethical, and humanitarian concerns associated with autonomous weapons.

The campaign uses various strategies, including public awareness campaigns, lobbying, and engagement with policymakers. It also conducts research and publishes reports addressing specific aspects of autonomous weapons. Their efforts have contributed to increased international attention and discussions on this critical issue.

Conclusion

Autonomous weapons present significant ethical challenges that must be addressed to safeguard human rights, maintain international peace and security, and uphold moral standards. Achieving a balance between technological advancements and ethical considerations requires interdisciplinary collaboration, international cooperation, and a commitment to meaningful human control. Only through informed public debates and proactive regulation can we ensure that autonomous weapons do not compromise our human values and principles.

Virtual Reality and Ethical Challenges

Virtual reality (VR) technology has rapidly advanced in recent years, allowing users to immerse themselves in computer-generated environments. It has found applications in various fields, including entertainment, education, healthcare, and training. However, like any emerging technology, VR presents its own set of ethical challenges. In this section, we will explore some of these challenges and discuss the ethical considerations surrounding virtual reality.

Privacy and Surveillance

One significant concern with VR is the potential invasion of privacy. When users enter a virtual environment, they often provide personal information such as their name, age, and even biometric data. This data can be collected and used for various purposes, including targeted advertising, behavior analysis, and even surveillance.

To address these concerns, it is essential for VR developers and service providers to implement strict privacy policies and ensure that users have control over their data. Clear consent mechanisms should be in place, and users should be informed about how their data is collected, stored, and used. Additionally, anonymity options should be provided to users who wish to preserve their privacy within virtual environments.

Virtual Crime and Harassment

Virtual reality provides a unique platform for social interaction and communication. However, this also means that virtual spaces can become breeding grounds for virtual crime and harassment. In some cases, users may experience virtual stalking, bullying, or even sexual harassment within a virtual environment.

To combat this issue, virtual platforms need to establish robust community guidelines and moderation systems. Users should be able to report and block abusive individuals, and appropriate actions should be taken against those who violate the rules. Virtual reality companies should also educate users about responsible behavior within virtual spaces and create a culture of inclusivity and respect.

Ethics in Virtual Reality Content

Virtual reality content can range from immersive educational experiences to violent and explicit simulations. While the potential for creativity and educational value is vast, there is also a risk of creating content that is harmful, offensive, or unethical.

To navigate this challenge, content creators and VR platforms should adhere to ethical guidelines and standards. They should consider the potential impact of their content on users and society as a whole. It is crucial to strike a balance between freedom of expression and protecting users from harmful or inappropriate experiences. Open discussions and collaborations with ethicists, psychologists, and other experts can help in developing responsible content guidelines.

Addiction and Psychological Impact

Virtual reality has the potential to create immersive experiences that can be highly captivating and addictive. Prolonged and excessive use of VR can lead to various psychological and physiological effects, including dizziness, disorientation, and even addiction.

To mitigate these risks, users should be educated about responsible VR usage and the potential risks associated with excessive immersion. VR platforms should also incorporate features that encourage breaks and limit extended usage. Additionally, mental health professionals and researchers should be more involved in studying the long-term effects of virtual reality on psychological well-being.

Accessibility and Inclusivity

Virtual reality technology has the potential to revolutionize the way we interact with digital content. However, it is crucial to consider accessibility and inclusivity when designing and developing VR experiences. Not everyone has equal access to the technology or can fully participate due to disabilities or other barriers.

Developers should strive to create VR experiences that are accessible to individuals with different abilities and needs. This includes features for individuals with visual or hearing impairments, as well as considerations for those with mobility limitations. Additionally, efforts should be made to ensure affordable access to VR technology and content for marginalized communities and developing regions.

Unrealistic Perceptions and Desensitization

Virtual reality can create vivid and realistic experiences that can blur the line between the virtual and real world. This can have unintended consequences, such as desensitization to violence, empathy erosion, or the reinforcement of harmful stereotypes.

It is crucial for content creators and VR platforms to be aware of these risks and design experiences that promote positive values, empathy, and understanding. Regulation and content rating systems should be implemented to prevent the distribution of harmful or unethical virtual experiences.

Conclusion

Virtual reality technology holds immense potential for transformative experiences and applications in various fields. However, as with any technology, there are ethical challenges that need to be addressed. Privacy, virtual crime, content ethics, addiction, accessibility, and perception distortion are among the key concerns.

By considering these ethical challenges and implementing responsible practices, virtual reality can continue to evolve in an ethical and inclusive manner. It is essential for stakeholders, including technology developers, policymakers, and users, to actively engage in discussions and collaborate to create a responsible and beneficial future for virtual reality.

Brain-Computer Interfaces and Ethical Considerations

Brain-computer interfaces (BCIs) have emerged as a groundbreaking technology, allowing direct communication between the brain and external devices. This field holds immense potential in various areas, including medicine, research, assistive technologies, and entertainment. However, along with this potential comes a range of ethical considerations that need to be carefully addressed. In this section, we will explore the ethical implications of brain-computer interfaces and the importance of responsible development and use.

Understanding Brain-Computer Interfaces

Before delving into the ethical considerations, let's first understand what brain-computer interfaces are and how they function. Brain-computer interfaces are systems that enable direct communication between the brain and an external device, bypassing traditional pathways such as muscles or nerves. They work by detecting and interpreting brain signals, which are then translated into commands that control the device.

BCIs can be invasive or non-invasive. Invasive BCIs require surgery to implant electrodes directly into the brain tissue, whereas non-invasive BCIs use external sensors to measure brain activity. Both approaches have their advantages and limitations, but the focus here will be on the broader ethical considerations applicable to BCIs as a whole.

Ethical Considerations

1. Privacy and Data Security: BCIs, particularly those that involve recording and analyzing brain activity, raise significant privacy concerns. Brain signals can reveal personal and sensitive information about an individual, such as thoughts, emotions, and intentions. It is crucial to ensure that the collection, storage, and transmission of brain data are done securely and with informed consent, protecting the privacy of users.

2. Informed Consent: Obtaining informed consent is vital in BCI research and applications. Users must receive comprehensive information about the risks, benefits, and potential outcomes of BCI use. Special attention should be given to vulnerable populations, such as individuals with cognitive impairments or minors, to ensure their rights are protected and their autonomy respected.

3. User Autonomy: BCIs have the potential to greatly enhance human capabilities, but they also raise questions about autonomy and agency. For instance, can a BCI user truly exercise free will if their thoughts or actions are influenced or manipulated by external factors? Careful consideration should be given to the potential impact on user autonomy, and safeguards must be in place to protect individuals from undue influence or coercion.

4. Equity and Accessibility: Like many emerging technologies, BCIs may exacerbate existing disparities. It is crucial to ensure equal access to this technology, regardless of socioeconomic status or disability. Ethical considerations should include affordability, availability, and accessibility to ensure that BCIs do not widen the gap between different groups in society.

5. Ethical Use of BCI Data: As BCIs continue to evolve, the data generated by these systems will become increasingly valuable. Organizations and researchers must use this data responsibly, adhering to established ethical guidelines and regulations. Clear policies must be in place to govern data ownership, sharing, and usage to protect individuals' privacy and prevent misuse.

Case Study: Brain-Computer Interfaces in Assistive Technologies

Let's consider a case study in which BCIs are used in assistive technologies for individuals with paralysis. BCIs can provide a means of communication and control for these individuals, enabling them to interact with their environment using their thoughts. This technology holds tremendous potential for improving the quality of life for people with disabilities.

However, several ethical considerations arise in this context. It is essential to ensure that individuals have fully understood the limitations, risks, and benefits of BCI use before incorporating them into their daily lives. Informed consent and ongoing support should be provided to ensure the empowerment and autonomy of users.

Additionally, the affordability and accessibility of assistive BCI technologies should be addressed. The high costs associated with developing and maintaining BCIs can create significant barriers for those who would benefit most from these technologies. Efforts should be made to make assistive BCIs affordable and available to all individuals with disabilities.

Ethical Guidelines and Regulation

To address the ethical considerations surrounding BCIs, it is essential to develop and follow ethical guidelines and regulations for their development and use. These guidelines should cover areas such as informed consent, privacy and data security, user autonomy, accessibility, and responsible data usage.

Furthermore, interdisciplinary collaboration among researchers, ethicists, policymakers, and representatives from impacted communities is crucial in shaping these guidelines. Open dialogue and exchange of ideas will help ensure that the ethical implications of BCIs are thoroughly examined from various perspectives.

Conclusion

Brain-computer interfaces hold immense promise in advancing medicine, research, and human-machine interactions. However, ethical considerations arise as these technologies become increasingly integrated into our lives. Privacy, informed consent, user autonomy, equity, and responsible data usage are among the key ethical concerns that require careful consideration.

As the development of BCIs continues, it is imperative that stakeholders actively engage in ethical discussions and implement robust guidelines and regulations. Only through responsible development, use, and regulation can we fully harness the potential of brain-computer interfaces while ensuring the protection of individual rights and well-being in an increasingly connected world.

Ethical Practices in Education

Ethics in Teaching and Classroom Management

Professionalism and Ethical Conduct of Teachers

In the field of education, teachers play a crucial role in shaping the minds and character of their students. To fulfill this responsibility effectively, teachers are expected to maintain a high level of professionalism and ethical conduct. This section explores the importance of professionalism in teaching, the ethical obligations teachers have towards their students, and the challenges they may encounter in upholding these standards.

The Significance of Professionalism in Teaching

Professionalism is a fundamental aspect of the teaching profession. It encompasses a teacher's commitment to maintain and improve their expertise, adhere to ethical standards, and demonstrate responsible behavior towards students, colleagues, and the community.

One key aspect of professionalism is continuous professional development. Teachers should actively engage in ongoing learning to enhance their knowledge and skills. By participating in workshops, conferences, and professional development programs, teachers can stay updated with the latest research and best practices in education. This not only benefits their own growth but also ensures that they provide their students with the most effective and up-to-date instruction.

Professionalism also includes maintaining a positive and respectful attitude towards students, regardless of their backgrounds or abilities. Teachers should create a safe and inclusive learning environment where all students feel valued and respected. This involves treating students fairly, addressing their individual needs, fostering a sense of belonging, and promoting equity and social justice.

Furthermore, teachers must demonstrate a strong work ethic and a commitment to their professional responsibilities. This includes being punctual, prepared for lessons, and responsive to student inquiries and concerns. Teachers should also communicate effectively with parents and collaborate with colleagues to support student learning.

Ethical Obligations of Teachers

In addition to professionalism, teachers have ethical obligations that guide their conduct towards their students. These obligations aim to ensure that teachers act in the best interests of their students and uphold the values of education.

First and foremost, teachers have a duty to provide a safe and nurturing environment for their students. This involves protecting students from physical, emotional, and psychological harm. Teachers should be aware of signs of abuse or neglect and report any concerns to the appropriate authorities. Additionally, teachers should promote positive behavior and teach students the importance of respect, empathy, and integrity.

Teachers also have an ethical obligation to maintain confidentiality and respect student privacy. They should handle student information with care and only share it with individuals who have a legitimate need to know. This includes discussing student performance, behavior, or personal issues only with relevant colleagues or parents/guardians.

Moreover, teachers are responsible for fostering academic honesty and ensuring that students understand the importance of intellectual integrity. Teachers should teach and reinforce ethical practices related to research, citation, and avoiding plagiarism. They should also model honesty and integrity in their own work and assessment practices.

Teachers are expected to treat all students fairly and without bias. They should avoid favoritism, discrimination, or any form of prejudice. Ensuring equitable opportunities for all students, regardless of their race, gender, socioeconomic status, or abilities, is an essential aspect of an ethical teacher's role.

Challenges in Upholding Professionalism and Ethics

While maintaining professionalism and ethical conduct is essential, teachers face various challenges in upholding these standards. One challenge is managing conflicts of interest, such as personal relationships with students or biased grading practices. Teachers should be aware of these potential conflicts and take measures to ensure objectivity and fairness.

Another challenge is navigating the boundaries between professional and personal relationships. Teachers must maintain appropriate boundaries with students to prevent any form of exploitation or unprofessional behavior. This includes avoiding favoritism, maintaining professionalism in communication and interactions, and refraining from sharing personal information or engaging in inappropriate relationships with students.

Teachers may also encounter situations where their personal beliefs or values conflict with the curriculum, school policies, or the diverse perspectives of their students. In such cases, teachers should strive to maintain objectivity, respect different viewpoints, and create an inclusive learning environment that encourages open dialogue and critical thinking.

Additionally, with the advancement of technology, teachers face ethical challenges related to the use of digital resources and communication platforms. They must navigate issues such as online privacy, cybersecurity, appropriate behavior on social media, and ensuring equitable access to digital resources for all students.

Conclusion

Professionalism and ethical conduct are foundational principles in the teaching profession. Teachers must continuously strive to enhance their expertise, maintain high ethical standards, and prioritize the best interests of their students. By upholding professionalism and ethics, teachers not only contribute to the development of their students but also foster a positive learning environment that promotes academic excellence, social growth, and ethical awareness.

Key Terms

- Professionalism

- Continuous professional development

- Inclusive education

- Equity and social justice

- Work ethic

- Duty of care

- Confidentiality

- Academic honesty

- Fairness and equality

- Conflicts of interest

- Boundaries

- Online privacy and cybersecurity

Resources

- Darling-Hammond, L., Burns, D., Campbell, C., Goodwin, A. L., Hammerness, K., Low, E. L., ... & Yuan, Z. (2017). *Teaching for equity and justice: Supporting educators' capacity to work effectively with diverse learners.* New York: Routledge.

- National Education Association. (2013). *Code of ethics of the Education Profession.* Retrieved from https://www.nea.org/advocating-for-change/new-from-nea/code-of-ethics.html

- Seldin, P., & Miller, J. E. (2014). *The supervisory relationship: A contemporary psychodynamic approach.* New York: Guilford Publications.

- UNESCO. (2019). *Ethics of teaching: Believing, knowing and doing what's right.* Retrieved from https://en.unesco.org/themes/ethics-education/good-practices/ethics-teaching

Exercises

1. Reflect on a situation where you observed an ethical dilemma in a classroom. Discuss how you would address the situation ethically and maintain professionalism.

2. Research and discuss the impact of teachers' ethical behavior on students' academic achievement and overall well-being.

3. Interview an experienced teacher and inquire about their strategies for upholding professionalism and ethics in their practice.

4. Explore your school's code of conduct or professional ethics guidelines. Identify key principles and discuss their significance in maintaining professionalism and ethical conduct.

Discussion Questions

1. How can teachers balance their personal beliefs and values with the need to provide an inclusive and unbiased learning environment?

2. What are some strategies that teachers can employ to manage conflicts of interest while grading students' work?

3. Discuss the ethical implications of the increasing use of technology in education and its impact on student-teacher relationships.

4. How can teachers promote academic honesty and integrity among students? Share specific strategies and examples.

Further Reading

+ Blase, J., & Blase, J. (2014). *Effective instructional leadership: Teachers' perspectives on how principals promote teaching and learning in schools.* New York: Routledge.

+ Harrison, C., Cochrane, M., & Carr, T. (Eds.). (2016). *Developing exemplary performance one person at a time.* New York: Routledge.

+ Strike, K. A., & Soltis, J. F. (2019). *The ethics of teaching.* New York: Teachers College Press.

Student-Teacher Relationships and Boundaries

Establishing and maintaining appropriate boundaries in student-teacher relationships is crucial in the field of education. Effective student-teacher relationships can significantly impact student learning, motivation, and overall well-being. However, crossing professional boundaries can lead to ethical issues and even harm to both students and teachers. In this section, we will explore the importance of student-teacher relationships, the boundaries that should be maintained, and strategies to navigate potential challenges.

Importance of Student-Teacher Relationships

Student-teacher relationships play a vital role in creating a positive and supportive learning environment. When students feel connected to their teachers, they are more likely to engage actively in the learning process and achieve better academic outcomes. A strong student-teacher relationship can foster a sense of trust, respect, and empathy, enabling teachers to better understand and address the individual needs of their students.

Research has shown that positive student-teacher relationships can enhance students' self-esteem, motivation, and engagement in school. Students who have a supportive relationship with their teachers are also less likely to exhibit behavioral problems or experience school-related stress. As educators, it is our responsibility to create a safe and supportive environment that promotes healthy student-teacher relationships.

Maintaining Boundaries

While it is crucial to establish positive and supportive relationships with students, it is equally important to maintain professional boundaries. Boundaries ensure that the interactions between teachers and students remain appropriate and ethical. Here are some key boundaries that should be followed:

1. **Physical Boundaries:** Teachers should avoid physical contact with students that may be misunderstood or inappropriate. Touching should only be used when it is necessary for the safety or well-being of the student, such as providing comfort during emotional distress or assisting with a physical task.

2. **Emotional Boundaries:** Teachers should be mindful of emotional boundaries by maintaining an appropriate level of emotional involvement. While it is important to build rapport and empathy with students, it is essential to avoid favoritism or emotional dependency.

3. **Communication Boundaries:** Teachers should establish clear guidelines for communication with students, both in person and online. All communication should be professional and related to academic or school-related matters. It is important to avoid personal, confidential, or intimate conversations with students.

4. **Privacy Boundaries:** Teachers must respect the privacy of their students. Confidential information shared by students should be kept confidential unless there are legal or safety concerns. Teachers should also be mindful of their online presence and ensure that they do not share students' personal information or engage in inappropriate online behaviors.

5. **Social Boundaries:** Teachers should exercise caution when interacting with students in social settings outside of the school environment. While it is

acceptable to attend school-sponsored events or activities, it is important to maintain appropriate boundaries and avoid situations that may compromise the professionalism of the student-teacher relationship.

By establishing and maintaining these boundaries, teachers can maintain a professional and ethical relationship with their students while creating a positive and supportive learning environment.

Navigating Challenges

Maintaining clear boundaries in student-teacher relationships can be challenging, especially in complex situations. It is important for educators to be aware of potential challenges and have strategies to navigate them effectively. Here are some common challenges and suggested strategies:

1. **Favoritism:** Teachers should make a conscious effort to treat all students fairly and equitably. It is essential to be aware of personal biases and avoid showing favoritism towards particular students. Developing inclusive teaching practices and providing equal opportunities for all students can help mitigate the risk of favoritism.

2. **Conflicts of Interest:** Teachers should avoid situations where personal or financial interests may conflict with their professional responsibilities. For example, accepting gifts from students or their families may create conflicts of interest. It is important to adhere to the school's policies and maintain professional integrity.

3. **Boundaries with Colleagues:** Teachers should establish clear boundaries with their colleagues to ensure that professional relationships are not compromised. It is important to avoid engaging in gossip or sharing confidential information about students or colleagues. Maintaining a collaborative and respectful working environment can help prevent boundary violations.

4. **Online Interactions:** With the increasing use of technology in education, teachers must be cautious when interacting with students online. It is important to use school-approved communication platforms and adhere to the school's guidelines for online interactions. Teachers should avoid communicating with students through personal social media accounts and maintain a professional online presence.

Navigating these challenges requires reflection, self-awareness, and adherence to ethical guidelines. By maintaining professional boundaries and addressing potential challenges proactively, teachers can promote healthy and productive student-teacher relationships.

Case Study

Consider the following case study:

Mr. Johnson, a high school teacher, has noticed that one of his female students, Sarah, often stays behind after class to discuss personal matters. Sarah seems to seek emotional support and advice from Mr. Johnson on a regular basis. While Mr. Johnson wants to be supportive, he is concerned that their interactions may be crossing professional boundaries.

In this case, Mr. Johnson should consider the following steps:

1. Reflect on the nature of his interactions with Sarah and analyze whether they are appropriate and within professional boundaries.

2. Strive to maintain a supportive and empathetic approach while ensuring that the conversations with Sarah remain focused on academic or school-related matters.

3. Encourage Sarah to seek support from the school's counseling services or other appropriate resources that can better address her personal needs.

4. Consult with a trusted colleague or mentor to gain perspective and guidance on how to navigate the situation.

5. If necessary, discuss the concerns with the school administration or seek professional development opportunities on maintaining appropriate boundaries.

By taking these steps, Mr. Johnson can address the potential boundary crossing and ensure that his interactions with Sarah remain professional and supportive.

Conclusion

Student-teacher relationships are instrumental in creating a positive and engaging learning environment. By maintaining clear boundaries, educators can develop meaningful connections with their students while upholding professional ethics. Navigating and addressing challenges in student-teacher relationships requires self-reflection, awareness, and adherence to ethical guidelines. By fostering healthy and appropriate relationships, teachers can contribute to the overall academic and personal development of their students.

Exercises

1. Reflect on your own experiences as a student or a teacher. Share an example of a positive student-teacher relationship and identify the boundaries that were maintained in that relationship.

2. Identify potential boundary issues in the following scenarios and suggest strategies to address them:

   + A high school teacher regularly socializes with their students outside of school.

   + A teacher accepts an expensive gift from a student's parent.

   + A teacher shares confidential student information with a colleague without consent.

3. Research and discuss the legal and professional consequences of crossing boundaries in student-teacher relationships. How can these consequences be avoided?

Additional Resources

+ *Boundaries in the Classroom: Balancing Openness, Flexibility, and Professionalism* by Kelley B. Taylor

+ *Boundaries in the Teacher-Student Relationship* by M. Hixon, R. Soares, and S. Reinharz

+ American Psychological Association (APA) Ethical Principles of Psychologists and Code of Conduct

+ National Education Association (NEA) Code of Ethics for Educators

Remember, establishing and maintaining appropriate boundaries in student-teacher relationships is crucial for the well-being of both students and teachers. As educators, we have a responsibility to create a safe and supportive learning environment that fosters healthy and ethical interactions.

Disciplinary Actions and Punishments

Disciplinary actions and punishments play a crucial role in maintaining discipline and order in educational institutions. They serve as a means of correcting behavior and teaching students the importance of accountability and responsibility. In this section, we will explore various aspects of disciplinary actions and punishments, including their purpose, principles, types, and ethical considerations.

Purpose of Disciplinary Actions

The primary purpose of disciplinary actions is to promote a safe and conducive learning environment that fosters the intellectual, emotional, and social development of students. Disciplinary actions aim to:

1. Dissuade students from engaging in misconduct or disruptive behavior.

2. Reinforce positive behavior and adherence to school rules and policies.

3. Protect the rights and well-being of all members of the educational community.

4. Teach students valuable life skills such as self-discipline, conflict resolution, and accountability.

Through appropriate disciplinary actions, educators can maintain a positive school climate that supports effective teaching and learning.

Principles of Disciplinary Actions

Disciplinary actions in educational settings should be guided by a set of principles that promote fairness, consistency, and the best interests of students. Some key principles include:

1. Proportionality: The severity of the disciplinary action should be proportional to the nature and severity of the offense committed.

2. Non-Discrimination: Disciplinary actions should be applied without bias or discrimination based on factors such as race, gender, religion, or socioeconomic status.

3. Due Process: Students should be afforded a fair and impartial process that includes the right to be heard, present evidence, and challenge the accusations against them.

4. Rehabilitation: The primary goal of disciplinary actions should be to help students learn from their mistakes and develop positive behavior patterns, rather than solely focusing on punishment.

5. Consistency: Disciplinary actions should be applied consistently across all students, ensuring that similar offenses receive similar consequences.

By upholding these principles, educators can ensure that their disciplinary actions are just and promote a sense of trust among students, parents, and the larger community.

Types of Disciplinary Actions

Disciplinary actions can take various forms, depending on the severity of the offense and the needs of the student. Some common types of disciplinary actions include:

1. Verbal Warning: This is a mild form of disciplinary action that involves a private conversation between the teacher and the student, highlighting the inappropriate behavior and consequences of further violations.

2. Detention: Students are required to stay after school for a specified period to reflect on their behavior and complete assigned tasks.

3. In-school Suspension: Students attend school but are isolated from their regular classes and peers, providing an opportunity for reflection and making up missed work.

4. Loss of Privileges: Students may lose certain privileges, such as participation in extracurricular activities or using electronic devices, to reinforce the consequences of their behavior.

5. Restitution: Students are required to repair any damage caused by their actions or make amends to those affected.

6. Community Service: Students engage in activities that benefit the school or larger community, fostering a sense of responsibility and empathy.

7. Parental Involvement: Parents may be invited to attend meetings or workshops to address their child's behavior and develop strategies for improvement.

8. Suspension: Students are temporarily removed from school for a designated period, during which they may be required to complete assignments and reflect on their behavior.

9. Expulsion: Students are permanently removed from the school due to severe or repeated violations of the school's code of conduct.

It is important for educators to consider the severity of the offense, the student's age and maturity level, and any underlying factors that may have contributed to the misconduct when determining the appropriate type of disciplinary action.

Ethical Considerations

When administering disciplinary actions, educators must adhere to ethical considerations to ensure fairness, dignity, and respect for students. Some ethical considerations in disciplinary actions include:

1. Confidentiality: Student disciplinary records should be kept confidential and only shared with relevant parties on a need-to-know basis.

2. Rehabilitation over Punishment: Disciplinary actions should focus on helping students develop positive behavior rather than inflicting unnecessary punishment.

3. Consistency and Equity: Disciplinary actions should be consistent and equitable, ensuring that similar behaviors receive similar consequences regardless of individual differences.

4. Respect and Dignity: Students should be treated with respect and dignity throughout the disciplinary process, with their rights and needs being taken into consideration.

5. Reflection and Restorative Justice: Disciplinary actions should provide opportunities for students to reflect on their behavior, make amends, and learn from their mistakes through restorative justice practices.

Educators should continuously reflect on their disciplinary practices to ensure they align with these ethical considerations and promote the well-being and growth of their students.

Addressing Challenges in Disciplinary Actions

Disciplinary actions can present challenges for educators due to various factors such as student resistance, complexity of situations, and potential negative impact on the student's academic progress. Here are some strategies for addressing these challenges:

1. Effective Communication: Establish open lines of communication with students, parents, and colleagues to address concerns, explain disciplinary actions, and collaborate on solutions.

2. Restorative Practices: Implement restorative justice practices, such as peer mediation or circles, to foster dialogue, healing, and resolution in the aftermath of a disciplinary incident.

3. Supportive Interventions: Provide students with appropriate support systems, such as counseling services, mentorship programs, or referral to external support agencies, to address underlying issues contributing to their behavior.

4. Professional Development: Engage in ongoing professional development and training on disciplinary strategies, restorative justice, and empathy-building techniques to enhance their effectiveness in handling disciplinary incidents.

5. Prevention and Proactive Measures: Implement proactive approaches, such as social-emotional learning programs, character education, and positive behavior reinforcement, to create a positive school climate and reduce the frequency of disciplinary incidents.

By proactively addressing challenges and adopting a holistic approach to disciplinary actions, educators can create a supportive and nurturing environment that promotes students' personal and academic growth.

Case Study: Addressing Bullying Incidents

Bullying is a prevalent issue in schools that requires careful consideration and appropriate disciplinary actions. Let's consider a case study to understand how disciplinary actions can be applied in addressing bullying incidents:

Case: Sarah, a 13-year-old student, has been consistently bullying her classmate, Emma, by spreading rumors and making hurtful comments. Emma's academic performance and emotional well-being have been significantly affected.

Disciplinary Actions:

1. Investigation: Conduct a thorough investigation to gather evidence and understand the full extent of the bullying incidents.

2. Student Support: Provide immediate support to Emma by offering counseling services and ensuring her safety.

3. Meeting with Parents: Organize a meeting with Sarah's parents to discuss the bullying incidents, the impact on the victim, and the consequences of the behavior.

4. Restorative Measures: Encourage Sarah to reflect on her actions, apologize to Emma, and participate in restorative justice practices, such as a mediated conversation between both parties.

5. Behavioral Contract: Develop a behavioral contract with Sarah, outlining expected behaviors, consequences for future violations, and support mechanisms.

6. Follow-up and Monitoring: Regularly check in with Emma to ensure her well-being and monitor Sarah's behavior to prevent further incidents.

7. Education and Prevention: Conduct workshops on bullying prevention and empathy-building for all students to raise awareness and foster a culture of respect and kindness.

In this case study, the disciplinary actions aim not only to address the immediate bullying incidents but also to support the victim, promote empathy and understanding in the bully, and prevent future occurrences. By addressing the root causes of the behavior and involving all stakeholders, educators can create a safe and inclusive learning environment.

Conclusion

Disciplinary actions and punishments are essential tools for educators to maintain discipline and ensure a conducive learning environment. By understanding the purpose, principles, types, and ethical considerations of disciplinary actions, educators can implement fair and effective strategies that promote positive behavior, accountability, and personal growth in students. Addressing challenges in disciplinary actions requires proactive measures, effective communication, and a focus on restorative justice. Through these efforts, educators can create a supportive and nurturing school climate that empowers students to become responsible and ethical individuals.

Inclusive Education and Ethical Obligations

Inclusive education is an approach that aims to ensure that all students, regardless of their abilities or disabilities, are able to fully participate in and benefit from the educational environment. It promotes diversity, equity, and empowerment, and recognizes that every student has the right to an education that meets their unique needs and abilities. Inclusive education not only benefits students with disabilities but also enhances the learning experience for all students by fostering a culture of understanding, respect, and acceptance.

Principles of Inclusive Education

There are several principles that underpin inclusive education and guide ethical obligations towards creating an inclusive learning environment:

1. **Equity and Access:** Inclusive education recognizes that every student has the right to equal educational opportunities. Schools and educational institutions must remove barriers and provide necessary resources and support for all students to participate and succeed.

2. **Individualized Support:** Inclusive education acknowledges that students have different strengths, needs, and learning styles. Teachers should provide appropriate accommodations, modifications, and specialized instruction to meet the diverse learning needs of students.

3. **Collaboration and Partnerships:** Inclusive education encourages collaboration among all stakeholders, including educators, parents, students, and community members. This collaborative approach helps create an inclusive school culture and ensures that decisions are made collectively, taking into account the perspectives and expertise of all involved.

4. **Social Integration:** Inclusive education promotes the social integration of students with disabilities into mainstream classrooms and school activities. It encourages peer support and fosters positive relationships among students, promoting an inclusive and accepting school environment.

5. **Emphasis on Strengths:** Inclusive education focuses on students' abilities and strengths rather than their disabilities. It values and supports the diverse talents, skills, and interests of every student, fostering their self-esteem and motivation to learn.

Ethical Obligations in Inclusive Education

Inclusive education comes with ethical obligations for educators, educational institutions, and society as a whole. These obligations include:

1. **Equal Opportunities:** Educators have an ethical obligation to provide equal opportunities for all students to access quality education. This means ensuring that students with disabilities are not discriminated against and have access to the same educational resources and opportunities as their peers.

2. **Respect for Diversity:** Educators should foster a culture of respect for diversity and create a learning environment that celebrates and values individual differences. They should promote positive attitudes towards students with disabilities and ensure that all students feel included and valued in the classroom.

3. **Individualized Instruction:** Educators have an ethical obligation to provide individualized instruction and support to students with disabilities. This may involve using different teaching strategies, providing assistive technologies, or adapting the curriculum to meet the students' unique needs.

4. **Collaboration and Communication:** Educators should collaborate with parents, special education professionals, and other stakeholders to ensure the success of inclusive education. Open and transparent communication is crucial in creating a partnership that supports the learning and well-being of students with disabilities.

5. **Advocacy and Empowerment:** Educators have an ethical obligation to advocate for the rights of students with disabilities and empower them to become active participants in their own education. This may involve promoting self-advocacy skills, providing opportunities for student input and decision-making, and challenging barriers to inclusion.

Example Scenario

To illustrate the ethical obligations in inclusive education, let's consider the case of Sarah, a 10-year-old student with a hearing impairment. Sarah uses a hearing aid and requires some accommodations to fully participate in the classroom.

The ethical obligations of Sarah's teacher and the school include:

1. Ensuring that Sarah has access to appropriate assistive technologies, such as a functioning hearing aid and a sound amplification system in the classroom.

2. Providing individualized support by using visual aids, providing clear instructions, and allowing extra time for Sarah to process information.

3. Collaborating with Sarah's parents and other professionals, such as a sign language interpreter or a speech therapist, to ensure that her unique needs are met.

4. Promoting an inclusive classroom environment by fostering understanding and empathy among Sarah's peers and encouraging them to communicate effectively with her.

5. Advocating for Sarah's rights and addressing any barriers or discriminatory practices that may hinder her full participation and inclusion in the school community.

By fulfilling these ethical obligations, educators and educational institutions can create an inclusive educational environment that supports the learning and development of all students, including those with disabilities.

Additional Resources

1. UNESCO Guidelines on Inclusion in Education: https://unesdoc.unesco.org/ark:/48223/pf0000221084

2. The Council for Exceptional Children: https://www.cec.sped.org/

3. The National Association of Special Education Teachers: https://www.naset.org/

4. The American Association of People with Disabilities: https://www.aapd.com/

5. "Inclusion in Education: Selected Key Issues" by Susie Miles & Ann-Marie Wykes

Academic Integrity and Ethical Cheating

Academic integrity is the foundation upon which the education system is built. It encompasses values such as honesty, fairness, trust, and responsibility. Academic integrity is essential for maintaining the credibility and quality of education. However, in recent years, the issue of ethical cheating has become a significant concern in educational institutions.

Understanding Academic Integrity

Academic integrity refers to the ethical principles and values that govern the behavior of students, educators, and researchers within the academic community. It involves upholding intellectual honesty, acknowledging the contributions of others, and respecting the rules and regulations set by educational institutions.

At the core of academic integrity is the concept of originality. Students are expected to produce their work, acknowledge the ideas and research findings of others through proper citation, and avoid any form of plagiarism. Plagiarism is the act of presenting someone else's ideas, words, or work as one's own without giving proper credit.

Types of Ethical Cheating

Ethical cheating refers to violations of academic integrity that occur intentionally and knowingly. It encompasses a range of dishonest practices that students may employ to gain an unfair advantage in their academic pursuits. Some common types of ethical cheating include:

- **Plagiarism:** Presenting someone else's work as one's own, without proper citation or attribution.

- **Cheating on Exams:** Using unauthorized resources, such as cheat sheets or electronic devices, during exams.

- **Collusion:** Working together with others to complete an assignment or exam when individual work is required.

- **Contract Cheating:** Hiring someone to complete an assignment or exam on one's behalf.

- **Fabrication of Data:** Falsifying research findings or experimental data to support one's claims.

Consequences of Ethical Cheating

Ethical cheating undermines the educational process and has serious consequences for both individual students and the academic community as a whole. Some of the consequences of ethical cheating include:

- **Loss of Learning:** Students who engage in ethical cheating miss out on the opportunity to develop and demonstrate essential skills and knowledge.

- **Diminished Academic Reputation:** Ethical cheating tarnishes the reputation of educational institutions and devalues the achievements of honest students.

- **Unfair Evaluation:** Ethical cheating skews the evaluation process, creating an uneven playing field for students who engage in honest academic work.

- **Legal and Professional Consequences:** In some cases, ethical cheating can have legal or professional repercussions, such as academic probation, expulsion, or damage to one's future career prospects.

Preventing and Addressing Ethical Cheating

Educational institutions play a vital role in preventing and addressing ethical cheating. Creating a culture of academic integrity requires a multidimensional approach that involves students, educators, administrators, and policymakers. Here are some strategies for preventing and addressing ethical cheating:

+ **Promote Awareness and Education:** Educate students about the importance of academic integrity, the consequences of ethical cheating, and the proper methods of citation and referencing.

+ **Strengthen Policies and Procedures:** Develop clear and comprehensive policies that explicitly state the expectations regarding academic integrity and outline the consequences for violations.

+ **Support Services and Resources:** Provide students with resources such as writing centers, citation guides, and tutorials on academic integrity to help them develop the necessary skills.

+ **Implement Technology Solutions:** Explore technologies that can help detect instances of plagiarism or cheating, such as plagiarism-checking software and remote proctoring tools.

+ **Promote a Culture of Trust and Respect:** Foster an environment where students feel supported and encouraged to engage in honest academic work, promoting a culture of trust and respect within the academic community.

Case Study: The Rise of Contract Cheating

One of the emerging challenges in academic integrity is the rise of contract cheating, where students pay others to complete their assignments or exams. This form of ethical cheating has become more prevalent due to the ease of accessing online platforms and essay mills, which offer customized essays for a fee.

Contract cheating not only undermines the true learning experience but also poses significant challenges in detection and prevention. Educational institutions must stay vigilant and adopt proactive measures to address this issue. This might include raising awareness among students about the risks and consequences of contract cheating, implementing stringent assessment methods, and fostering a supportive environment that encourages students to seek help when facing academic difficulties.

Conclusion

Maintaining academic integrity is crucial for the credibility and quality of education. Ethical cheating poses a serious threat to the principles of honesty and fairness within the academic community. By promoting awareness, strengthening policies, and fostering a culture of integrity, educational institutions can mitigate the prevalence of ethical cheating and uphold the values of academic excellence.

Ethical Considerations in Educational Policy

Equity and Access to Education

In today's society, the concepts of equity and access to education are of utmost importance. Education is widely recognized as a fundamental right, and every individual should have an equal opportunity to access high-quality education regardless of their background, race, gender, socioeconomic status, or disability. Unfortunately, in many parts of the world, educational opportunities are not distributed equitably, leading to significant disparities and hindering social progress. In this section, we will explore the principles, challenges, and strategies related to achieving equity and access to education.

Understanding Equity in Education

Equity in education refers to the concept of fairness and justice in providing educational opportunities for all individuals. While equality focuses on treating everyone the same, equity recognizes that individuals have different needs and aims to address these differences in order to ensure equal outcomes. Achieving educational equity requires targeting resources, support, and opportunities to those who need them most, in order to level the playing field and create a fair and inclusive educational system.

Challenges to Equity and Access

Several factors contribute to the lack of equity and access to education. These challenges can vary across countries and regions, but some common issues include:

- **Socioeconomic disparities:** Socioeconomic status often determines the quality of education one can access. Students from low-income families may face barriers such as lack of resources, inadequate infrastructure, and limited access to technology and educational materials.

- **Gender inequality:** In many societies, girls face significant obstacles to education, including cultural norms, early marriage, gender-based violence, and discrimination. Ensuring gender equality in education is crucial for achieving social and economic development.

- **Rural and remote areas:** Students living in rural and remote areas often have limited access to educational facilities, qualified teachers, and resources. The geographical location can create disparities in educational opportunities, leading to educational disadvantage for these students.

- **Disabilities and special needs:** Students with disabilities and special needs often encounter barriers in accessing education due to physical, sensory, or intellectual impairments. Inclusive education practices and supportive services are necessary to ensure equitable opportunities for these students.

- **Discrimination and marginalization:** Discrimination based on race, ethnicity, religion, language, or social background can perpetuate educational inequity. Minority and marginalized communities often face prejudice, stereotypes, and unequal treatment, leading to limited access to quality education.

Strategies for Promoting Equity and Access

Addressing the challenges of equity and access in education requires a multi-faceted approach involving policymakers, educators, and communities. Here are some strategies that can be implemented:

1. **Equitable funding:** Ensuring adequate and equitable distribution of financial resources is crucial for reducing educational disparities. Governments should prioritize funding to schools and districts serving disadvantaged communities, providing them with additional resources and support.

2. **Inclusive policies and practices:** Education systems should adopt inclusive policies that promote diversity, equality, and non-discrimination. This includes fostering inclusive classrooms, accommodating students with diverse needs, and providing appropriate support services.

3. **Quality teacher training:** Investing in teacher training programs that emphasize culturally responsive pedagogy, inclusive teaching practices, and strategies to address diverse learning needs. Well-trained and culturally competent teachers are essential for providing equitable education.

4. **Early intervention and support**: Early childhood education and targeted interventions can help close the achievement gap. Providing access to quality pre-school education, remedial support, and educational resources for disadvantaged students can mitigate the impact of socioeconomic barriers.

5. **Technology and digital literacy:** Embracing technology in education can help bridge the access gap. Providing access to digital devices, internet connectivity, and digital literacy training enable students from underserved areas to access educational resources and online learning opportunities.

6. **Community engagement**: Collaboration between schools, families, and communities is vital in promoting equitable education. Engaging parents and community members in decision-making processes, fostering a supportive learning environment, and encouraging community involvement can contribute to improved access and outcomes.

Real-World Example: The "One Laptop per Child" Initiative

An example of a program aiming to improve access to education is the "One Laptop per Child" (OLPC) initiative. This project, launched in 2005, aims to provide affordable laptop computers to children in developing countries. By providing access to technology and digital resources, OLPC aims to bridge the digital divide and enhance educational opportunities for disadvantaged children.

The OLPC initiative recognizes the importance of not only providing hardware but also developing appropriate software and educational content tailored to the needs of the target communities. Additionally, the program prioritizes teacher training and community engagement to ensure the effective integration of technology in the learning process.

While the OLPC initiative has faced challenges and criticism, it serves as an innovative approach to addressing access to education in underprivileged areas. It highlights the potential of technology in overcoming barriers and promoting equity in education.

Exercises

1. Research and analyze a case study related to a successful equity and access initiative in education. Discuss the key factors contributing to its success and the lessons that can be learned from it.

2. Identify one major challenge to equity and access in education in your country or region. Propose a targeted solution to address this challenge, considering the specific context and needs of the affected population.

3. Form a group discussion with your classmates and brainstorm innovative ideas or technologies that can improve access to education for marginalized or disadvantaged groups. Share and discuss your ideas, considering the feasibility and potential impact of each proposal.

Key Takeaways

Achieving equity and access to education is essential for social progress and inclusive development. While numerous challenges exist, strategies like equitable funding, inclusive policies and practices, teacher training, early intervention, technology integration, and community engagement can help overcome these obstacles. The "One Laptop per Child" initiative serves as an example of an innovative approach to addressing access to education. By promoting equity in education, we can create a society where every individual has an equal opportunity to thrive and contribute to the betterment of the world.

Standardized Testing and Ethical Implications

Standardized testing has become a widespread practice in educational systems around the world. It is a method of assessment that involves administering the same test to all students in a standardized manner, allowing for a comparison of their performance. While standardized testing is often seen as a way to measure student achievement and hold schools accountable, it also raises several ethical implications that need to be addressed.

The Purpose of Standardized Testing

Before we delve into the ethical implications, it is essential to understand the purpose of standardized testing. Proponents argue that standardized tests provide an objective and consistent measure of student performance. They believe that these tests help identify areas of academic strength and weakness, hold schools accountable for student outcomes, and contribute to educational equity by ensuring that all students are judged by the same standards.

Issues of Fairness and Equity

However, one of the key ethical concerns surrounding standardized testing is its impact on fairness and equity in education. Some argue that these tests put certain groups of students at a disadvantage. For instance, standardized tests may not accurately measure the diverse range of skills, knowledge, and abilities that students possess. This can particularly affect students from disadvantaged backgrounds who may not have had access to the same resources and opportunities as their peers.

Additionally, standardized tests tend to be biased towards certain cultural, socioeconomic, and linguistic backgrounds. This bias could lead to the underrepresentation of students from marginalized groups and reinforce existing inequalities in the educational system. It may also put significant pressure on English language learners and students with disabilities, who may struggle to perform well on standardized tests due to language barriers or the inability to access appropriate accommodations.

Narrowing of Curriculum

Another ethical concern associated with standardized testing is the potential narrowing of the curriculum. The emphasis on preparing students for these tests may lead educators to prioritize teaching only what is tested, neglecting other valuable aspects of education such as critical thinking, creativity, and problem-solving skills. This narrow focus on test preparation can hinder students' overall development and limit their educational opportunities.

High-Stakes Nature

Standardized testing is often high-stakes, meaning that the results can have significant consequences for students, teachers, and schools. Ethical concerns arise when these test scores are used as the sole determinant for important decisions such as student promotion, graduation, teacher evaluations, and school funding. Relying solely on test scores to make high-stakes decisions can lead to unfair and inaccurate judgments, as it fails to consider the multiple factors that contribute to student and school success.

Teaching to the Test

The pressure to achieve higher test scores can also lead to "teaching to the test." This practice involves focusing classroom instruction primarily on the content and format of the test, rather than promoting deep understanding and meaningful learning. Teachers may feel compelled to use instructional methods that prioritize test-taking strategies and rote memorization, ultimately compromising the quality of education and the development of students' critical-thinking skills.

Ethical Considerations and Solutions

To address the ethical implications of standardized testing, it is crucial to have a comprehensive approach that goes beyond relying solely on test scores. Here are some potential solutions:

+ **Multiple Measures of Assessment:** Incorporate a range of assessment methods, such as performance-based assessments, portfolios, projects, and teacher evaluations, to better capture a student's abilities and potential.

+ **Fairness and Equity:** Ensure that standardized tests are culturally and linguistically fair, accommodating the diverse needs of students. Consider providing appropriate accommodations and linguistic support for English language learners and students with disabilities.

+ **Curriculum Enrichment:** Encourage a broader curriculum that promotes critical thinking, problem-solving, creativity, and social-emotional development, rather than solely focusing on test preparation.

+ **Transparency and Accountability:** Provide clarity and transparency regarding the purpose and use of standardized tests. Communicate the limitations and potential biases associated with these tests to students, parents, and educators.

+ **Professional Development:** Offer professional development opportunities for educators to develop assessment literacy, allowing them to make informed decisions about how to best assess student learning and progress.

+ **Balancing High-Stakes Decisions:** Consider multiple indicators of student achievement and school performance when making high-stakes decisions. Avoid relying solely on standardized test scores for consequences such as student promotion, graduation, and teacher evaluations.

By addressing these ethical considerations and implementing appropriate solutions, we can strive for a more equitable and balanced assessment system that promotes meaningful learning and supports the holistic development of all students. It is crucial to continually reconsider the purpose and impact of standardized testing to ensure that it aligns with our ethical obligations in education.

School Choice and Ethical Challenges

School choice is a controversial topic in education that raises various ethical challenges. It refers to the policy or practice that allows parents or guardians to choose the school their child will attend, often extending beyond the traditional public school system to include charter schools, private schools, and homeschooling. While school choice offers the potential for increased flexibility and access to education, it also raises significant ethical considerations that must be carefully addressed.

Equity and Access to Education

One of the primary ethical challenges associated with school choice is the issue of equity and access to education. Proponents argue that school choice promotes fairness by providing parents with more options for their child's education, particularly for families who feel disadvantaged by their neighborhood school. However, critics argue that school choice exacerbates existing educational inequalities by diverting resources from public schools, which are often left with higher proportions of disadvantaged students.

To address this ethical challenge, it is important to ensure that school choice policies are designed in a way that does not disproportionately disadvantage certain students or communities. This could involve implementing mechanisms to redistribute resources to public schools that may be negatively impacted by school choice initiatives. Additionally, efforts should be made to ensure that all schools, regardless of their funding source or organizational structure, meet certain minimum standards of quality and provide equitable access to educational opportunities for all students.

Social Segregation and Inequality

Another ethical challenge associated with school choice is the potential for increased social segregation and inequality. Critics argue that school choice can lead to the creation of homogenous schools that are segregated along racial, socioeconomic, or ideological lines. This can reinforce existing inequalities and limit opportunities for social integration and understanding.

To address this ethical challenge, school choice policies should prioritize diversity and inclusion. This could involve implementing mechanisms to ensure that schools accepting public funding or participating in school choice programs have policies and practices that promote diversity and prevent discrimination. Additionally, efforts should be made to provide students with opportunities for cross-cultural interactions and understanding, such as through inter-school exchanges or shared extracurricular activities.

Quality Control and Accountability

Ensuring quality control and accountability in schools is another ethical challenge associated with school choice. With a diverse range of educational options available, it is crucial to ensure that all schools meet certain standards of quality and provide students with a high-quality education. Without proper oversight and accountability, there is a risk that some schools may prioritize profit or personal ideology over the well-being and educational outcomes of students.

To address this ethical challenge, school choice policies should establish clear criteria and standards for school evaluation and accountability. This could involve regular assessments of student performance, teacher qualifications, and school facilities. Additionally, mechanisms should be in place to address and rectify issues of underperformance or inadequate provision of educational services.

Informed Decision Making

Promoting informed decision making is another ethical consideration in the context of school choice. When parents or guardians are given the autonomy to choose their child's school, it is essential that they have access to accurate and comprehensive information about the schools available to them. This includes information about school performance, curriculum, teaching methods, and extracurricular opportunities.

To address this ethical challenge, school choice policies should prioritize transparency and information sharing. This could involve developing comprehensive school profiles or report cards that provide easy-to-understand information about each school's performance and offerings. Additionally, efforts should be made to provide parents with guidance and support in navigating the school choice process, ensuring that they have the necessary resources to make informed decisions that align with their child's needs and aspirations.

In conclusion, while school choice offers potential benefits such as increased flexibility and access to education, it also raises significant ethical challenges. These challenges include equity and access to education, social segregation and inequality, quality control and accountability, and informed decision making. By addressing these ethical considerations, policymakers can strive to create a school choice system that promotes fairness, diversity, and educational excellence for all students.

Teacher Evaluation Systems and Ethical Issues

In the field of education, teacher evaluation plays a crucial role in assessing the performance and effectiveness of educators. Teacher evaluation systems are designed to provide feedback, support professional growth, and ensure accountability. However, there are many ethical considerations that arise when implementing these systems. This section explores the ethical issues surrounding teacher evaluation and discusses strategies for addressing them.

The Importance of Teacher Evaluation

Effective teacher evaluation is essential for maintaining high standards of education. It helps identify areas for improvement, promotes professional development, and ensures that students receive quality instruction. Teacher evaluation systems provide valuable feedback to educators, helping them enhance their teaching practices and ultimately improve student outcomes.

Ethical Principles in Teacher Evaluation

When developing and implementing teacher evaluation systems, it is important to consider the following ethical principles:

1. **Fairness:** Evaluation systems should be fair and unbiased, treating all teachers equitably. They should not discriminate based on factors such as race, gender, age, or socio-economic status.

2. **Transparency:** The evaluation process should be transparent, with clear criteria and guidelines. Teachers should have a clear understanding of how they will be evaluated and what standards they need to meet.

3. **Confidentiality:** Teacher evaluation should ensure the privacy and confidentiality of teachers' personal and professional information. Evaluation results should only be shared with authorized individuals and used for legitimate purposes.

Ethical Issues in Teacher Evaluation

Despite the importance of teacher evaluation, several ethical issues can arise during its implementation. It is essential to address these issues to ensure a fair and effective evaluation process. Some of the common ethical issues include:

1. **Bias and Subjectivity:** One of the major concerns in teacher evaluation is the presence of bias and subjectivity. Evaluators may have personal biases that can influence their assessment of teachers. To mitigate this issue, evaluation systems should incorporate clear and objective criteria, multiple evaluators, and training to reduce bias.

2. **Standardization vs. Individualization:** Balancing standardization and individualization is a challenge in teacher evaluation. On one hand, standardized evaluation criteria ensure consistency and comparability. On the other hand, educators argue that individualization is necessary to consider diverse teaching contexts and student populations. Striking a balance between these two approaches is crucial to ensure a fair evaluation process.

3. **Narrow Focus on Student Achievement:** Many teacher evaluation systems heavily rely on student achievement data, such as standardized test scores, as a measure of effectiveness. This narrow focus can lead to a limited assessment of teachers' overall impact on student learning and neglect other crucial aspects, such as classroom environment and student engagement. Evaluation systems should consider multiple measures of teacher effectiveness, including qualitative observations and feedback from students and colleagues.

4. **Professional Judgment:** Teacher evaluation systems often struggle to strike the right balance between relying on objective measures and allowing for professional judgment. Overreliance on quantitative data and rigid evaluation criteria can undermine the professional judgment of educators. It is important to give teachers the autonomy to exercise their professional expertise while maintaining accountability through appropriate evaluation measures.

5. **Stress and Negative Impact:** Teacher evaluation can lead to increased stress and anxiety among educators. In some cases, it may have a negative impact on teachers' mental well-being and job satisfaction. It is crucial to

implement evaluation systems that support the professional growth and well-being of teachers, rather than creating a culture of fear and punishment.

Addressing Ethical Issues in Teacher Evaluation

To address the ethical issues associated with teacher evaluation, educators, policymakers, and administrators can take the following steps:

1. **Clear Guidelines and Training:** Provide clear guidelines and training on evaluation criteria, procedures, and potential biases. Training should focus on evidence-based practices and strategies for reducing bias in evaluation.

2. **Multiple Measures:** Utilize multiple measures of teacher effectiveness, including qualitative observations, student feedback, and peer evaluations, in addition to quantitative measures, such as student achievement data. This holistic approach provides a more comprehensive and accurate assessment of teaching performance.

3. **Collaborative Approach:** Involve teachers in the design and implementation of evaluation systems. Encourage collaboration and open dialogue between evaluators and teachers to ensure a shared understanding of expectations and foster a sense of ownership in the process.

4. **Continuous Professional Development:** Provide ongoing professional development opportunities that focus on enhancing teaching practices, addressing areas for improvement, and building the skills needed for effective evaluation.

5. **Supportive School Culture:** Foster a supportive school culture that values professional growth and well-being. Recognize and reward exemplary teaching practices, establish mentoring programs, and promote a collaborative environment that encourages teachers to share best practices and learn from one another.

Conclusion

Teacher evaluation is a crucial component of effective education systems, but it also raises important ethical considerations. By implementing fair and transparent evaluation systems, addressing bias and subjectivity, and promoting a collaborative and supportive culture, educators can ensure that teacher evaluation is conducted ethically and contributes to the continuous improvement of teaching practices.

Maintaining a balance between accountability and professional judgment is key to fostering a positive and empowering evaluation process.

Funding and Resource Allocation in Education

Funding and resource allocation play a crucial role in the education sector, as they directly impact the quality and accessibility of education. In this section, we will explore the various aspects of funding education, including the sources of funding, the challenges in resource allocation, and strategies to ensure equitable distribution of resources.

Sources of Funding

Education funding can come from various sources, including government allocations, private contributions, and international aid.

Government Allocations: Governments allocate funds for education through their national budgets. These funds are typically collected through taxes and other revenue sources. The government has a responsibility to ensure that education is adequately funded to promote equal opportunities for all students.

Private Contributions: Private organizations, philanthropic foundations, and individuals also contribute towards education funding. These contributions can take the form of scholarships, grants, or endowments. Private funding helps supplement government allocations and can support innovative educational programs.

International Aid: Developing countries often receive financial assistance from international organizations and donor countries to support their education systems. This aid aims to fill funding gaps and improve the quality of education in these countries by providing resources such as textbooks, teacher training, and infrastructure development.

Challenges in Resource Allocation

While funding is essential, effective resource allocation is equally important to ensure that resources are distributed equitably and efficiently. However, several challenges can hinder optimal resource allocation in education.

Budget Constraints: Limited funding often poses a significant challenge in resource allocation. Educational institutions may struggle to meet their needs due to budgetary constraints, leading to inadequate infrastructure, shortage of teaching staff, and insufficient learning materials.

Inequitable Distribution: Unequal distribution of resources is a prevalent issue, especially in regions with socioeconomic disparities. Schools in economically disadvantaged areas may lack proper facilities and resources, resulting in educational inequalities.

Mismatched Priorities: Sometimes, resource allocation does not align with the actual needs of educational institutions. This can occur due to bureaucratic processes, lack of accurate data on student needs, or insufficient communication between policymakers and education providers.

Strategies for Equitable Resource Allocation

To address the challenges in resource allocation, various strategies can be implemented to ensure equitable distribution and optimize the use of available resources.

Needs-Based Allocation: Resource allocation should be based on the specific needs of each educational institution. This requires accurate data collection and analysis to identify areas that require additional resources, such as schools with high student populations or those in underserved communities.

Transparent and Accountable Processes: Transparent processes are essential to enhance accountability and prevent corruption in resource allocation. Establishing clear guidelines and criteria for resource distribution can help ensure fairness and reduce favoritism.

Investment in Human Resources: Allocating resources to attract, train, and retain qualified teachers is crucial for providing quality education. Investing in teacher professional development, competitive salaries, and supportive working environments can significantly impact the quality of education.

Infrastructure Development: Adequate infrastructure is essential for effective teaching and learning. Resource allocation should consider improving and maintaining school facilities, including classrooms, libraries, laboratories, and technology resources.

Partnerships and Collaboration: Collaboration between the government, private sector, and community organizations can enhance resource allocation efforts. Public-private partnerships and community involvement can leverage additional resources and expertise to support education initiatives.

Case Study: Resource Allocation in a Developing Country

Let's consider the case of a developing country, XYZ, which faces challenges in resource allocation in its education system. The country has limited funds, and a significant portion of the population lives in rural areas with limited access to quality education.

To address these challenges, the government of XYZ can implement the following strategies:

Needs Assessment: Conduct a comprehensive needs assessment to identify areas that require immediate attention, such as schools in remote areas, where infrastructure and teaching resources are lacking.

Effective Budget Planning: Develop a transparent and realistic budget plan that allocates funds based on the identified needs. This plan should prioritize investments in infrastructure, teacher training, and student support programs.

Public-Private Partnerships: Foster partnerships with private organizations to leverage additional funding and resources. Encourage corporate social responsibility initiatives to support rural schools and provide scholarships for underprivileged students.

Teacher Training and Recruitment: Allocate resources to improve teacher training programs and incentivize qualified teachers to work in rural areas. This can include offering competitive salaries, providing housing facilities, and career development opportunities.

Technology Integration: Invest in technology infrastructure and provide schools in remote areas with access to digital learning resources. This can bridge the educational gap between urban and rural areas and enhance the quality of education.

Community Engagement: Involve local communities in educational decision-making processes and resource allocation. This can ensure that resources are distributed effectively and empower communities to take ownership of their children's education.

By implementing these strategies, XYZ can significantly improve resource allocation and enhance the quality of education, fostering a more equitable and inclusive education system.

Conclusion

Funding and resource allocation are critical aspects of education. Adequate funding from various sources, including government allocations, private contributions, and international aid, is essential. However, effective resource allocation is equally crucial, as it can address inequalities and ensure that resources are distributed equitably. By implementing transparent and needs-based allocation processes, investing in human resources and infrastructure, and fostering partnerships and community engagement, education systems can overcome challenges and provide quality education for all.

Ethical Issues in Educational Research

Informed Consent and Ethical Approval

In research involving human participants, it is essential to prioritize their autonomy and protect their rights and well-being. Informed consent and ethical approval are two critical components of this process, ensuring that participants are fully informed about the research and have voluntarily given their consent to participate. Additionally, ethical approval ensures that the research meets ethical standards and guidelines set by relevant institutions or regulatory bodies.

Informed Consent

Informed consent is the process by which researchers provide participants with all the relevant information regarding the study so that they can make an informed decision about whether or not to participate. It is important to note that informed consent is an ongoing process and not just a one-time event. It involves a series of steps to ensure that participants have a comprehensive understanding of the research.

The process of obtaining informed consent typically includes the following elements:

1. **Presentation of Information:** Researchers must provide participants with clear and understandable information about the purpose, procedures, risks, benefits, and any potential discomforts associated with the study. This information should be presented in a language and format that participants can comprehend.

2. **Voluntary Participation:** Participants must be informed that their involvement in the study is entirely voluntary and that they have the right to withdraw at any time without facing any negative consequences.

3. **Understanding and Comprehension:** Researchers must ensure that participants have understood the information provided. This can be assessed through a process of discussion, questionnaires, or other appropriate means. Researchers should use plain language and avoid technical jargon to enhance participants' understanding.

4. **Capacity to Consent:** Researchers should assess the participants' capacity to provide informed consent. This involves determining if they have the ability

to understand the information, make a decision based on that understanding, and communicate their choice.

5. **Documentation:** Participants who provide informed consent should sign a consent form or provide their consent in a documented manner. This serves as evidence that informed consent was obtained. However, it is important to note that the process of obtaining informed consent is not just about getting a signature but ensuring participants truly understand and freely choose to participate.

Ethical Approval

Ethical approval is the formal process by which research proposals are reviewed and approved by relevant ethical review boards or committees. The purpose of ethical approval is to ensure that research involving human participants adheres to ethical principles and guidelines.

The ethical approval process typically involves the following steps:

1. **Submission of Research Proposal:** Researchers submit their research proposals to the appropriate ethical review board or committee. The proposal should provide detailed information about the study's objectives, methodology, recruitment procedures, data collection process, and measures to protect participants' rights and well-being.

2. **Ethical Review Board Evaluation:** The ethical review board carefully evaluates the research proposal to determine if it meets ethical standards. The evaluation considers various aspects, such as the potential risks and benefits to participants, the informed consent process, the confidentiality and privacy measures, and the researchers' qualifications.

3. **Ethics Review Decision:** Based on the evaluation, the ethical review board makes a decision regarding the approval of the research proposal. The decision can be approval, conditional approval (with specific modifications or requirements), deferral (seeking further clarification or information), or rejection (if the study poses significant ethical concerns that cannot be adequately addressed).

4. **Monitoring and Oversight:** Upon approval, researchers are usually required to provide progress reports and updates to the ethical review board. This helps ensure that the study continues to adhere to ethical standards

throughout its duration. In some cases, the ethical review board may conduct periodic site visits to ensure compliance.

It is important to note that ethical approval is not a one-time process but an ongoing commitment. Researchers have a responsibility to inform the ethical review board of any changes in the study design, procedures, or potential risks that may arise during the course of the research.

Challenges and Considerations

Obtaining informed consent and ethical approval can present various challenges and considerations in research involving human participants. Some of these include:

- **Vulnerable Populations:** Certain populations, such as children, individuals with cognitive impairments, or those with limited decision-making capacity, require special considerations in obtaining informed consent. In such cases, additional safeguards and procedures may be necessary to protect their rights and well-being.

- **Language and Cultural Barriers:** Researchers must consider participants' language and cultural backgrounds when providing information and obtaining informed consent. Translations of consent forms and plain language explanations may be needed to ensure comprehension for participants with diverse linguistic or cultural backgrounds.

- **Privacy and Confidentiality:** Researchers must implement measures to protect participants' privacy and confidentiality, both during the data collection process and in any subsequent data analysis and reporting. Participants have the right to know how their data will be used and protected.

- **Dynamic Nature of Consent:** In some cases, participants' circumstances or understanding of the research may change over time. Researchers should regularly reassess participants' understanding and ensure ongoing informed consent throughout the study period.

Overall, informed consent and ethical approval are fundamental in safeguarding the rights and well-being of participants in research involving human subjects. Researchers must adhere to ethical principles and guidelines to ensure the ethical conduct of their studies and contribute to the advancement of knowledge while upholding the principles of respect, beneficence, and justice.

Case Study: Informed Consent in Clinical Trials

Consider a clinical trial aimed at evaluating the effectiveness of a new medication for a particular medical condition. Informed consent plays a crucial role in ensuring the rights and well-being of participants in such trials.

The informed consent process in this case would involve presenting participants with information about the purpose of the trial, the potential risks and benefits of the medication, alternative treatment options, and the voluntary nature of participation. The participants would also be informed about the data collection procedures, the duration of the trial, and any potential side effects or adverse reactions that they may experience.

To ensure comprehension, researchers can use visual aids, clear language, and allow ample time for participants to ask questions and seek clarification. The consent process should be ongoing throughout the trial, and participants should be informed of any new developments or changes that may arise during the course of the study.

In addition to obtaining informed consent from the participants, ethical approval for the clinical trial would be required. The ethical review board or committee would evaluate the trial protocol, assessing factors such as participant selection criteria, monitoring procedures, data management, and the potential risks and benefits of the trial.

The research team would also need to address any concerns related to participant recruitment, ensuring that vulnerable populations are not unduly coerced or targeted for participation. Privacy and confidentiality measures should be in place to protect participants' personal health information.

By obtaining informed consent and ethical approval, the researchers in this case can conduct the clinical trial in an ethical and responsible manner, ensuring that participants are well-informed and protected throughout the study journey.

Conclusion

Informed consent and ethical approval are crucial aspects of research involving human participants. They serve to protect the rights, autonomy, and well-being of individuals involved in research studies. Researchers must ensure that participants have all the relevant information required to make an informed decision about their involvement in the study. Ethical approval, on the other hand, involves the review of research proposals to ensure that they meet ethical standards and guidelines. Together, these processes help maintain the integrity and ethical conduct of research involving human subjects.

Confidentiality and Anonymity of Participants

In research studies, ensuring the confidentiality and anonymity of participants is crucial for maintaining ethical standards. Confidentiality refers to the protection of participants' personal information, while anonymity refers to the concealment of their identity. By safeguarding these aspects, researchers can create a safe and trusted environment for participants to share sensitive information without fear of repercussions or breaches of privacy.

The Importance of Confidentiality

Respecting confidentiality is essential because it fosters trust between researchers and participants. When participants believe that their personal information will be handled with care and kept confidential, they are more likely to provide honest and accurate responses. This is particularly important in studies that involve sensitive topics such as mental health, substance abuse, or personal relationships.

Adhering to confidentiality guidelines is also crucial for protecting participants' privacy rights. In many jurisdictions, privacy laws and regulations require researchers to obtain informed consent, inform participants about the purpose of data collection, and reassure them that their information will be kept confidential. Failure to meet these requirements may result in legal consequences, damage to participants' well-being, and reputational harm to the researcher or institution.

Ensuring Confidentiality in Research

To ensure confidentiality, researchers employ various measures:

- **Data encryption and secure storage:** Research data should be stored securely, using encryption techniques if necessary, to prevent unauthorized access. Physical safeguards, such as locked filing cabinets or password-protected databases, can help protect sensitive information.

- **Anonymizing data:** Researchers should remove any personally identifiable information (PII) that could link participants to their responses. This includes names, addresses, phone numbers, email addresses, and other identifying details. Data should be assigned unique identifiers or codes to maintain anonymity.

- **Limited access:** Researchers should restrict access to research data to authorized personnel only. This ensures that only those directly involved in the research process have access to the confidential information. Access should be granted on a need-to-know basis.

* **Confidentiality agreements:** Researchers may require participants, collaborators, and team members to sign confidentiality agreements to legally bind them to protect participants' personal information.

* **Secure data transfer:** When sharing or transferring research data, researchers should use secure transmission methods, such as encrypted email or secure file transfer protocols, to prevent unauthorized access or interception.

Ethical Considerations in Anonymity

Anonymity goes beyond confidentiality by protecting participants' identities, even from the researchers themselves. Researchers must consider the potential benefits and risks associated with anonymity before deciding the level of identity concealment in a study.

While anonymity ensures participants' privacy, it can also limit opportunities for follow-up or longitudinal studies. Without knowing participants' identities, researchers cannot establish a direct relationship or provide personalized support. However, in certain studies involving highly sensitive or stigmatized topics, anonymity is necessary to protect participants from potential harm or social repercussions.

When designing research protocols that involve anonymity, researchers must:

* **Clearly communicate anonymity:** Researchers must inform participants that their identities will not be recorded or traceable in any way. This ensures transparency and informed consent.

* **Collect data without identifiers:** To ensure anonymity, researchers must refrain from collecting any personally identifiable information. Special care should be taken to avoid inadvertent collection of such data, especially in online surveys or digital platforms.

* **Use secure data storage and processing:** Anonymized data should still be stored securely to prevent re-identification. Researchers must make efforts to remove or encrypt any indirect identifiers that could potentially link data to individuals.

* **Protect against unintended re-identification:** Researchers should assess the risk of re-identification by considering the uniqueness or rareness of certain

participant characteristics.   Data release agreements should restrict third-party attempts to re-identify participants.

It is important to note that despite researchers' best efforts, complete anonymity cannot always be guaranteed. As technology evolves, re-identification techniques may become more sophisticated, potentially compromising the confidentiality and anonymity of participants. Researchers must stay informed about emerging risks and take necessary precautions to mitigate them.

Case Study: Anonymity in a Mental Health Research Study

To illustrate the practical application of confidentiality and anonymity principles, let's consider a case study involving a mental health research study:

Dr. Smith is conducting a study on the prevalence of anxiety disorders among college students. The study involves administering an anonymous online survey to gather information about participants' mental health experiences. Dr. Smith has implemented several measures to ensure confidentiality and anonymity:

+ The survey does not ask for any personally identifiable information such as names or email addresses.

+ Participants are assigned unique identification numbers to link their responses without revealing their identities.

+ The survey platform is hosted on a secure server with encrypted data transmission.

+ After data collection, Dr. Smith removes any demographic or contextual data that could potentially identify participants.

+ The anonymized data is stored in a password-protected database accessible only by Dr. Smith and authorized team members.

By following these confidentiality and anonymity measures, Dr. Smith ensures that participants' personal information remains protected, allowing for honest and accurate responses without fear of privacy breaches.

Ethical Training and Oversight

Maintaining confidentiality and anonymity requires researchers to have a strong understanding of ethical principles, laws, and regulations governing research conduct. Ethical training and oversight play a crucial role in ensuring researchers adhere to the highest standards of confidentiality and anonymity.

Research institutions should provide comprehensive training programs to educate researchers about the importance of confidentiality and anonymity, guidelines for data management, and best practices for protecting participants' personal information. Institutional Review Boards (IRBs) or Research Ethics Committees (RECs) should review and approve research protocols to ensure compliance with ethical standards. These oversight bodies play a crucial role in safeguarding participants' rights and holding researchers accountable for ethical breaches.

Conclusion

Confidentiality and anonymity are paramount in research to protect participants' privacy and foster trust. Researchers must implement robust measures to ensure the confidentiality of personal information and employ anonymity when necessary. By following ethical guidelines, researchers can maintain the participants' trust and contribute to the responsible advancement of knowledge.

[References to be included in the final version.]

Ethical Data Collection and Analysis

Ethical data collection and analysis are fundamental aspects of any research study or investigation. In this section, we will explore the principles, guidelines, and considerations involved in ensuring the ethicality of data collection and analysis in various fields of study.

Principles of Ethical Data Collection

The collection of data plays a crucial role in generating reliable and valid research findings. However, it is essential to follow ethical principles to protect the rights and privacy of individuals involved in the study. Here are some key principles of ethical data collection:

1. **Informed Consent:** Before collecting data from participants, it is important to obtain informed consent. Researchers should provide detailed information about the study's purpose, methods, potential risks, benefits, and confidentiality measures. Participants should have the freedom to decline participation or withdraw from the study at any point without facing negative consequences.

2. **Voluntary Participation:** Participation in research should be voluntary, without any form of coercion or undue influence. Researchers should ensure that individuals are not pressured or compelled to participate against their will.

3. **Anonymity and Confidentiality:** Researchers should protect the privacy and confidentiality of participants by utilizing methods that preserve anonymity. This includes removing personally identifiable information from data and storing it securely. Researchers must also ensure that participants' data is kept confidential and is only accessible to authorized personnel.

4. **Minimization of Harm:** Researchers should take measures to minimize the potential harm or discomfort that participants may experience during data collection. This includes addressing any potential risks, providing appropriate support or resources, and prioritizing participants' well-being throughout the research process.

5. **Avoidance of Deception:** Researchers should be transparent about the purpose and nature of the study. Deception should only be used when absolutely necessary, and the potential benefits should outweigh any harm caused. In such cases, researchers must provide a thorough debriefing after the study to ensure participants fully understand the reasons for deception.

6. **Respect for Cultural Considerations:** Researchers should be mindful of cultural norms, beliefs, and customs, particularly when working with diverse populations. It is essential to adapt data collection methods to be sensitive and respectful to the cultural context of the participants. This includes considering language barriers, traditions, and potential power dynamics.

Ethical Considerations in Data Analysis

Once data has been collected, it is crucial to analyze it ethically, ensuring that the findings accurately reflect the research objectives while respecting the privacy and rights of the participants. Here are some ethical considerations in data analysis:

1. **Anonymization and Confidentiality:** Researchers must ensure that any personally identifiable information is removed or sufficiently anonymized before commencing data analysis. This ensures the protection of participants' privacy and confidentiality. Additionally, the data must be stored securely to prevent unauthorized access.

2. **Data Transparency and Reproducibility:** It is essential to maintain transparency in data analysis by providing detailed documentation of the analysis process. This includes describing the methods, software tools, and algorithms used. By promoting reproducibility, other researchers can verify the findings and further contribute to the field.

3. **Avoidance of Bias:** Researchers must be aware of potential biases that could influence the data analysis process. This includes confirmation bias, selection bias, or any other form of bias that may result in skewed or unreliable results. Transparency and sound methodology can help mitigate bias and increase the validity of the analysis.

4. **Responsible Data Interpretation:** Researchers should interpret the results accurately, making sure not to overstate or misinterpret the findings. Honesty and integrity are essential when reporting the outcomes, especially when dealing with sensitive or high-stakes research topics.

5. **Protection of Intellectual Property:** Researchers should respect intellectual property rights and give appropriate credit to the original authors or creators of any data, software, or methodologies used in the analysis. Plagiarism should be strictly avoided.

   In the context of data analysis, it is important to note that ethical considerations extend beyond individual research studies. With the increasing use of big data and data sharing, ethical issues such as data ownership, consent for data sharing, and data anonymization become more complex and demanding. Researchers must stay informed about evolving ethical guidelines and legislation, adapting their practices accordingly.

Examples of Ethical Data Collection and Analysis

Let's consider a hypothetical example to illustrate the ethical considerations in data collection and analysis. Suppose a team of researchers is conducting a study on the impact of a new educational intervention program on student achievement. Here's how they could incorporate ethical practices:

1. The researchers obtain informed consent from students, parents, and teachers, clearly explaining the study's objectives and methodology. They ensure that participation is voluntary and that participants can withdraw at any time.

2. To protect privacy, the researchers assign unique identification codes to participants instead of using their names. Personally identifiable information, such as addresses or phone numbers, is kept separate from the research data to maintain confidentiality.

3. The researchers employ a randomized control trial design, ensuring fairness and avoiding selection bias. They allocate students randomly to the intervention and control groups to minimize confounding variables.

4. Data collection instruments, such as surveys or tests, are designed with cultural sensitivity and language appropriateness to cater to the diverse student population. The researchers consult with local educators and specialists to ensure the instruments are inclusive and respectful.

5. During the data analysis process, the researchers use robust statistical techniques to minimize biases and accurately measure the intervention's effects. They document their analysis methods thoroughly, allowing other researchers to replicate their findings.

6. The researchers interpret the results objectively, acknowledging any limitations or potential conflicts of interest. They refrain from making exaggerated claims or overgeneralizing the findings.

By adhering to ethical principles throughout the study, the researchers ensure the integrity, validity, and social acceptability of their research findings.

Resources for Ethical Data Collection and Analysis

For researchers and practitioners looking to gain a deeper understanding of ethical data collection and analysis, numerous resources provide guidelines, frameworks, and case studies. Here are some notable resources:

+ **The Belmont Report:** Published by the National Commission for the Protection of Human Subjects of Biomedical and Behavioral Research, the Belmont Report provides ethical principles and guidelines for research involving human subjects.

+ **The Association for Computing Machinery (ACM) Code of Ethics:** The ACM provides a comprehensive code of ethics for professionals in the field of computing, including guidelines for responsible data collection and analysis.

+ **The European Union General Data Protection Regulation (GDPR):** The GDPR outlines legal and ethical requirements for data collection and handling, particularly within the European Union. It addresses privacy concerns and provides guidelines for informed consent, data anonymization, and individual rights.

+ **Ethics Guidelines for Statistical Practice:** The American Statistical Association offers comprehensive guidelines for statisticians, including ethical practices for data collection, analysis, and reporting.

+ **Institutional Review Boards (IRBs):** Many institutions have IRBs that review and approve research proposals involving human subjects. These boards ensure compliance with ethical standards and provide guidance on data collection and analysis.

Researchers should consult these resources and engage in discussions with their peers and advisors to stay updated on the latest ethical considerations in data collection and analysis in their respective fields.

Exercises

To reinforce the concepts discussed in this section, here are some exercises for reflection and application:

1. Select a research study of your interest and evaluate its ethical considerations in data collection and analysis. Identify the principles that were followed and any gaps or areas for improvement.

2. Imagine you are designing a survey to collect data on a sensitive topic. Outline the steps you would take to ensure the privacy and anonymity of participants.

3. Research and analyze an ethical case study related to data collection and analysis. Identify the ethical dilemmas faced by the researchers and propose alternative approaches to address those dilemmas.

By engaging in these exercises, you will develop a deeper understanding of the ethical dimensions inherent in data collection and analysis, preparing you for responsible and impactful research practices.

Summary

In this section, we explored the principles and considerations for ethical data collection and analysis. We discussed the importance of informed consent, voluntary participation, anonymity, and confidentiality in data collection. We also explored the vital role of transparency, bias avoidance, responsible interpretation, and protection of intellectual property in ethical data analysis. Finally, we provided examples, highlighted available resources, and offered exercises to consolidate the concepts covered. By adhering to ethical practices in data collection and analysis, researchers can generate reliable and meaningful findings while upholding the rights and privacy of study participants.

Reporting and Dissemination of Research Findings

In the field of educational research, the reporting and dissemination of research findings play a crucial role in advancing knowledge and informing educational practices. This section focuses on the ethical considerations that researchers need to take into account when reporting and sharing their research findings with the broader academic community and the public.

Importance of Research Reporting

Reporting research findings is vital for the progress of the scientific field and the improvement of educational practices. It allows other researchers to critically evaluate the study, replicate the research, and build upon the existing knowledge. Additionally, research reporting enables policymakers, educators, and other stakeholders to make informed decisions based on evidence.

Proper research reporting ensures transparency, accuracy, reliability, and accountability. It enhances the credibility and integrity of the research, thereby strengthening the confidence of the scientific community and the wider society in the findings and the researchers themselves. Moreover, transparent reporting helps to identify potential biases, conflicts of interest, or ethical lapses, promoting responsible conduct in research.

Ethical Considerations in Reporting

Ethical considerations in reporting research findings involve several key areas that researchers must address to uphold the highest standards of integrity and avoid misrepresentation or misuse of data. These considerations include:

Accuracy and Validity Researchers have an ethical responsibility to accurately report their findings, ensuring that they are valid and reliable. This requires providing a detailed description of the research design, methodology, data collection procedures, and analysis techniques used. Researchers should also report any limitations or potential sources of error in their study, allowing readers to assess the validity and generalizability of the findings.

Honesty and Objectivity Researchers must report their findings honestly and objectively, without distorting or selectively presenting the data to favor a particular outcome or interpretation. They should clearly distinguish between empirical evidence and personal opinions, avoiding any form of bias or misrepresentation. If any conflicts of interest exist, researchers should disclose them transparently to maintain the integrity and credibility of their work.

Clarity and Accessibility To ensure the effective dissemination of research findings, it is essential to present them in a clear and accessible manner. Researchers should use plain language and avoid unnecessary jargon or technical terminology. It is also crucial to provide sufficient context and explain the implications of the findings, making them understandable and relevant to both academic and non-academic audiences.

Protection of Participants When reporting research findings, researchers must safeguard the privacy and confidentiality of the participants involved. Any identifying information should be carefully anonymized or pseudonymized to ensure that individuals cannot be identified. Researchers should also consider the potential impact of their findings on the participants' well-being and reputations, taking appropriate measures to minimize any potential harm.

Acknowledgment and Attribution Researchers should acknowledge the contributions of all individuals and organizations that have supported or collaborated on the research. This includes giving credit to co-authors, funders, research participants, and institutions. Proper attribution ensures transparency, fairness, and recognition of intellectual and practical contributions, promoting a culture of collaboration and ethical research practices.

Best Practices in Research Reporting

To promote responsible and ethical reporting, researchers are encouraged to adhere to established best practices in research reporting. These practices include:

Adherence to Reporting Guidelines   Researchers should familiarize themselves with and follow relevant reporting guidelines specific to their field or research design. Examples include the CONSORT (Consolidated Standards of Reporting Trials) statement, the STROBE (Strengthening the Reporting of Observational Studies in Epidemiology) statement, and the COREQ (Consolidated Criteria for Reporting Qualitative Research) checklist. These guidelines provide a structured framework for reporting different types of research studies, ensuring transparency and consistency in reporting.

Pre-registration of Studies   Pre-registration involves publicly documenting key aspects of a research study, including the research question, study design, methodology, and analysis plan, prior to data collection. By pre-registering their studies, researchers commit to conducting and reporting their research findings transparently and according to their initially stated intentions. Pre-registration helps prevent selective reporting and publication bias, enhancing the integrity and reproducibility of research.

Data Sharing   Researchers are encouraged to share their data and make it available to the scientific community, whenever possible and appropriate. Data sharing allows others to verify the findings, conduct additional analyses, and promote collaboration. However, researchers must consider data protection and privacy issues when sharing sensitive or identifiable data. They should also establish clear protocols for data sharing, including data access agreements, to ensure proper use and attribution.

Open Access Publishing   Open access publishing promotes the widespread dissemination of research findings by making them freely accessible to anyone, anywhere. Researchers should consider publishing their work in open access journals or depositing their manuscripts in open repositories, allowing the public, policymakers, educators, and practitioners to access and benefit from their research without restrictions. Open access publishing increases the visibility and impact of research and fosters global knowledge exchange.

Engagement with Stakeholders   Researchers should actively engage with stakeholders such as policymakers, educators, and practitioners to share their research findings effectively and ensure they are relevant and actionable. This can involve presenting findings at conferences, workshops, or policy briefings, and collaborating with stakeholders to translate research into practice. Engaging stakeholders promotes the ethical use of research findings and enhances the understanding and application of evidence-based practices in education.

Case Study: Reporting and Dissemination of a Classroom-Based Intervention Study

Consider a case where a researcher conducted a classroom-based intervention study to evaluate the effectiveness of a new teaching strategy on students' math achievement. The study involved several schools, teachers, and students, and the researcher collected quantitative data on students' math scores.

To report and disseminate the research findings ethically, the researcher would follow these steps:

1. Ensure accuracy and validity: The researcher would provide a detailed description of the study design, including the random assignment of participants, the intervention protocol, and the data collection procedures. The statistical analysis methods used would be described, along with any potential limitations or sources of error.

2. Maintain honesty and objectivity: The researcher would present the findings objectively, without selectively reporting or interpreting the data to favor the new teaching strategy. Any conflicts of interest, such as financial or personal relationships with the intervention developers, would be disclosed transparently.

3. Ensure clarity and accessibility: The research findings would be presented in a clear and accessible manner, using plain language and avoiding unnecessary jargon. The implications of the findings for educators and policymakers would be explained, making them relevant and understandable to a wide audience.

4. Protect participant privacy: The researcher would ensure that the students' identities are protected by anonymizing or pseudonymizing their data. Any identifying information would be removed, and the researcher would consider the potential impact of the findings on the participants' well-being and reputations.

5. Acknowledge contributions: The researcher would acknowledge the contributions of the participating schools, teachers, and students. Co-authors, funders, and institutions that supported the research would also be acknowledged in the research report.

By following these ethical considerations and best practices, the researcher can contribute to the advancement of knowledge in education, promote evidence-based decision-making, and foster an ethical research culture.

Exercises

1. Identify and explain the potential ethical issues that can arise when reporting research findings in education.

2. Discuss the importance of open access publishing in the context of educational research. What are the potential benefits and challenges associated with open access publishing?

3. Imagine you are a researcher conducting a study on a sensitive topic in education. What steps would you take to protect the privacy and confidentiality of the participants when reporting your research findings?

4. Consider a scenario where a researcher encounters unexpected findings that contradict their initial hypotheses. How should the researcher approach the reporting and interpretation of these unexpected findings ethically?

5. Explore and critically evaluate the ethical considerations associated with sharing research data in education. What are the potential benefits and challenges of data sharing?

Further Reading

1. Dixon, P., & Kalaitzidis, T. (2019). Reporting and sharing research data: A guide for researchers. Educational Studies, 45(4), 361-378.

2. Nosek, B. A., Ebersole, C. R., DeHaven, A. C., & Mellor, D. (2018). The preregistration revolution. Proceedings of the National Academy of Sciences, 115(11), 2600-2606.

3. Committee on Publication Ethics. (2018). COPE Ethical Guidelines for Peer Reviewers. Retrieved from https://publicationethics.org/files/ Ethic_all_REVISED_2.pdf

4. Pope, C., Mays, N., & Popay, J. (2007). Synthesizing qualitative and quantitative health evidence: A guide to methods. McGraw-Hill International.

Remember, ethical research reporting is not just a responsibility but an opportunity to contribute to the advancement of knowledge and the improvement of educational practices. Upholding ethical standards in reporting ensures the credibility, transparency, and impact of your research findings.

Student and Parent Involvement in Research

Student and parent involvement in research is an essential aspect of ethical educational research practices. In this section, we will explore the importance of including students and parents in the research process, the benefits they bring, and the ethical considerations involved.

Importance of Student Involvement

Involving students in educational research offers several advantages. First and foremost, it empowers students to actively participate in the construction of knowledge. By engaging them in the research process, students develop critical thinking skills, gain a deeper understanding of the subject matter, and enhance their problem-solving abilities. Additionally, involving students helps researchers gain insights into the student experience, ensuring that the research is relevant and addresses their needs.

Student involvement in research can take various forms. They can participate in data collection, analysis, and interpretation, thereby becoming active contributors to the research findings. Involving students can also lead to increased motivation and engagement with the subject matter, as they see the real-world relevance of their contributions. Furthermore, research involvement can foster a sense of ownership and responsibility among students, as they recognize their impact on the research outcomes.

Engaging Parents in the Research Process

In addition to student involvement, including parents in educational research is crucial for a comprehensive understanding of the educational ecosystem. Parents play a significant role in their children's education, and their perspectives and insights are invaluable. By involving parents in the research process, researchers can gain a deeper understanding of the home environment, parental involvement practices, and the influence of family dynamics on student learning outcomes.

Including parents in the research process can facilitate collaboration between schools and families, promoting a holistic approach to education. Parents can provide valuable feedback, suggestions, and concerns that can inform educational policies, curriculum development, and teaching strategies. Their involvement also enhances transparency and establishes trust between researchers, schools, and families.

It is important to note that involving parents in research requires careful consideration of ethical guidelines. Privacy and confidentiality must be prioritized, ensuring that any personal information shared by parents is protected. Informed consent should be obtained, clearly explaining the purpose and nature of the research, as well as the rights and responsibilities of all parties involved.

Ethical Considerations

When involving students and parents in research, it is crucial to adhere to ethical principles and guidelines. The following considerations should be taken into account:

1. **Consent and Voluntary Participation:** Researchers must obtain informed consent from both students and parents, ensuring they understand the nature of the research, their rights, and the potential risks and benefits of participation. Participation should always be voluntary, and participants should have the right to withdraw at any time without consequence.

2. **Protection of Privacy and Confidentiality:** Identifiable information should be treated with utmost care to protect the privacy and confidentiality of the participants. Researchers should use secure storage systems and employ appropriate anonymization techniques when reporting research findings.

3. **Respect for Autonomy and Diversity:** Researchers should respect the autonomy of students and parents, considering their individual perspectives, values, and cultural backgrounds. Diversity should be embraced, and the research process should be inclusive and sensitive to the needs of all participants.

4. **Transparent Communication:** Researchers should maintain open and transparent communication with students and parents, providing regular updates on the progress of the research and ensuring that any questions or concerns are addressed promptly. Clear channels of communication should be established to facilitate meaningful engagement.

5. **Benefits and Safeguards:** Researchers should ensure that the benefits of student and parent involvement outweigh any potential risks. Safeguards should be in place to protect the well-being and rights of the participants, and researchers should actively work to minimize any potential harm or discomfort.

Example: Student-Parent Partnership in Early Childhood Education Research

To illustrate the importance of student and parent involvement in research, let's consider a specific example: a study on the impact of family engagement in early childhood education. In this research project, researchers collaborate with both students and parents to explore the relationship between parental involvement practices and children's academic achievement.

The study involves students in data collection by using surveys specifically designed for their age group to gauge their perception of parental involvement.

Students also participate in focus group discussions, where they can share their experiences and insights regarding their parents' involvement in their education.

Parents are invited to participate through informative meetings, where researchers explain the research objectives, methodology, and potential benefits. Informed consent is obtained from parents who decide to participate. They are encouraged to share their perspectives, experiences, and challenges related to their involvement in their child's early education.

Throughout the research process, researchers maintain regular communication with both students and parents, providing updates and addressing any concerns or questions. The collected data remains confidential and is used solely for research purposes, with all identifying information removed.

The research findings include insights from both students and parents, shedding light on effective strategies for promoting family engagement in early childhood education. The involvement of students and parents not only contributes to the validity and richness of the research but also empowers them as active stakeholders in their children's education.

Resources and Further Reading

If you are interested in exploring research on student and parent involvement further, consider the following resources:

- Epstein, J.L., Sanders, M.G., Simon, B.S., Salinas, K.C., Jansorn, N.R., & Van Voorhis, F.L. (2002). School, family, and community partnerships: Your handbook for action. Corwin Press.

- Henderson, A.T., & Mapp, K.L. (2002). A new wave of evidence: The impact of school, family, and community connections on student achievement. National Center for Family & Community Connections with Schools.

- Clark, A.M. (2019). Student-Parent Relationships in Early Elementary Education: Understanding Socialization Processes. Journal of Child and Family Studies, 28(5), 1332-1344.

These resources provide practical guidance, research-based strategies, and insights into the benefits of student and parent involvement in education. They can serve as a starting point for educators, researchers, and policymakers interested in promoting ethical practices that support meaningful student and parent engagement in research.

Overall, involving students and parents in educational research fosters a collaborative approach to knowledge construction, ensures the relevance of research findings, and strengthens the connection between educational institutions and the broader community. Ethical considerations guide this involvement, protecting the rights and well-being of all participants and promoting a culture of transparency, inclusivity, and respect.

Ethical Engagement with Technology in Education

Digital Literacy and Cyber Ethics

In today's digital age, where technology is an integral part of our lives, it is essential to have a good understanding of digital literacy and cyber ethics. Digital literacy refers to the ability to use and navigate digital technologies effectively, while cyber ethics focuses on ethical considerations and responsible behavior in the digital realm.

Importance of Digital Literacy

Digital literacy is crucial in our modern society for a variety of reasons. First and foremost, it enables individuals to access, evaluate, and utilize information effectively. With the vast amount of information available online, being digitally literate allows one to discern reliable sources, fact-check information, and make informed decisions.

Moreover, digital literacy empowers individuals to communicate, collaborate, and express themselves in the digital world. Proficiency in using digital tools and platforms opens up opportunities for networking, creating content, and engaging with others on social media or online communities.

Furthermore, digital literacy is essential for success in education and the workplace. Many educational institutions and employers expect individuals to be adept at using digital tools for research, communication, and problem-solving. Without proficiency in digital literacy, individuals may find themselves at a disadvantage in these domains.

Key Aspects of Digital Literacy

Digital literacy encompasses various areas of competence. Here are some key aspects that individuals need to develop:

Technical Skills: Digital literacy entails having the technical skills to navigate and utilize digital devices, applications, and software. This includes proficiency in using operating systems, word processors, spreadsheets, web browsers, search engines, and other digital tools relevant to one's field or interests.

Information Literacy: Being digitally literate also means having the ability to evaluate and critically analyze information found online. This involves understanding factors like source credibility, biases, currency, and relevance. Developing strong information literacy skills enables individuals to make informed decisions and avoid falling victim to misinformation or fake news.

Media Literacy: In today's digital landscape, individuals are constantly exposed to various forms of media such as images, videos, and advertisements. Digital literacy involves being able to navigate and interpret media messages critically. This includes understanding the techniques used to influence and manipulate audiences and being aware of issues like media ownership, bias, and representation.

Online Communication: Effective digital literacy also involves knowing how to communicate appropriately and responsibly online. This includes understanding netiquette (internet etiquette), being mindful of one's tone and language in digital conversations, and respecting others' privacy and boundaries. It also includes being aware of the potential risks associated with online communication, such as cyberbullying and online scams.

Ethical Considerations in the Digital Realm

As we engage with technology and the digital world, it is crucial to adhere to ethical principles and practices. Here are some key ethical considerations in the digital realm:

Respect for Privacy: Respecting and safeguarding the privacy of individuals when using digital technologies is of utmost importance. This includes obtaining proper consent for collecting personal information, ensuring secure data storage and transmission, and being aware of privacy settings when sharing information online. It also implies refraining from invading others' privacy by unauthorized access to their personal data.

Digital Security: Protecting digital devices, networks, and systems from unauthorized access and cyber threats is essential. This involves using strong passwords, enabling two-factor authentication, keeping software up to date, and being cautious of phishing attempts and malicious software. It also includes respecting intellectual property rights and refraining from unauthorized copying, distribution, or modification of digital content.

Digital Citizenship: Being a responsible digital citizen means using technology and the internet in a manner that promotes positive engagement and contributes to the well-being of the online community. This involves treating others with respect, kindness, and empathy, practicing good digital etiquette, and promoting inclusivity and diversity in online spaces. It also means being aware of the consequences of one's digital actions and taking responsibility for them.

Critical Thinking: Engaging with digital content critically and thoughtfully is crucial to combat misinformation and fake news. Developing a habit of fact-checking, verifying sources, and critically analyzing information before sharing or acting upon it helps maintain integrity and credibility in the digital realm. It also involves being mindful of one's own biases and being open to diverse perspectives.

Teaching Digital Literacy and Cyber Ethics

Educators play a vital role in promoting digital literacy and teaching cyber ethics to students. Here are some strategies that can be employed in educational settings:

Integration of Technology: Infusing technology into the curriculum and classroom activities helps students develop digital literacy skills organically. By using various digital tools and platforms for research, collaboration, and creative projects, students gain hands-on experience and become familiar with digital best practices.

Media Literacy Education: Incorporating media literacy into the curriculum helps students critically analyze media messages and develop a discerning eye for media manipulation and bias. This involves engaging students in activities such as analyzing advertisements, deconstructing news articles, and creating media projects to promote media literacy skills.

Cyber Ethics Discussions: Engaging students in open discussions about cyber ethics and the ethical implications of digital behavior fosters critical thinking and ethical decision-making. Teachers can present real-world ethical dilemmas related to digital technology and guide students in analyzing the consequences of different choices.

Digital Citizenship Programs: Implementing digital citizenship programs in schools provides students with guidelines and skills to navigate the digital world responsibly. These programs cover topics such as online safety, responsible social media use, cyberbullying prevention, and digital rights and responsibilities.

Parental and Community Engagement: Involving parents and the wider community in conversations about digital literacy and cyber ethics enhances the impact of educational efforts. Schools can organize workshops or informational sessions for parents to increase awareness and equip them with strategies to support their children's digital literacy development.

Teaching digital literacy and cyber ethics goes beyond imparting technical skills. It involves nurturing critical thinking, ethical decision-making, and responsible behavior in digital spaces. By integrating these principles into education, we can empower individuals to thrive in the digital age while upholding ethical values and fostering a safe and inclusive digital community.

Note: For additional resources, tips, and activities related to promoting digital literacy and cyber ethics, refer to the "Digital Citizenship" website maintained by Common Sense Education (`https://www.commonsense.org/education/digital-citizenship`).

Conclusion

Digital literacy and cyber ethics are essential skills in today's technology-driven world. By developing proficiency in digital literacy and adhering to ethical considerations, individuals can effectively navigate the digital realm, make informed decisions, and contribute to a positive and responsible digital community. Educators play a crucial role in promoting digital literacy and teaching cyber ethics by integrating technology, fostering critical thinking, and engaging students in discussions about ethical dilemmas in the digital age.

Responsible Use of Social Media by Educators

In today's digital age, social media has become an integral part of our lives, including the field of education. Educators have started using social media platforms to connect with students, collaborate with colleagues, and share resources. However, the use of social media in the education sector comes with its own set of ethical considerations and responsibilities. In this section, we will explore the importance of responsible use of social media by educators and discuss key guidelines to ensure ethical behavior.

Importance of Responsible Use

Social media platforms offer educators a unique opportunity to engage with students outside the classroom, build a community, and share valuable educational content. It can enhance learning experiences, promote collaboration, and provide a platform for ongoing professional development. However, it is crucial for educators to understand the ethical implications and potential risks associated with their social media presence.

Responsible use of social media by educators is important for several reasons:

1. Protecting student privacy: Educators must be mindful of the personal information they disclose about their students online. Respect for privacy is vital to maintain trust and ensure the safety of students.

2. Maintaining professionalism: Educators should uphold high standards of professionalism in their online interactions, just as they would in the physical classroom. This includes maintaining appropriate boundaries, refraining from engaging in discussions that may compromise their professional reputation, and ensuring that their online behavior aligns with their role as educators.

3. Promoting digital citizenship: Educators play a crucial role in modeling responsible online behavior for their students. By demonstrating ethical use of social media, educators can help students develop a positive digital footprint, understand online safety, and engage in respectful online communication.

4. Avoiding conflicts of interest: Educators must be aware of the potential conflicts of interest that may arise when using social media. They should not endorse or promote products, services, or organizations that may compromise their professional integrity or impartiality.

Guidelines for Responsible Use

To ensure responsible use of social media by educators, it is essential to establish clear guidelines and best practices. Here are some key guidelines for educators to follow:

1. Privacy settings and security: Educators should familiarize themselves with the privacy settings of social media platforms they use and adjust them according to their preferences. It is important to limit access to personal information and ensure that only appropriate individuals can view and interact with their content.

2. Separate personal and professional accounts: Educators should consider maintaining separate personal and professional accounts on social media platforms. This helps to maintain a clear distinction between personal and professional interactions, ensuring that professional content is easily accessible and does not get mixed with personal posts.

3. Think before posting: Educators should exercise caution and think critically before posting anything online. They should be mindful of the potential impact of their posts on students, colleagues, and the overall educational community. It is important to ensure that the content shared is accurate, respectful, and appropriate for the intended audience.

4. Respect confidentiality and student privacy: Educators should always prioritize student privacy and confidentiality. They should avoid sharing any information that could identify individual students without obtaining the necessary consent. Even when sharing student work or achievements, it is important to ensure that personal information is not disclosed without consent.

5. Engage in respectful and professional communication: When interacting with students, colleagues, parents, or the wider community on social media, educators should maintain a respectful and professional tone. It is important to engage in constructive discussions and avoid engaging in online conflicts or heated debates.

6. Stay informed about school policies: Educators should familiarize themselves with their school's social media policies and guidelines. They should ensure compliance with these policies and seek clarification if they have any doubts or concerns.

Addressing Challenges and Concerns

Despite following guidelines, educators may face challenges and concerns when using social media. It is important to address these effectively to ensure responsible use. Here are some common challenges and potential solutions:

1. Cyberbullying and inappropriate behavior: Educators should be vigilant about monitoring their social media platforms regularly. If they encounter cyberbullying, inappropriate behavior, or any content that violates ethical standards, they should promptly address the issue by reporting it to the platform and seeking support from relevant authorities.

2. Maintaining work-life balance: It is important for educators to establish boundaries between their personal and professional lives. They should allocate specific times for engaging with social media and prioritize their well-being. Educators should be mindful of not letting social media use interfere with their personal life or overwhelm them.

3. Handling negative feedback: Educators may receive negative feedback or criticism on social media. It is important to respond calmly and professionally, using the opportunity to engage in constructive dialogue and demonstrate professionalism. Educators should listen to concerns, provide clarification if needed, and, if appropriate, move the discussion offline to ensure privacy and address the issue effectively.

Conclusion

Social media can be a powerful tool for educators, but it also comes with ethical responsibilities. Responsible use of social media by educators involves protecting student privacy, maintaining professionalism, promoting digital citizenship, and avoiding conflicts of interest. By following guidelines for responsible use and addressing challenges effectively, educators can harness the potential of social media while upholding ethical standards in the field of education.

Remember, as an educator, your online presence reflects your role as a professional and your commitment to ethical conduct. Embrace social media as a tool for positive impact, engage responsibly, and always prioritize the well-being of your students and the integrity of the education profession.

Further Reading

- Davis, V. (2017). *Cultivating Communication in the Classroom: Future-Ready Skills for Secondary Students*. Thousand Oaks, CA: Corwin Press.

- Ribble, M. (2017). *Digital Citizenship in Schools*. Eugene, OR: International Society for Technology in Education.

- Solomon, G., & Schrum, L. (2013). *Web 2.0: How-To for Educators*. Eugene, OR: International Society for Technology in Education.

- Vander Ark, T. (2016). *Getting Smart: How Digital Learning is Changing the World*. San Francisco, CA: Jossey-Bass.

- Westheimer, J., & Kahne, J. (2004). What kind of citizen? The politics of educating for democracy. *American Educational Research Journal*, 41(2), 237-269.

Discussion Questions

1. What are some potential risks associated with the use of social media by educators?

2. How can educators balance their personal and professional accounts on social media platforms?

3. What steps can educators take to ensure student privacy and confidentiality on social media?

4. What are some strategies educators can use to address negative feedback or criticism on social media?

5. How can educators promote responsible digital citizenship among their students through social media?

Ethical Considerations

When discussing responsible use of social media, it is essential to consider ethical considerations related to privacy, confidentiality, and professional conduct. Educators must prioritize the well-being and privacy of their students and avoid engaging in any online behavior that may compromise their professional integrity. By adhering to ethical guidelines, educators can ensure a positive and safe online learning environment.

Data Privacy and Security in Educational Technology

Data privacy and security are critical concerns in the realm of educational technology. With the increasing reliance on digital platforms for teaching and learning, the protection of sensitive information becomes paramount. This section will explore the concepts and challenges associated with data privacy and security in educational technology, as well as provide practical strategies for safeguarding information.

Understanding Data Privacy and Security

Data privacy refers to the control and protection of personal information. In the context of educational technology, this includes student records, assessment data, and any other data collected during the learning process. Data security, on the other hand, refers to the measures taken to safeguard the information from unauthorized access, disclosure, or modification.

In the digital age, data privacy and security face various challenges. Educational institutions must ensure compliance with data protection laws, such as the General Data Protection Regulation (GDPR) in the European Union or the Family Educational Rights and Privacy Act (FERPA) in the United States. Additionally, technological advancements and the increasing use of cloud-based services raise concerns about data breaches and cyber-attacks.

Legal and Ethical Considerations

Educational institutions have a legal and ethical obligation to protect student data. It is essential to have clear policies and procedures in place to ensure compliance with privacy laws and standards. These policies should outline the purpose and scope of data collection, specify who has access to the data, and establish protocols for data retention and disposal.

Transparency and informed consent are crucial aspects of data privacy. Students, parents, and educators should be well-informed about the types of data collected, the purposes for which it is used, and the safeguards in place to protect it. By obtaining explicit consent, educational institutions can ensure that data is collected and used in an ethical and responsible manner.

Strategies for Data Privacy and Security

To ensure data privacy and security in educational technology, consider the following strategies:

1.   Data Encryption: Encrypting sensitive data ensures that even if it is intercepted, it cannot be read without the decryption key. Utilize encryption protocols when storing and transmitting data to minimize the risk of unauthorized access.

2. Access Controls: Implement strong authentication measures to verify the identity of users accessing data. This can include the use of strong passwords, multi-factor authentication, and role-based access control to limit the information accessible to different users.

3. Secure Storage: Store data in secure servers or cloud platforms that comply with industry standards for data protection. Regularly back up data to prevent loss and consider redundancy measures to ensure continuity in case of system failure.

4.   Regular Security Audits: Conduct regular security audits to identify vulnerabilities and potential threats. This can include penetration testing, vulnerability scans, and code reviews to assess the robustness of the educational technology systems.

5. Staff Training and Awareness: Educate faculty, staff, and students about data privacy and security best practices. Provide training on recognizing phishing attempts, using secure passwords, and handling personal information with care.

6.   Data Minimization: Collect and retain only the data necessary for educational purposes. Avoid unnecessary or excessive data collection to reduce the risk of improper use or disclosure.

7.   Vendor and Third-Party Assessments: When utilizing third-party educational technology vendors, assess their privacy and security practices. Ensure they comply with relevant data protection laws and have robust security measures in place.

Case Study: Protecting Student Data in a Learning Management System

Consider the case of a school district implementing a learning management system (LMS) to facilitate online learning. The LMS contains student records, grades, and other sensitive information. To protect student data privacy and security:

1. The district enforces strict access controls, allowing only authorized users with unique login credentials to access the LMS.

2. The LMS data is encrypted using industry-standard encryption protocols, ensuring that any data transmitted between the users' devices and the system is secure.

3. The district regularly conducts security audits of the LMS to identify and address any vulnerabilities. They engage an independent security firm to perform penetration testing to ensure the system's robustness.

4. All staff members receive comprehensive training on data privacy and security best practices. They are educated on topics such as recognizing phishing attempts, selecting strong passwords, and handling student data responsibly.

5. The district has a clear data retention and disposal policy in place. Data is retained only for as long as necessary and securely disposed of when no longer needed.

By implementing these strategies, the school district ensures the privacy and security of student data in their educational technology system.

Resources

To further explore the topic of data privacy and security in educational technology, consider the following resources:

- **Data Security and Privacy in Educational Technology:** A comprehensive guide that explores best practices and strategies for safeguarding student data in educational technology, written specifically for educators and administrators.

- **GDPR and Education:** A resource specifically designed to help educational institutions understand and comply with the General Data Protection Regulation (GDPR) in the European Union.

- **FERPA and Student Privacy:** A guide that explains the Family Educational Rights and Privacy Act (FERPA) and its implications for student privacy in the United States.

- **Data Privacy in the Age of Digital Learning:** This book discusses the ethical and legal considerations related to data privacy in the context of digital learning.

Conclusion

Data privacy and security are paramount when it comes to educational technology. As educational institutions increasingly rely on digital platforms, it is essential to implement robust strategies to safeguard student data. By complying with legal requirements, adopting best practices, and promoting a culture of data privacy, educators can ensure the protection and ethical use of student information in educational technology systems.

Exercises: 1. Research and describe a real-life case of a data breach in the educational sector. Discuss the implications and lessons learned from the incident.

2. Identify three specific ways in which educational institutions can promote awareness and educate students about data privacy and security.

3. Consider an emerging technology, such as virtual reality or augmented reality, and discuss potential data privacy and security concerns associated with its use in education. Provide recommendations to mitigate these concerns.

4. Conduct a privacy impact assessment for an educational technology system of your choice. Identify potential privacy risks and recommend measures to address them.

5.   Create a data privacy policy for a hypothetical educational institution. Outline the key principles, procedures, and responsibilities related to data privacy and security.

Online Learning and Equity Considerations

In recent years, online learning has gained significant popularity, especially in the field of education. With the advent of technology, learning has become more accessible and convenient, breaking down geographical barriers and providing opportunities for continuous education. However, as online learning continues to expand, it is crucial to consider the equity implications associated with this mode of education.

Equity in Online Learning

Equity in education refers to the concept of fairness and equal opportunity for all students, regardless of their background, socioeconomic status, or geographical location. In the context of online learning, equity is important to ensure that every student has the necessary resources and support to fully participate and succeed in their educational journey. However, achieving equity in online learning poses several challenges.

1. Access to Technology and Internet Connectivity

One of the fundamental factors influencing equity in online learning is access to technology and reliable internet connectivity. Not all students have the same level of access to these resources, which can create a digital divide and hinder their ability to engage in online learning effectively. Students from low-income households or rural areas may face difficulties in accessing and affording the necessary devices, such as computers or tablets, and a stable internet connection. This disparity can result in unequal educational opportunities and negatively impact the learning outcomes of these students.

To address this issue, it is crucial for educational institutions and policymakers to invest in bridging the digital divide. This can be achieved by providing financial assistance or subsidies for technology devices and internet access to students from disadvantaged backgrounds. Collaboration with internet service providers can also be explored to ensure affordable internet connectivity options are available to all students.

2. Digital Literacy and Technological Skills

Equitable access to online learning also requires students to possess the necessary digital literacy skills to navigate digital platforms and effectively utilize the available technology. This includes skills such as computer literacy, internet research skills, online communication, and the ability to critically evaluate online content. Students who lack these skills may struggle to fully participate in online learning activities and may require additional support to develop their digital literacy.

Educators play a crucial role in addressing this challenge by integrating digital literacy skills into the curriculum and providing training and support to students. This can involve teaching students how to effectively search for information online, critically evaluate online sources, and use digital tools for collaboration and communication. By equipping students with digital literacy skills, educational institutions can ensure that all students are prepared to succeed in an online learning environment.

3. Support for Diverse Learning Needs

Equity in online learning also involves addressing the diverse learning needs of students. Students with disabilities, English language learners, and students from culturally diverse backgrounds may require additional support to fully participate and thrive in online learning environments. It is essential to ensure that resources, instructional materials, and learning platforms are designed to accommodate the unique needs of all students.

Educators can promote equity in online learning by providing accommodations, such as closed captions for videos, alternative text for images, and accessible learning materials. Additionally, fostering a culturally responsive and inclusive learning environment can help students feel valued and supported.

Collaborating with special education teachers, language specialists, and other support staff can further enhance the provision of equitable opportunities for all students.

Addressing Equity Considerations in Online Learning

To promote equity in online learning, educators and educational institutions can implement several strategies and practices. Here are some approaches that can contribute to an equitable online learning environment:

1. Flexible Learning Options

Offering flexible learning options can help address equity concerns by accommodating the diverse needs of students. This can include providing both synchronous and asynchronous learning opportunities, allowing students to access educational materials and participate in activities at their own pace. Offering multiple modes of engagement can benefit students with varying learning styles and time commitments, ensuring that everyone has an opportunity to succeed.

2. Personalized Support

Personalized support plays a crucial role in promoting equity in online learning. Educational institutions can implement student support services to provide individualized assistance to students who may face challenges in online learning. This can involve assigning mentors or academic advisors to guide and support students throughout their learning journey. Additionally, providing access to tutoring services, online office hours, and virtual study groups can further enhance the personalized support offered to students.

3. Promoting Collaboration and Peer Interaction

Collaboration and peer interaction are integral components of the learning process. To ensure equity in online learning, educational institutions can promote collaborative activities and peer interaction through group projects, virtual discussions, and online forums. These interactions provide students with the opportunity to learn from their peers, exchange ideas, and engage in collective learning experiences. Moreover, fostering a sense of community and belonging can contribute to a more equitable online learning environment.

4. Ongoing Assessment and Feedback

Fair and timely assessment is vital to promoting equity in online learning. Providing clear assessment criteria, offering multiple assessment formats (such as quizzes, projects, and presentations), and utilizing technology-enabled assessment tools can help accommodate diverse learning styles and abilities. Additionally, providing prompt and constructive feedback to students can support their learning progress and ensure equity in evaluation.

5. Continuous Professional Development for Educators

Equitable online learning requires educators who are knowledgeable and skilled in leveraging technology effectively and addressing the diverse needs of students. Therefore, it is crucial for educators to engage in continuous professional development focused on online pedagogy, accessibility, cultural competence, and digital literacy. This can be achieved through workshops, conferences, online courses, and collaborative learning communities. By investing in professional development opportunities for educators, educational institutions can enhance the quality of online instruction and promote equity.

Conclusion

As online learning continues to evolve, it is imperative to ensure that equity remains a central consideration. By addressing the challenges related to access, digital literacy, and support for diverse learners, educational institutions can develop robust strategies to promote equity in online learning. Emphasizing flexible learning options, personalized support, collaboration, ongoing assessment, and continuous professional development can contribute to an inclusive and equitable online learning experience for all students. It is through these concerted efforts that we can harness the full potential of online learning and provide equitable educational opportunities for learners around the world.

Ethical Considerations in AI in Education

In recent years, the integration of artificial intelligence (AI) technologies in education has gained significant attention. AI has the potential to revolutionize the way we teach and learn, providing personalized learning experiences, automated assessments, and intelligent tutoring systems. However, along with the numerous benefits AI brings to education, there are also ethical considerations that need to be carefully addressed. In this section, we will explore various ethical considerations in the use of AI in education and discuss ways to mitigate potential risks.

Privacy and Data Security

One of the primary ethical concerns in AI in education is privacy and data security. AI systems used in education often collect and process vast amounts of sensitive student data, including personal information, academic performance, and even behavioral patterns. It is crucial to ensure that this data is collected and stored securely, and that proper consent is obtained from students and their parents or guardians.

Educational institutions and AI developers must adhere to strict data protection regulations, such as the General Data Protection Regulation (GDPR), to safeguard student privacy. They should implement robust encryption and authentication measures to prevent unauthorized access to student data.

Furthermore, transparency and informed consent are essential. Students and their parents should be informed about the type of data collected, how it will be used, and who will have access to it. It is crucial to establish clear policies and guidelines regarding data usage, retention, and sharing, to build trust between educational institutions, AI providers, and students.

Algorithmic Bias and Fairness

AI algorithms used in education may unintentionally perpetuate biases and inequalities. Machine learning algorithms learn from historical data, which may reflect societal biases, stereotypes, and discrimination. If these biases are not addressed, AI systems can reinforce existing inequalities and limit opportunities for certain groups of students.

To address this issue, it is essential to develop and train AI models on diverse and unbiased datasets. AI developers should carefully evaluate the training data to identify and mitigate any biases. Regular audits and evaluations should be conducted to ensure fairness and equity in the AI algorithms used in education.

Additionally, it is crucial to involve diverse stakeholders, including students, teachers, and educational policymakers, in the design and implementation of AI systems. This collaborative approach can help identify and rectify any potential biases and ensure that the AI technologies in education promote inclusivity and equal opportunities for all learners.

Accountability and Responsibility

Another ethical consideration in AI in education is accountability and responsibility. As AI systems become increasingly autonomous and make decisions impacting students' educational journeys, it is essential to establish clear lines of accountability.

Educational institutions should clearly define the roles and responsibilities of AI systems, teachers, and administrators. While AI can provide valuable support, it should not replace human educators. Teachers should retain the autonomy to make informed decisions regarding student progress and well-being, rather than blindly following AI recommendations.

Moreover, AI systems should be designed in a way that allows for transparency and interpretability. Students, teachers, and educational stakeholders should understand how AI algorithms arrive at their recommendations or decisions, enabling them to question and challenge the system when necessary.

Ethical Use of Learning Analytics

Learning analytics involves the collection and analysis of data from educational activities to improve teaching and learning. AI plays a significant role in analyzing these data and providing valuable insights. However, the ethical use of learning analytics requires careful consideration.

Educational institutions should ensure that the use of learning analytics respects students' autonomy and privacy. Data should be collected and analyzed with a clear educational purpose, and students should have the option to opt-out if they feel uncomfortable with their data being used for analytics.

Furthermore, it is crucial to use learning analytics in an ethical manner that benefits students' learning outcomes. AI should not be used solely for surveillance or punitive purposes. Instead, it should be used to support students' progress, provide personalized feedback, and identify potential areas for improvement.

Equitable Access and Digital Divide

The ethical consideration of equitable access is crucial in the context of AI in education. While AI has the potential to enhance learning experiences, it is essential to ensure that all students have equal access to these technologies.

Educational institutions and policymakers should work towards bridging the digital divide by providing necessary resources, infrastructure, and training to students from disadvantaged backgrounds. Access to high-quality AI-powered educational tools should not be limited to those who can afford it but should be made available to all learners, irrespective of their socioeconomic status.

Moreover, it is vital to recognize that not all students may have the same level of digital literacy or experience with AI technologies. Educational institutions should prioritize digital literacy education, ensuring that students and teachers are adequately trained to use AI tools effectively and ethically.

In conclusion, the integration of AI in education holds immense potential for enhancing teaching and learning experiences. However, careful consideration of ethical considerations is essential to ensure that AI technologies are used in a responsible and equitable manner. By addressing privacy concerns, mitigating biases, establishing accountability, and promoting equitable access, we can harness the power of AI in education while ensuring the well-being and autonomy of students.

Ethical Leadership in Education

Role of School Leaders in Promoting Ethical Practices

School leaders play a crucial role in promoting ethical practices within educational institutions. As the guiding force behind the school's mission and vision, they have the responsibility to cultivate an ethical culture that permeates all aspects of the educational environment. In this section, we will explore the key responsibilities and strategies that school leaders can employ to promote ethical behavior among staff, students, and the wider school community.

Setting the Ethical Tone

School leaders set the tone for ethical behavior through their own actions and behavior. They serve as role models, demonstrating integrity, fairness, and ethical decision-making. By adhering to high ethical standards in their interactions with staff, students, parents, and the wider community, school leaders create a culture of accountability and trust.

To promote ethical practices, school leaders should be transparent in their communication and decision-making processes. They should foster an environment where diverse perspectives are valued and ethical dilemmas are openly discussed. By involving stakeholders in decision-making processes, school leaders can ensure that ethical considerations are given due attention.

Educating and Training Staff

School leaders have a responsibility to educate and train their staff on ethical practices. Professional development programs should include training on ethical decision-making, recognizing ethical dilemmas, and understanding the impact of decisions on students and the school community.

School leaders should establish a code of conduct or a set of ethical guidelines that clearly outline the expected behavior for staff members. Regular workshops and trainings can help staff members understand and internalize these ethical standards. Furthermore, school leaders should create opportunities for ongoing reflection and discussion on ethical issues to enhance staff members' ethical awareness.

Fostering Ethical Behavior among Students

School leaders play a vital role in fostering ethical behavior among students. They can do so by incorporating ethics education into the curriculum and providing opportunities for students to engage in ethical discussions and reflection. This can be achieved through dedicated ethics classes or by integrating ethical concepts into existing subjects.

School leaders can also establish a student-led ethics club or committee to encourage students to take an active role in promoting ethical behavior within the school community. This allows students to develop leadership skills while addressing ethical concerns and fostering a sense of responsibility.

Additionally, school leaders should establish a supportive and inclusive school climate that values diversity, promotes empathy, and cultivates a moral compass in students. By fostering positive relationships and modeling ethical behavior, school leaders can inspire students to act ethically and empathetically towards others.

Collaborating with Parents and the Community

School leaders should actively engage parents and the wider community in promoting ethical practices. They can organize workshops, seminars, or parent-teacher conferences to discuss ethical issues and share strategies for promoting ethical behavior at home and in the community.

By establishing partnerships with community organizations and local businesses, school leaders can provide students with real-world examples of ethical practices and the importance of ethical behavior in various contexts. These collaborations can also support the development of internship and mentoring programs that expose students to ethical role models and provide them with opportunities to practice ethical decision-making in real-life situations.

Assessing and Monitoring Ethical Practices

School leaders should regularly assess and monitor the ethical practices within their institution. This can be done through ethical audits, surveys, or focus groups to gather feedback from staff, students, parents, and the wider community. The data collected can be used to identify areas of improvement and inform the development of targeted interventions to address any ethical concerns.

Furthermore, school leaders should establish mechanisms for reporting ethical violations or concerns, ensuring the confidentiality and protection of whistleblowers. By responding promptly and effectively to reports of ethical misconduct, they can demonstrate their commitment to maintaining an ethical environment and reinforce the importance of ethical behavior.

Addressing Ethical Challenges

Ethical challenges are inevitable in any educational institution. School leaders must be prepared to address these challenges promptly and effectively. This requires a clear understanding of ethical frameworks, legal obligations, and relevant policies.

When faced with ethical dilemmas, school leaders should rely on established decision-making models and consult with ethical experts or professional networks, if necessary. They should prioritize the well-being and best interests of students and the wider school community when making difficult decisions.

School leaders should also be proactive in addressing ethical concerns that may arise from external influences, such as societal changes, technology advancements, or evolving educational policies. They should stay informed about emerging ethical issues, engage in ongoing professional development, and adapt their strategies to ensure the continued promotion of ethical practices in changing contexts.

Summary

In summary, school leaders play a vital role in promoting ethical practices within educational institutions. By setting the ethical tone, educating and training staff, fostering ethical behavior among students, collaborating with parents and the community, assessing and monitoring ethical practices, and addressing ethical challenges, school leaders can create an ethical culture that permeates all aspects of the educational environment. Through their actions and decisions, they shape the ethical climate and ensure that ethical values are upheld within the school community.

Ethical Decision Making in Educational Institutions

In educational institutions, ethical decision making plays a crucial role in ensuring the well-being and development of students, maintaining professional integrity, and fostering a positive learning environment. It involves a thoughtful and systematic approach to addressing ethical dilemmas and conflicts that may arise in various aspects of education. In this section, we will explore the key principles and frameworks for ethical decision making in educational institutions.

Principles of Ethical Decision Making

Ethical decision making in educational institutions is guided by several core principles that help educators and administrators navigate complex situations and make informed choices. These principles include:

1. **Respect for Autonomy:** Recognizing and respecting the rights of students, parents, and colleagues to make their own decisions and choices.

2. **Beneficence:** Promoting the well-being and best interests of students and the educational community as a whole.

3. **Non-maleficence:** Ensuring that actions do not cause harm to students, parents, or other stakeholders.

4. **Justice:** Striving for fairness and equitable treatment of all individuals, regardless of their background or circumstances.

5. **Integrity:** Acting with honesty, transparency, and adherence to professional and ethical standards.

These principles serve as a foundation for ethical decision making and guide educators and administrators in resolving conflicts and dilemmas that may arise in their day-to-day work.

Frameworks for Ethical Decision Making

Several frameworks can be employed to guide and structure the process of ethical decision making in educational institutions. These frameworks provide a systematic approach to analyzing ethical issues and making informed choices. Some commonly used frameworks include:

1. **The Six-step Model for Ethical Decision Making**: This model, developed by the Josephson Institute, provides a step-by-step process for examining ethical dilemmas. The steps include recognizing the ethical issue, gathering relevant information, identifying alternative actions, considering the consequences, making a decision, and reflecting on the outcome.

2. **The Ethical Decision-making Process**: This process, proposed by the National Education Association (NEA), involves six stages: defining the problem, gathering information, identifying the stakeholders, considering the available options, making a decision, and evaluating the decision.

3. **The Potter Box Model**: This model, developed by Ralph Potter, offers a framework for ethical decision making based on four key elements: facts, values, principles, and loyalties. Educators and administrators analyze the situation by examining the relevant facts, identifying the underlying values at stake, considering ethical principles, and considering the loyalties to different stakeholders.

These frameworks provide educators and administrators with a structured approach to navigating ethical dilemmas and making well-informed decisions.

Case Studies and Examples

To illustrate the application of ethical decision making in educational institutions, let's consider a few case studies:

1. **Case Study 1: Confidentiality and Student Safety**: A teacher becomes aware that one of her students is being physically abused at home. The teacher is torn between maintaining the confidentiality of the student and ensuring the safety of the child. How should the teacher navigate this ethical dilemma?

2. **Case Study 2: Inclusive Education and Resource Allocation**: A school is faced with limited resources and must make decisions about the allocation of these resources to support students with diverse learning needs. How can the school uphold the principles of justice and inclusivity in this decision-making process?

3. **Case Study 3: Personal Relationships and Professional Boundaries**: A teacher develops a close friendship with a student's parent outside of the educational setting. This relationship starts to blur professional boundaries

and raises concerns among other parents and colleagues. How should the teacher handle this situation ethically?

These case studies highlight the complex nature of ethical decision making in educational institutions and the need for critical thinking, empathy, and a strong ethical framework to guide educators and administrators in making the right choices.

Resources and Professional Development

To support ethical decision making in educational institutions, educators and administrators can engage in professional development and access resources that promote ethical practices. Some valuable resources include:

- **Ethics Codes and Guidelines:** Many educational organizations and professional associations have established ethics codes and guidelines that outline the expected standards of conduct. These codes provide valuable insights and guidance for ethical decision making.

- **Ethics Training Programs:** Educational institutions can offer ethics training programs to help educators and administrators enhance their understanding of ethical principles and decision-making frameworks. These programs enable professionals to develop the skills needed to navigate ethical challenges effectively.

- **Collaborative Forums and Discussion Groups:** Creating spaces for educators and administrators to engage in discussions and share experiences related to ethical decision making can foster a supportive and reflective culture. Collaborative forums and discussion groups can provide opportunities for learning from one another and seeking advice on ethical dilemmas.

By utilizing these resources and engaging in ongoing professional development, educators and administrators can strengthen their ability to make ethical decisions and create a nurturing educational environment for all stakeholders.

Conclusion

Ethical decision making in educational institutions is a complex and essential process that involves respecting the autonomy of individuals, promoting the well-being of students, upholding principles of fairness and justice, and acting with integrity. By following the principles and frameworks discussed in this section, educators and administrators can navigate ethical dilemmas and make informed choices that contribute to the overall ethical and moral development of their educational communities.

Professional Development for Ethical Educators

Professional development plays a crucial role in helping educators enhance their skills and knowledge in order to provide ethical guidance to their students. It enables teachers to stay updated with the latest research and best practices in ethics education, and equips them with the tools and strategies they need to effectively teach and model ethical behavior. In this section, we will explore the importance of professional development for ethical educators and provide practical guidance on how educators can engage in ongoing professional development.

Importance of Professional Development

Ethics education is not a static field; it is constantly evolving in response to societal changes, new research, and emerging ethical challenges. In order to effectively address these challenges, educators must continuously update their knowledge and skills through professional development opportunities. Here are some key reasons why professional development is essential for ethical educators:

- **Knowledge Enhancement:** Professional development allows educators to deepen their understanding of ethical theories, principles, and frameworks. It helps educators stay up-to-date with the latest research and scholarly publications in ethics education, enabling them to incorporate new knowledge and insights into their teaching practice.

- **Strategic Teaching Approaches:** Professional development equips educators with a wide range of teaching strategies and approaches specifically designed to promote moral development and ethical decision-making in students. Through professional development, educators can learn how to engage students in meaningful ethical discussions, facilitate ethical dilemmas, and promote critical thinking skills.

- **Role Modeling:** Educators serve as role models for their students. Professional development provides teachers with opportunities to reflect on their own values and beliefs, and to develop a stronger sense of self-awareness. This self-reflection enables educators to model ethical behavior in their interactions with students and colleagues.

+ **Ethics Integration:** Professional development helps educators integrate ethics across different subject areas and disciplines. It provides teachers with strategies for incorporating ethical considerations into their curriculum, enabling students to develop a holistic understanding of ethics and its relevance in various contexts.

+ **Collaborative Learning:** Professional development often involves opportunities for educators to collaborate and learn from one another. Through collaboration, educators can share their experiences, reflect on their teaching practice, and exchange ideas and strategies for teaching ethics effectively.

Engaging in Ongoing Professional Development

To engage in ongoing professional development as an ethical educator, consider the following strategies:

+ **Attend Workshops and Conferences:** Attend workshops, conferences, and seminars that focus on ethics education. These events provide opportunities to learn from experts in the field, engage in interactive sessions, and network with other educators who share similar interests.

+ **Join Professional Organizations:** Join professional organizations that focus on ethics education, such as the Association for Moral Education or the Ethics and Education Research Group. These organizations often offer resources, publications, and professional development opportunities specifically tailored to ethical educators.

+ **Read Ethical Literature:** Stay updated with the latest research and literature in ethics education by reading scholarly publications, books, and journals. This will help you expand your knowledge and gain new perspectives on ethical issues in education.

+ **Participate in Online Courses:** Take advantage of online courses and webinars on ethics education. Many reputable organizations and universities offer online courses that cover various aspects of ethics education, allowing educators to learn at their own pace and schedule.

+ **Join or Start a Professional Learning Community:** Establish or join a professional learning community focused on ethics education. This can be a group of like-minded educators who meet regularly to discuss ethical issues, share resources, and engage in collaborative learning.

+ **Reflect on Teaching Practice:** Regularly reflect on your teaching practice and seek feedback from colleagues, students, and mentors. Reflective practice allows you to identify areas for improvement and to continuously refine your teaching approaches.

+ **Engage in Action Research:** Conduct action research in your classroom to explore the effectiveness of different ethical teaching strategies. Collect data, analyze results, and reflect on the impact of your teaching methods on students' ethical development.

+ **Mentorship and Coaching:** Seek mentoring and coaching from experienced ethical educators. Mentors can provide guidance, support, and constructive feedback to help you enhance your teaching practice.

+ **Utilize Online Resources:** Take advantage of online resources that provide lesson plans, case studies, and other teaching materials related to ethics education. These resources can supplement your professional development and support your teaching endeavors.

Case Study: Building Ethical Competence through Professional Development

Let's consider the case of Ms. Johnson, a high school teacher who wants to enhance her skills in teaching ethics to her students. She decides to engage in ongoing professional development and adopts some of the strategies mentioned above.

Ms. Johnson attends a national ethics education conference, where she participates in workshops on integrating ethics across different subject areas. She also joins an online course offered by a renowned university, focusing on ethical decision-making models for teachers. In addition, she becomes a member of a professional learning community dedicated to ethics education, where she collaborates with other educators to develop and refine ethical teaching strategies.

Through her professional development journey, Ms. Johnson gains valuable insights into ethics education and expands her teaching repertoire. She learns the importance of case-based approaches in ethical discussions and incorporates real-life ethical dilemmas into her lesson plans. She also understands the significance of fostering a safe and inclusive classroom environment that encourages open dialogue and respectful disagreement.

Ms. Johnson's professional development efforts culminate in the creation of a school-wide initiative on ethics education. With the support of her school administration, she leads professional learning sessions for her colleagues, sharing her knowledge and experiences. As a result, the entire school community becomes more ethically competent, with teachers equipped to guide students in ethical reasoning and decision-making.

Conclusion

Professional development plays a crucial role in preparing ethical educators to effectively teach and model ethical behavior. By enhancing their knowledge, skills, and teaching approaches, educators can make a significant impact on the ethical development of their students.   Through ongoing professional development, educators can stay updated with the latest research, collaborate with peers, and continuously improve their teaching practice, ultimately creating a culture of ethics in educational institutions.   So, let's embark on the journey of professional development and become ethical educators committed to nurturing the ethical minds of the future generation.

Ethical Challenges for School Leaders

As school leaders, educators and administrators, individuals are faced with a range of ethical challenges in their roles. These challenges require them to navigate complex situations and make decisions that uphold ethical principles while also considering the well-being and best interests of their students, staff, and wider community. In this section, we will explore some of these ethical challenges and discuss strategies for addressing them.

Maintaining Student Safety

One of the primary responsibilities of school leaders is to ensure the safety and well-being of their students. This encompasses a wide range of areas, including physical safety, emotional well-being, and protection from harm. School leaders must grapple with issues such as bullying, violence, and abuse that can occur within the school environment.

To address these challenges, school leaders must:

+ Implement and enforce comprehensive policies and procedures for preventing and addressing bullying, harassment, and violence.

+ Foster a positive and inclusive school culture that promotes respect, empathy, and tolerance.

- Provide training and professional development opportunities for teachers and staff that focus on recognizing and addressing safety concerns.

- Ensure effective communication channels are in place for students, parents, and staff to report safety concerns and seek support.

- Collaborate with external agencies and organizations to provide necessary resources and interventions to support at-risk students.

Promoting Equity and Inclusion

School leaders have a responsibility to promote equity and inclusion in their schools, ensuring that all students have equal access to opportunities and resources. This involves addressing issues of discrimination, prejudice, and unconscious bias that may exist within the school community.

To address these challenges, school leaders must:

- Develop and implement policies and practices that promote diversity, equity, and inclusion in all aspects of the school's operations.

- Regularly assess and review the school's practices to identify and eliminate any barriers that may prevent equitable access and opportunities for students.

- Provide professional development and training for staff to raise awareness of unconscious bias and develop culturally responsive teaching practices.

- Foster partnerships with community organizations and stakeholders to support equity initiatives and engage families in the school community.

- Ensure that the school's curriculum reflects diverse perspectives and experiences, promoting inclusivity and challenging stereotypes.

Maintaining High Standards of Professional Conduct

School leaders serve as role models for their staff and students and are expected to uphold high standards of professional conduct. They are responsible for creating an ethical culture within the school community and ensuring that all members adhere to professional codes of conduct.

To address these challenges, school leaders must:

- Lead by example and demonstrate integrity, honesty, and transparency in all interactions and decision-making processes.

+ Establish and communicate clear expectations for staff conduct, including guidelines for ethical behavior and professionalism.

+ Provide professional development and training opportunities for staff to enhance their understanding of professional ethics and standards.

+ Implement systems for monitoring and addressing misconduct or ethical breaches, ensuring fair and consistent disciplinary processes.

+ Foster a supportive environment where staff can seek guidance and support when faced with ethical dilemmas.

Navigating Conflicting Stakeholder Interests

School leaders often face situations where the interests of various stakeholders, such as students, parents, teachers, and the wider community, may conflict. Balancing these interests while upholding ethical principles is a key challenge faced by school leaders.

To address these challenges, school leaders must:

+ Maintain open and transparent communication channels with all stakeholders, ensuring their voices are heard and their concerns are addressed.

+ Seek input from all stakeholders when making decisions that may impact them, fostering a sense of ownership and collaboration.

+ Clearly articulate the school's mission, values, and priorities to provide a framework for decision-making during conflicting situations.

+ Consider the long-term implications of decisions and their impact on all stakeholders, aiming for outcomes that promote the greater good.

+ Seek guidance from professional organizations, educational networks, or mentors to navigate complex ethical dilemmas.

Addressing Educational Inequities

School leaders have a responsibility to address educational inequities and ensure that all students have access to a high-quality education. This involves identifying and addressing factors that may contribute to inequities, such as resource allocation, teacher quality, and curriculum design.

To address these challenges, school leaders must:

+ Conduct regular assessments to identify inequities in educational outcomes and opportunities across student groups.

+ Allocate resources in a fair and equitable manner, ensuring that all students have access to necessary support and enrichment programs.

+ Recruit and retain highly qualified teachers who are committed to promoting equity and closing achievement gaps.

+ Develop and implement targeted interventions and strategies to support struggling students and address educational disparities.

+ Advocate for policies and funding that promote educational equity at local, state, and national levels.

In conclusion, school leaders face numerous ethical challenges in their roles, from maintaining student safety to promoting equity and inclusion, and from upholding professional conduct to navigating conflicting stakeholder interests. Addressing these challenges requires a commitment to ethical principles, ongoing reflection, and continuous professional development. By prioritizing ethical practices, school leaders can create an environment where all members of the school community thrive and succeed.

Ethical Cultures in Educational Organizations

In educational institutions, creating and fostering ethical cultures is of paramount importance. An ethical culture refers to the shared values, norms, and behaviors that guide the actions of individuals within an organization. It sets the tone for how people should behave, make decisions, and interact with one another. By promoting an ethical culture, educational organizations can ensure the well-being of all stakeholders, including students, teachers, administrators, and the broader community.

Importance of an Ethical Culture

The establishment of an ethical culture in educational organizations is essential for several reasons. First and foremost, it serves as a moral compass, providing a framework for ethical decision-making and behavior. It helps individuals within the organization to determine what is right and wrong, and encourages them to act in line with ethical principles.

Furthermore, an ethical culture contributes to a positive and supportive learning environment. When students and teachers feel that they are part of an ethical community, they experience a sense of belonging and trust. This, in turn, leads to improved academic outcomes and overall satisfaction.

Moreover, an ethical culture promotes transparency and accountability. By fostering an environment of openness and honesty, educational organizations can ensure that actions are aligned with the organization's core values. This can help prevent unethical behavior such as cheating, plagiarism, or discrimination.

Finally, an ethical culture enhances the reputation of educational institutions. When an organization is known for its ethical practices, it attracts and retains high-quality students, teachers, and staff. It also builds trust and credibility within the community, leading to stronger partnerships and support from external stakeholders.

Components of an Ethical Culture

Creating an ethical culture in educational organizations requires a comprehensive approach that encompasses several key components. These components include:

Ethical Leadership   Leaders in educational organizations play a crucial role in promoting an ethical culture. By demonstrating ethical behavior and serving as role models, they set the tone for the entire institution. Ethical leaders uphold the values of integrity, honesty, and fairness, and actively communicate and reinforce the importance of ethical conduct to all members of the organization.

Clear Ethical Policies and Procedures   Educational organizations must establish clear and concise ethical policies and procedures that outline the expected behavior of all stakeholders. These policies should cover a wide range of areas, including academic integrity, respect for diversity, confidentiality, and professional conduct. By providing explicit guidelines, organizations can ensure that everyone understands the ethical expectations and consequences of non-compliance.

Ethics Training and Education   To foster an ethical culture, educational organizations should provide ongoing training and education on ethics to all members of the community. This can include workshops, seminars, or online modules that address topics such as ethical decision-making, conflict resolution, and ethical considerations in research and teaching. Through such initiatives, individuals are equipped with the knowledge and skills to navigate ethical challenges effectively.

Communication and Collaboration Open and honest communication is vital for maintaining an ethical culture. Educational organizations should encourage dialogue and collaboration among stakeholders, enabling them to voice their concerns or seek guidance on ethical matters. This can be facilitated through regular meetings, anonymous reporting mechanisms, or designated ethics committees. By fostering a culture of open communication, ethical dilemmas can be addressed promptly and fairly.

Recognition and Rewards Recognizing and rewarding ethical behavior is a powerful way to reinforce an ethical culture. Educational organizations should acknowledge and celebrate individuals or groups who consistently demonstrate exemplary ethical conduct. This can be done through awards, scholarships, or public recognition. By showcasing ethical role models, organizations inspire others to embrace and uphold ethical values.

Challenges in Establishing an Ethical Culture

While creating an ethical culture is desirable, it is not without its challenges. Educational organizations may face obstacles that can hinder the development of an ethical culture. Some common challenges include:

Resistance to Change Instituting an ethical culture requires a shift in mindset and behavior. Resistance to change may emerge from individuals who are comfortable with the status quo or fear the unknown. Overcoming this resistance requires effective change management strategies, such as providing clear justifications for the change, addressing concerns, and involving stakeholders in the decision-making process.

Lack of Resources Building and sustaining an ethical culture requires adequate resources, including funding, time, and personnel. Educational organizations may face resource constraints that limit their ability to invest in ethics training, policy development, or the maintenance of ethical initiatives. Seeking external funding, leveraging partnerships, and prioritizing ethics within budget allocations can help address this challenge.

Ethical Dilemmas and Conflicts Educational organizations, like any other institution, are bound to encounter ethical dilemmas and conflicts. Balancing competing interests and values can be complex and requires careful consideration.

Establishing clear processes for addressing ethical dilemmas, such as ethical committees or ombudsman offices, can assist in resolving conflicts and ensuring fairness.

Case Study: Promoting an Ethical Culture in a High School

To illustrate the practical application of promoting an ethical culture in an educational organization, let's consider the case of a high school facing prevalent issues of cheating and dishonesty among students.

To tackle this challenge, the school implements a multifaceted approach:

1. **Leadership Engagement:** The school principal takes a strong stance against cheating, emphasizing the importance of ethics in education through regular communication with students, parents, and teachers. They establish a zero-tolerance policy for cheating and set an example by consistently exhibiting ethical behavior.

2. **Ethics Education:** The school incorporates ethical education into the curriculum, offering courses or workshops that teach students about the consequences of dishonesty, the value of integrity, and strategies for ethical decision-making.

3. **Clear Policies and Procedures:** The school develops a comprehensive academic integrity policy that outlines the expectations for students and the consequences for dishonest behavior. This policy is communicated clearly to all stakeholders, including teachers and parents.

4. **Support Systems:** The school establishes an anonymous reporting mechanism, such as an online platform, where students can report incidents of cheating or academic dishonesty. The school ensures that these reports are addressed promptly and with confidentiality.

5. **Ethical Role Models:** The school identifies students who consistently exhibit ethical behavior and recognizes them publicly as role models. This recognition motivates other students to follow their example and promotes a culture of honesty and integrity.

Through the implementation of these strategies, the high school creates an ethical culture that discourages cheating and cultivates values of integrity and honesty among its students. This, in turn, contributes to a positive learning environment and prepares students for ethical decision-making in their future endeavors.

Conclusion

Establishing an ethical culture in educational organizations is essential for fostering a positive learning environment and guiding ethical behavior among all stakeholders. By prioritizing ethical leadership, clear policies, ethics education, communication, and recognition, educational organizations can create an ethical culture that promotes trust, accountability, and integrity. However, challenges such as resistance to change, resource constraints, and ethical dilemmas must be addressed to ensure the sustained development of an ethical culture. Through a concerted effort, educational organizations can instill ethical values that will benefit their students, teachers, and the broader community.

Index

Milton Keynes UK
Ingram Content Group UK Ltd.
UKHW022031230824
447344UK00012B/855

9 781779 613264